(Not feeling well.)

Wow! We made it to the tenth volume!
Before the series began, I thought,
"I guess it'll be over in about eight
volumes." Time slips away so mercilessly.

Ryu Fujisaki

Ryu Fujisaki's *Worlds* came in second place for the
prestigious 40th Tezuka Award. His *Psycho +*, *Wāqwāq* and
Hoshin Engi have all run in *Weekly Shonen Jump* magazine,
and *Hoshin Engi* anime is available on DVD in Japan and
North America. A lover of science fiction, literature and
history, Fujisaki has made *Hoshin Engi* a mix of genres that
truly showcases his amazing art and imagination.

HOSHIN ENGI VOL. 10
The SHONEN JUMP Manga Edition

STORY AND ART BY RYU FUJISAKI

Based on the novel *Hoshin Engi*, translated by Tsutomu Ano,
published by Kodansha Bunko

Translation & Adaptation/Tomo Kimura
Touch-up Art & Lettering/HudsonYards
Design/Matt Hinrichs
Editor/Jonathan Tarbox

Editor in Chief, Books/Alvin Lu
Editor in Chief, Magazines/Marc Weidenbaum
VP, Publishing Licensing/Rika Inouye
VP, Sales & Product Marketing/Gonzalo Ferreyra
VP, Creative/Linda Espinosa
Publisher/Hyoe Narita

Printed in the U.S.A.

Published by VIZ Media, LLC
P.O. Box 77010
San Francisco, CA 94107

SHONEN JUMP Manga Edition
10 9 8 7 6 5 4 3 2 1
First printing, December 2008

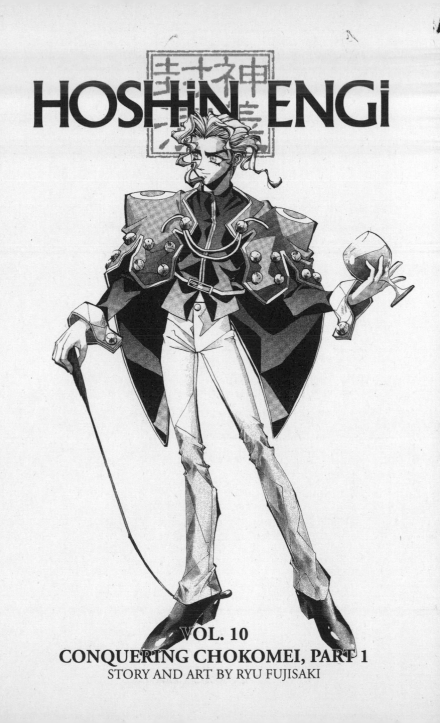

HOSHIN ENGI

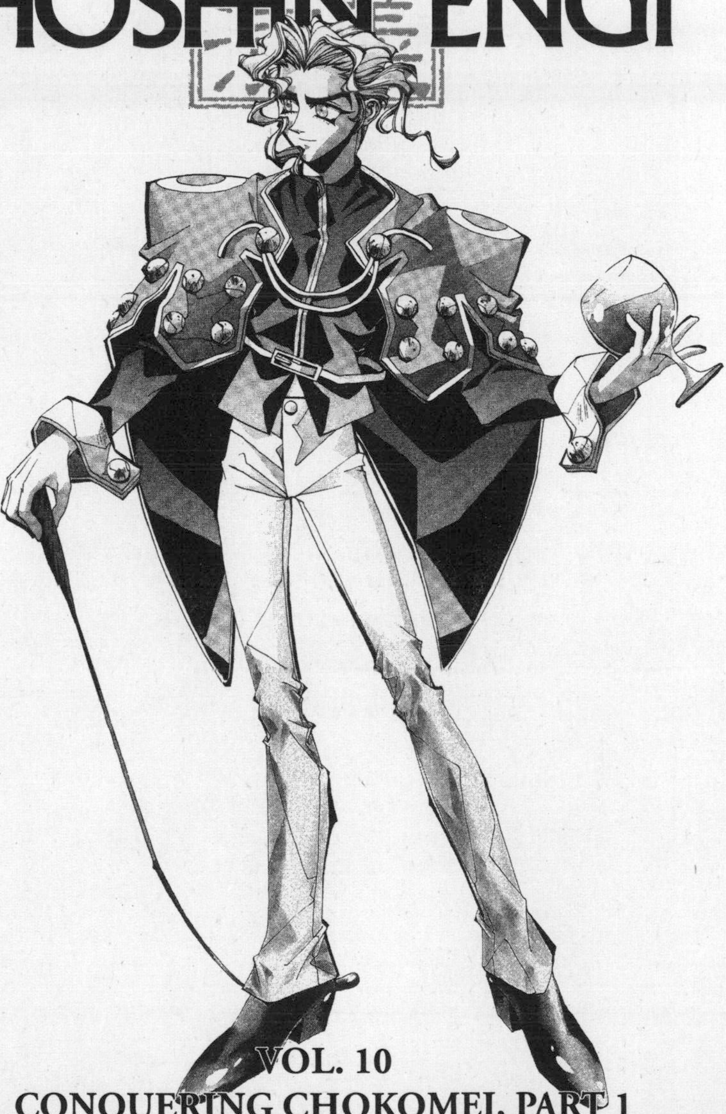

VOL. 10
CONQUERING CHOKOMEI, PART 1
STORY AND ART BY RYU FUJISAKI

THE CHARACTERS

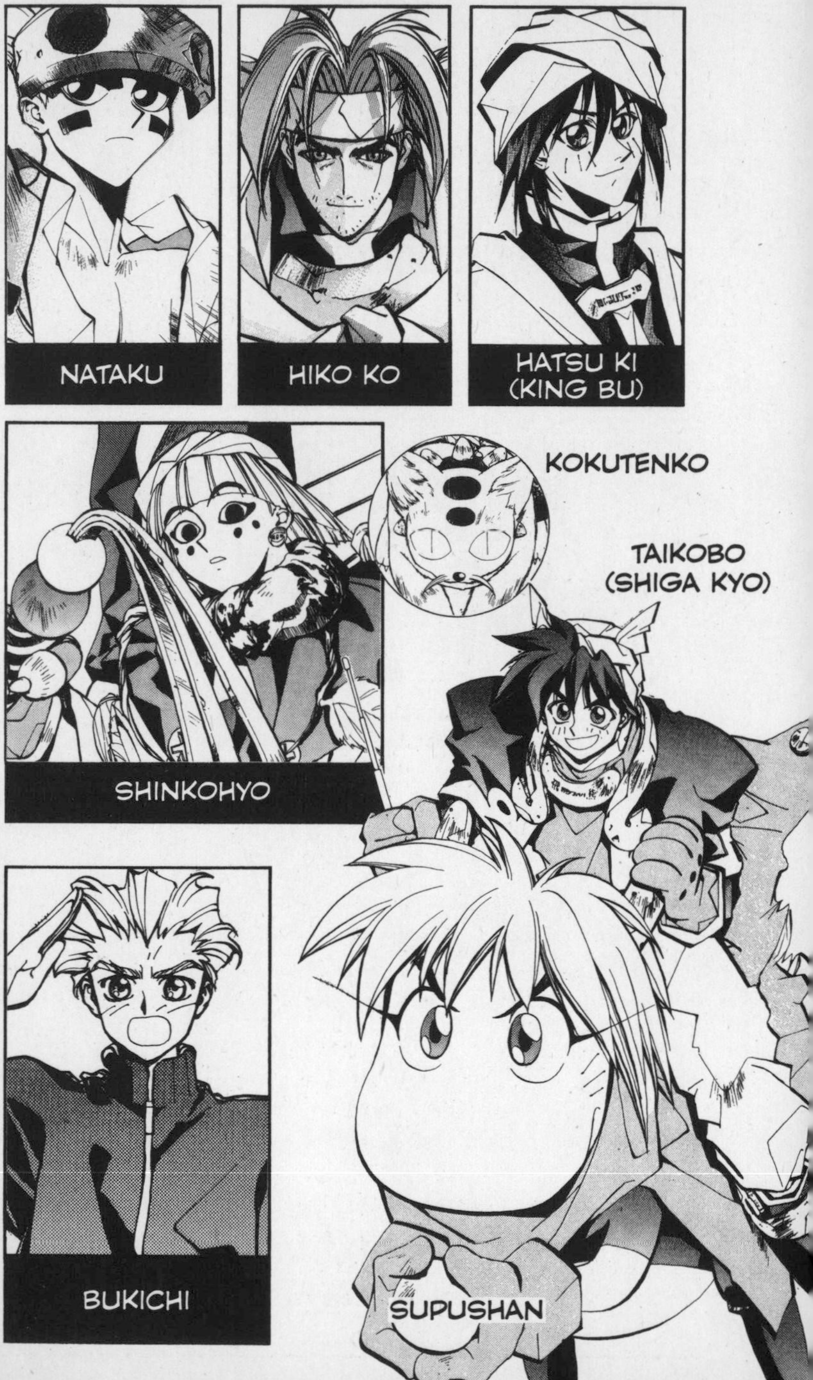
HATSU KI
(KING BU)
HIKO KO
NATAKU
KOKUTENKO
TAIKOBO
(SHIGA KYO)
SHINKOHYO
SUPUSHAN
BUKICHI

DAKKI

KING CHU

CHOKOMEI

INCHI

INCHON

The Story Thus Far

Ancient China, over 3,000 years ago. It is the era of the Yin Dynasty.

After King Chu, the emperor, married the beautiful Dakki, the good king was no longer himself, and became an unmanly and foolish ruler. Dakki, a *Sennyo* with a wicked heart, took control of Yin and the country fell into chaos.

To save the human world, the Hoshin Project was put into action. The project will seal evil Sennin and Doshi into the Shinkai, and cause Seihakuko Sho Ki to set up a new dynasty to replace Yin. Taikobo, who was chosen to execute this project, acts to install Sho Ki's heir Hatsu Ki as the next king. Hatsu Ki takes the title King Bu and declares Seiki is now the Kingdom of Zhou, effectively declaring war against Yin. But Inchon, the Crown Prince of Yin who was supposed to ally with Zhou, returns to Yin instead. Now the battle between Yin and Zhou finally begins!

HOSHiN ENGi

VOL. 10
CONQUERING CHOKOMEI, PART 1

CONTENTS

Chapter 80

THE PRINCES' CHOICE, PART 4

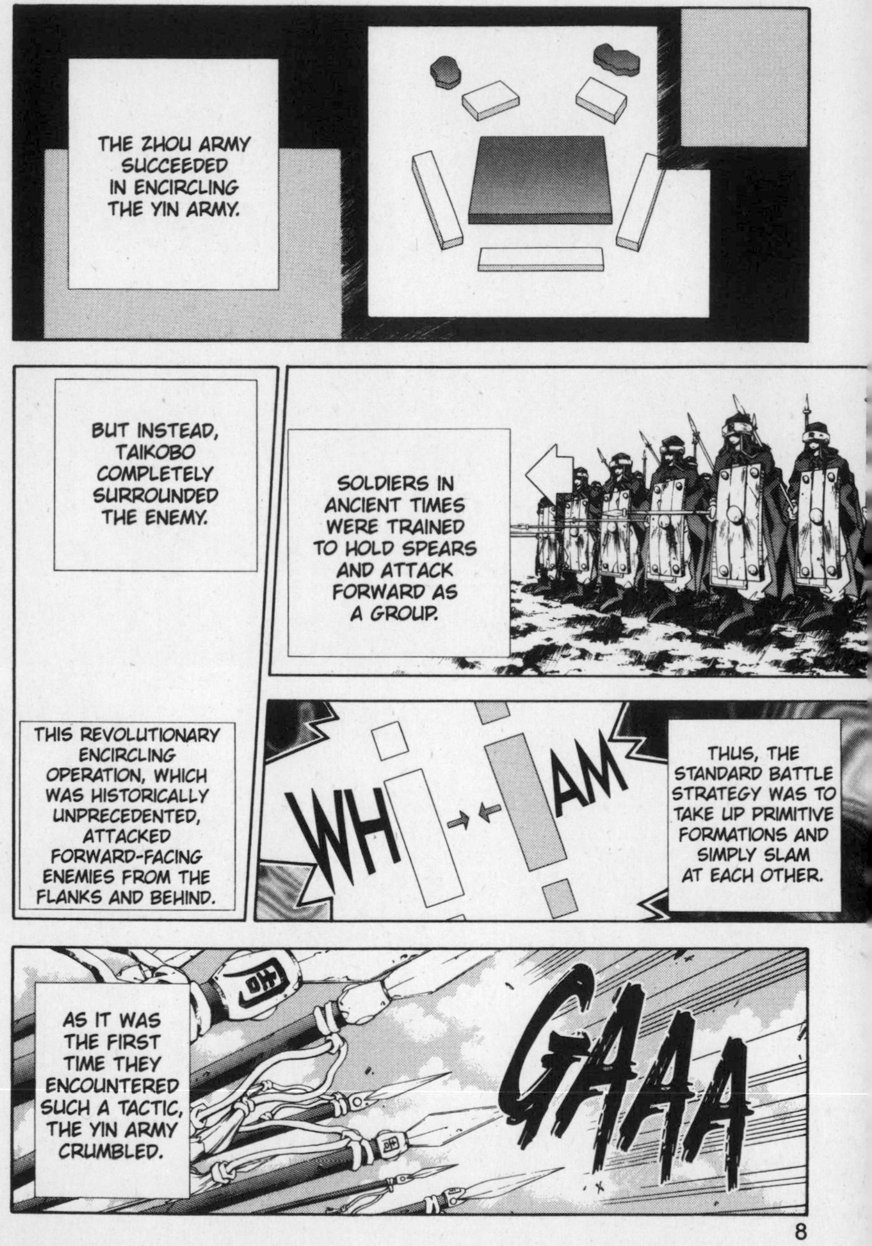
THE ZHOU ARMY SUCCEEDED IN ENCIRCLING THE YIN ARMY.
SOLDIERS IN ANCIENT TIMES WERE TRAINED TO HOLD SPEARS AND ATTACK FORWARD AS A GROUP.
THUS, THE STANDARD BATTLE STRATEGY WAS TO TAKE UP PRIMITIVE FORMATIONS AND SIMPLY SLAM AT EACH OTHER.
WHAM
BUT INSTEAD, TAIKOBO COMPLETELY SURROUNDED THE ENEMY.
THIS REVOLUTIONARY ENCIRCLING OPERATION, WHICH WAS HISTORICALLY UNPRECEDENTED, ATTACKED FORWARD-FACING ENEMIES FROM THE FLANKS AND BEHIND.
GAAA
AS IT WAS THE FIRST TIME THEY ENCOUNTERED SUCH A TACTIC, THE YIN ARMY CRUMBLED.

READ THIS WAY

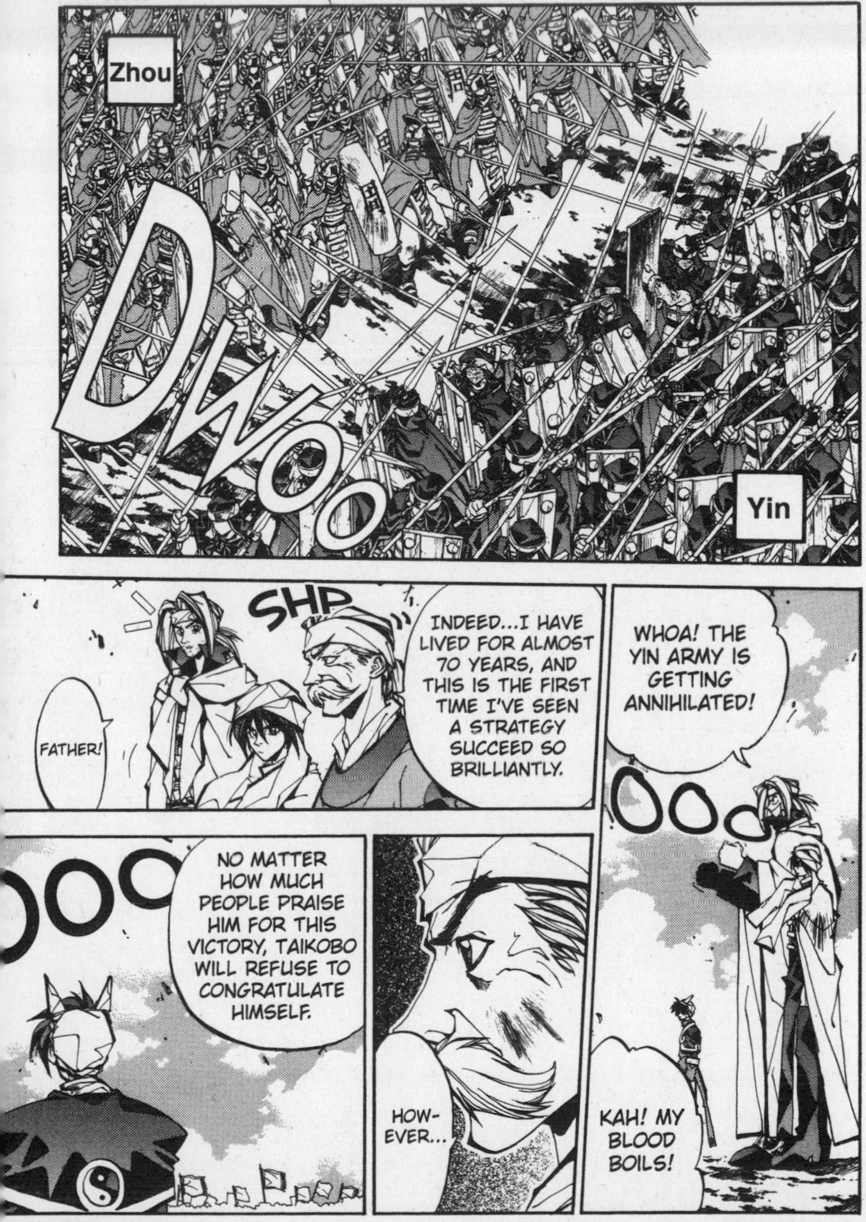
Zhou
DWOOO
Yin
WHOA! THE YIN ARMY IS GETTING ANNIHILATED!
INDEED...I HAVE LIVED FOR ALMOST 70 YEARS, AND THIS IS THE FIRST TIME I'VE SEEN A STRATEGY SUCCEED SO BRILLIANTLY.
SHP
FATHER!
OOO
KAH! MY BLOOD BOILS!
HOW-EVER...
OOO
NO MATTER HOW MUCH PEOPLE PRAISE HIM FOR THIS VICTORY, TAIKOBO WILL REFUSE TO CONGRATULATE HIMSELF.

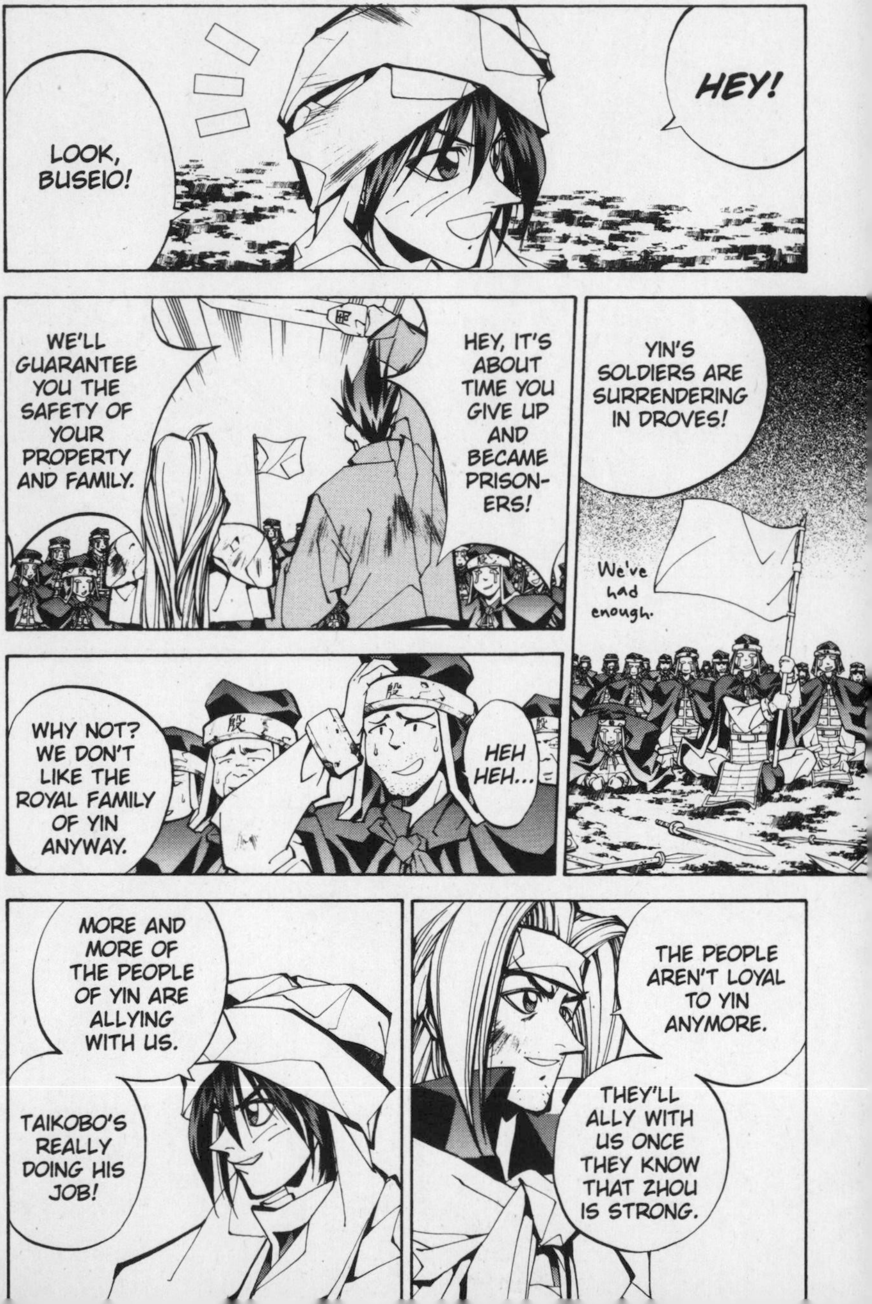
HEY!
LOOK, BUSEIO!
YIN'S SOLDIERS ARE SURRENDERING IN DROVES!
We've had enough.
HEY, IT'S ABOUT TIME YOU GIVE UP AND BECAME PRISON-ERS!
WE'LL GUARANTEE YOU THE SAFETY OF YOUR PROPERTY AND FAMILY.
HEH HEH...
WHY NOT? WE DON'T LIKE THE ROYAL FAMILY OF YIN ANYWAY.
THE PEOPLE AREN'T LOYAL TO YIN ANYMORE.
THEY'LL ALLY WITH US ONCE THEY KNOW THAT ZHOU IS STRONG.
MORE AND MORE OF THE PEOPLE OF YIN ARE ALLYING WITH US.
TAIKOBO'S REALLY DOING HIS JOB!

READ THIS WAY

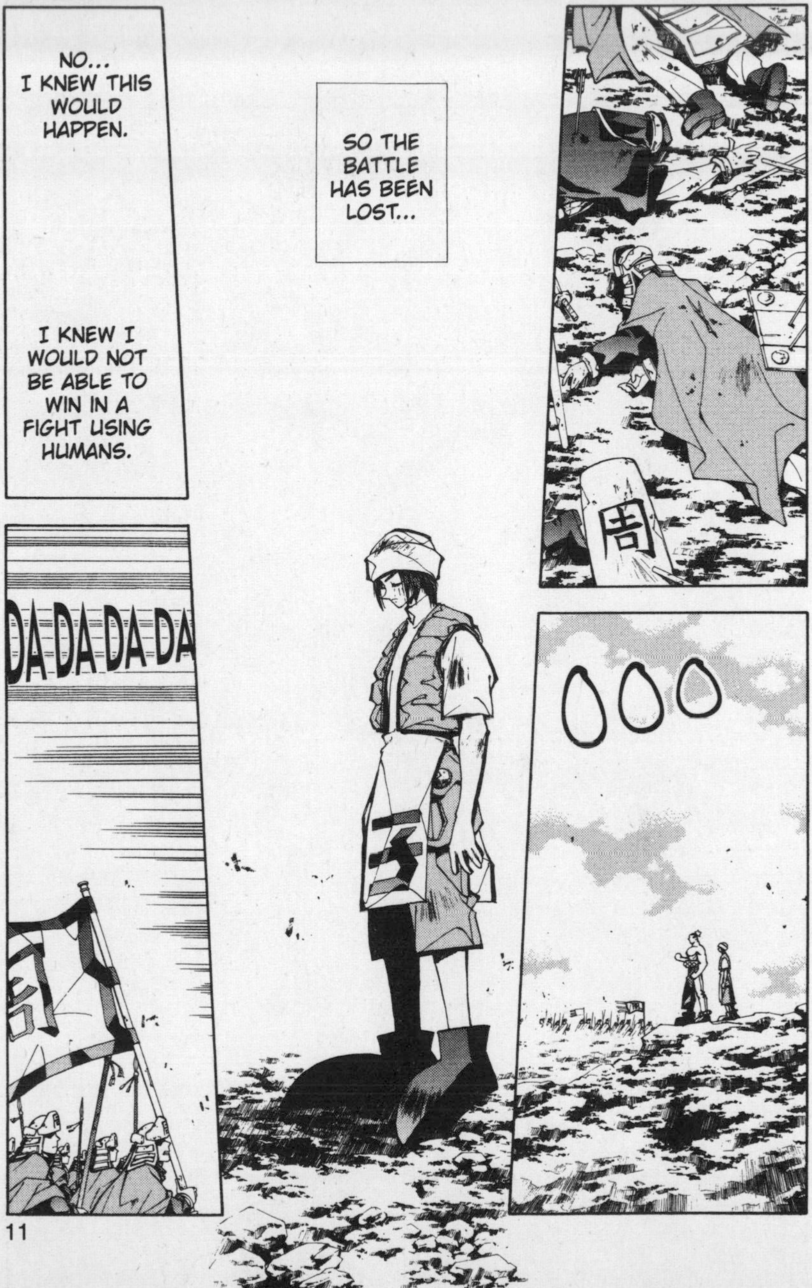

周
SO THE BATTLE HAS BEEN LOST...
NO... I KNEW THIS WOULD HAPPEN.
I KNEW I WOULD NOT BE ABLE TO WIN IN A FIGHT USING HUMANS.
DA DA DA DA

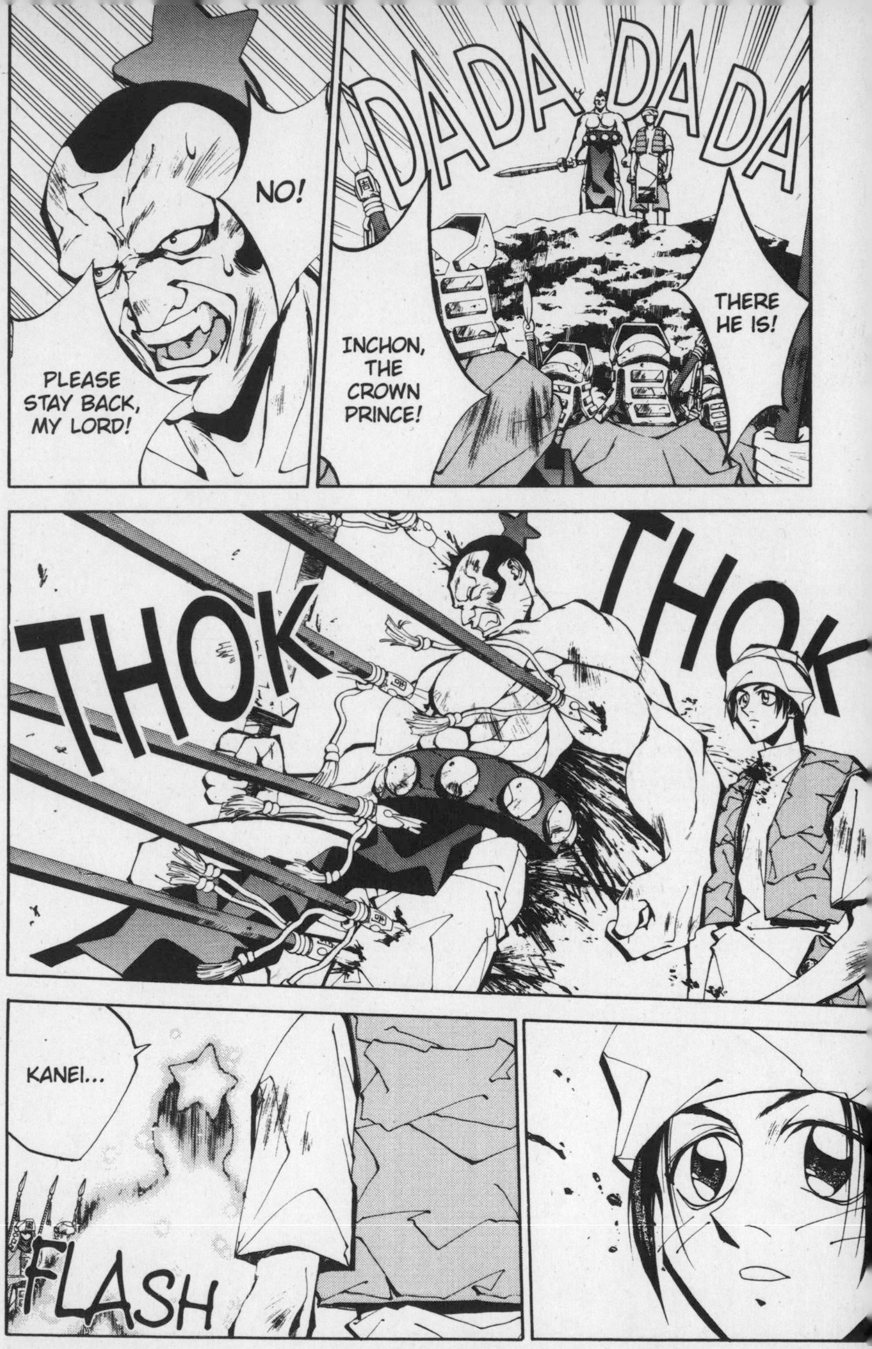
DADA DADA DADA
THERE HE IS!
INCHON, THE CROWN PRINCE!
NO!
PLEASE STAY BACK, MY LORD!
THOK THOK
KANEI...
FLASH

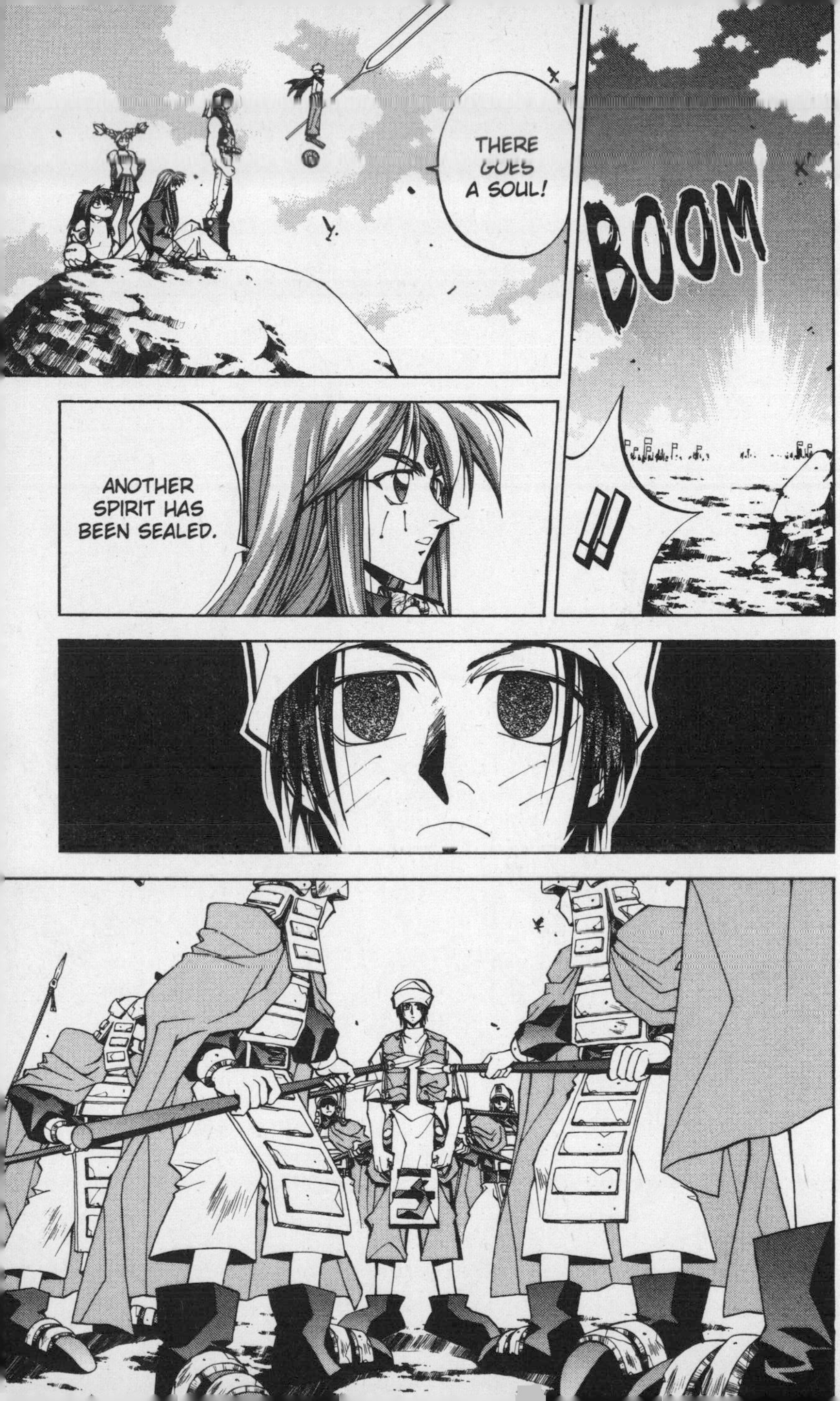
BOOM
!!
THERE GOES A SOUL!
ANOTHER SPIRIT HAS BEEN SEALED.

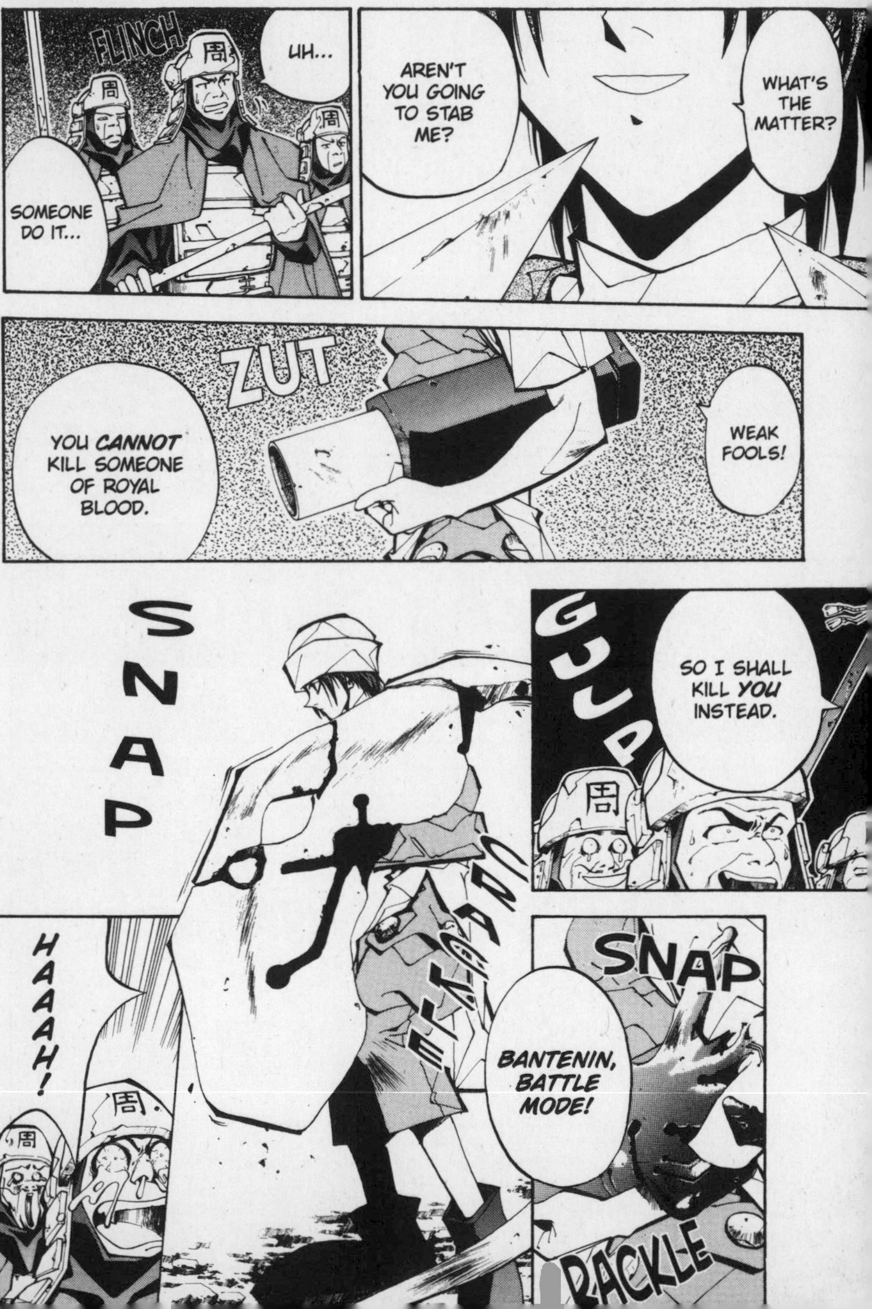
WHAT'S THE MATTER?
AREN'T YOU GOING TO STAB ME?
FLINCH
UH...
SOMEONE DO IT...
WEAK FOOLS!
ZUT
YOU *CANNOT* KILL SOMEONE OF ROYAL BLOOD.
SO I SHALL KILL *YOU* INSTEAD.
GULP
SNAP
SNAP
BANTENIN, BATTLE MODE!
RACKLE
CRACKLE
HAAAAH!

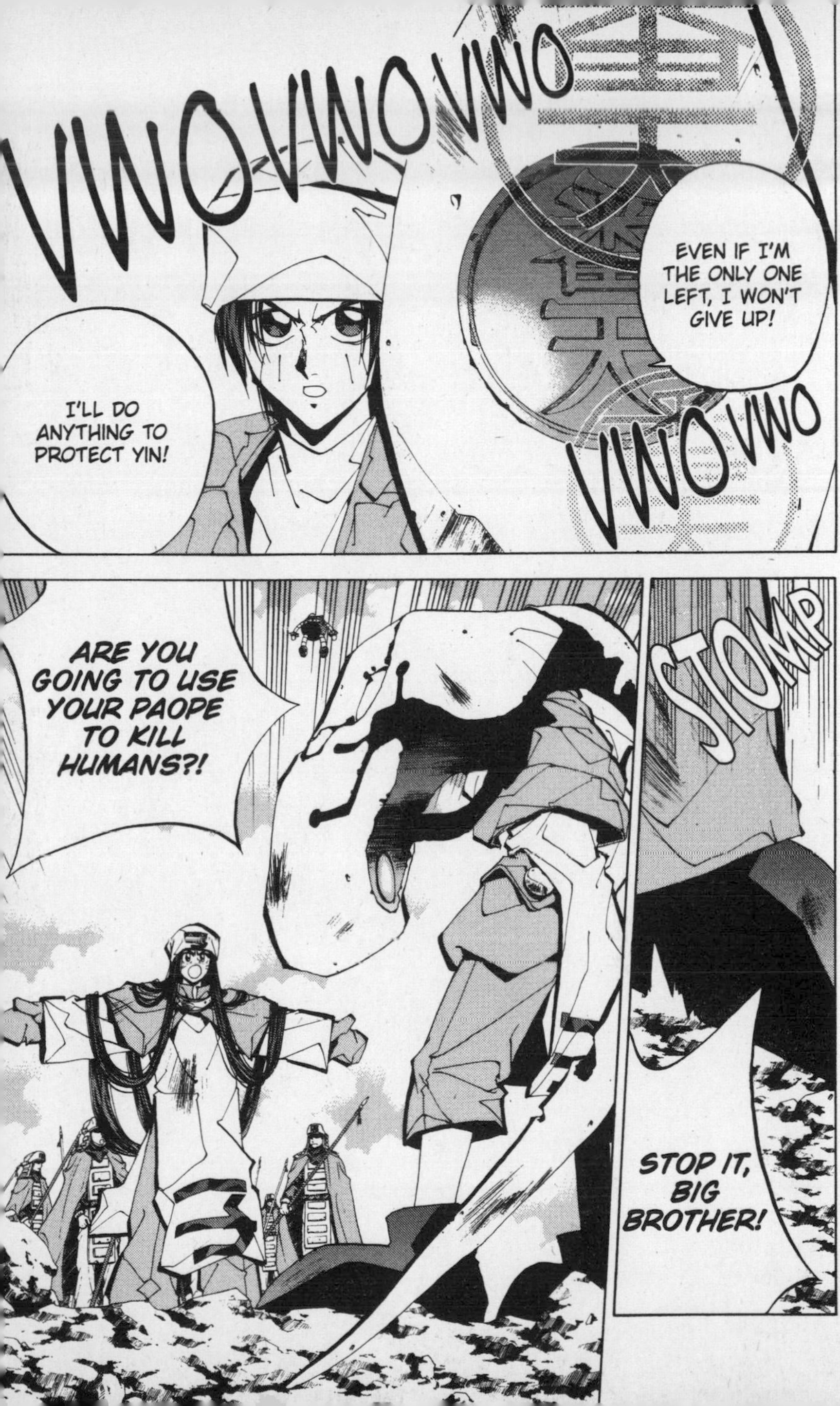
VWOVWOVWO
EVEN IF I'M THE ONLY ONE LEFT, I WON'T GIVE UP!
VWOVWO
I'LL DO ANYTHING TO PROTECT YIN!
STOMP
STOP IT, BIG BROTHER!
ARE YOU GOING TO USE YOUR PAOPE TO KILL HUMANS?!

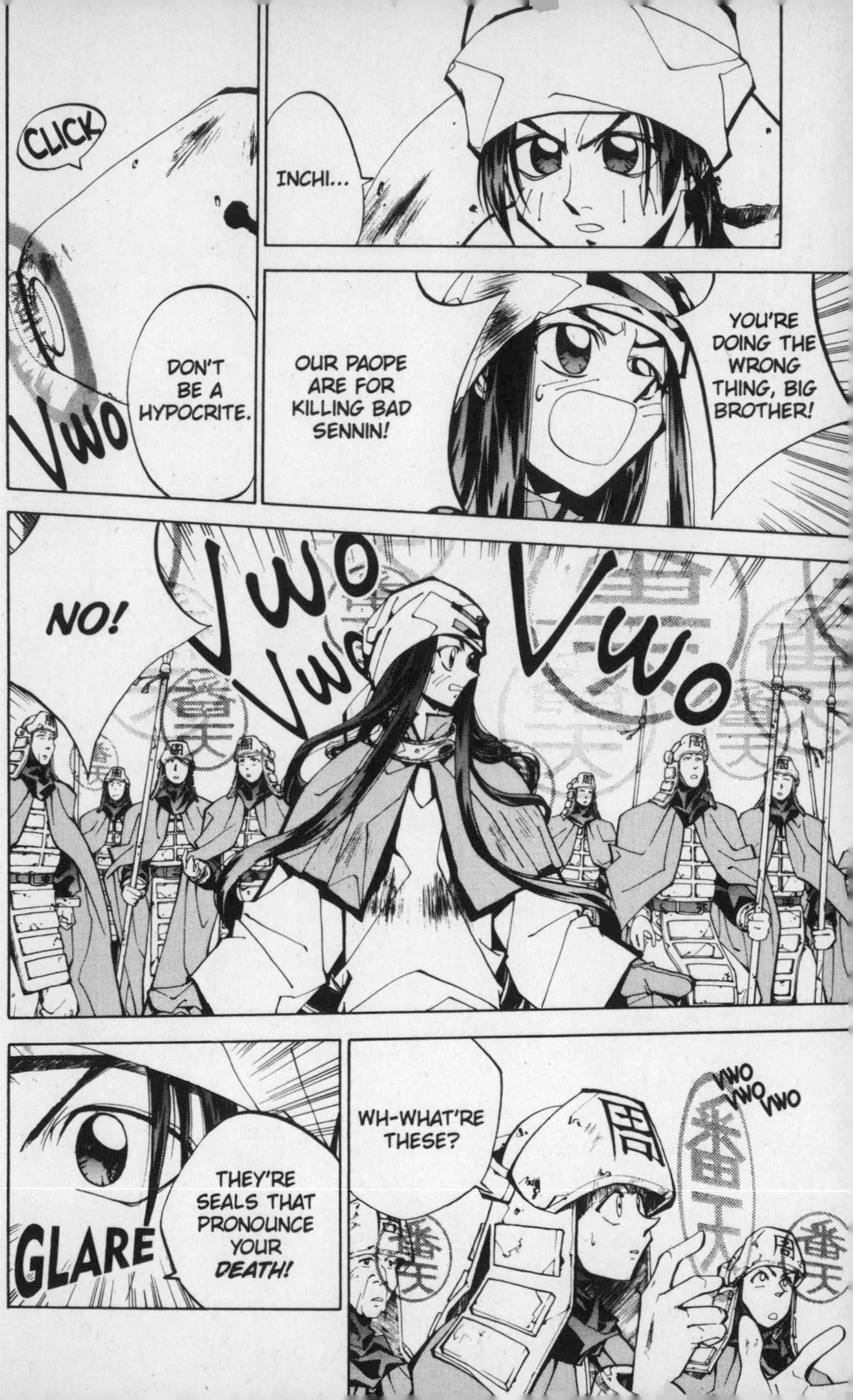
INCHI...
CLICK
YOU'RE DOING THE WRONG THING, BIG BROTHER!
OUR PAOPE ARE FOR KILLING BAD SENNIN!
DON'T BE A HYPOCRITE.
VWO
VWO
VWO
VWO
NO!
VWO VWO VWO
WH-WHAT'RE THESE?
THEY'RE SEALS THAT PRONOUNCE YOUR *DEATH!*
GLARE

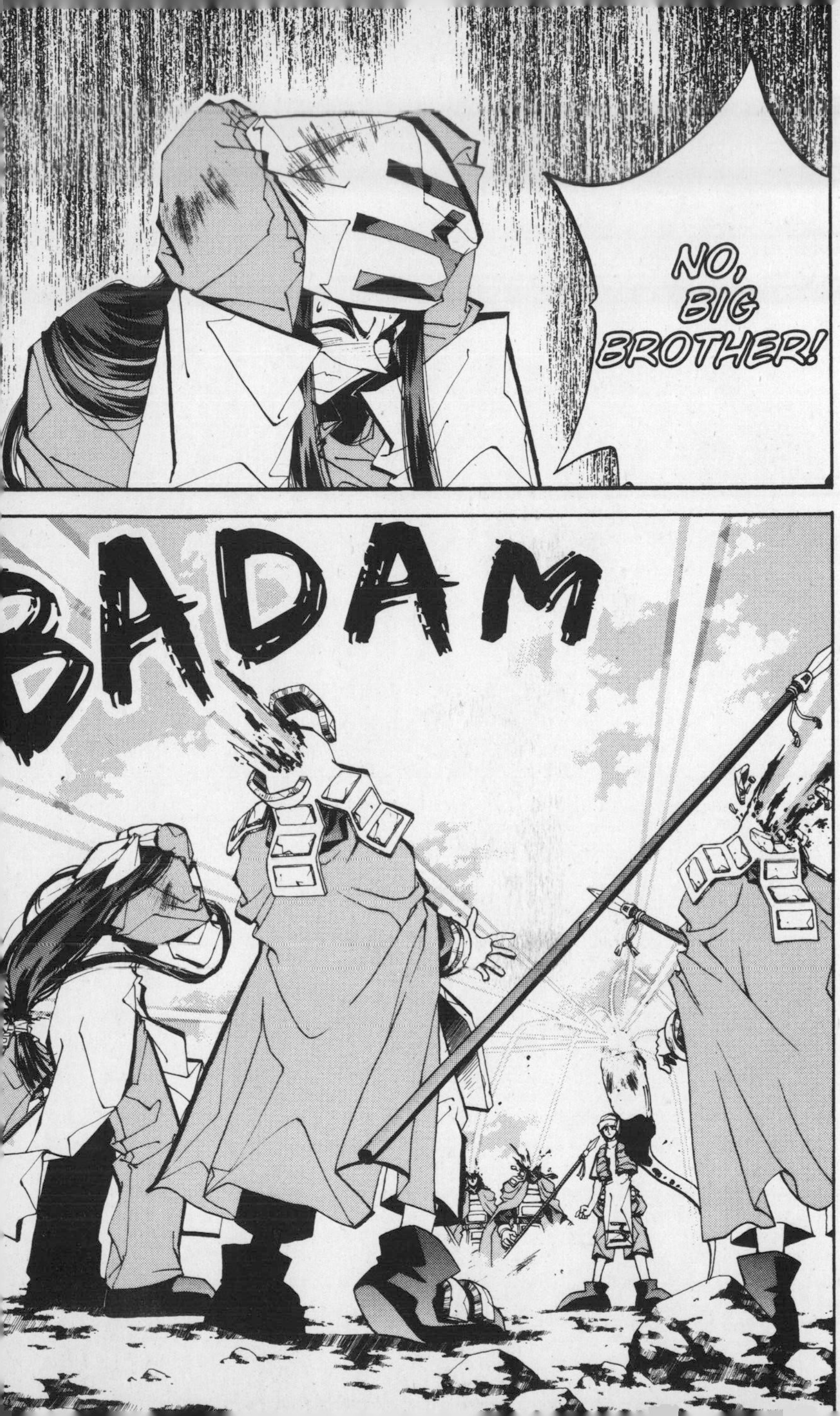
NO, BIG BROTHER!
BADAM

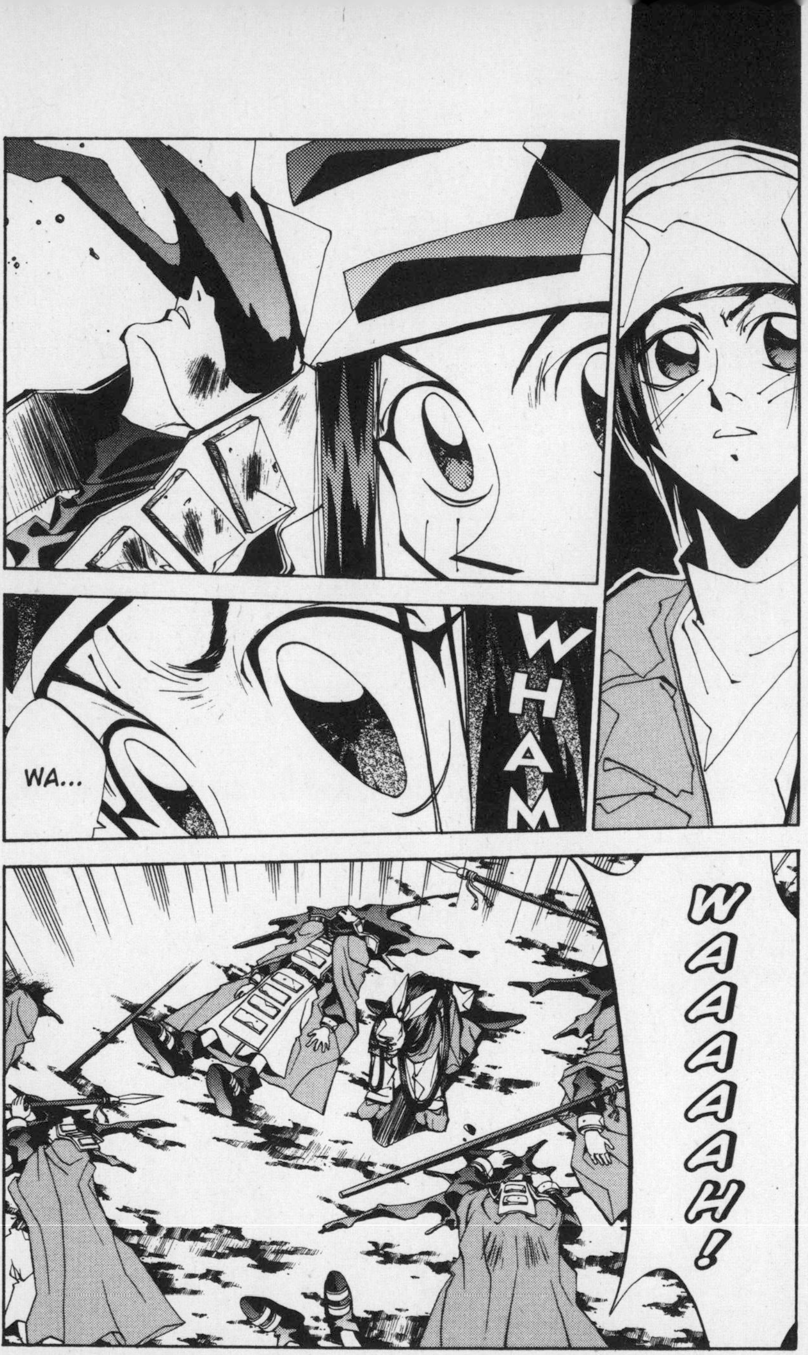
WHAM
WA...
WAAAAAAAAH!

READ THIS WAY

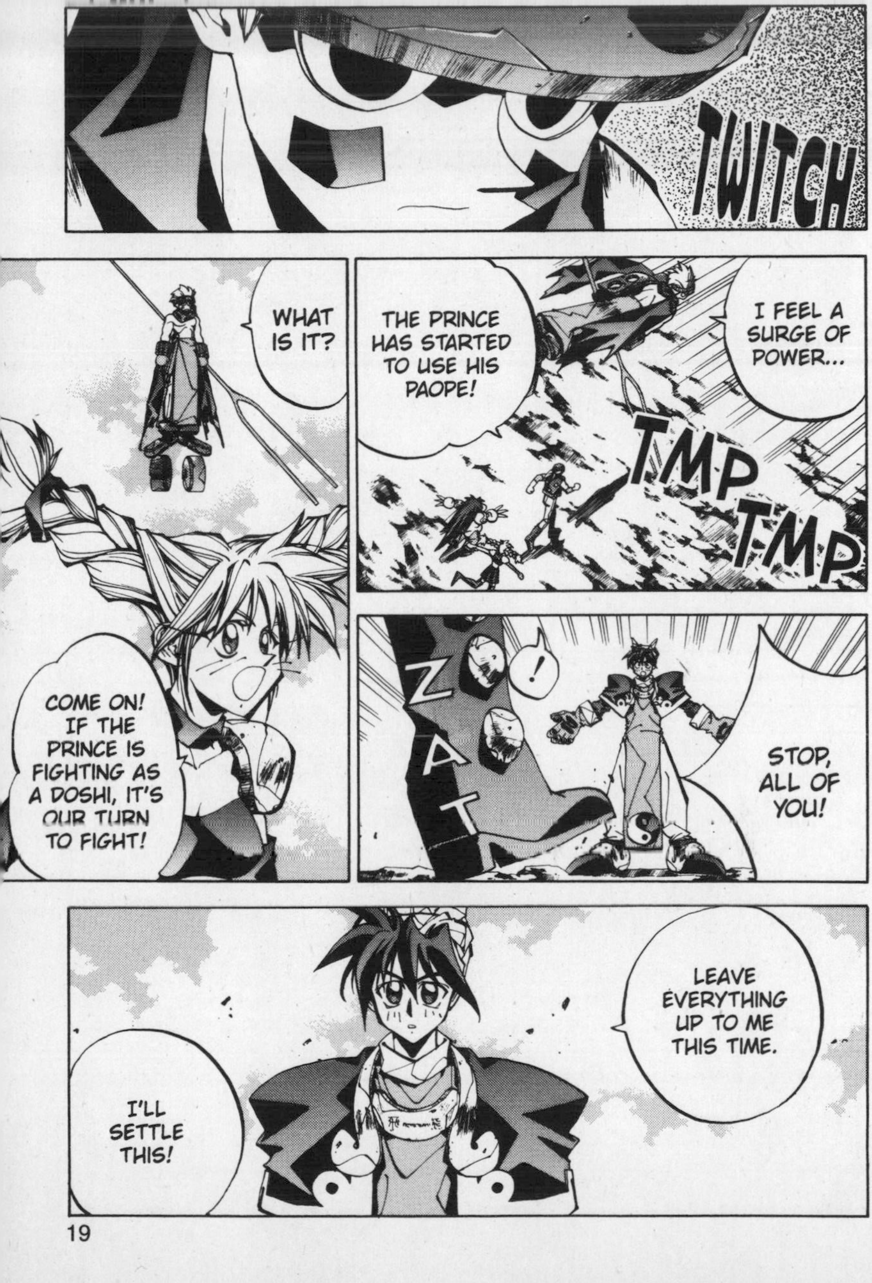
TWITCH
I FEEL A SURGE OF POWER...
THE PRINCE HAS STARTED TO USE HIS PAOPE!
TMP TMP
STOP, ALL OF YOU!
!
ZAT
WHAT IS IT?
COME ON! IF THE PRINCE IS FIGHTING AS A DOSHI, IT'S OUR TURN TO FIGHT!
LEAVE EVERYTHING UP TO ME THIS TIME.
I'LL SETTLE THIS!

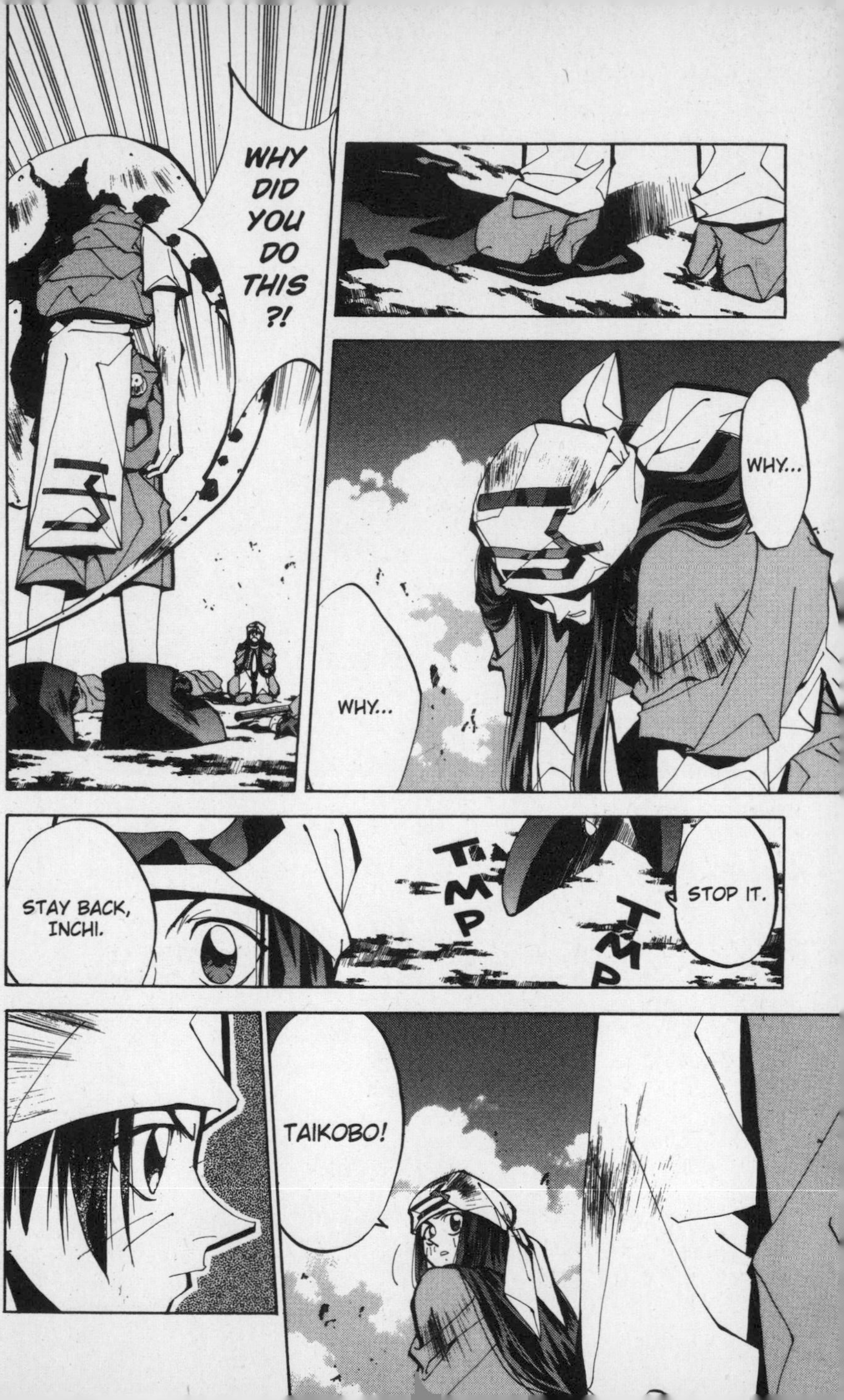
WHY...
WHY...
WHY DID YOU DO THIS?!
STOP IT.
TMP
TMP
STAY BACK, INCHI.
TAIKOBO!

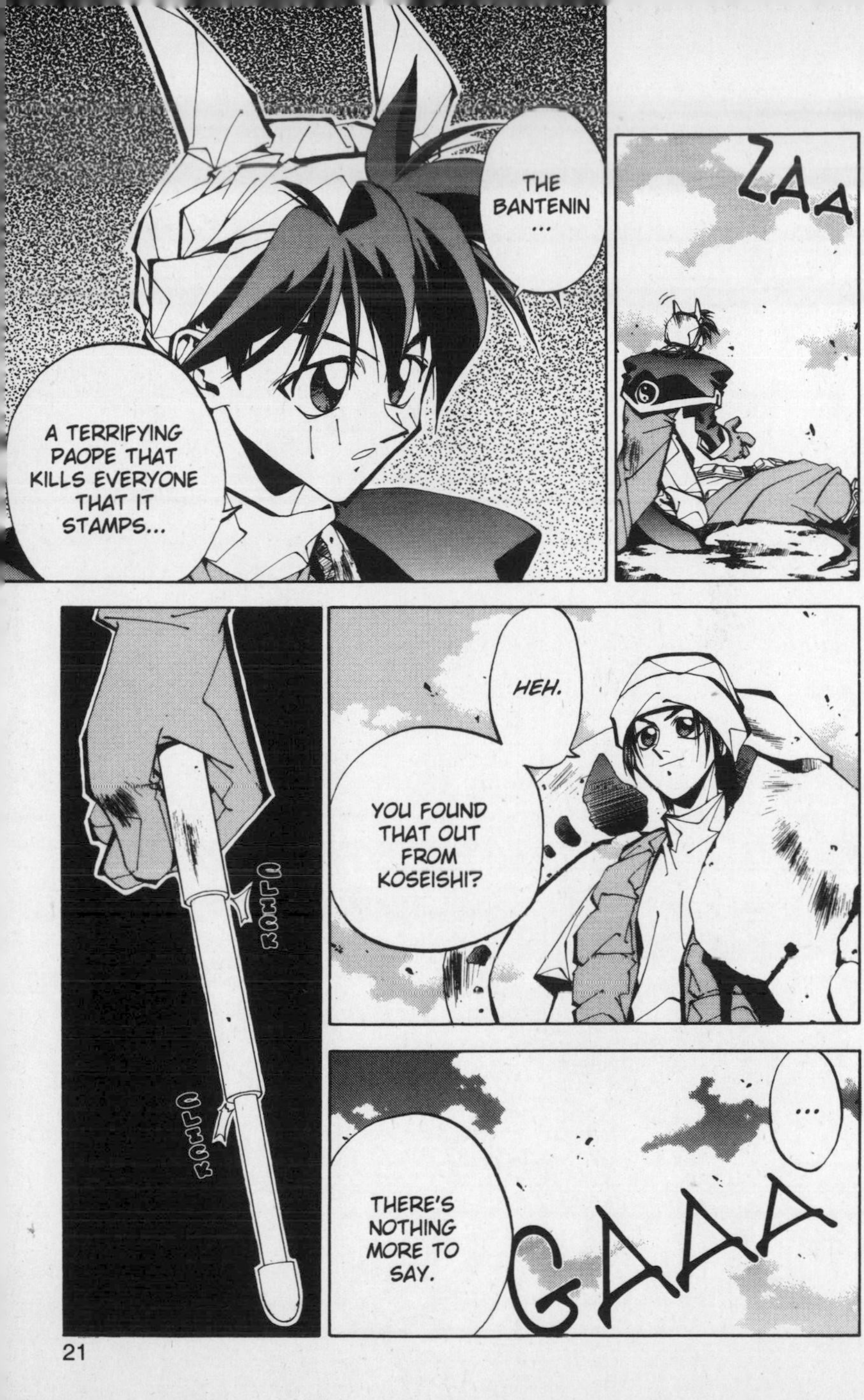
ZAA
THE BANTENIN ...
A TERRIFYING PAOPE THAT KILLS EVERYONE THAT IT STAMPS...
HEH.
YOU FOUND THAT OUT FROM KOSEISHI?
...
THERE'S NOTHING MORE TO SAY.
GAAA
CLICK
CLICK

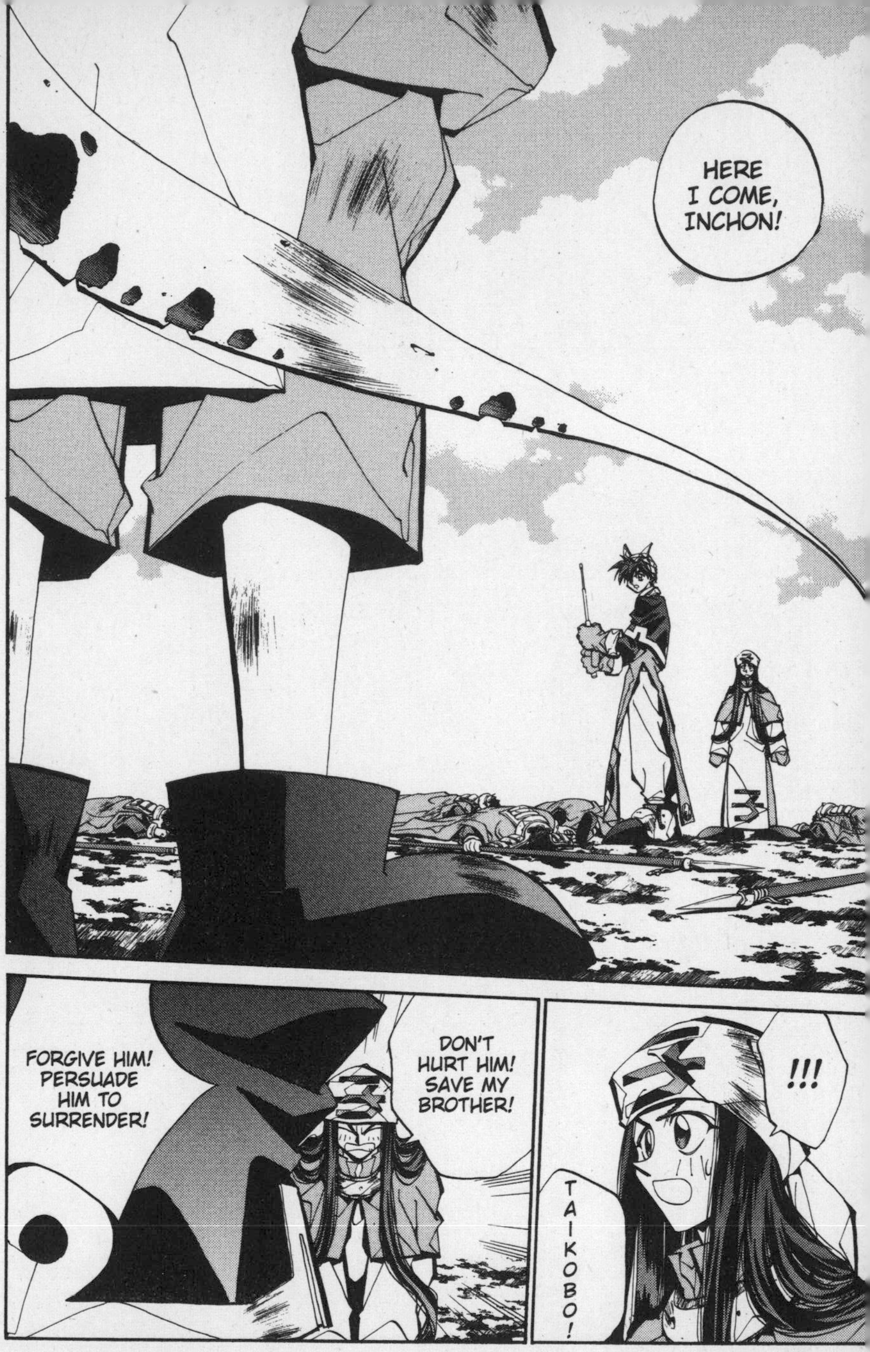
HERE I COME, INCHON!
!!!
TAIKOBO!
DON'T HURT HIM! SAVE MY BROTHER!
FORGIVE HIM! PERSUADE HIM TO SURRENDER!

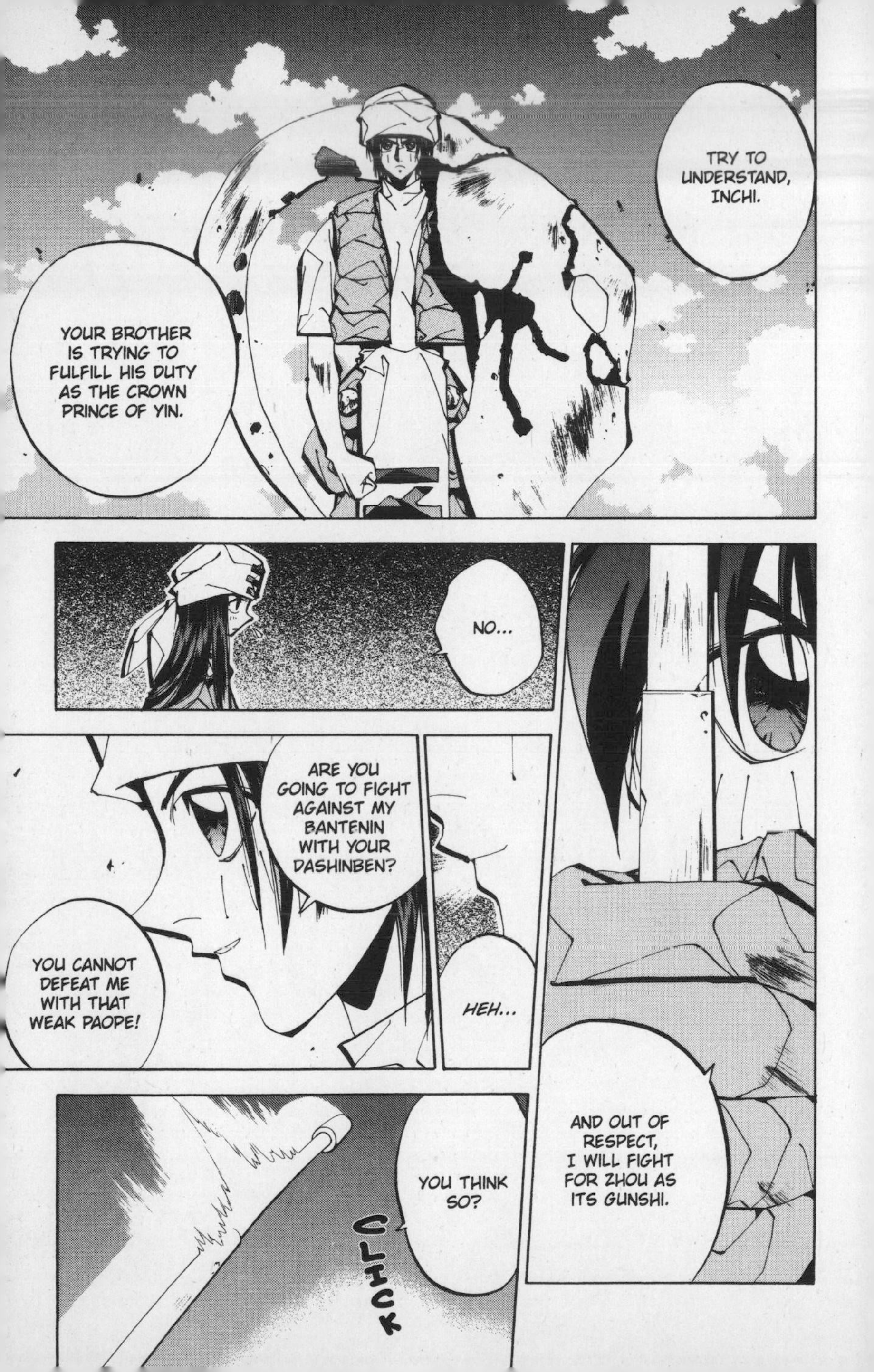
TRY TO UNDERSTAND, INCHI.
YOUR BROTHER IS TRYING TO FULFILL HIS DUTY AS THE CROWN PRINCE OF YIN.
AND OUT OF RESPECT, I WILL FIGHT FOR ZHOU AS ITS GUNSHI.
NO...
ARE YOU GOING TO FIGHT AGAINST MY BANTENIN WITH YOUR DASHINBEN?
YOU CANNOT DEFEAT ME WITH THAT WEAK PAOPE!
HEH...
YOU THINK SO?
CLICK

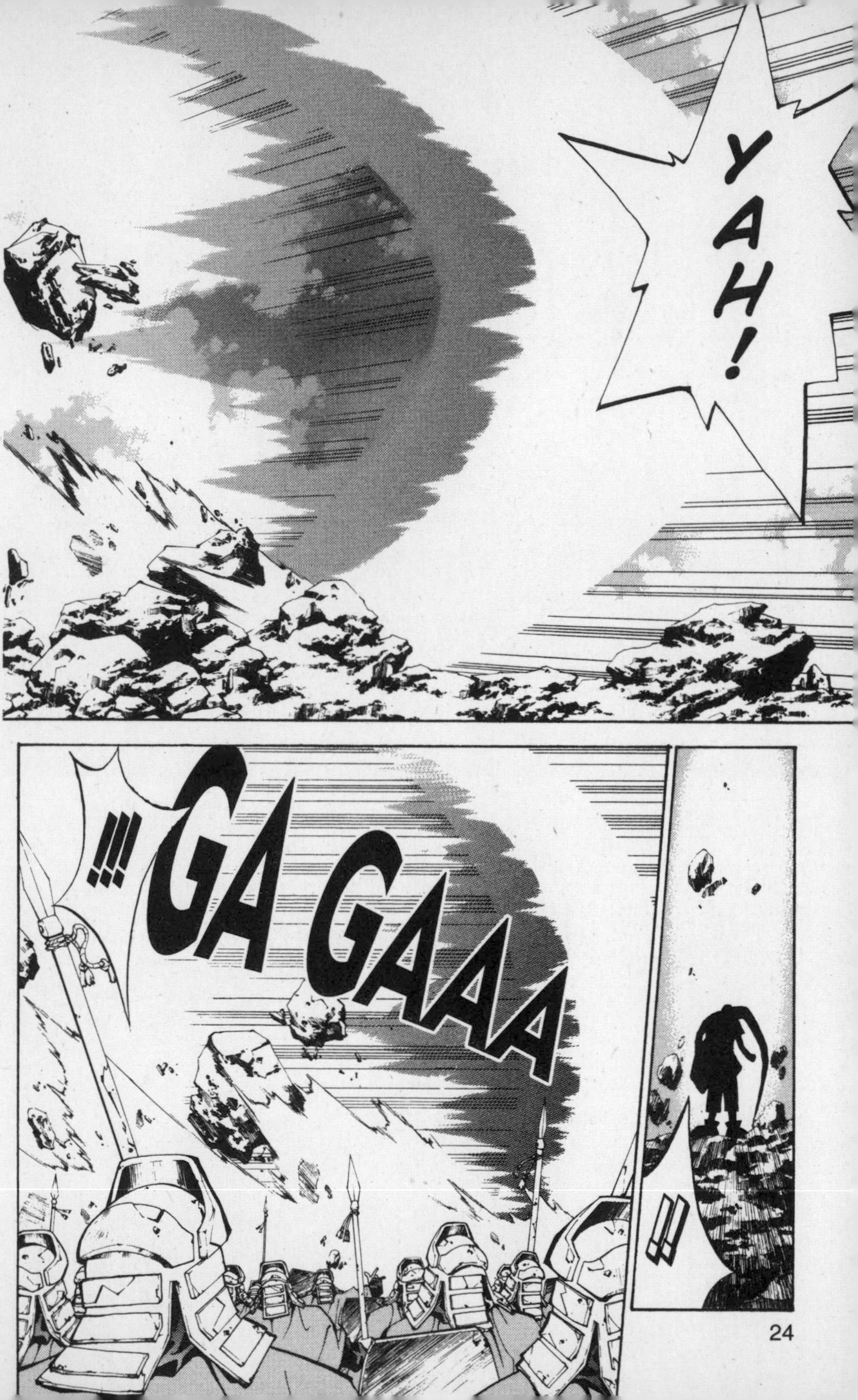
YAH!
!!
!!! GA GAAA

READ THIS WAY

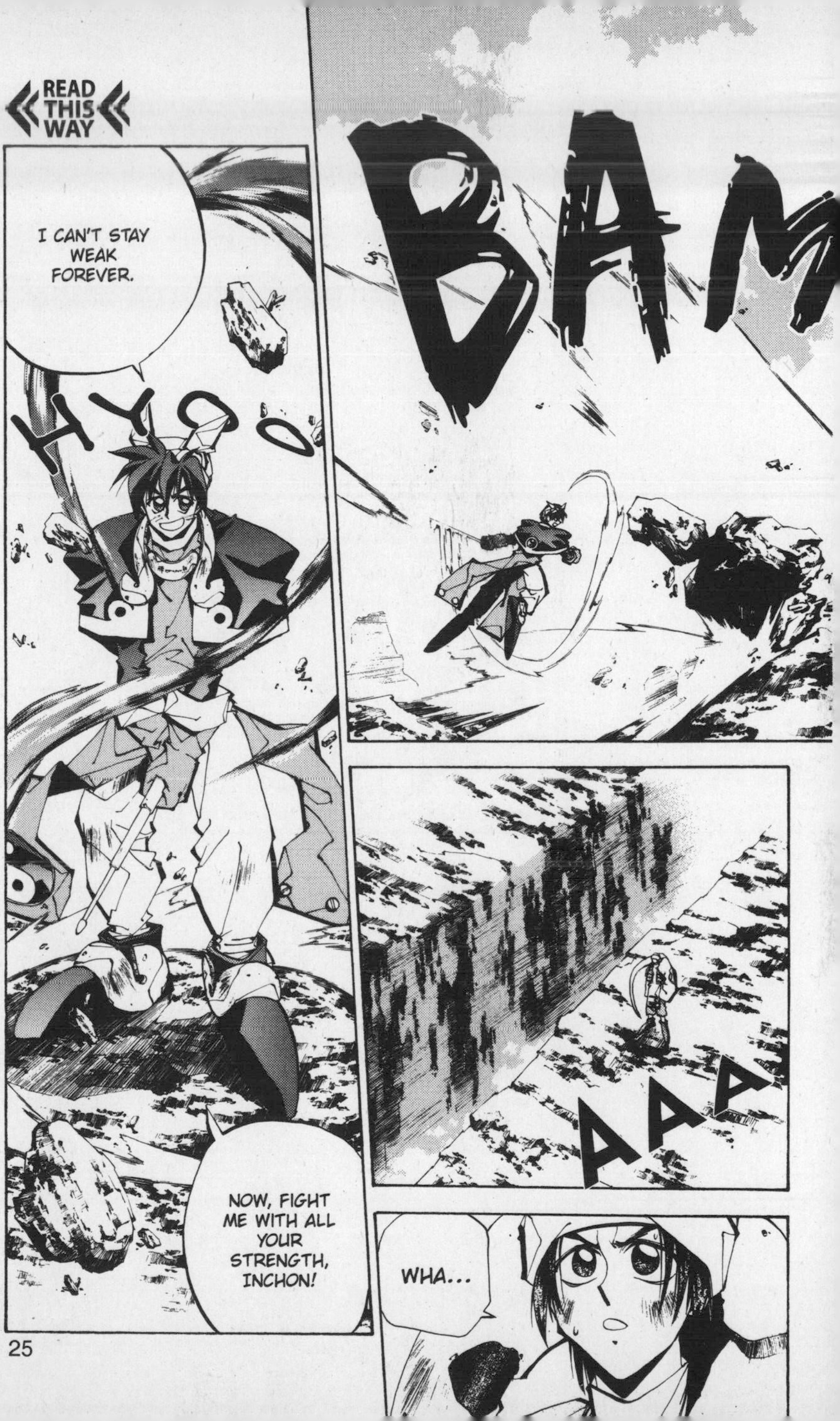
BAM
AAP
WHA...
I CAN'T STAY WEAK FOREVER.
NOW, FIGHT ME WITH ALL YOUR STRENGTH, INCHON!

封神演義

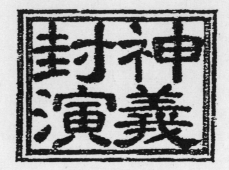

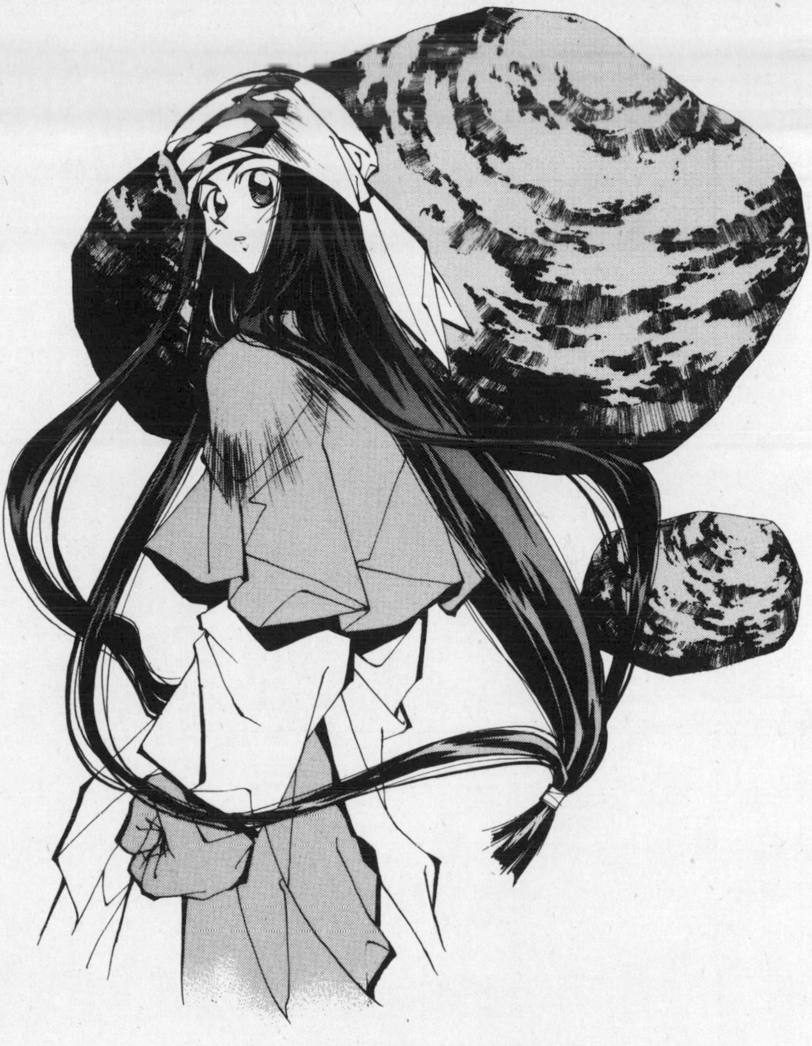

Chapter 81

THE PRINCES' CHOICE, PART 5

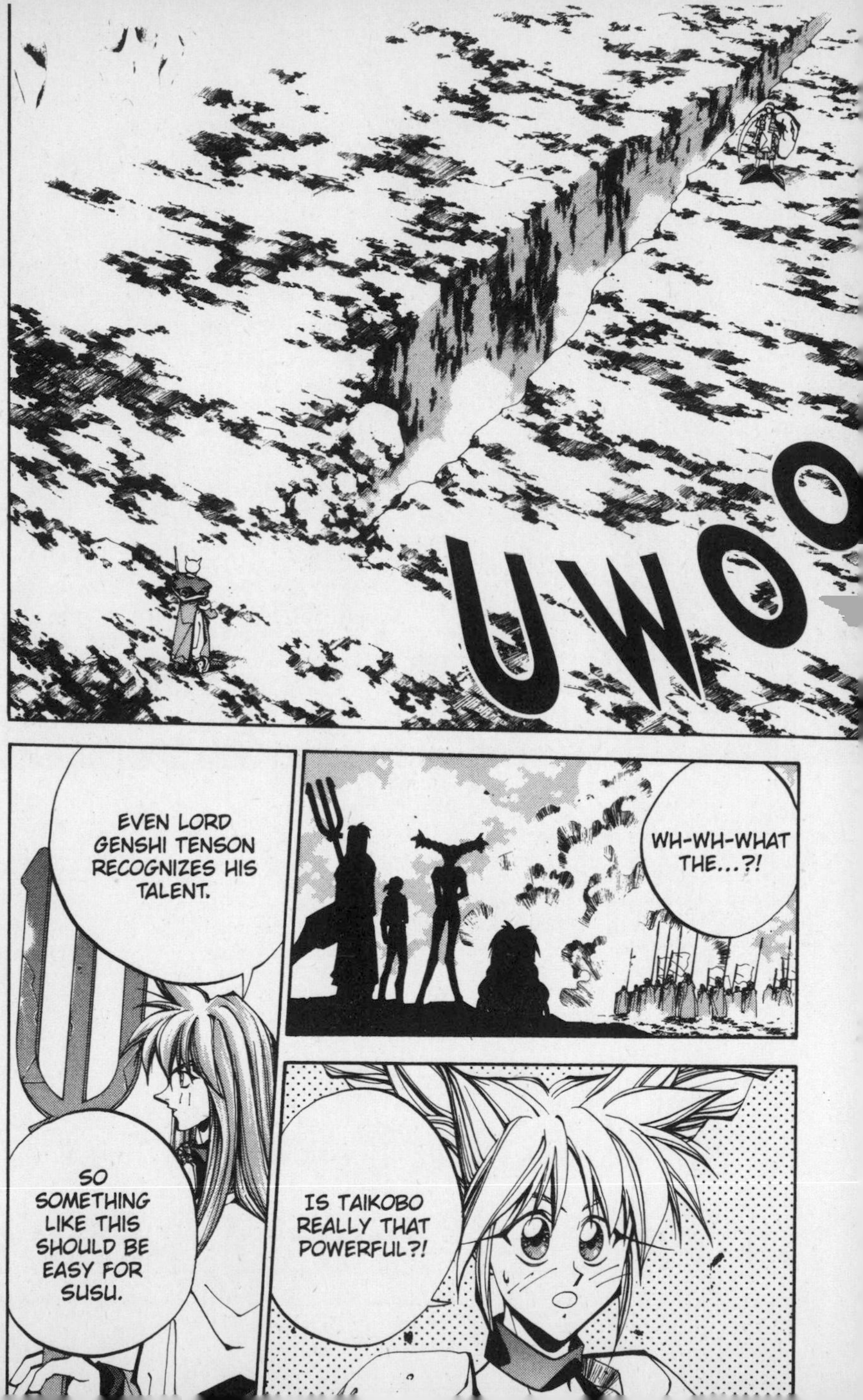
UWOO
WH-WH-WHAT THE...?!
IS TAIKOBO REALLY THAT POWERFUL?!
EVEN LORD GENSHI TENSON RECOGNIZES HIS TALENT.
SO SOMETHING LIKE THIS SHOULD BE EASY FOR SUSU.

READ THIS WAY

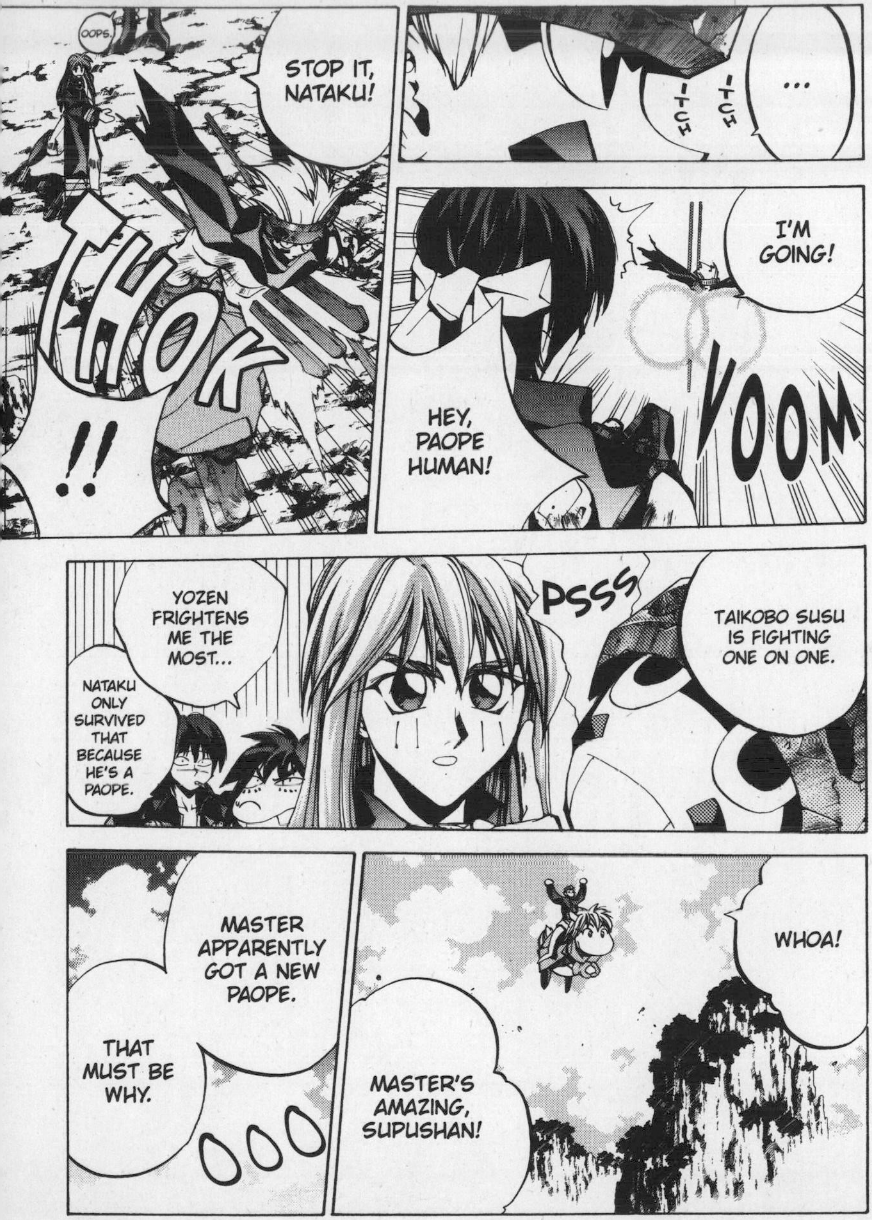
...
ITCH ITCH
I'M GOING!
VOOM
HEY, PAOPE HUMAN!
STOP IT, NATAKU!
OOPS.
THOK!!
TAIKOBO SUSU IS FIGHTING ONE ON ONE.
PSSS
YOZEN FRIGHTENS ME THE MOST...
NATAKU ONLY SURVIVED THAT BECAUSE HE'S A PAOPE.
WHOA!
MASTER'S AMAZING, SUPUSHAN!
MASTER APPARENTLY GOT A NEW PAOPE.
THAT MUST BE WHY.

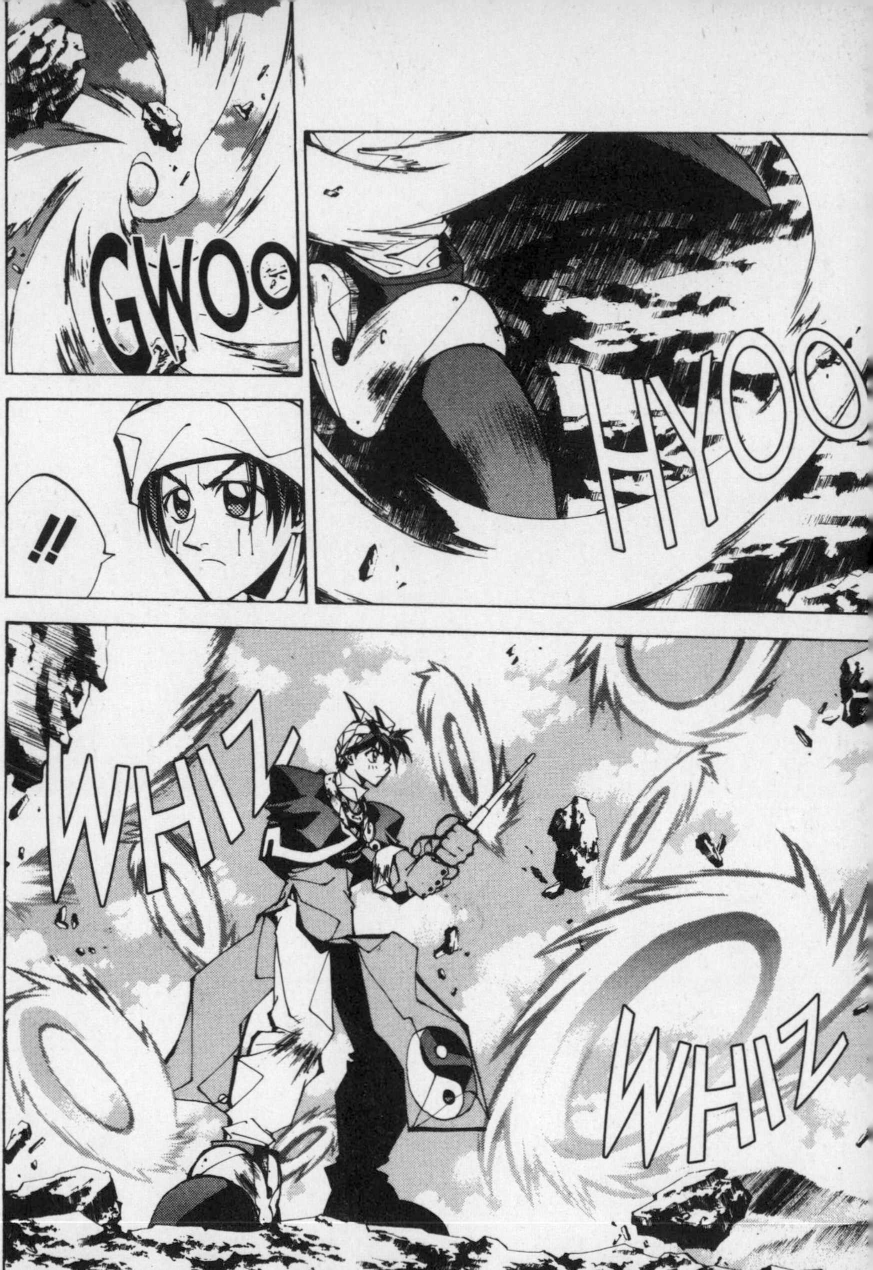
HYOO
GWOO
!!
WHIZ
WHIZ

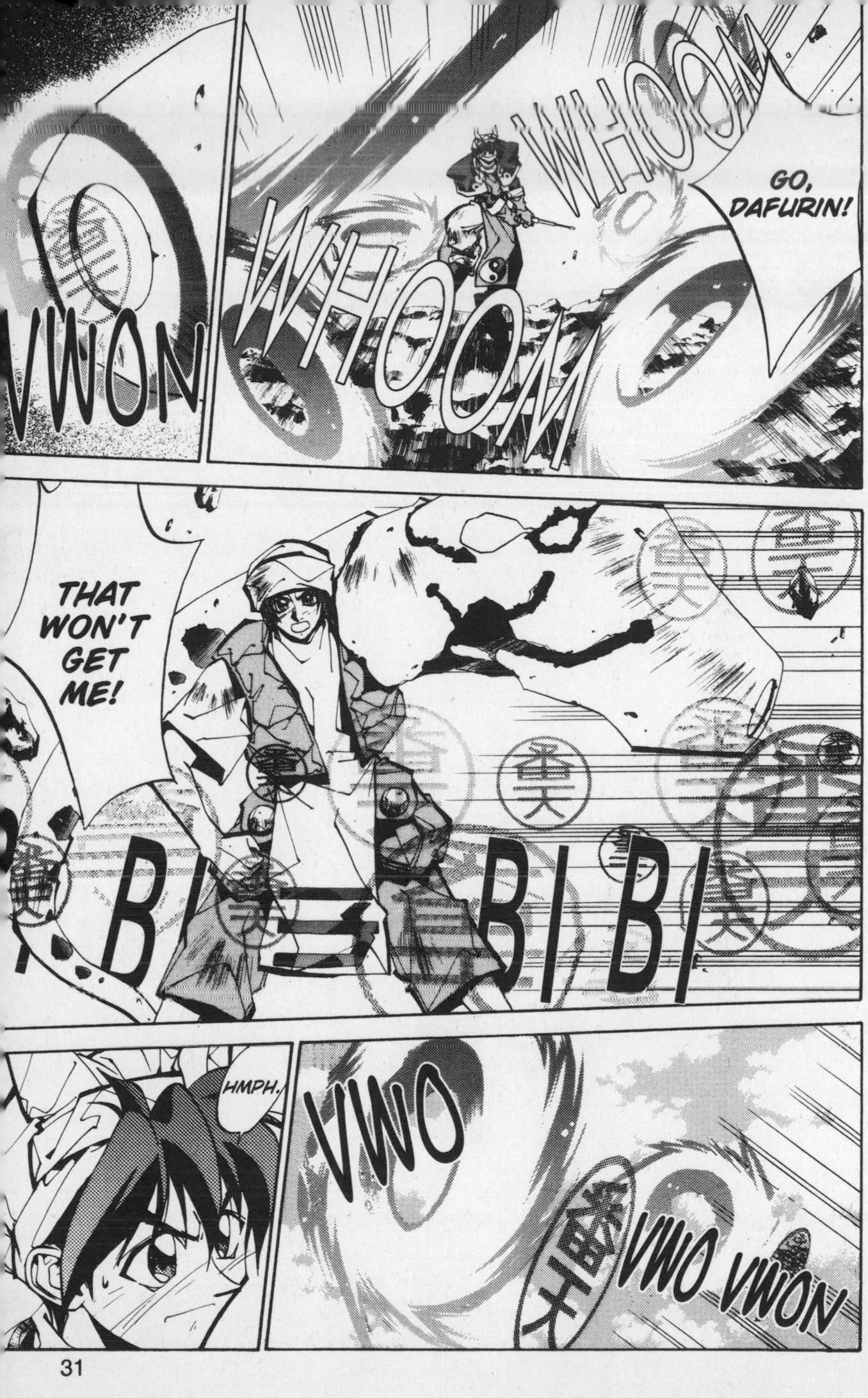
GO, DAFURIN!
WHOOM
WHOOM
VWON
THAT WON'T GET ME!
BI BI BI
VWO
VWO VWON
HMPH.

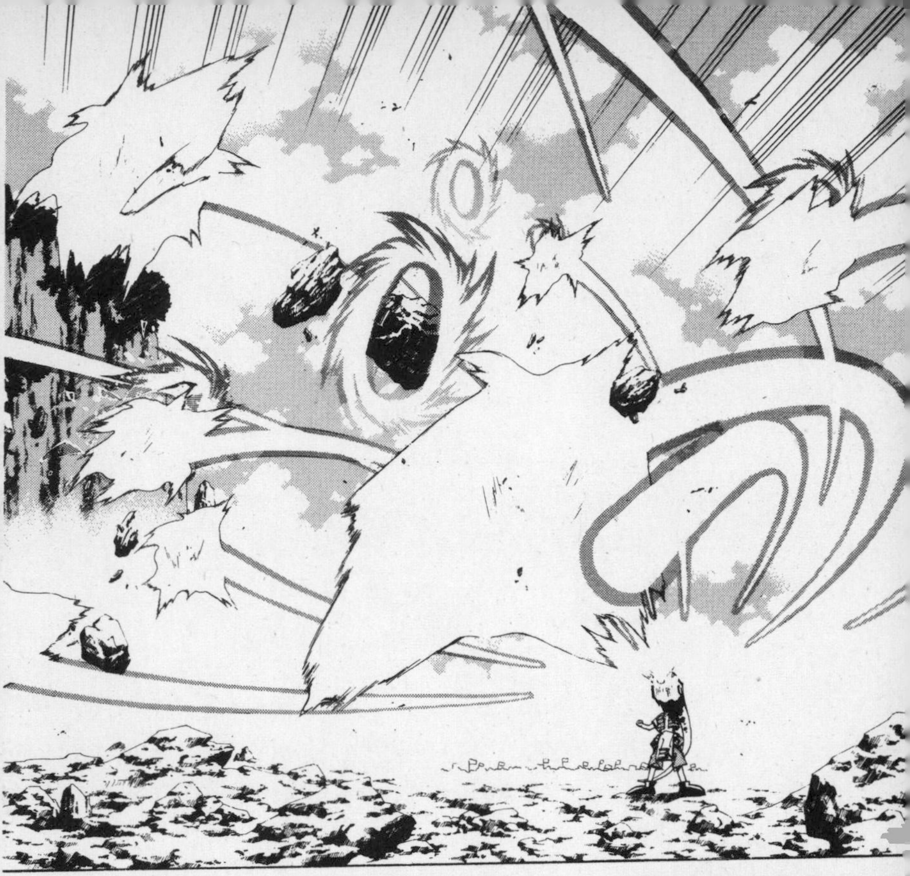

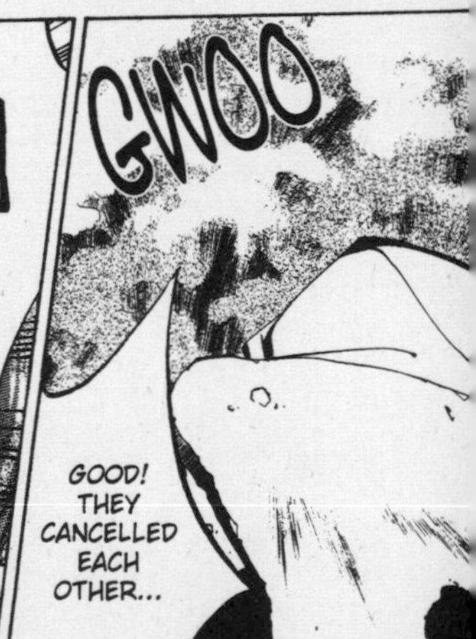
GWOO
GOOD! THEY CANCELLED EACH OTHER...

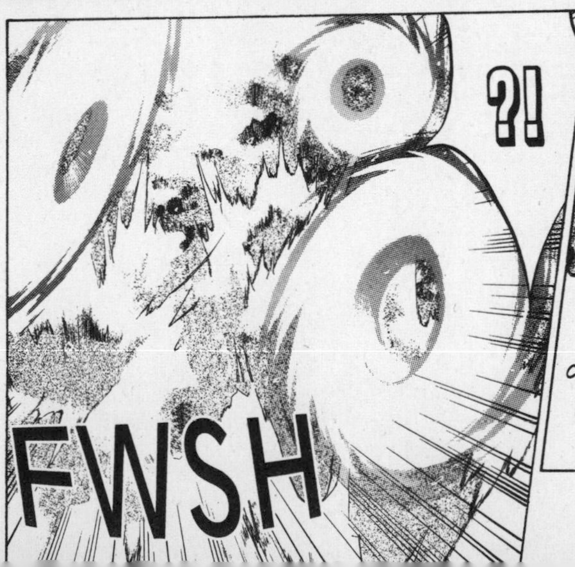
?!
FWSH

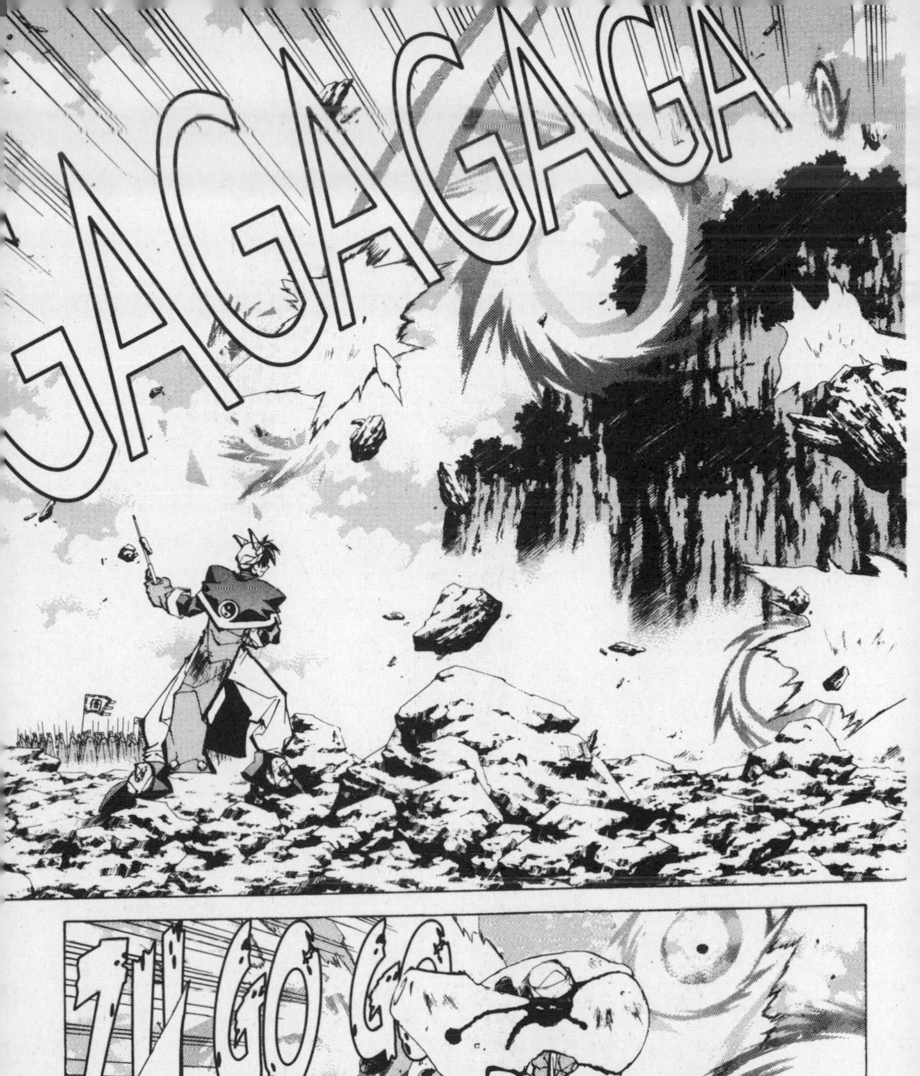
GAGAGAGA
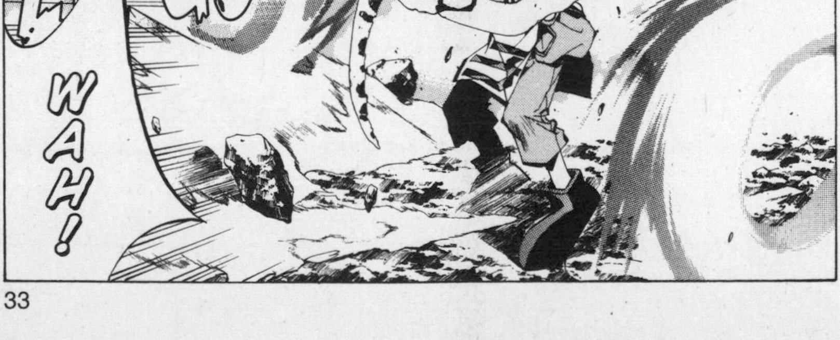
GOGO
WAH!

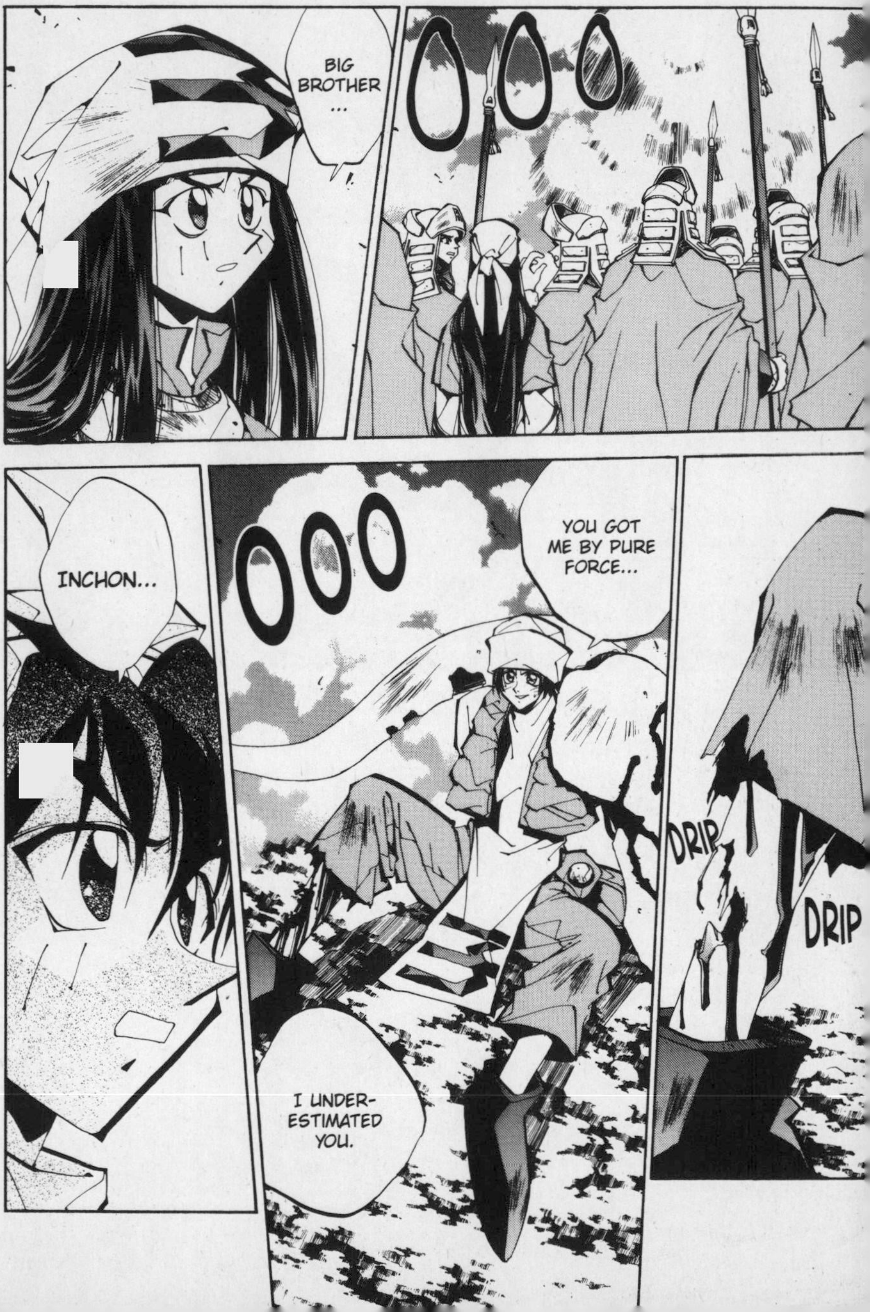
BIG BROTHER ...
DRIP
DRIP
YOU GOT ME BY PURE FORCE...
I UNDER-ESTIMATED YOU.
INCHON...

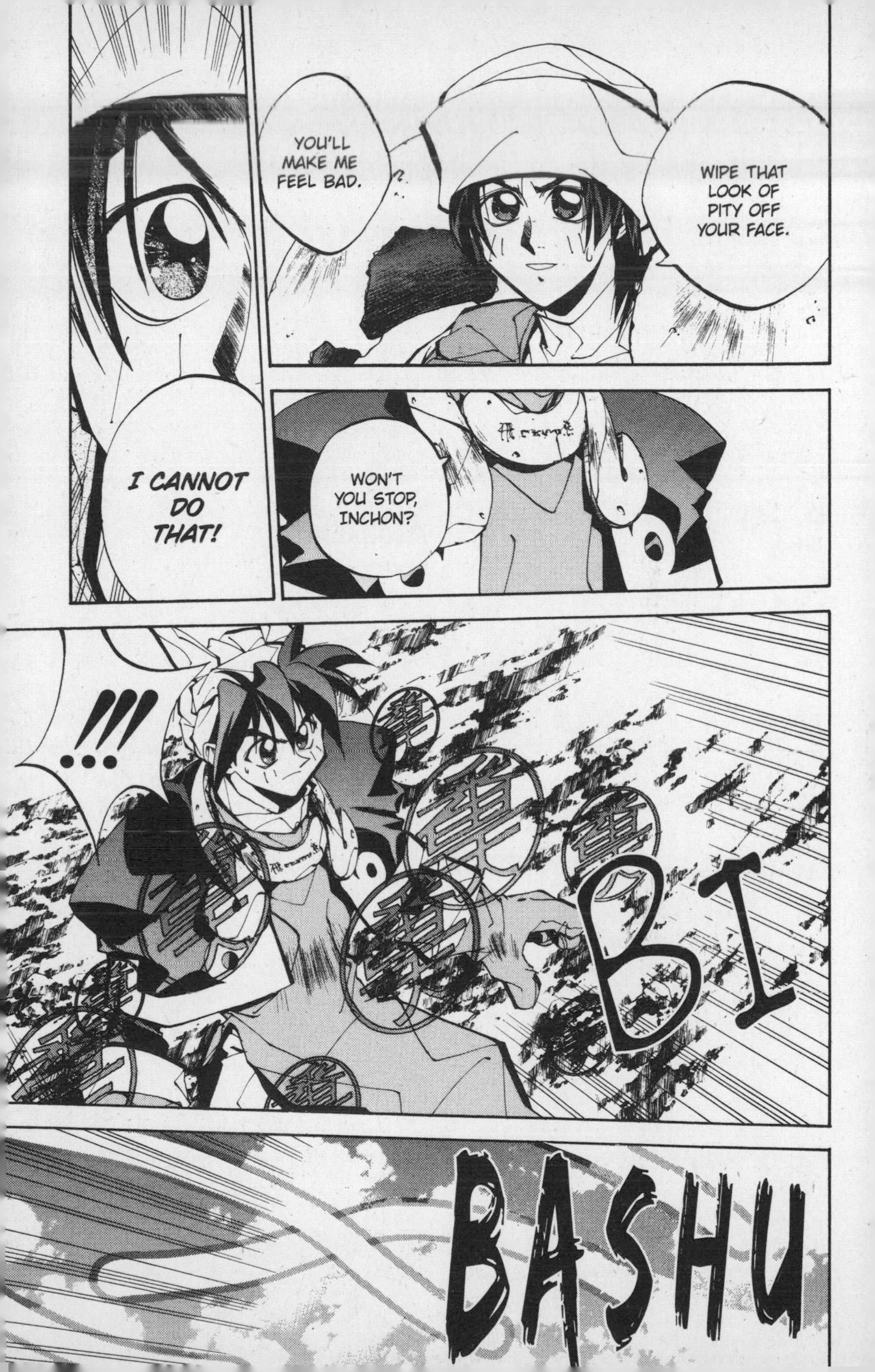
WIPE THAT LOOK OF PITY OFF YOUR FACE.
YOU'LL MAKE ME FEEL BAD.
WON'T YOU STOP, INCHON?
I CANNOT DO THAT!
...!!!
BI
BASHU

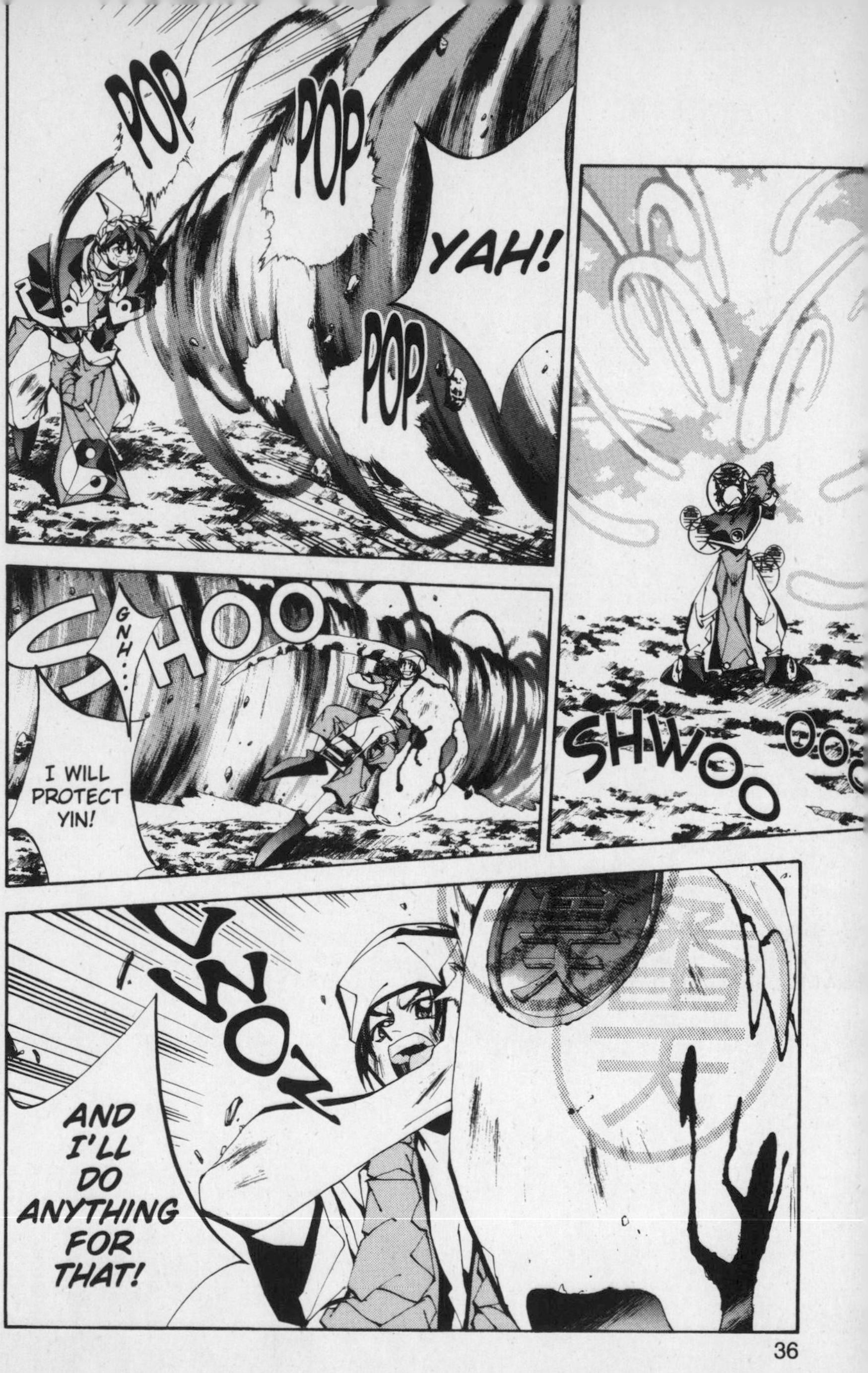
SHWOOOOO
POP
POP
YAH!
POP
GNH...
CHOO
I WILL PROTECT YIN!
AND I'LL DO ANYTHING FOR THAT!

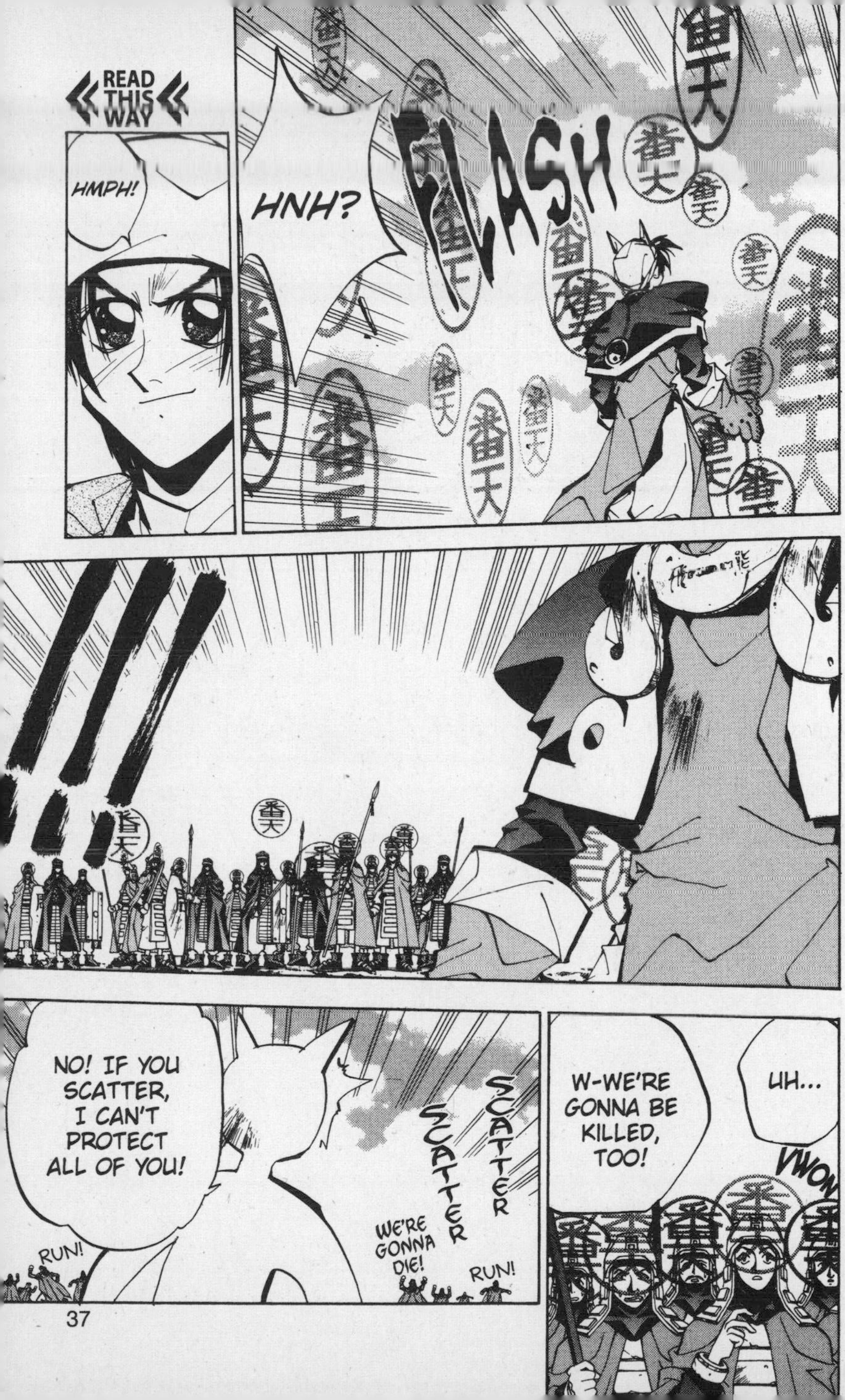
READ THIS WAY
HNH?
FLASH
HMPH!
UH...
W-WE'RE GONNA BE KILLED, TOO!
VWON
NO! IF YOU SCATTER, I CAN'T PROTECT ALL OF YOU!
SCATTER
SCATTER
WE'RE GONNA DIE!
RUN!
RUN!

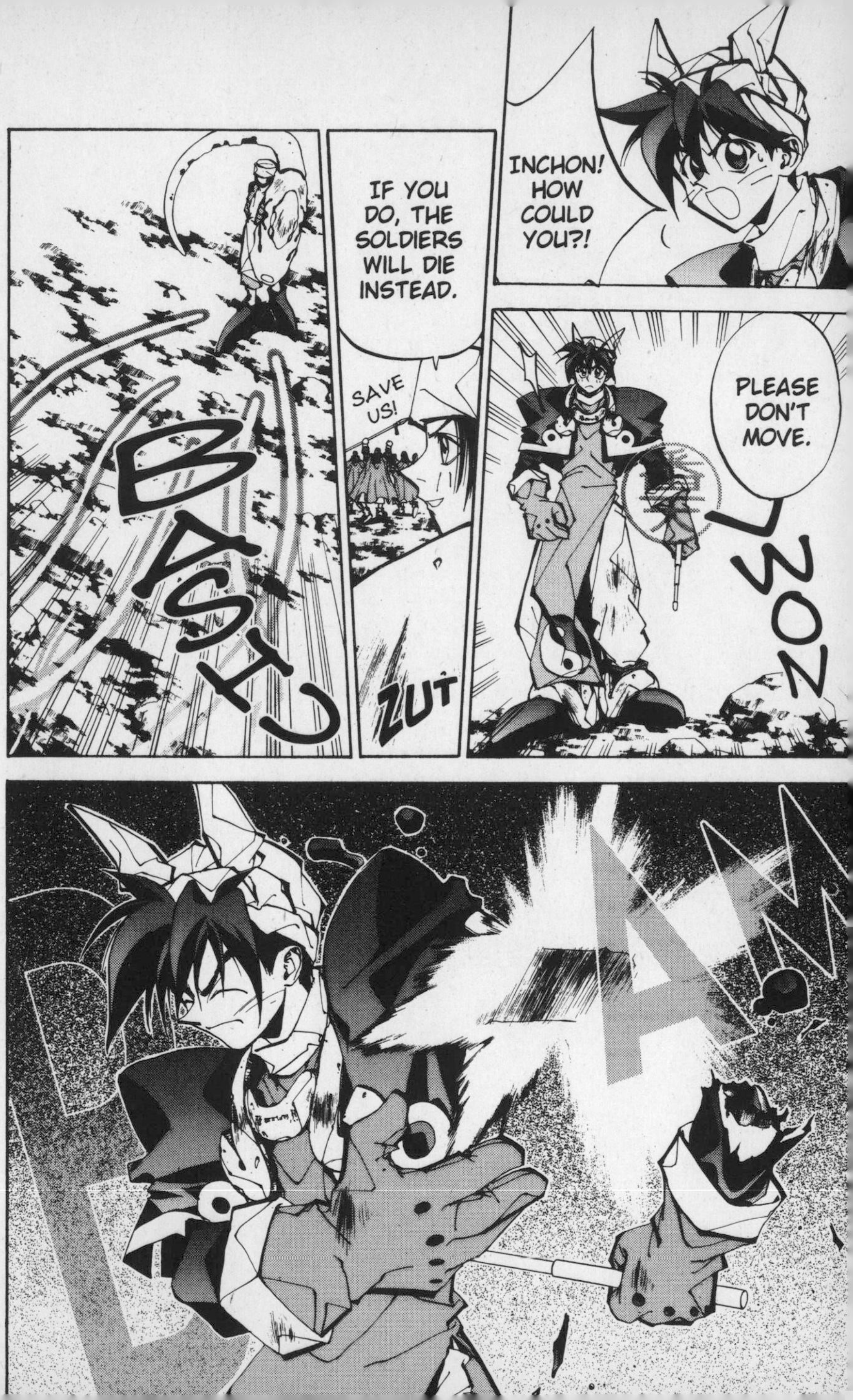
INCHON! HOW COULD YOU?!
PLEASE DON'T MOVE.
WON
IF YOU DO, THE SOLDIERS WILL DIE INSTEAD.
SAVE US!
ZUT
BASH

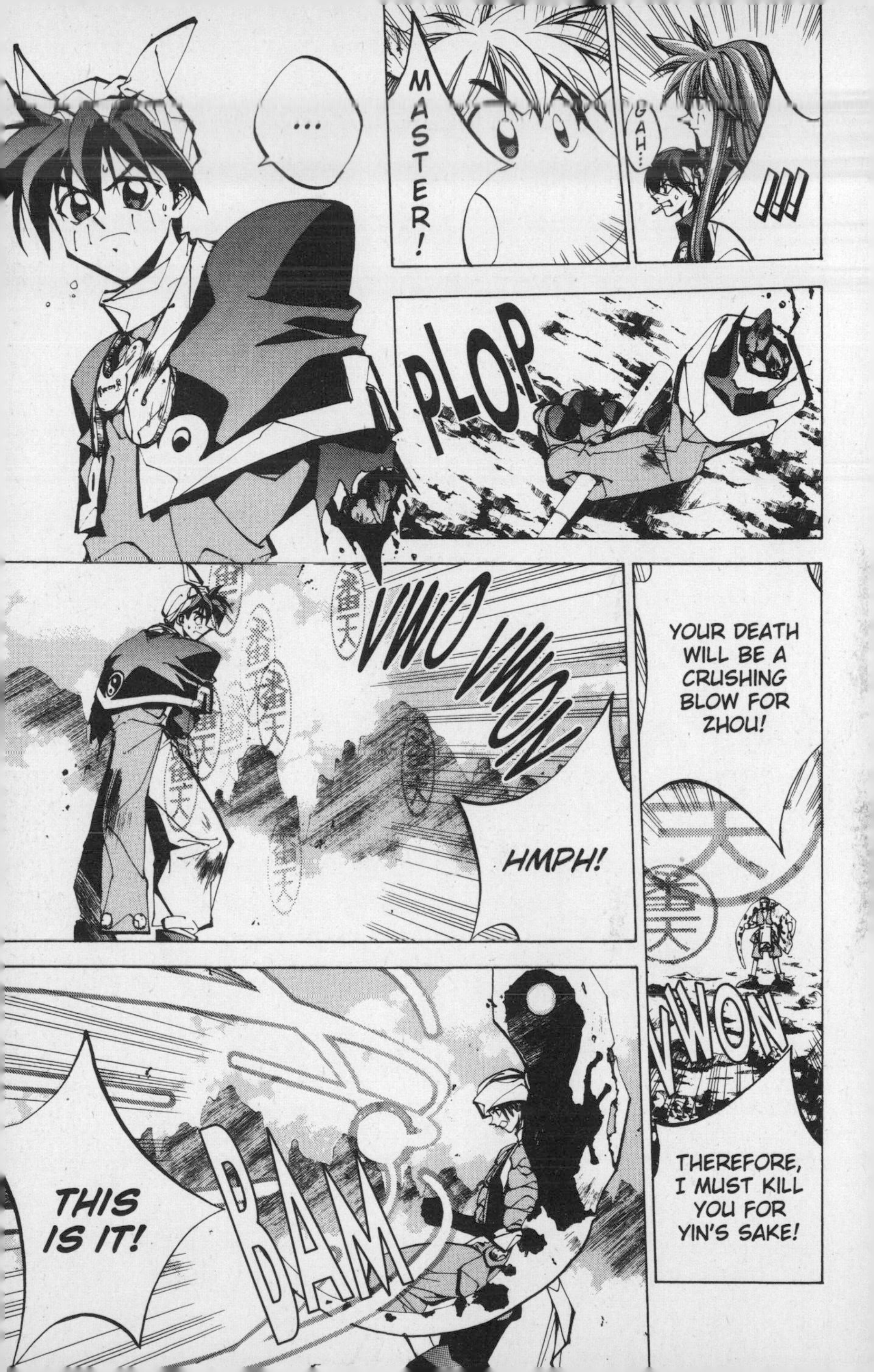
GAH...
!!!
MASTER!
PLOP
...
YOUR DEATH WILL BE A CRUSHING BLOW FOR ZHOU!
VWON
THEREFORE, I MUST KILL YOU FOR YIN'S SAKE!
VWO VWON
HMPH!
BAM
THIS IS IT!

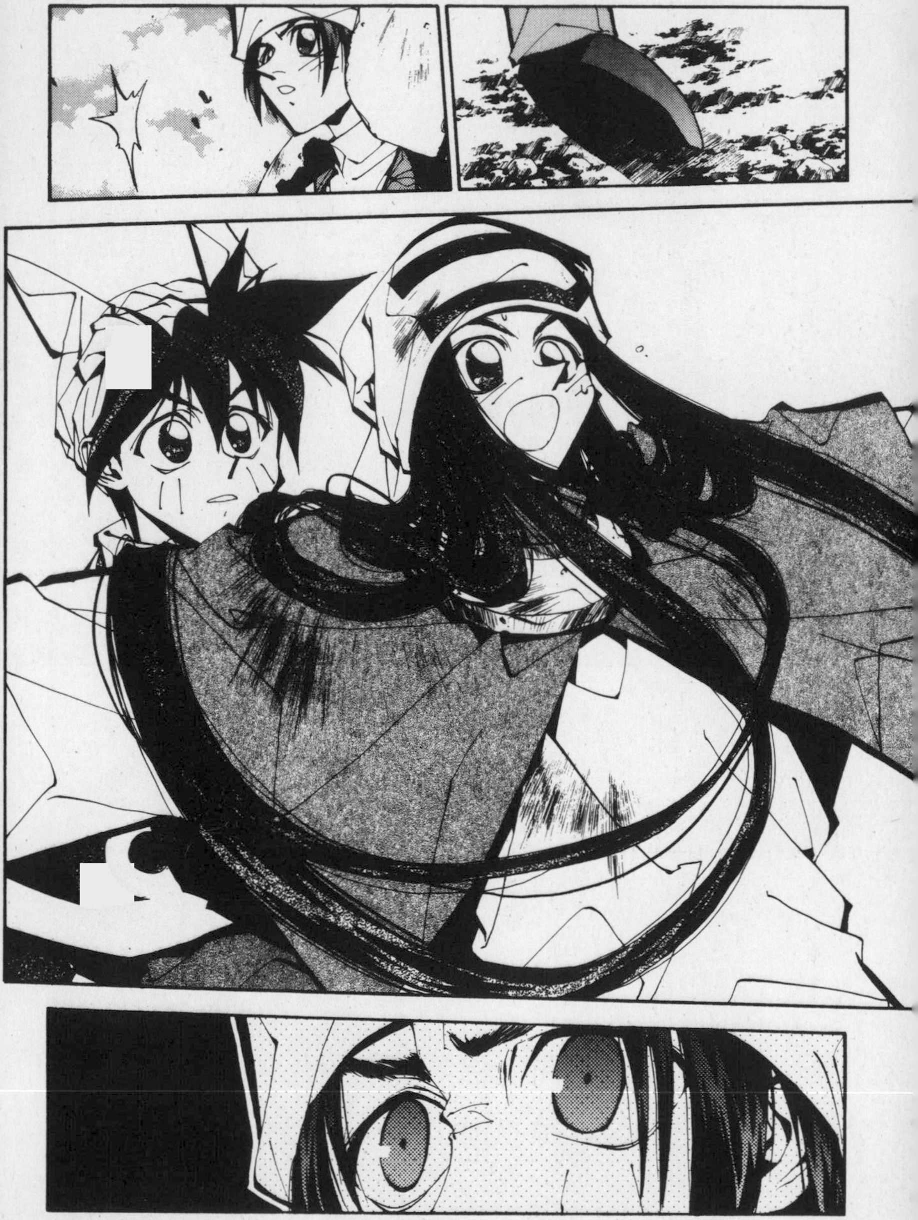

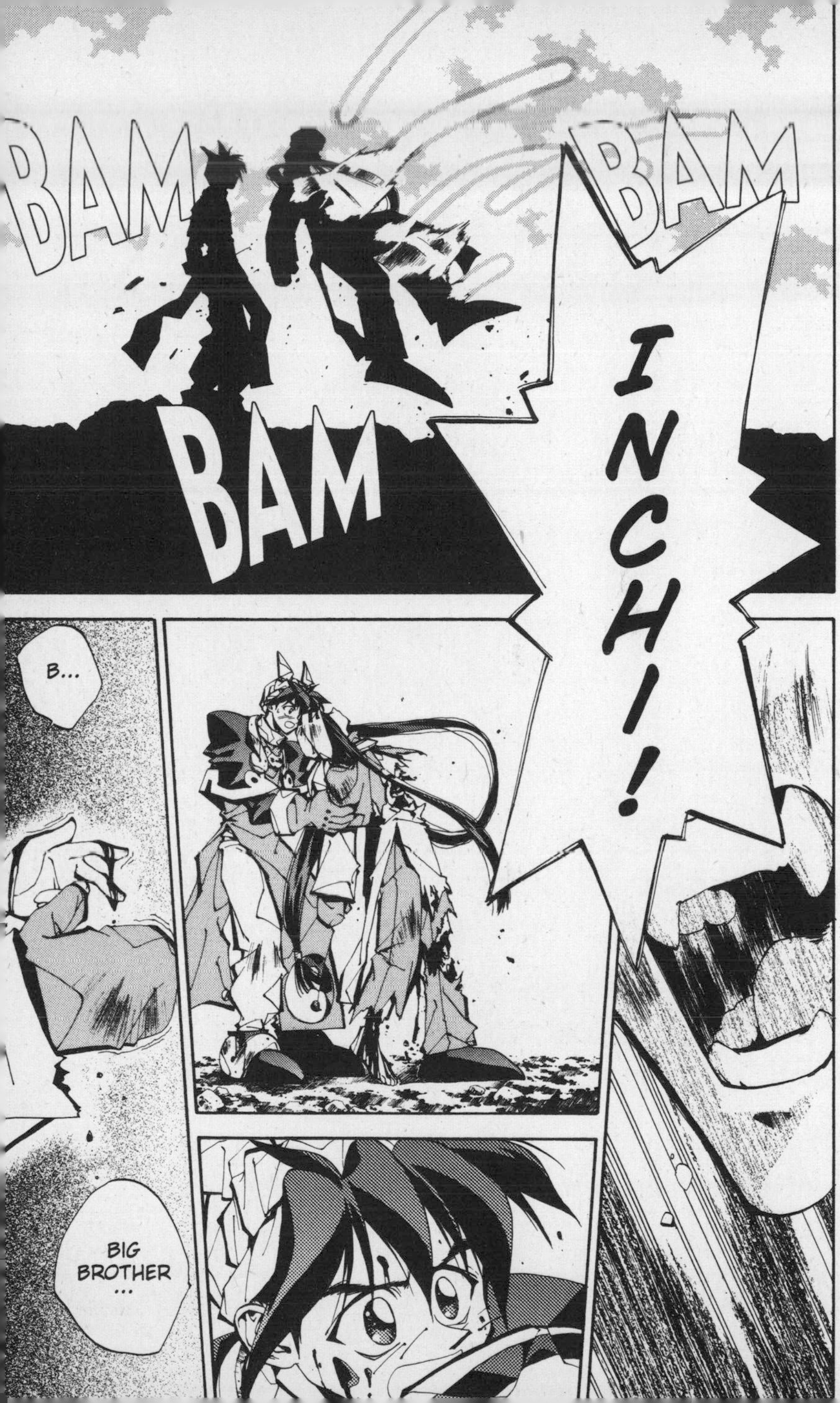
BAM
BAM
BAM
INCHI!
B...
BIG BROTHER...

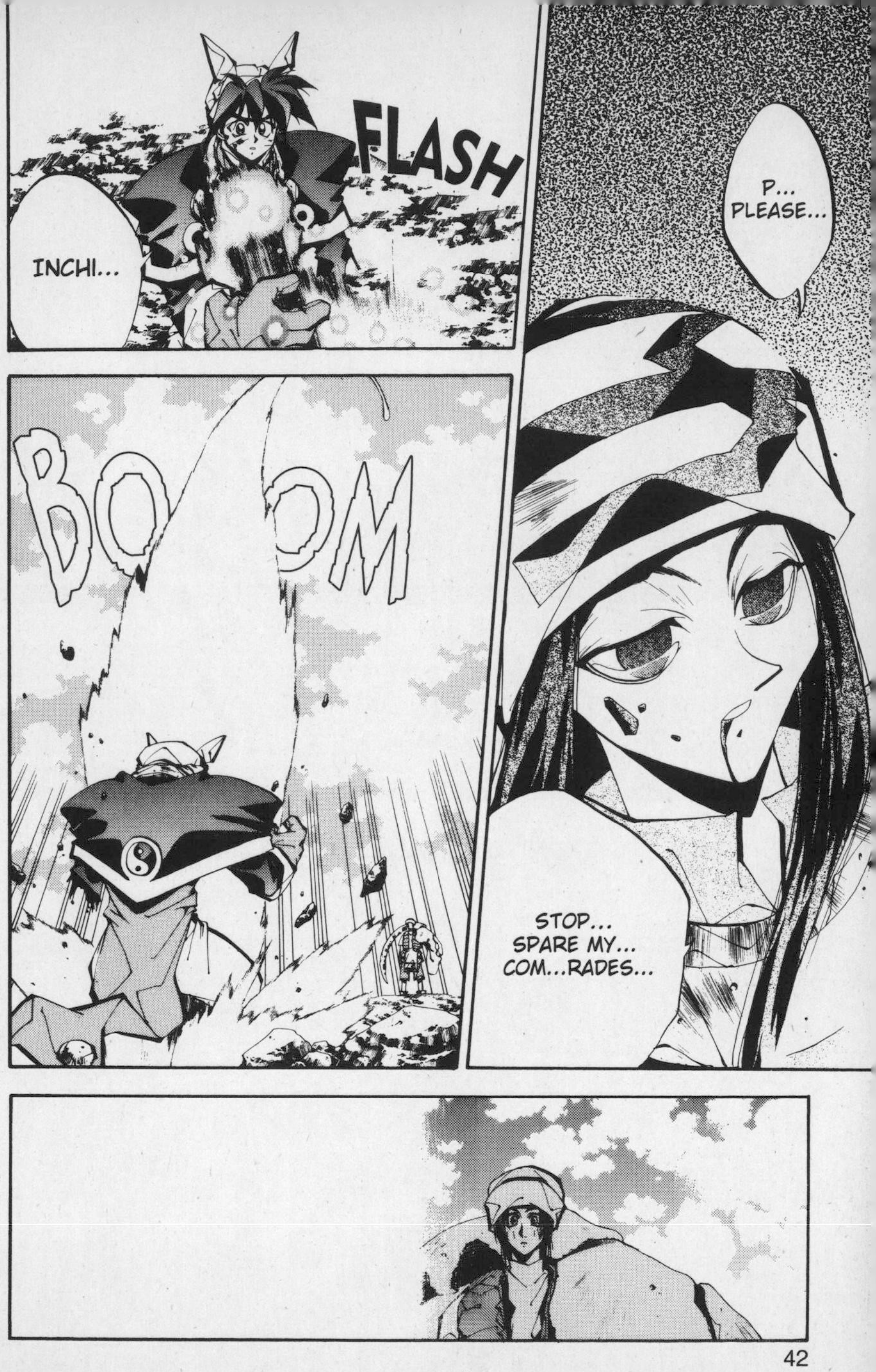
P...
PLEASE...
STOP...
SPARE MY...
COM...RADES...
FLASH
INCHI...
BOOM

READ THIS WAY

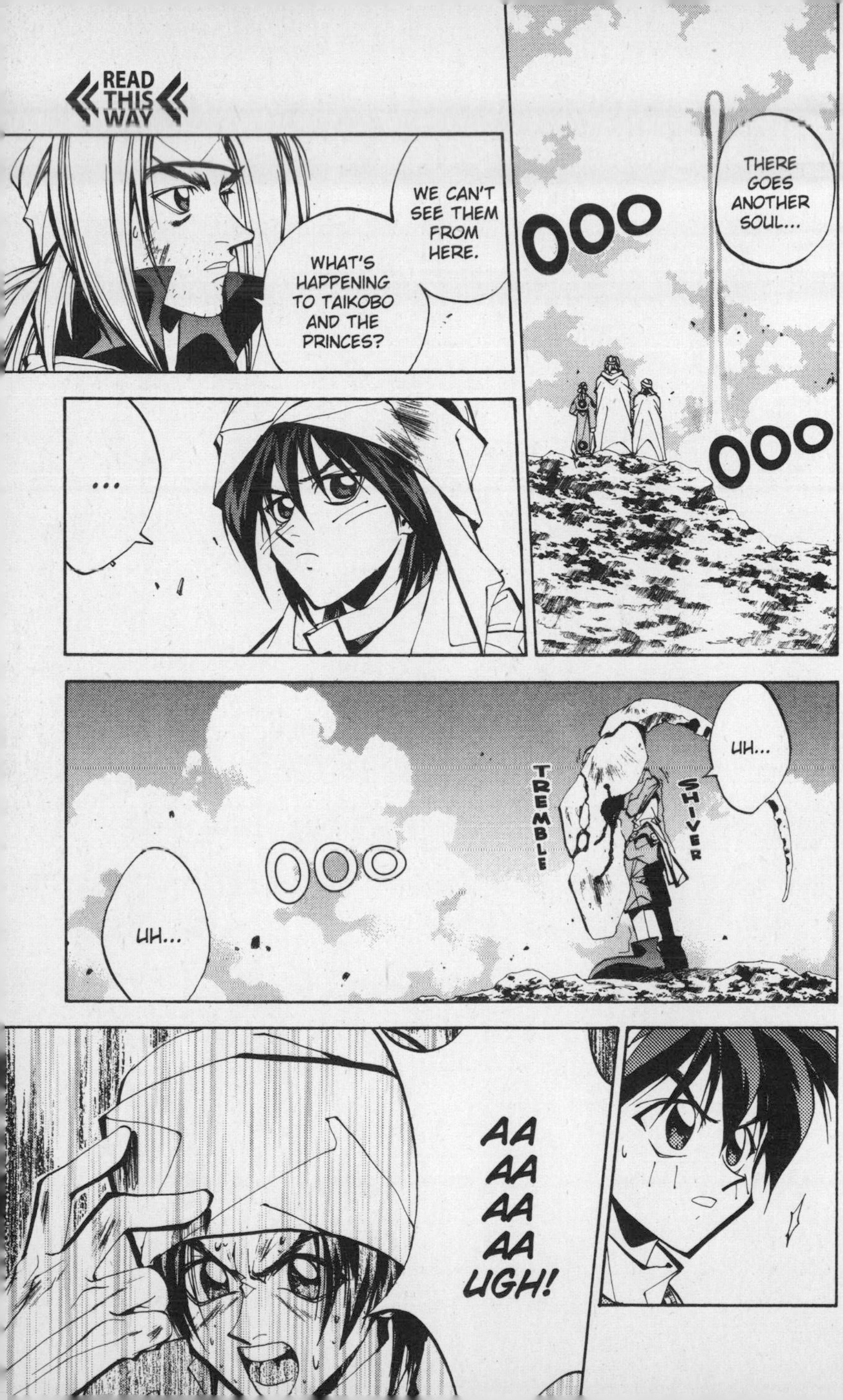
THERE GOES ANOTHER SOUL...
OOO
OOO
WE CAN'T SEE THEM FROM HERE.
WHAT'S HAPPENING TO TAIKOBO AND THE PRINCES?
...
UH...
SHIVER
TREMBLE
OOO
UH...
AAAAAAAAUGH!

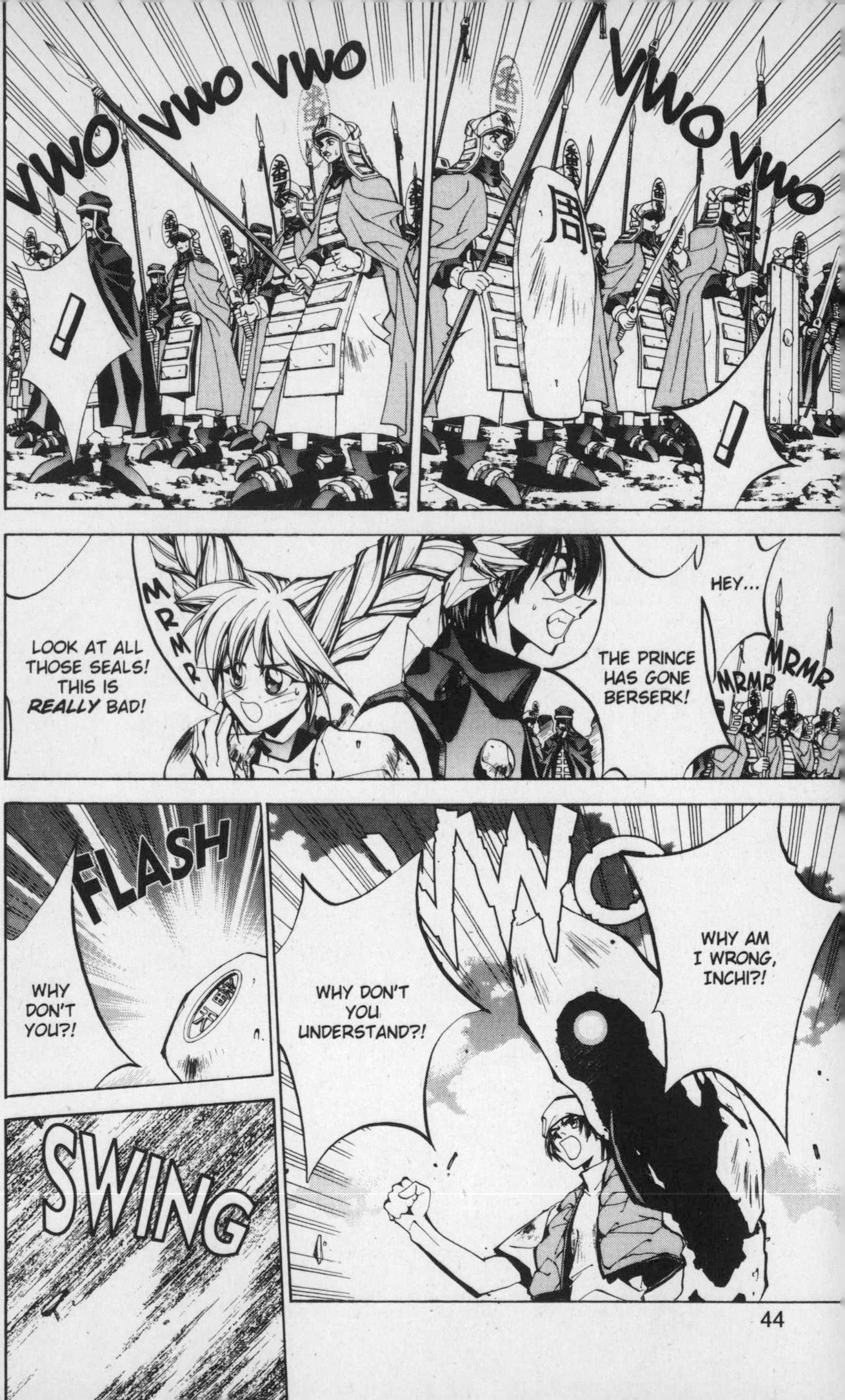
VWO VWO
!
VWO VWO VWO
!
HEY...
THE PRINCE HAS GONE BERSERK!
MRMR
MRMR
MRMR
LOOK AT ALL THOSE SEALS! THIS IS *REALLY* BAD!
VWO
WHY AM I WRONG, INCHI?!
WHY DON'T YOU UNDERSTAND?!
FLASH
WHY DON'T YOU?!
SWING

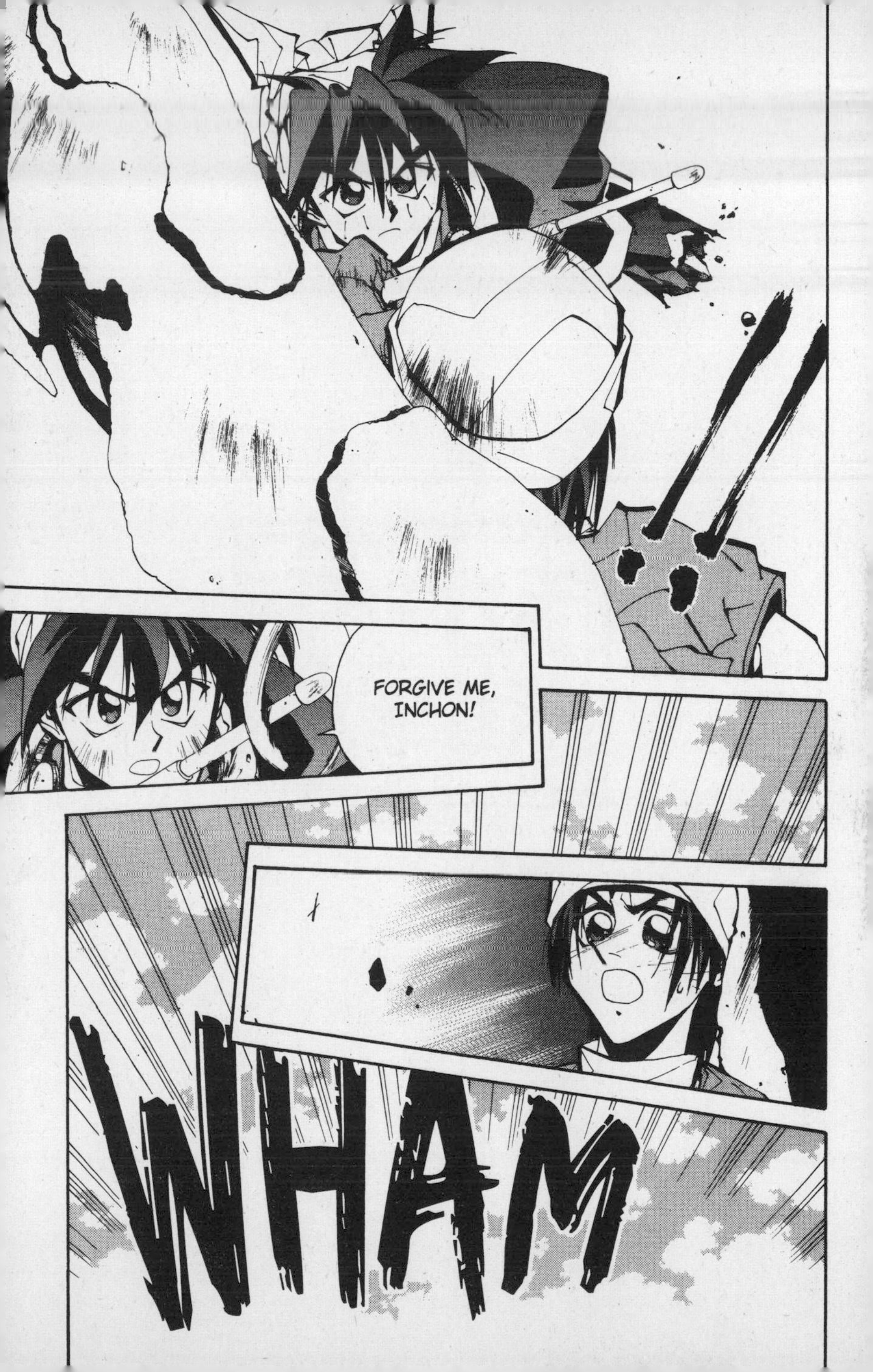
FORGIVE ME, INCHON!
WHAM

封神演義

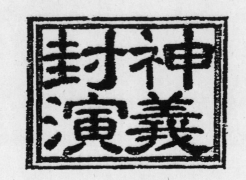

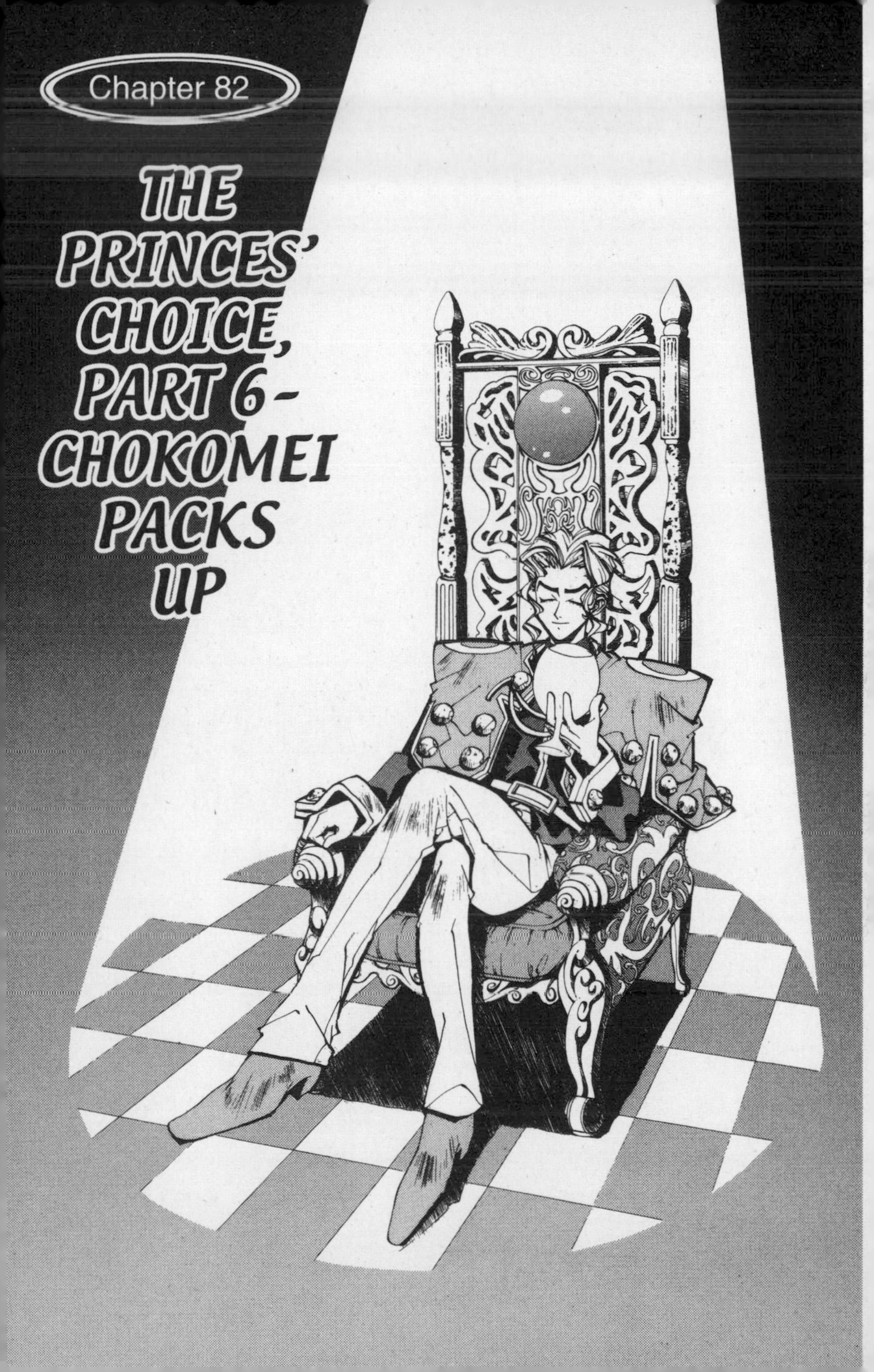
Chapter 82
THE PRINCES' CHOICE, PART 6 - CHOKOMEI PACKS UP

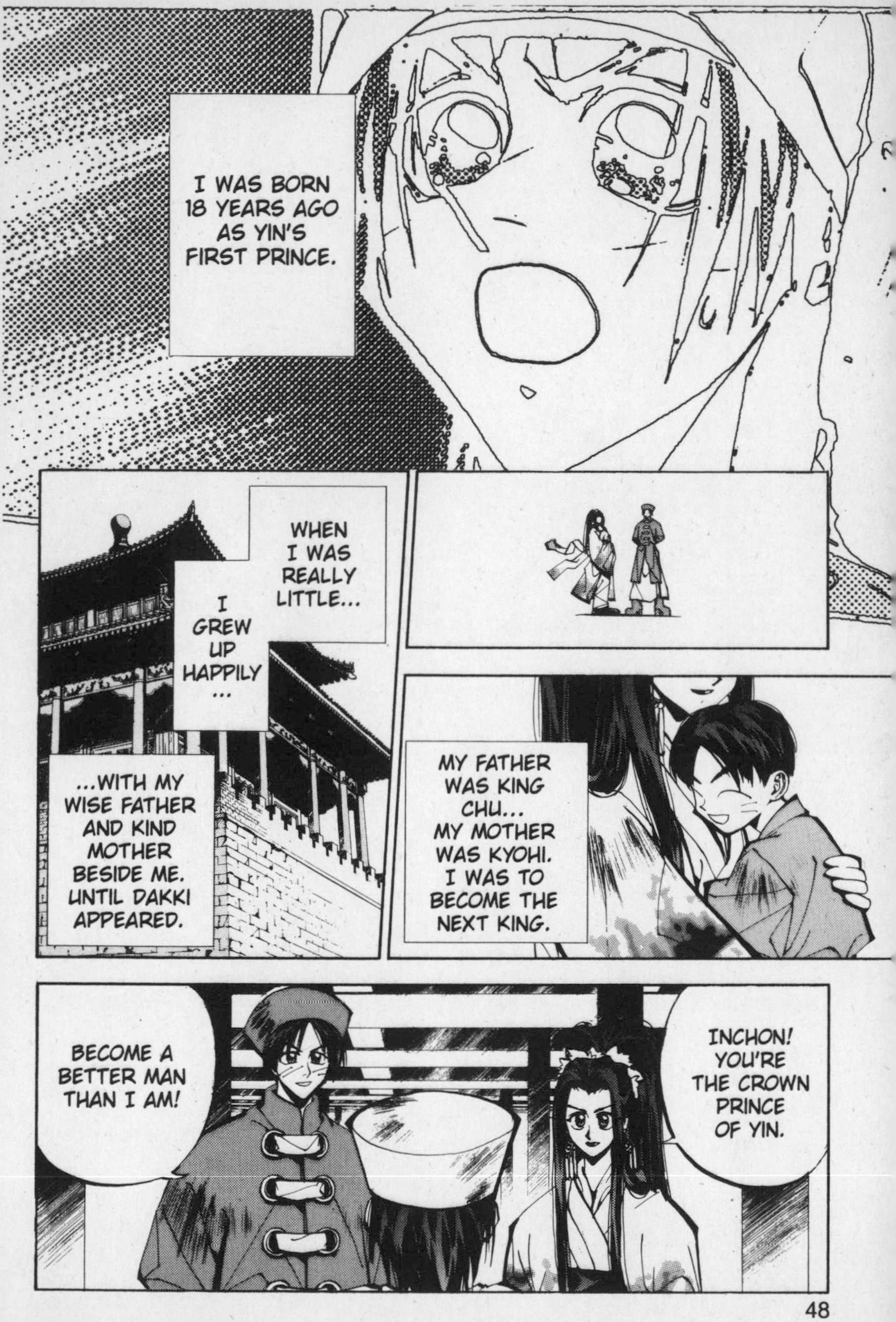
I WAS BORN 18 YEARS AGO AS YIN'S FIRST PRINCE.
MY FATHER WAS KING CHU... MY MOTHER WAS KYOHI. I WAS TO BECOME THE NEXT KING.
WHEN I WAS REALLY LITTLE...
I GREW UP HAPPILY...
...WITH MY WISE FATHER AND KIND MOTHER BESIDE ME. UNTIL DAKKI APPEARED.
INCHON! YOU'RE THE CROWN PRINCE OF YIN.
BECOME A BETTER MAN THAN I AM!

READ THIS WAY

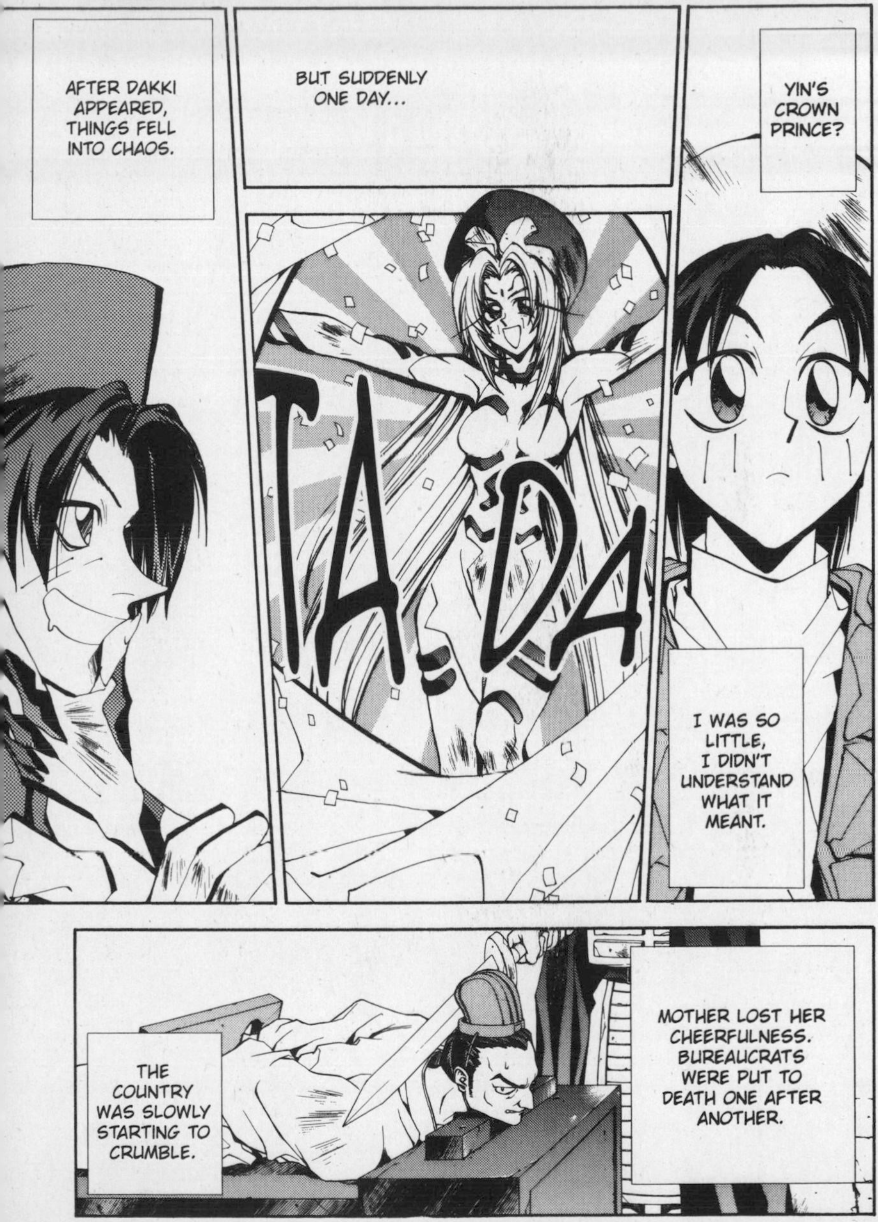

YIN'S CROWN PRINCE?
I WAS SO LITTLE, I DIDN'T UNDERSTAND WHAT IT MEANT.
BUT SUDDENLY ONE DAY...
TA-DA
AFTER DAKKI APPEARED, THINGS FELL INTO CHAOS.
MOTHER LOST HER CHEERFULNESS. BUREAUCRATS WERE PUT TO DEATH ONE AFTER ANOTHER.
THE COUNTRY WAS SLOWLY STARTING TO CRUMBLE.

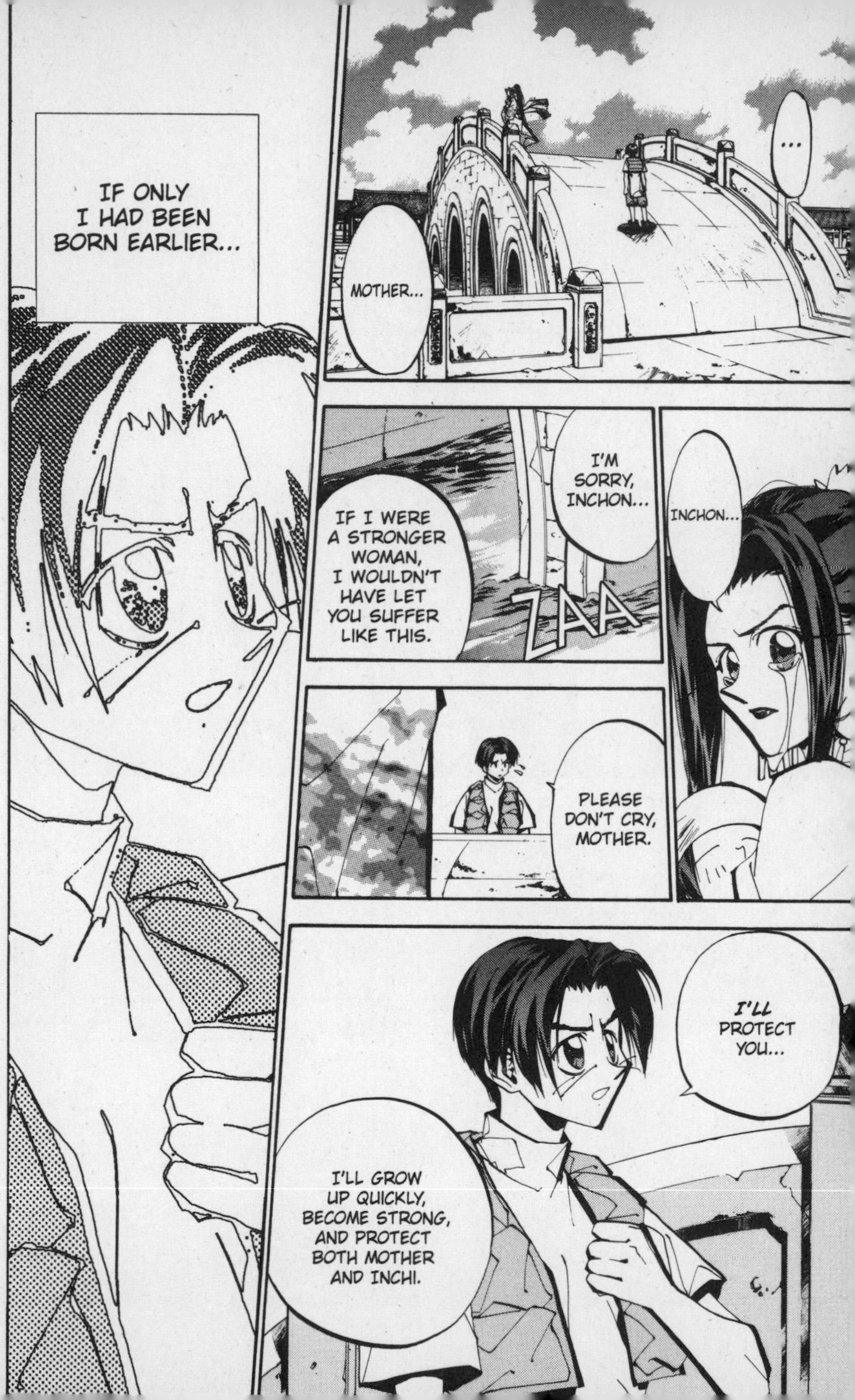
...
MOTHER...
INCHON...
I'M SORRY, INCHON...
IF I WERE A STRONGER WOMAN, I WOULDN'T HAVE LET YOU SUFFER LIKE THIS.
ZAA
PLEASE DON'T CRY, MOTHER.
I'LL PROTECT YOU...
I'LL GROW UP QUICKLY, BECOME STRONG, AND PROTECT BOTH MOTHER AND INCHI.
IF ONLY I HAD BEEN BORN EARLIER...

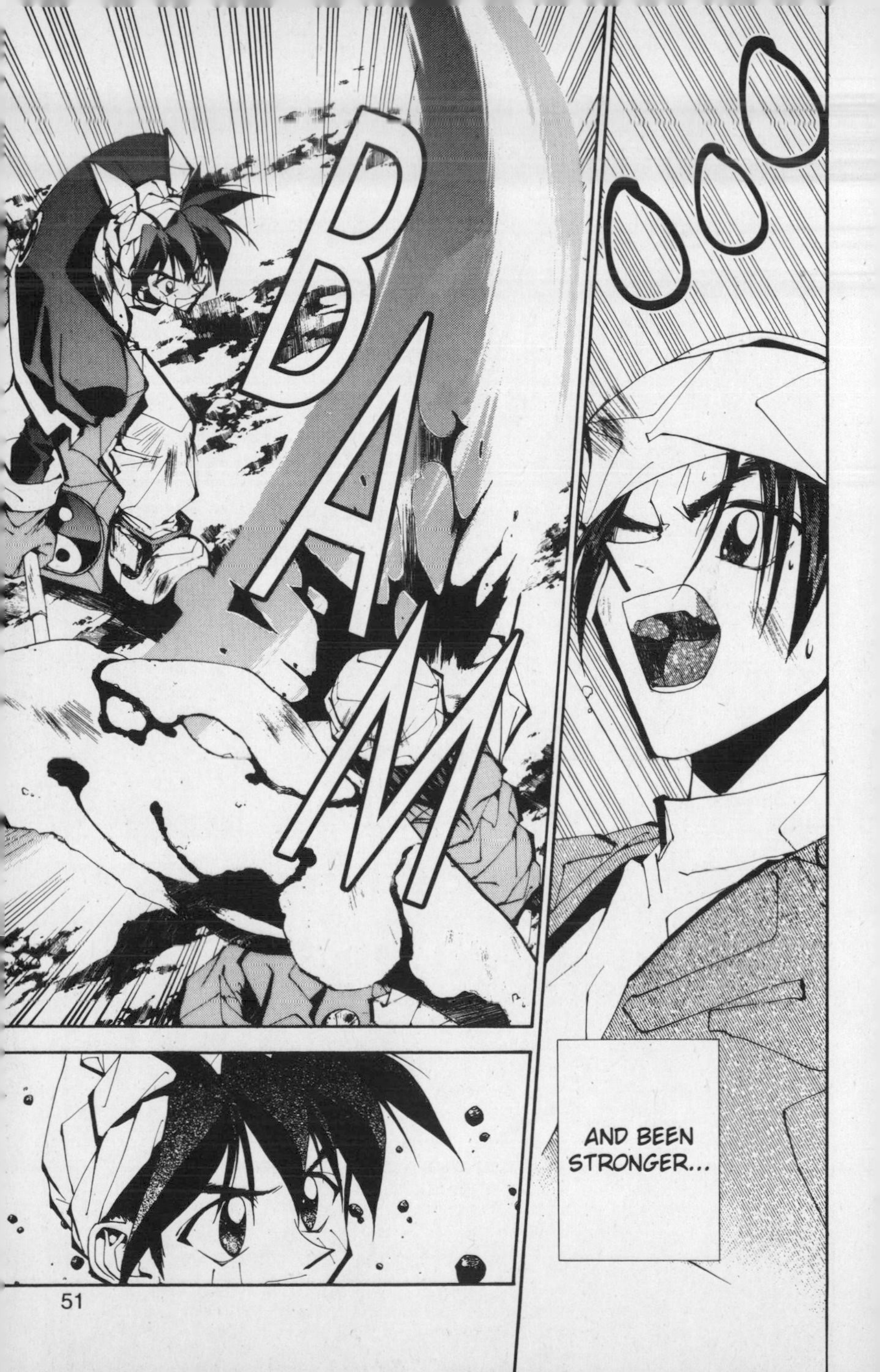
OOOO
AND BEEN STRONGER...
BAM

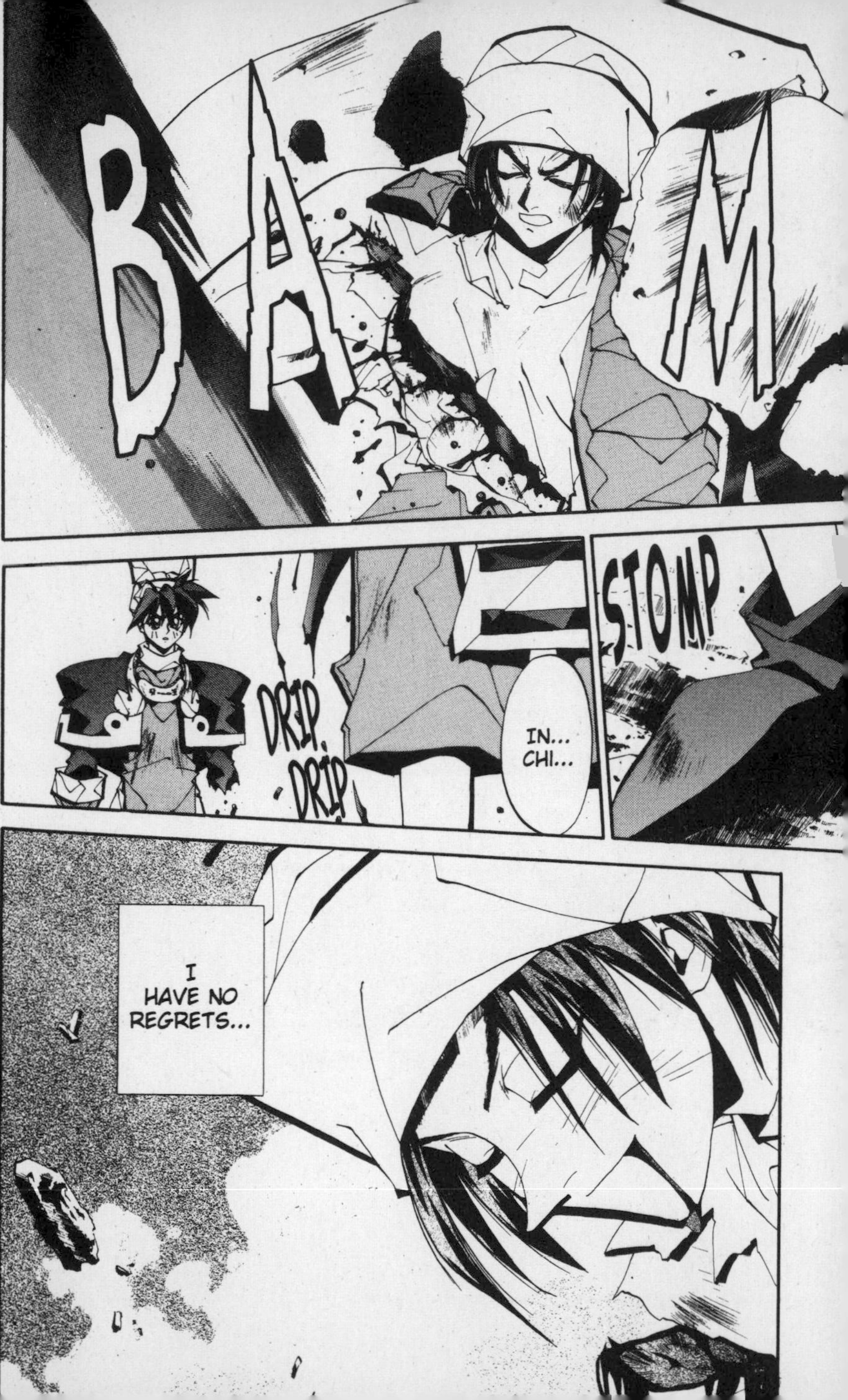
BAM
STOMP
IN... CHI...
DRIP DRIP
I HAVE NO REGRETS...

READ THIS WAY

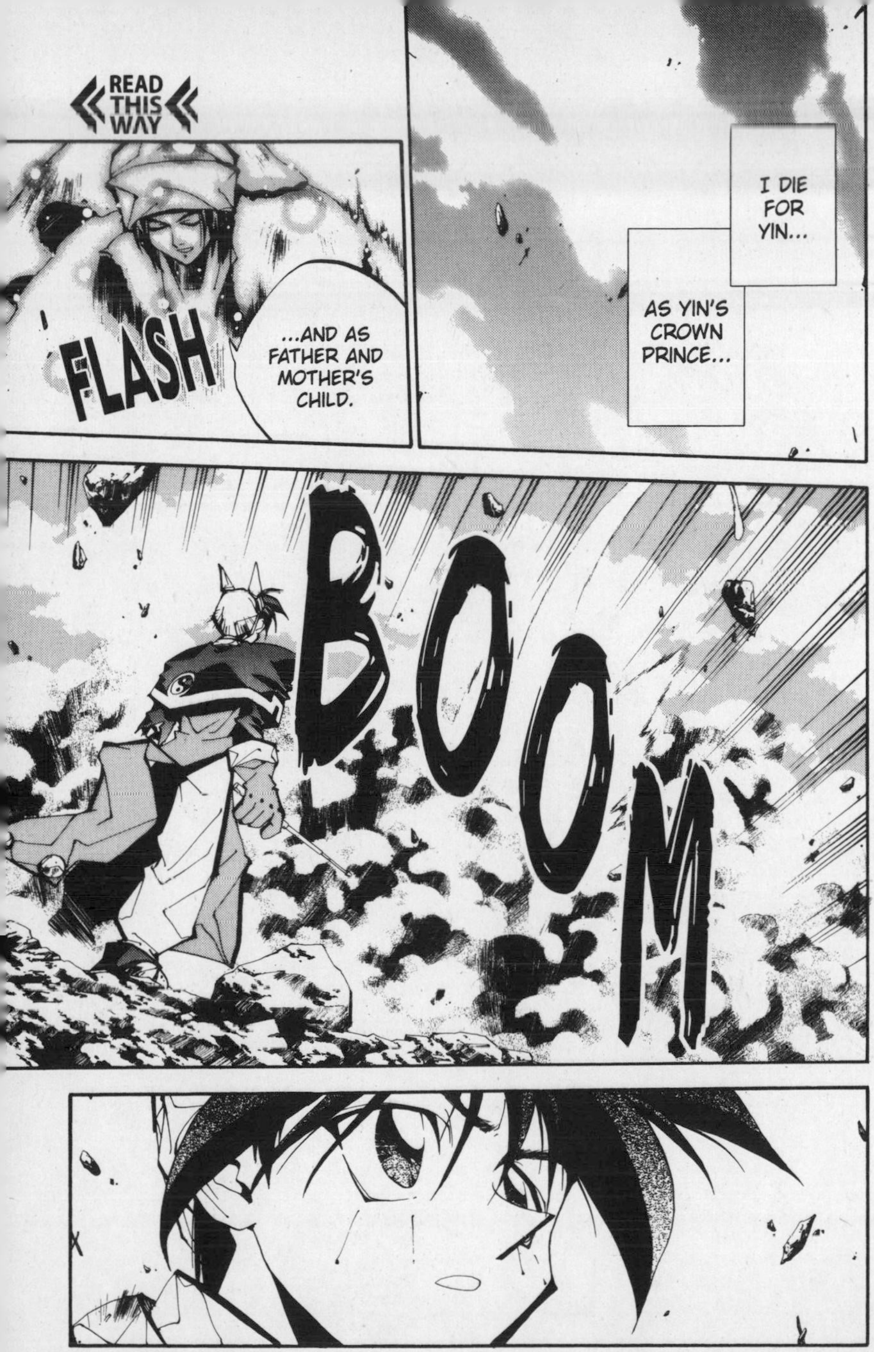
I DIE FOR YIN...
AS YIN'S CROWN PRINCE...
...AND AS FATHER AND MOTHER'S CHILD.
FLASH
BOOM

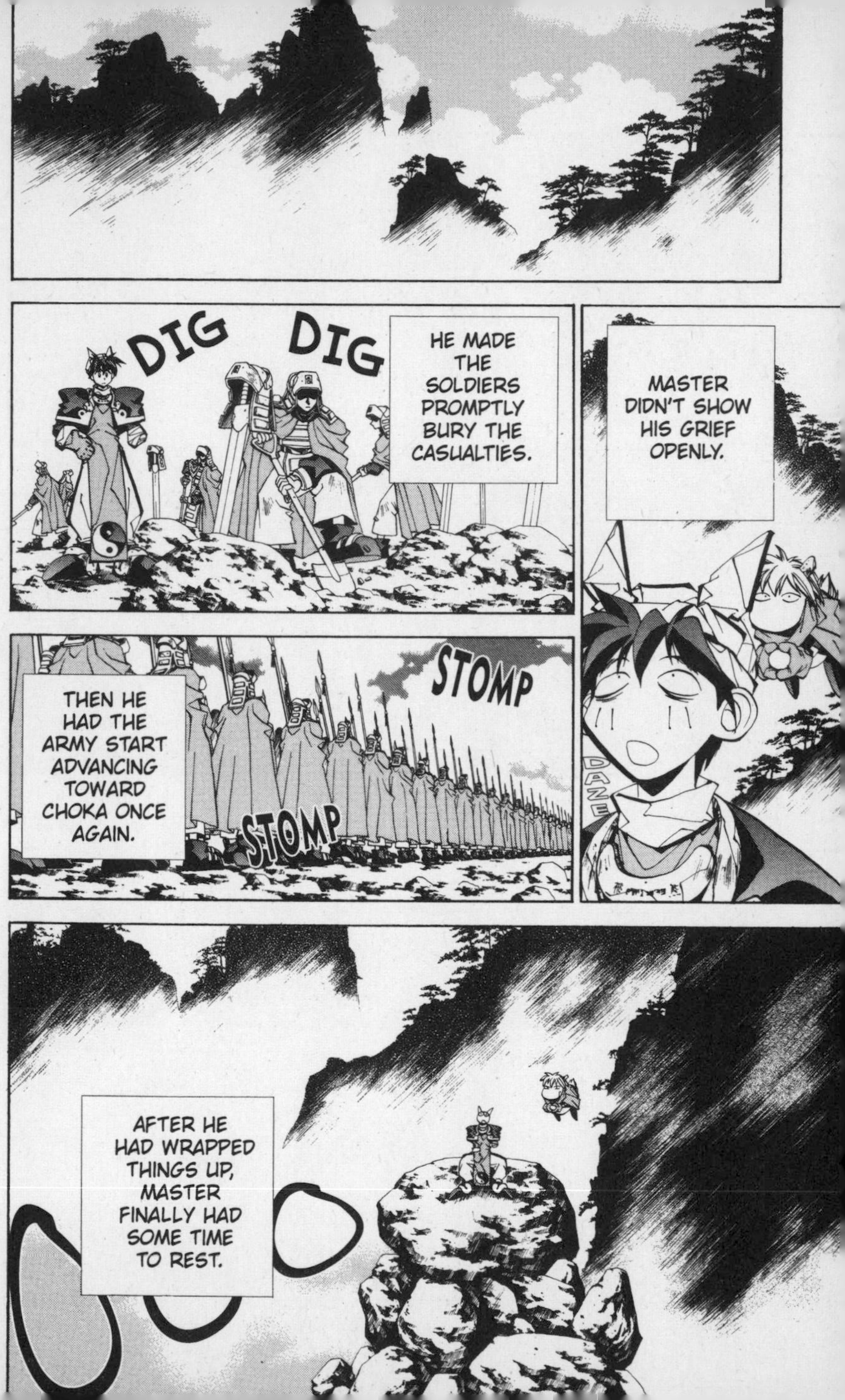
MASTER DIDN'T SHOW HIS GRIEF OPENLY.
DAZE
DIG DIG
HE MADE THE SOLDIERS PROMPTLY BURY THE CASUALTIES.
STOMP
THEN HE HAD THE ARMY START ADVANCING TOWARD CHOKA ONCE AGAIN.
STOMP
AFTER HE HAD WRAPPED THINGS UP, MASTER FINALLY HAD SOME TIME TO REST.

READ THIS WAY

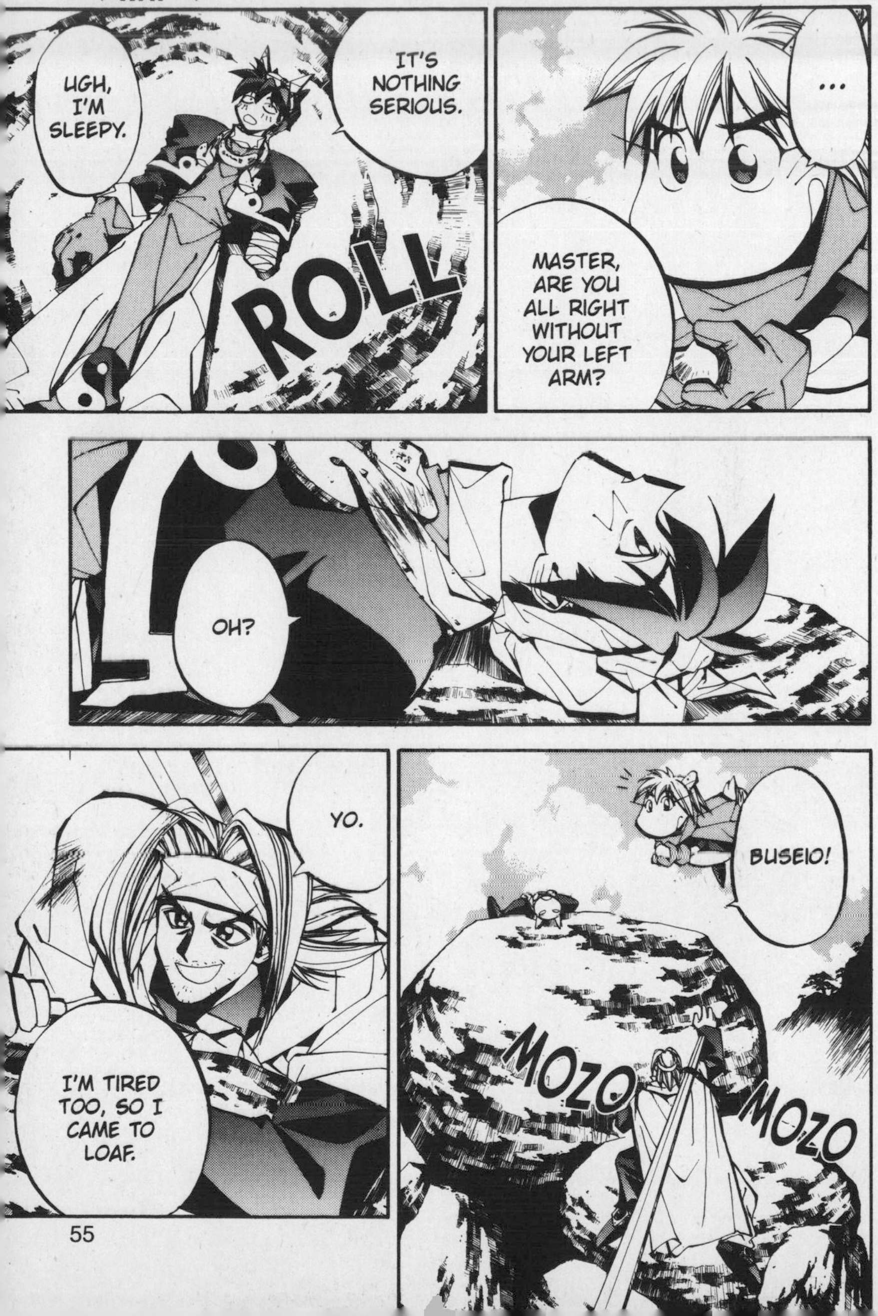
...
MASTER, ARE YOU ALL RIGHT WITHOUT YOUR LEFT ARM?
IT'S NOTHING SERIOUS.
UGH, I'M SLEEPY.
ROLL
OH?
BUSEIO!
MOZO
MOZO
YO.
I'M TIRED TOO, SO I CAME TO LOAF.

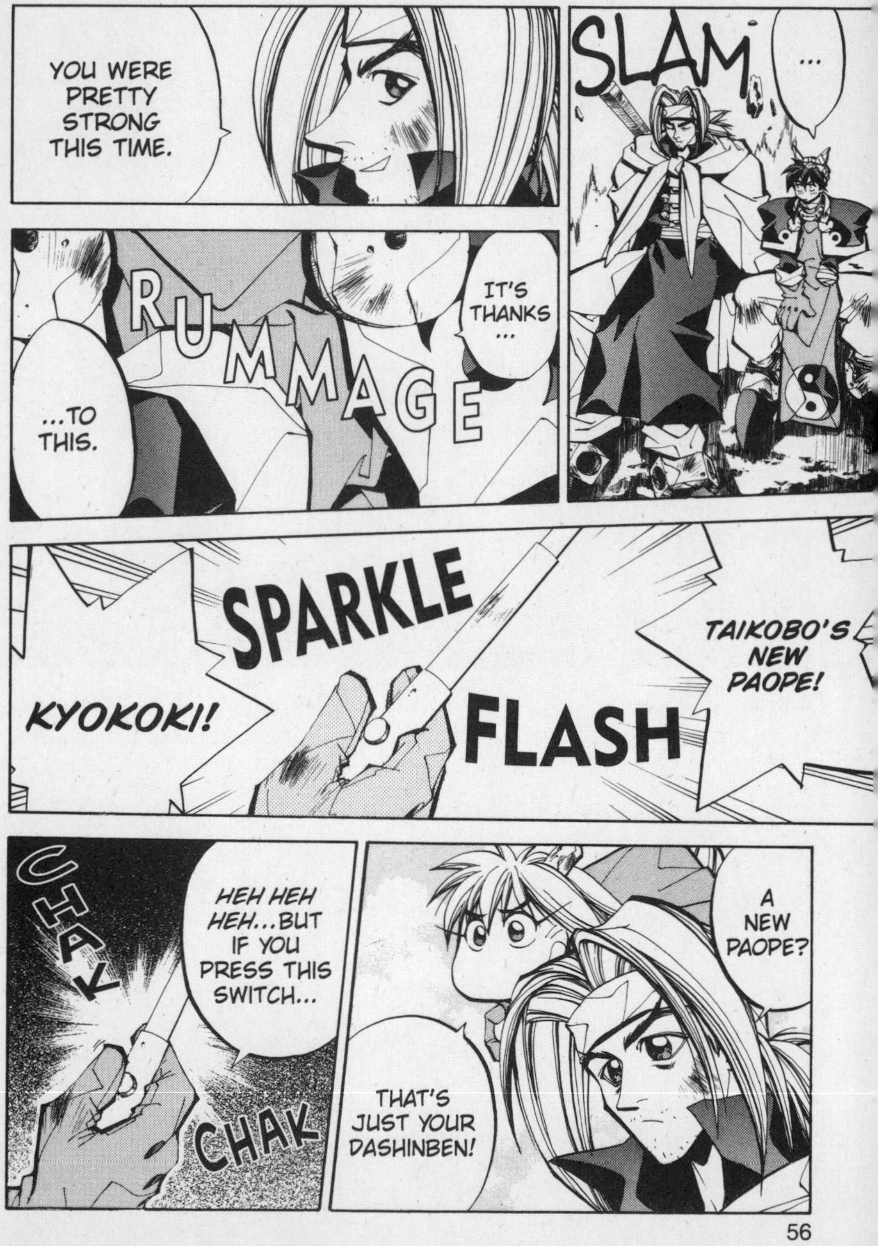
SLAM
...
YOU WERE PRETTY STRONG THIS TIME.
IT'S THANKS...
RUMMAGE
...TO THIS.
SPARKLE
TAIKOBO'S NEW PAOPE!
KYOKOKI!
FLASH
A NEW PAOPE?
THAT'S JUST YOUR DASHINBEN!
CHAK
HEH HEH HEH...BUT IF YOU PRESS THIS SWITCH...
CHAK

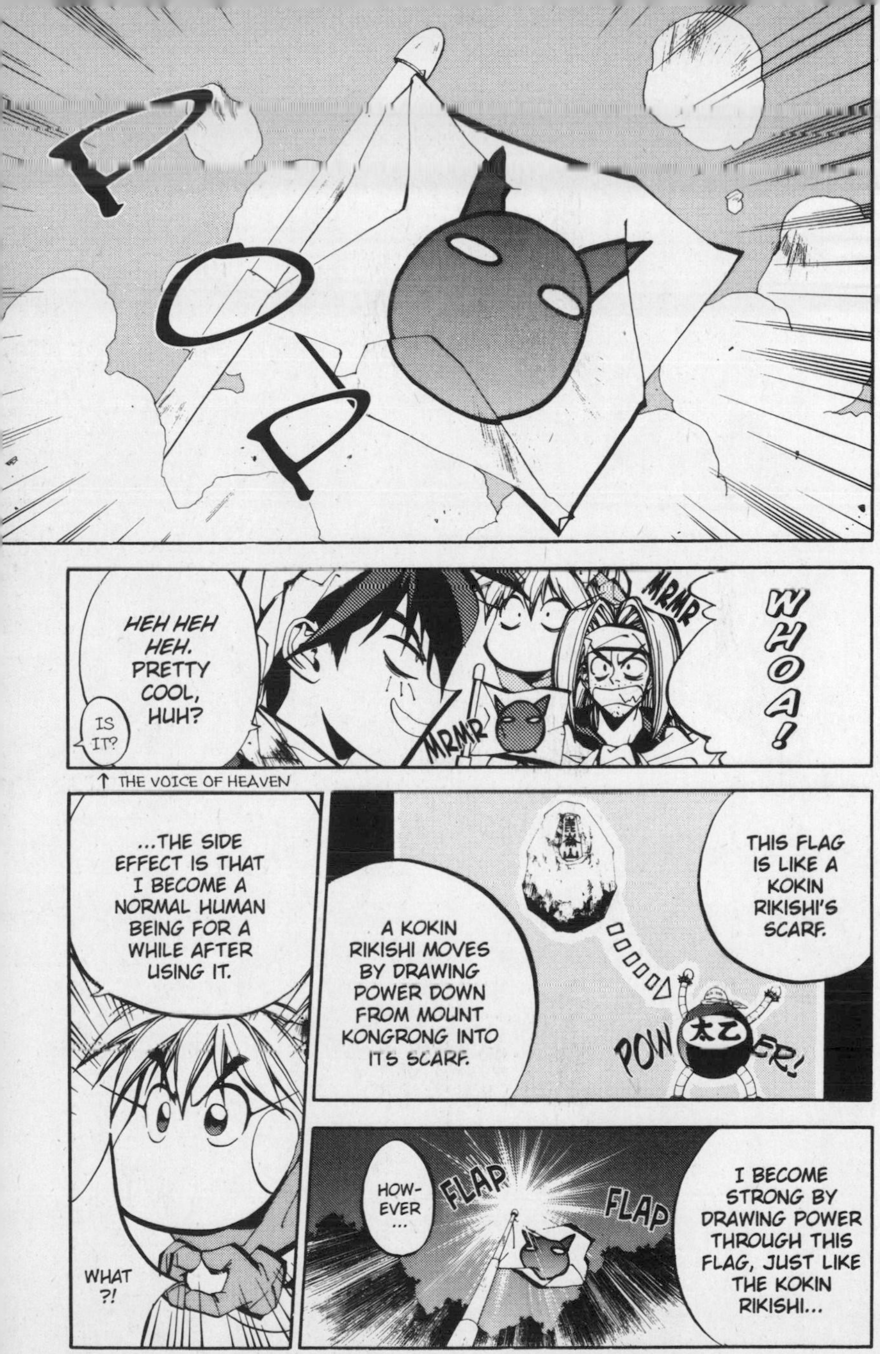
POP
WHOA!
MRMR
HEH HEH HEH. PRETTY COOL, HUH?
IS IT?
MRMR
↑ THE VOICE OF HEAVEN
THIS FLAG IS LIKE A KOKIN RIKISHI'S SCARF.
A KOKIN RIKISHI MOVES BY DRAWING POWER DOWN FROM MOUNT KONGRONG INTO ITS SCARF.
POW ER!
I BECOME STRONG BY DRAWING POWER THROUGH THIS FLAG, JUST LIKE THE KOKIN RIKISHI...
FLAP
FLAP
HOW-EVER...
...THE SIDE EFFECT IS THAT I BECOME A NORMAL HUMAN BEING FOR A WHILE AFTER USING IT.
WHAT?!

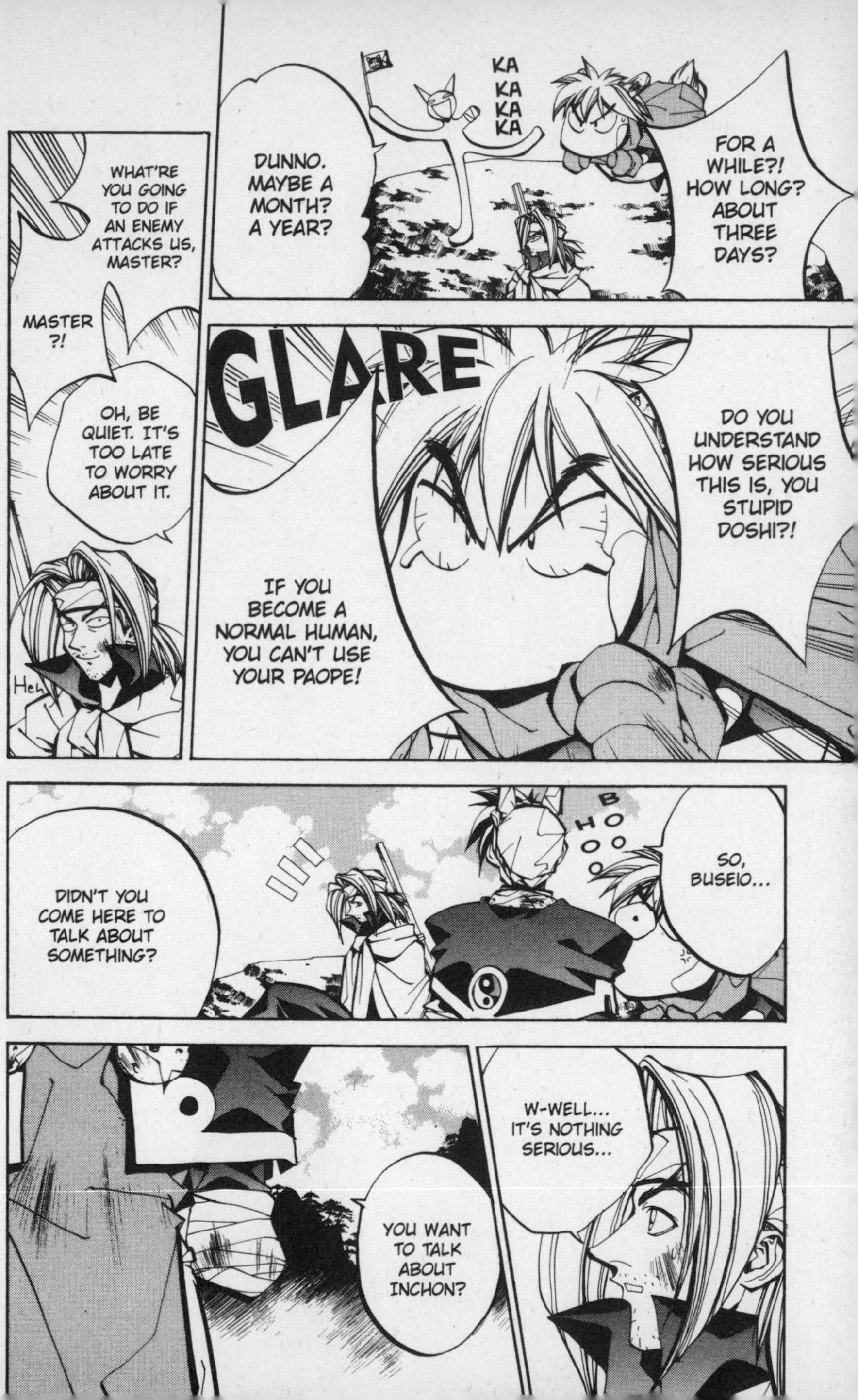
FOR A WHILE?! HOW LONG? ABOUT THREE DAYS?
KA KA KA KA
DUNNO. MAYBE A MONTH? A YEAR?
DO YOU UNDERSTAND HOW SERIOUS THIS IS, YOU STUPID DOSHI?!
GLARE
IF YOU BECOME A NORMAL HUMAN, YOU CAN'T USE YOUR PAOPE!
WHAT'RE YOU GOING TO DO IF AN ENEMY ATTACKS US, MASTER?
MASTER ?!
OH, BE QUIET. IT'S TOO LATE TO WORRY ABOUT IT.
Heh
SO, BUSEIO...
BHOOOO
DIDN'T YOU COME HERE TO TALK ABOUT SOMETHING?
W-WELL... IT'S NOTHING SERIOUS...
YOU WANT TO TALK ABOUT INCHON?

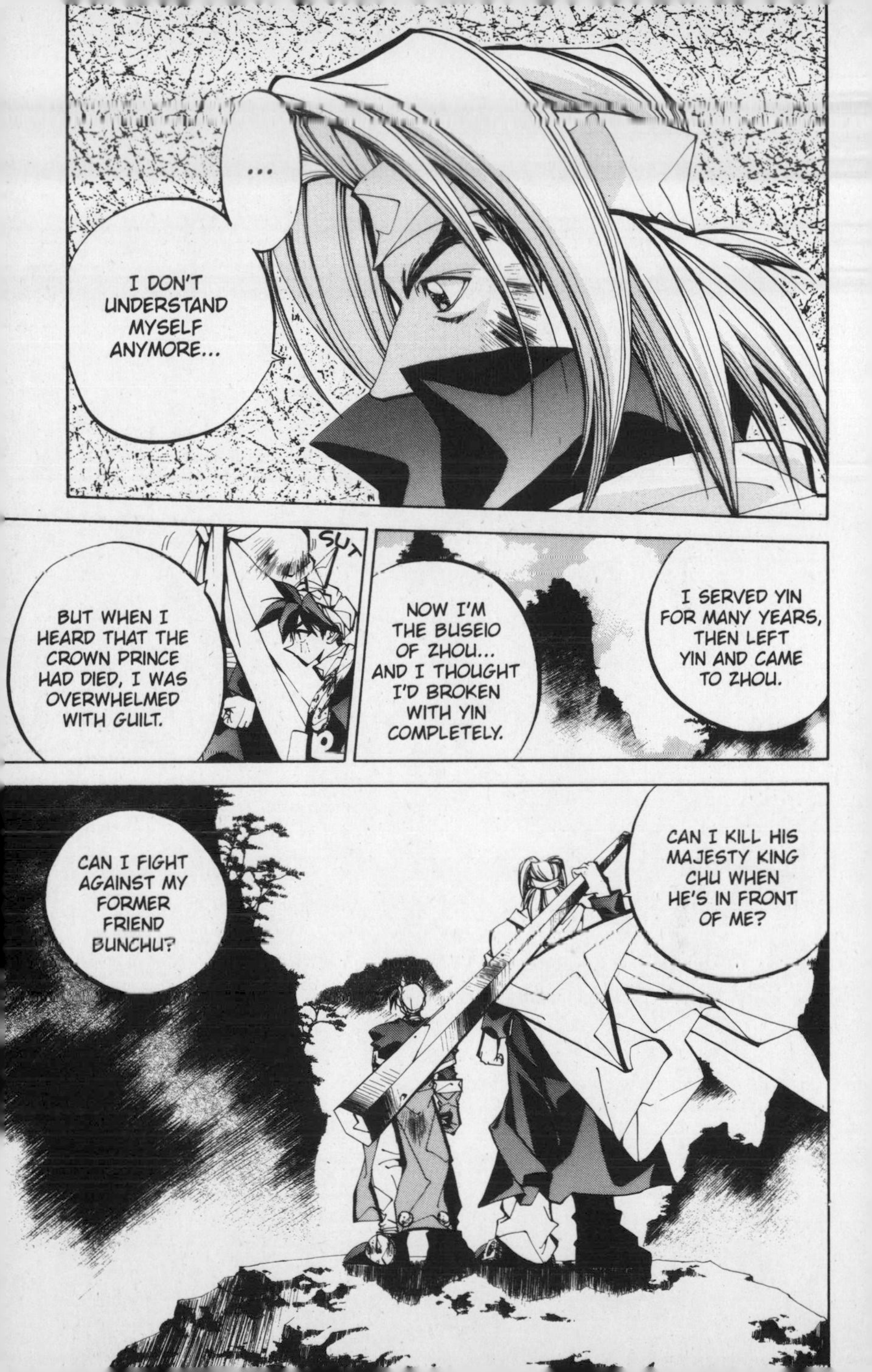
...
I DON'T UNDERSTAND MYSELF ANYMORE...
I SERVED YIN FOR MANY YEARS, THEN LEFT YIN AND CAME TO ZHOU.
NOW I'M THE BUSEIO OF ZHOU... AND I THOUGHT I'D BROKEN WITH YIN COMPLETELY.
SUT
BUT WHEN I HEARD THAT THE CROWN PRINCE HAD DIED, I WAS OVERWHELMED WITH GUILT.
CAN I KILL HIS MAJESTY KING CHU WHEN HE'S IN FRONT OF ME?
CAN I FIGHT AGAINST MY FORMER FRIEND BUNCHU?

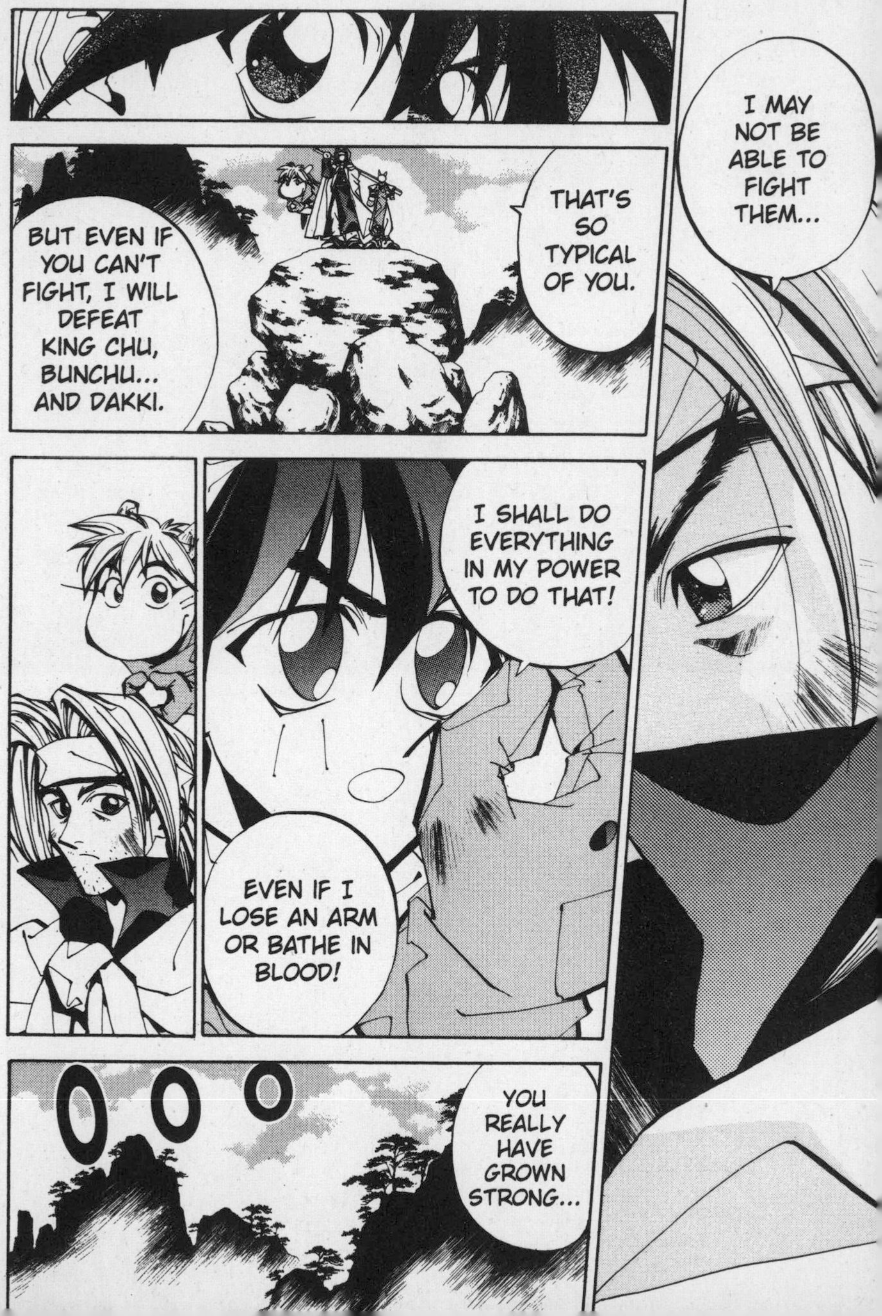
I MAY NOT BE ABLE TO FIGHT THEM...
THAT'S SO TYPICAL OF YOU.
BUT EVEN IF YOU CAN'T FIGHT, I WILL DEFEAT KING CHU, BUNCHU... AND DAKKI.
I SHALL DO EVERYTHING IN MY POWER TO DO THAT!
EVEN IF I LOSE AN ARM OR BATHE IN BLOOD!
YOU REALLY HAVE GROWN STRONG...

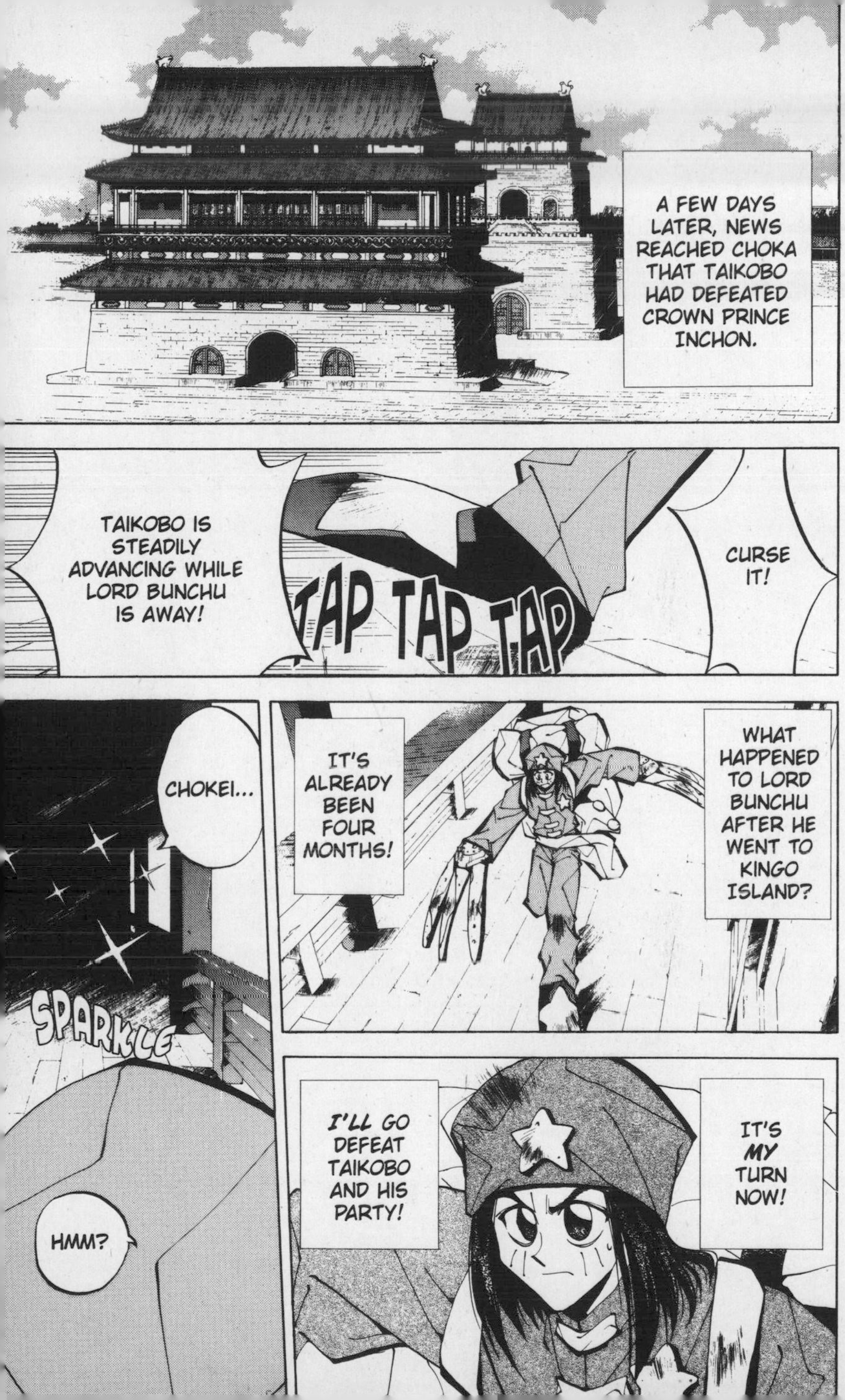
A FEW DAYS LATER, NEWS REACHED CHOKA THAT TAIKOBO HAD DEFEATED CROWN PRINCE INCHON.
CURSE IT!
TAP TAP TAP
TAIKOBO IS STEADILY ADVANCING WHILE LORD BUNCHU IS AWAY!
WHAT HAPPENED TO LORD BUNCHU AFTER HE WENT TO KINGO ISLAND?
IT'S ALREADY BEEN FOUR MONTHS!
IT'S *MY* TURN NOW!
I'LL GO DEFEAT TAIKOBO AND HIS PARTY!
CHOKEI...
SPARKLE
HMM?

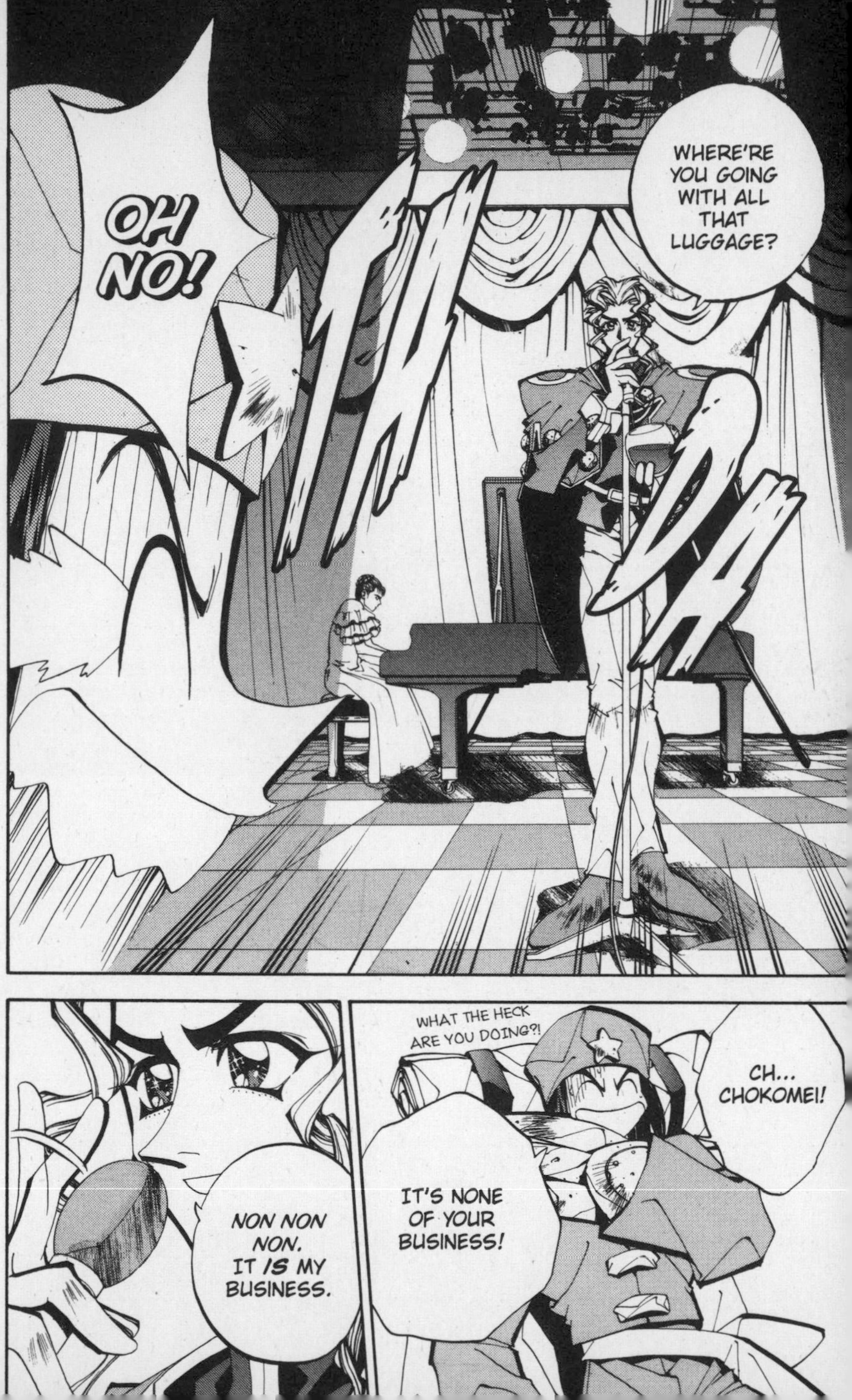
WHERE'RE YOU GOING WITH ALL THAT LUGGAGE?
OH NO!
CH... CHOKOMEI!
WHAT THE HECK ARE YOU DOING?!
IT'S NONE OF YOUR BUSINESS!
NON NON NON. IT *IS* MY BUSINESS.

READ THIS WAY

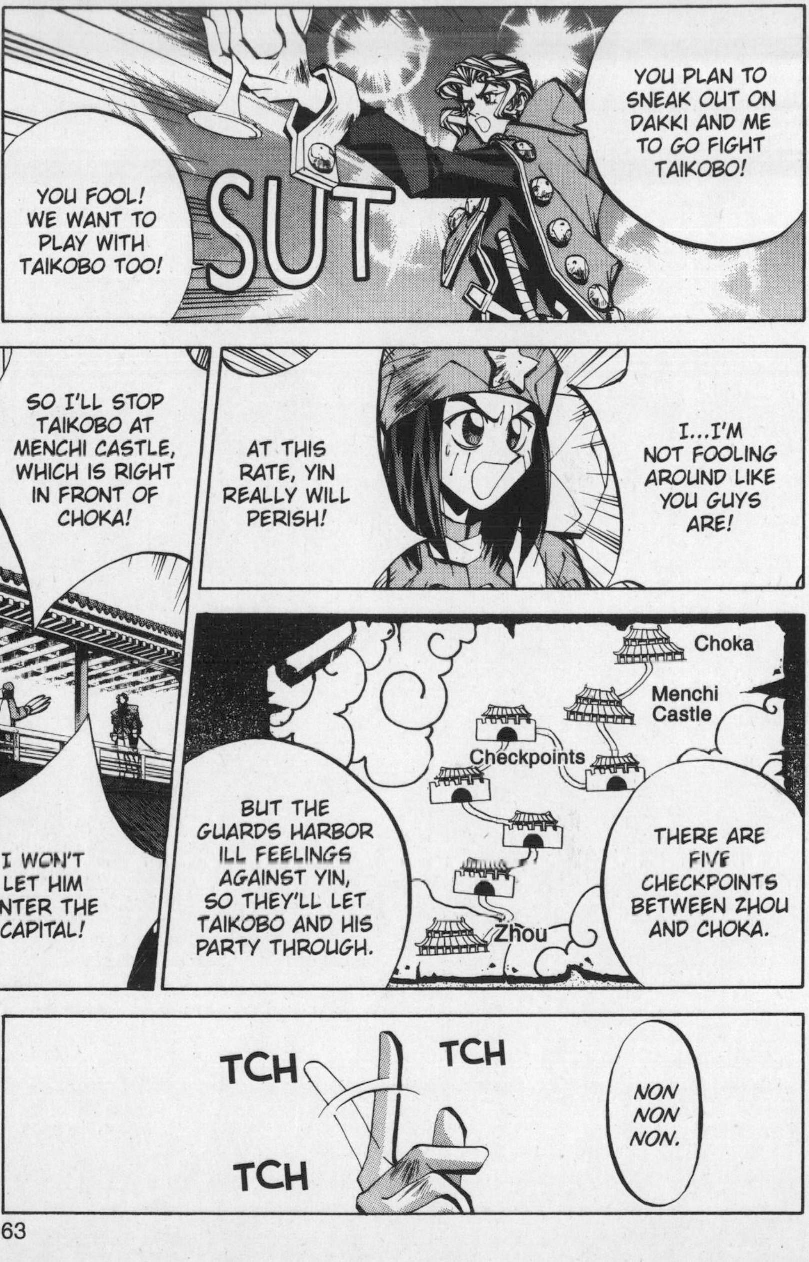
YOU PLAN TO SNEAK OUT ON DAKKI AND ME TO GO FIGHT TAIKOBO!
SUT
YOU FOOL! WE WANT TO PLAY WITH TAIKOBO TOO!
I...I'M NOT FOOLING AROUND LIKE YOU GUYS ARE!
AT THIS RATE, YIN REALLY WILL PERISH!
Choka
Menchi Castle
Checkpoints
Zhou
THERE ARE FIVE CHECKPOINTS BETWEEN ZHOU AND CHOKA.
BUT THE GUARDS HARBOR ILL FEELINGS AGAINST YIN, SO THEY'LL LET TAIKOBO AND HIS PARTY THROUGH.
SO I'LL STOP TAIKOBO AT MENCHI CASTLE, WHICH IS RIGHT IN FRONT OF CHOKA!
I WON'T LET HIM ENTER THE CAPITAL!
NON NON NON.
TCH
TCH
TCH

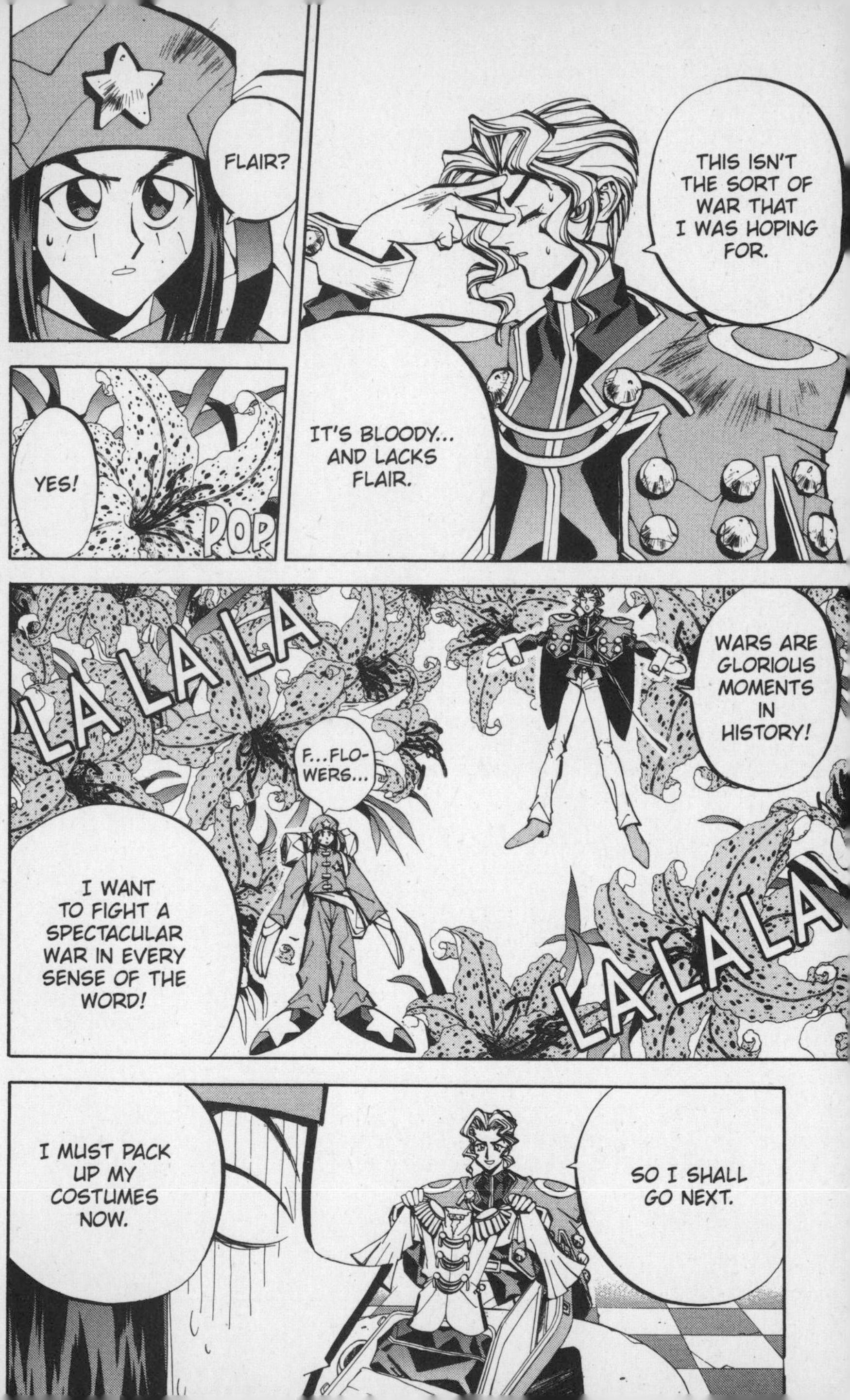
THIS ISN'T THE SORT OF WAR THAT I WAS HOPING FOR.
IT'S BLOODY... AND LACKS FLAIR.
FLAIR?
YES!
POP
WARS ARE GLORIOUS MOMENTS IN HISTORY!
I WANT TO FIGHT A SPECTACULAR WAR IN EVERY SENSE OF THE WORD!
F...FLO-WERS...
LA LA LA
LA LA LA
SO I SHALL GO NEXT.
I MUST PACK UP MY COSTUMES NOW.

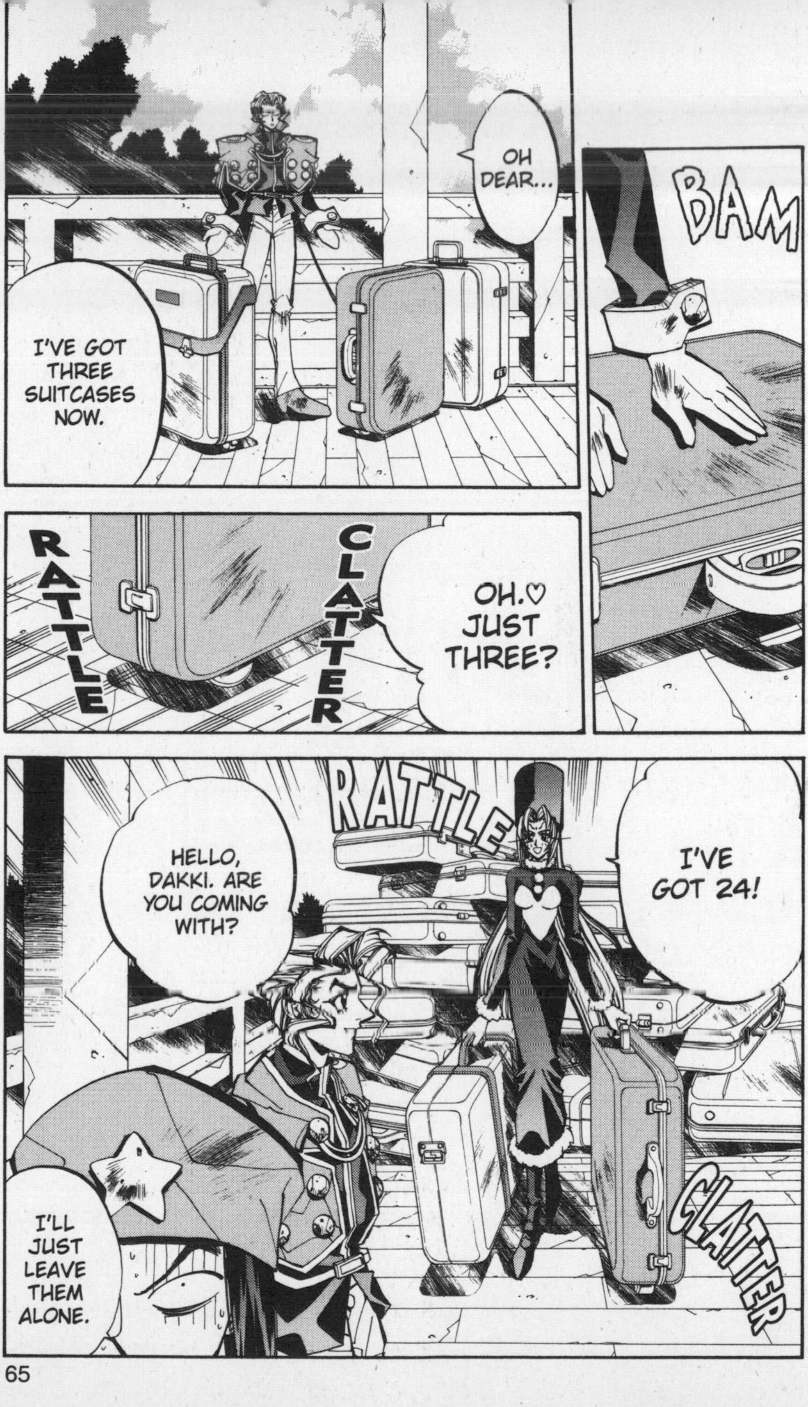
BAM
OH DEAR...
I'VE GOT THREE SUITCASES NOW.
OH.♡ JUST THREE?
CLATTER
RATTLE
I'VE GOT 24!
RATTLE
HELLO, DAKKI. ARE YOU COMING WITH?
CLATTER
I'LL JUST LEAVE THEM ALONE.

封神演義

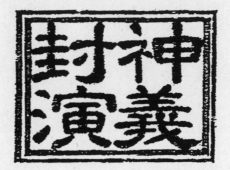

Chapter 83

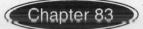

THE GIANT CHOKOMEI

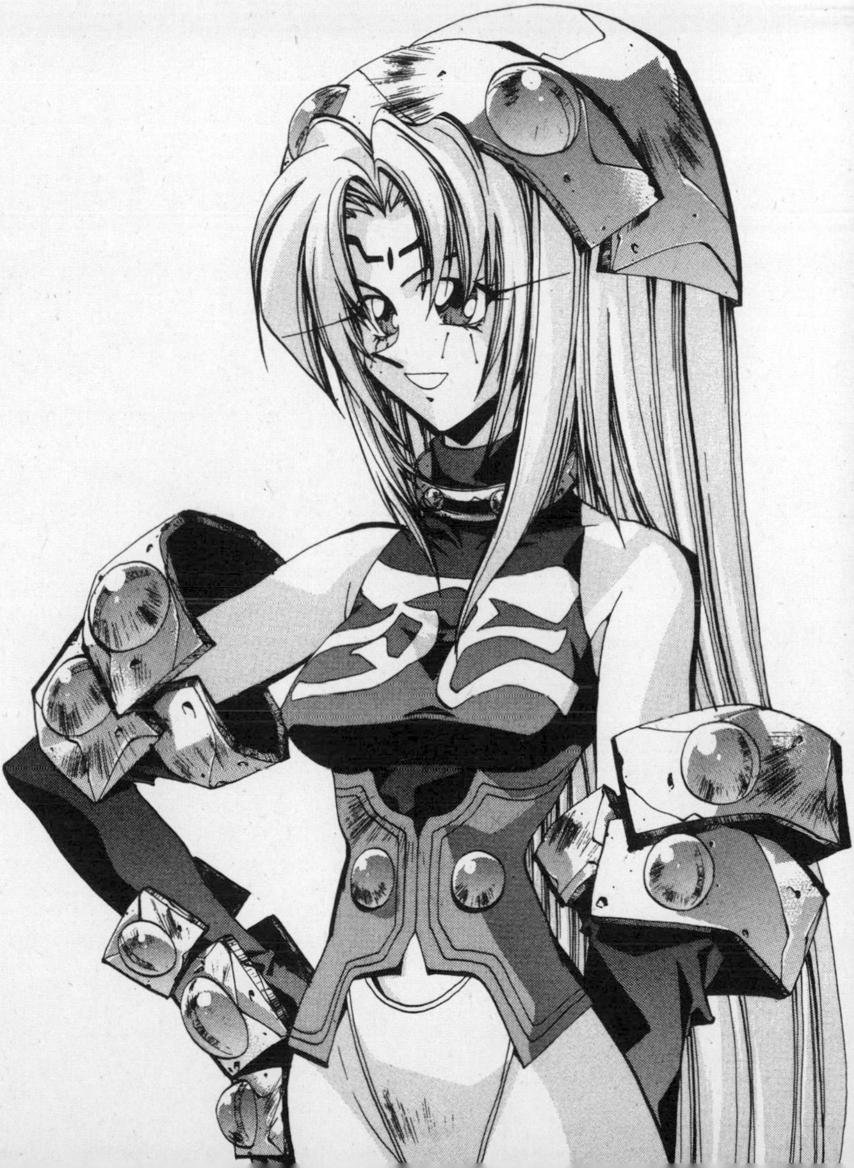

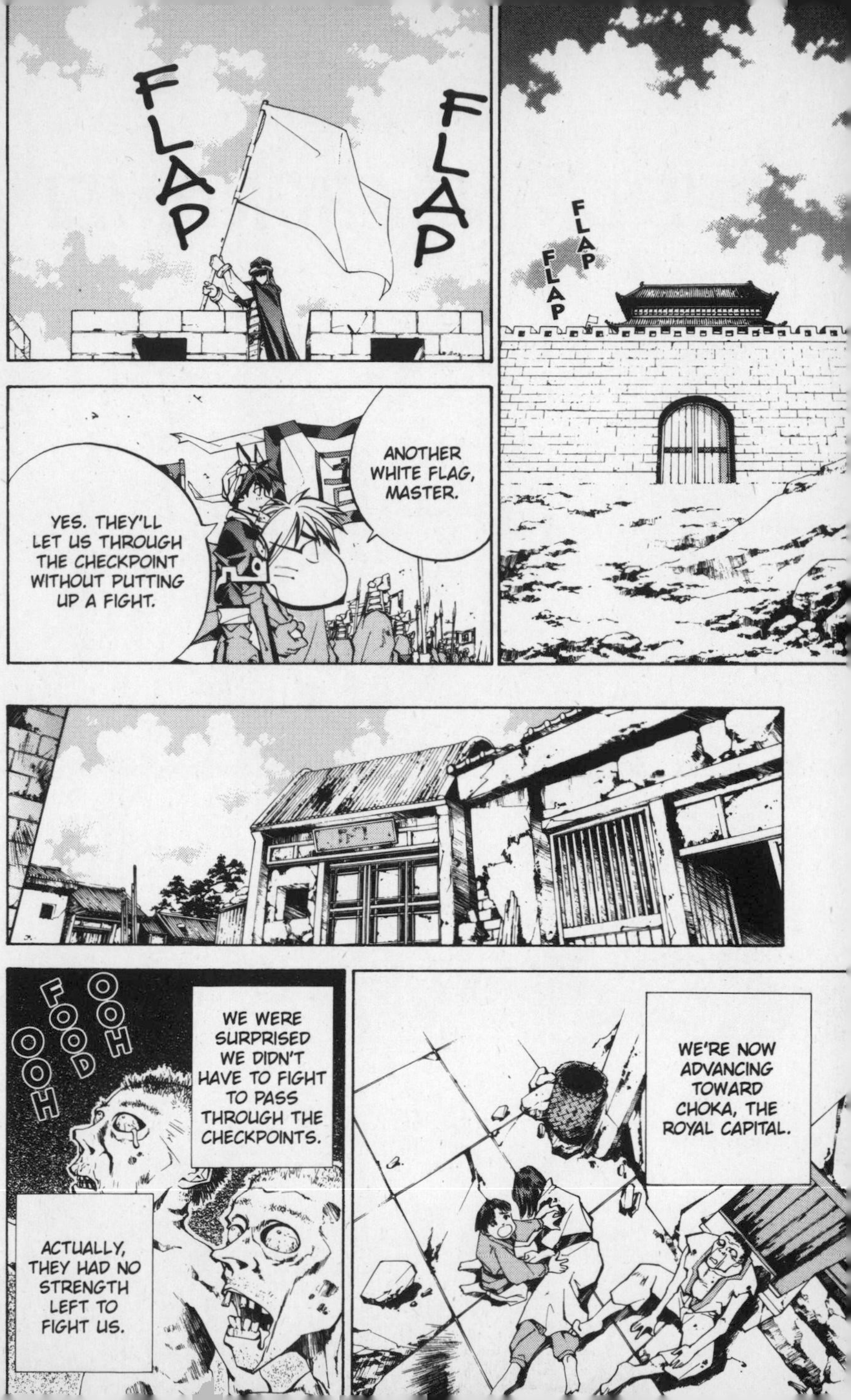

FLAP
FLAP
FLAP
FLAP
ANOTHER WHITE FLAG, MASTER.
YES. THEY'LL LET US THROUGH THE CHECKPOINT WITHOUT PUTTING UP A FIGHT.
WE'RE NOW ADVANCING TOWARD CHOKA, THE ROYAL CAPITAL.
WE WERE SURPRISED WE DIDN'T HAVE TO FIGHT TO PASS THROUGH THE CHECKPOINTS.
OOOH
FOOD
OOOH
ACTUALLY, THEY HAD NO STRENGTH LEFT TO FIGHT US.

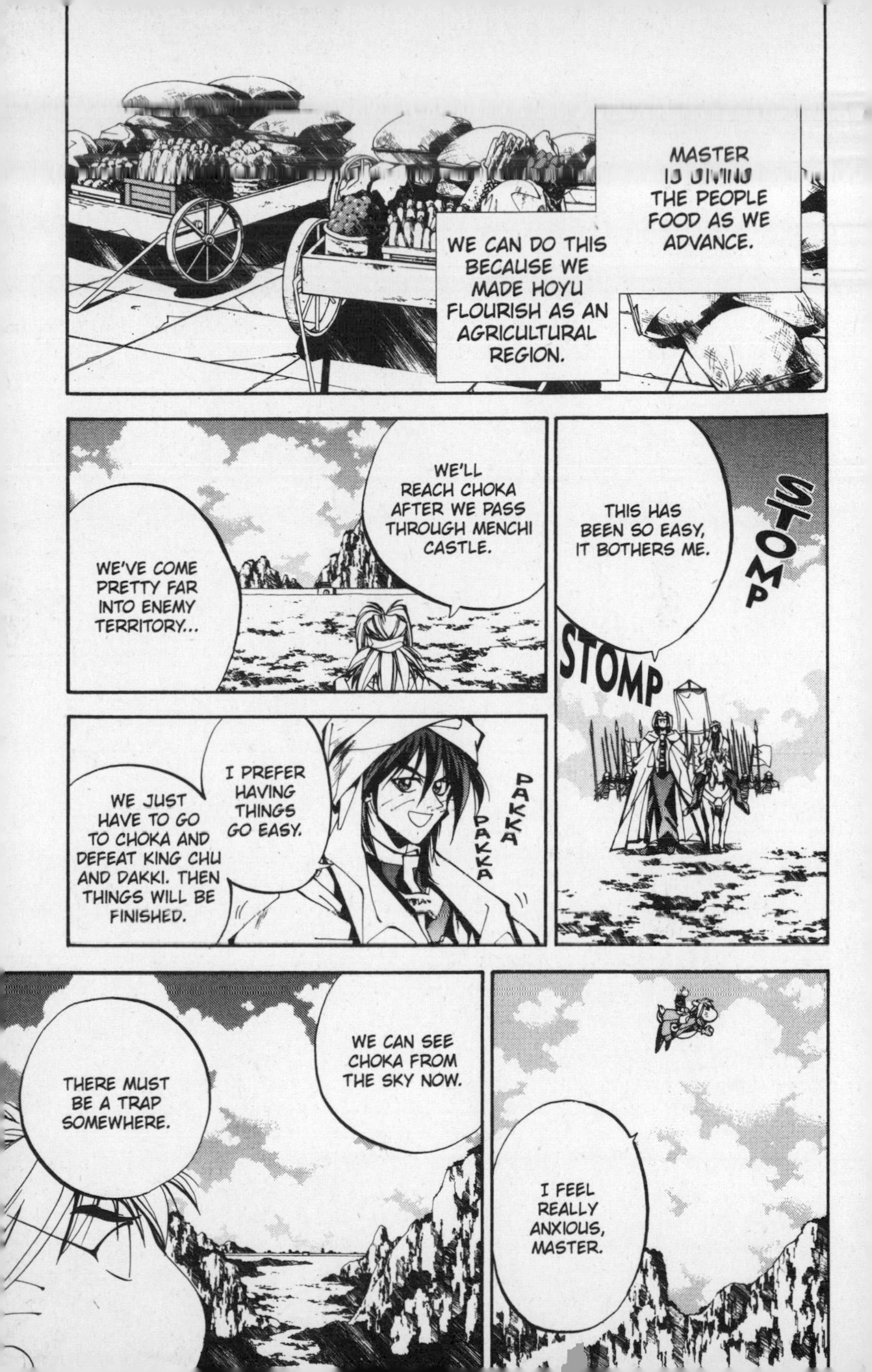
MASTER IS GIVING THE PEOPLE FOOD AS WE ADVANCE.
WE CAN DO THIS BECAUSE WE MADE HOYU FLOURISH AS AN AGRICULTURAL REGION.
THIS HAS BEEN SO EASY, IT BOTHERS ME.
STOMP
STOMP
WE'LL REACH CHOKA AFTER WE PASS THROUGH MENCHI CASTLE.
WE'VE COME PRETTY FAR INTO ENEMY TERRITORY...
PAKKA
PAKKA
I PREFER HAVING THINGS GO EASY.
WE JUST HAVE TO GO TO CHOKA AND DEFEAT KING CHU AND DAKKI. THEN THINGS WILL BE FINISHED.
I FEEL REALLY ANXIOUS, MASTER.
WE CAN SEE CHOKA FROM THE SKY NOW.
THERE MUST BE A TRAP SOMEWHERE.

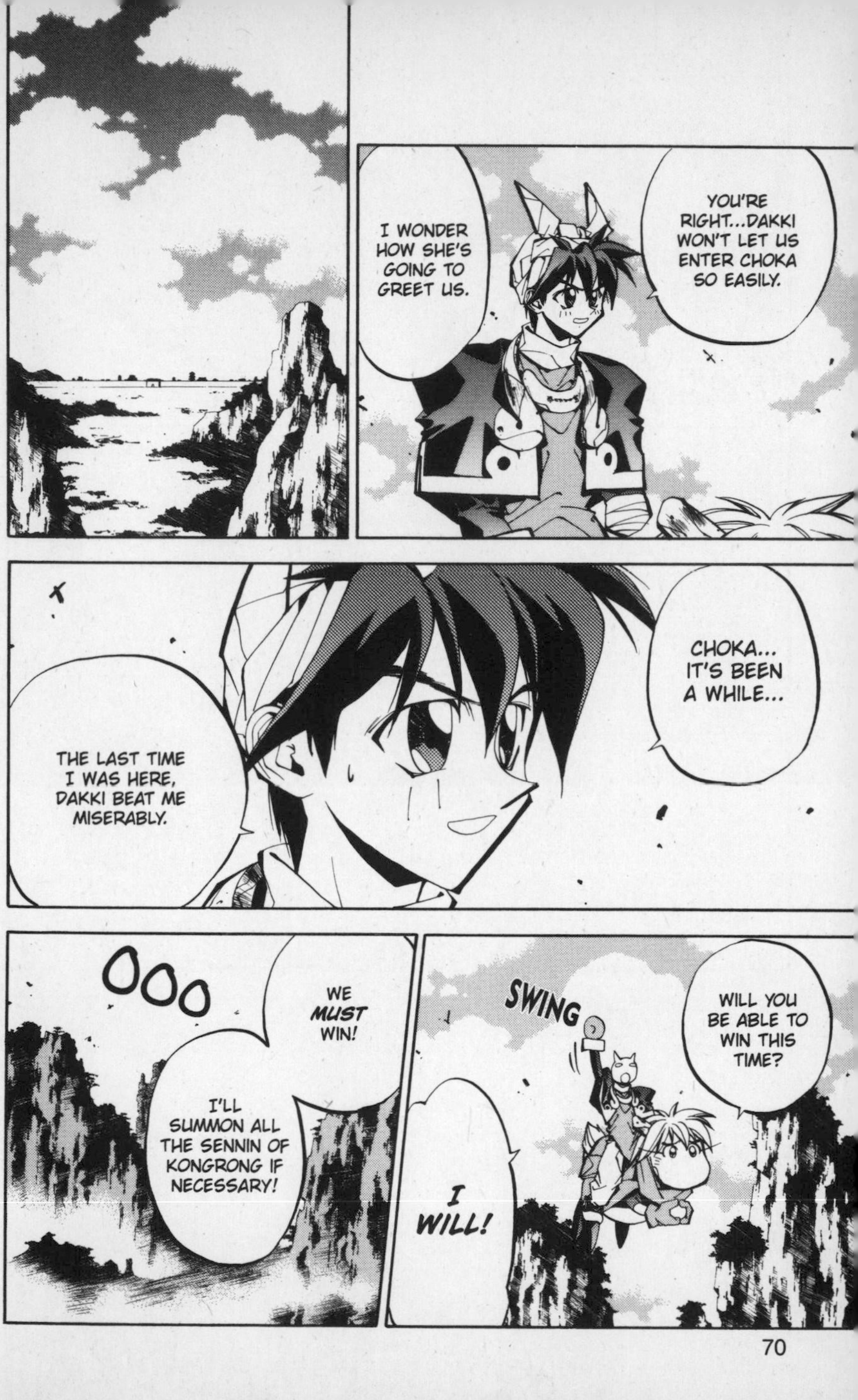
YOU'RE RIGHT...DAKKI WON'T LET US ENTER CHOKA SO EASILY.
I WONDER HOW SHE'S GOING TO GREET US.
CHOKA... IT'S BEEN A WHILE...
THE LAST TIME I WAS HERE, DAKKI BEAT ME MISERABLY.
WILL YOU BE ABLE TO WIN THIS TIME?
SWING
I WILL!
WE MUST WIN!
OOO
I'LL SUMMON ALL THE SENNIN OF KONGRONG IF NECESSARY!

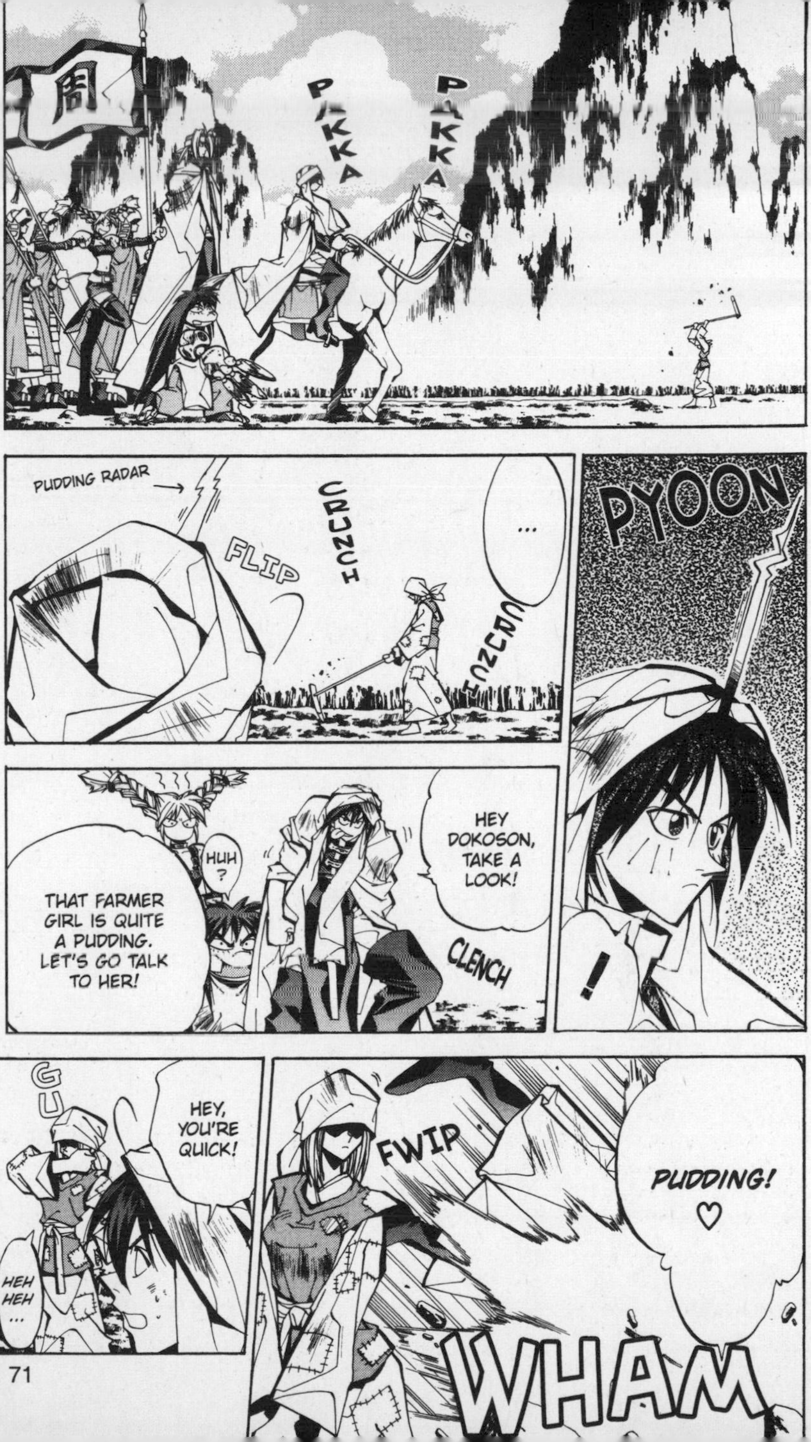
PAKKA
PAKKA
PYOON
!
...
CRUNCH
CRUNCH
FLIP
PUDDING RADAR
HEY DOKOSON, TAKE A LOOK!
CLENCH
HUH?
THAT FARMER GIRL IS QUITE A PUDDING. LET'S GO TALK TO HER!
PUDDING! ♡
FWIP
WHAM
HEY, YOU'RE QUICK!
GU
HEH HEH ...

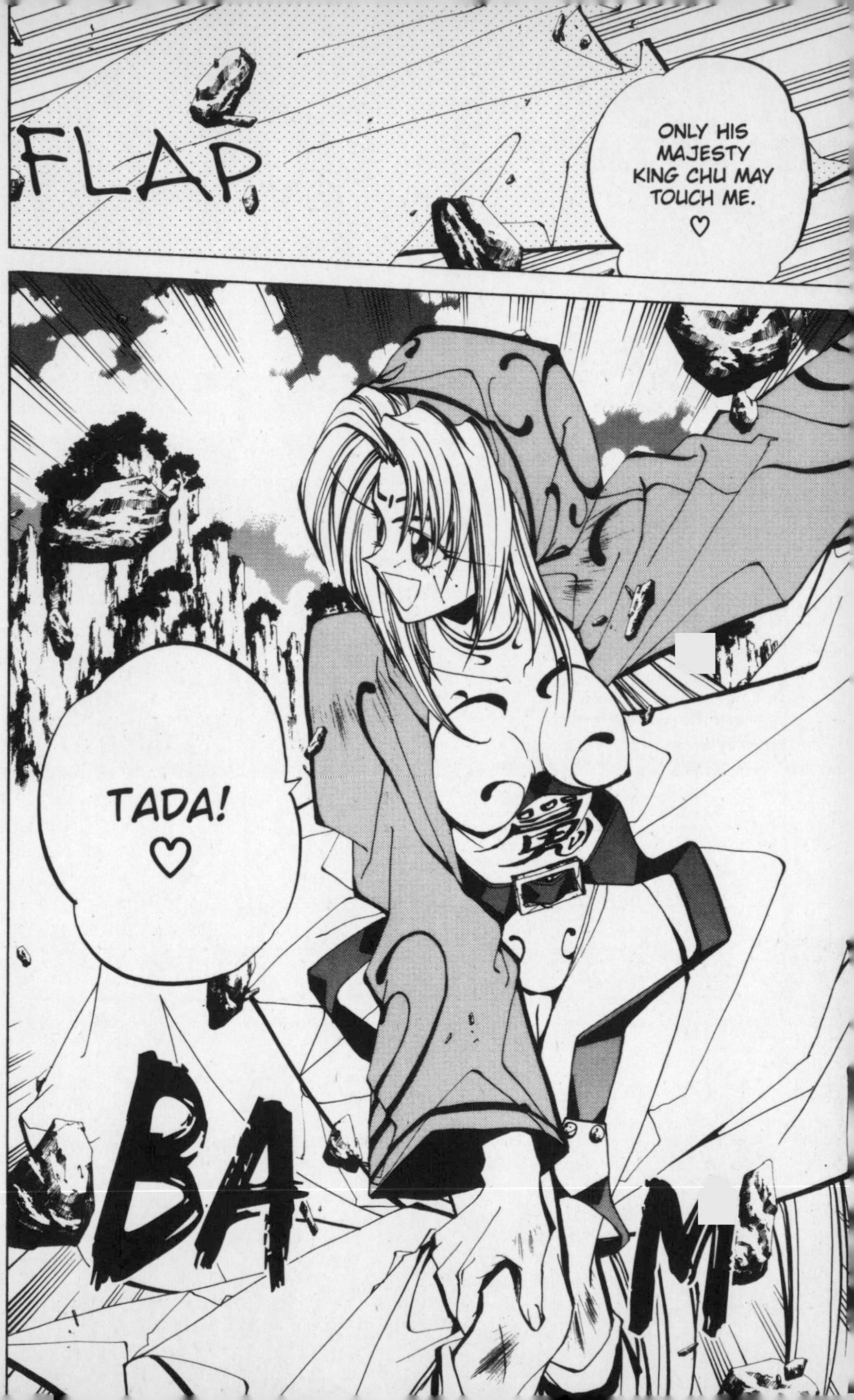
ONLY HIS MAJESTY KING CHU MAY TOUCH ME. ♡
FLAP
TADA! ♡
BAM!

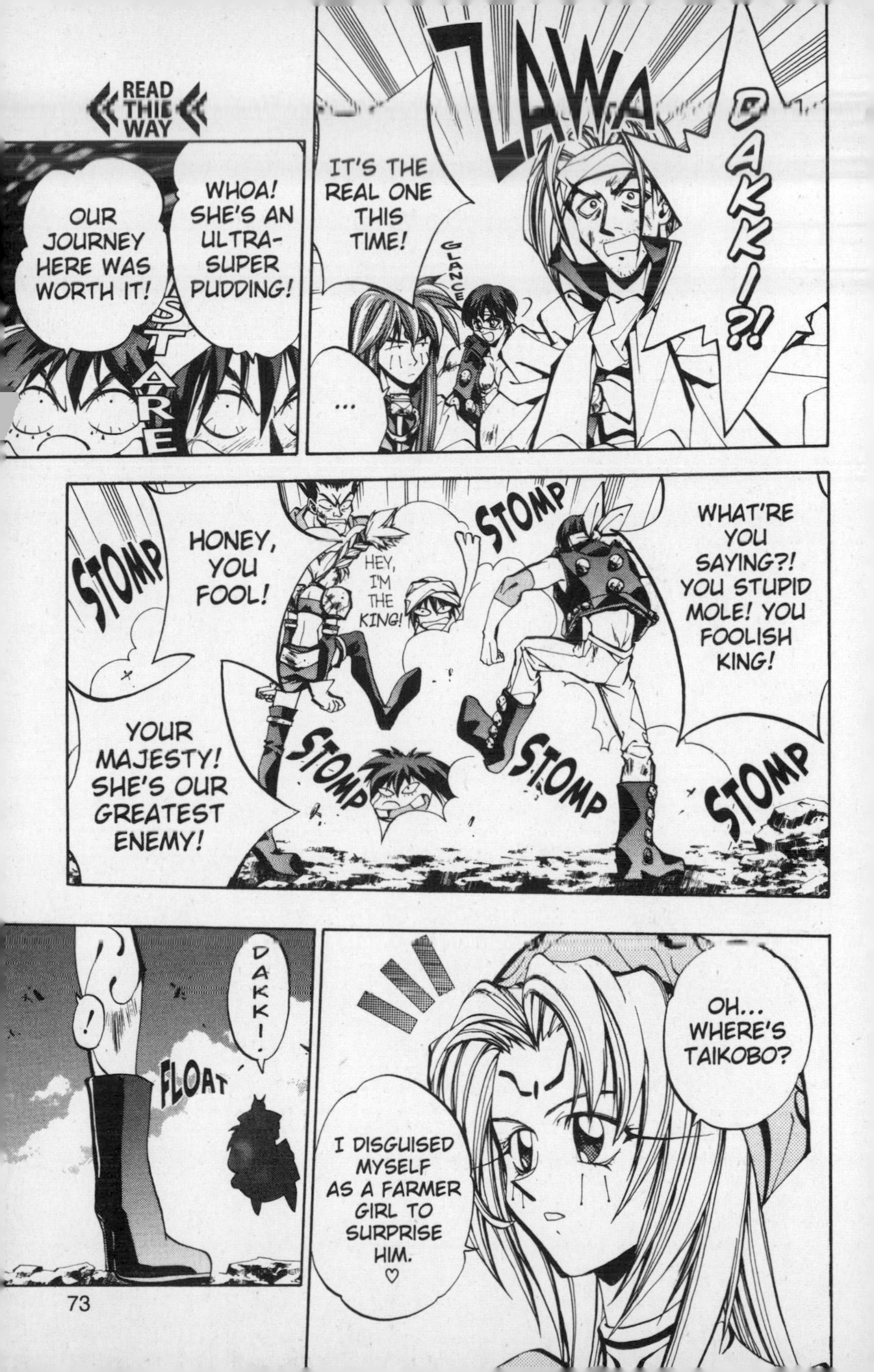
READ THIS WAY
ZAWA
DAKKI?!
IT'S THE REAL ONE THIS TIME!
GLANCE
...
WHOA! SHE'S AN ULTRA-SUPER PUDDING!
OUR JOURNEY HERE WAS WORTH IT!
STARE
WHAT'RE YOU SAYING?! YOU STUPID MOLE! YOU FOOLISH KING!
STOMP
STOMP
HEY, I'M THE KING!
HONEY, YOU FOOL!
STOMP
STOMP
STOMP
YOUR MAJESTY! SHE'S OUR GREATEST ENEMY!
OH... WHERE'S TAIKOBO?
I DISGUISED MYSELF AS A FARMER GIRL TO SURPRISE HIM. ♡
DAKKI!
FLOAT
!

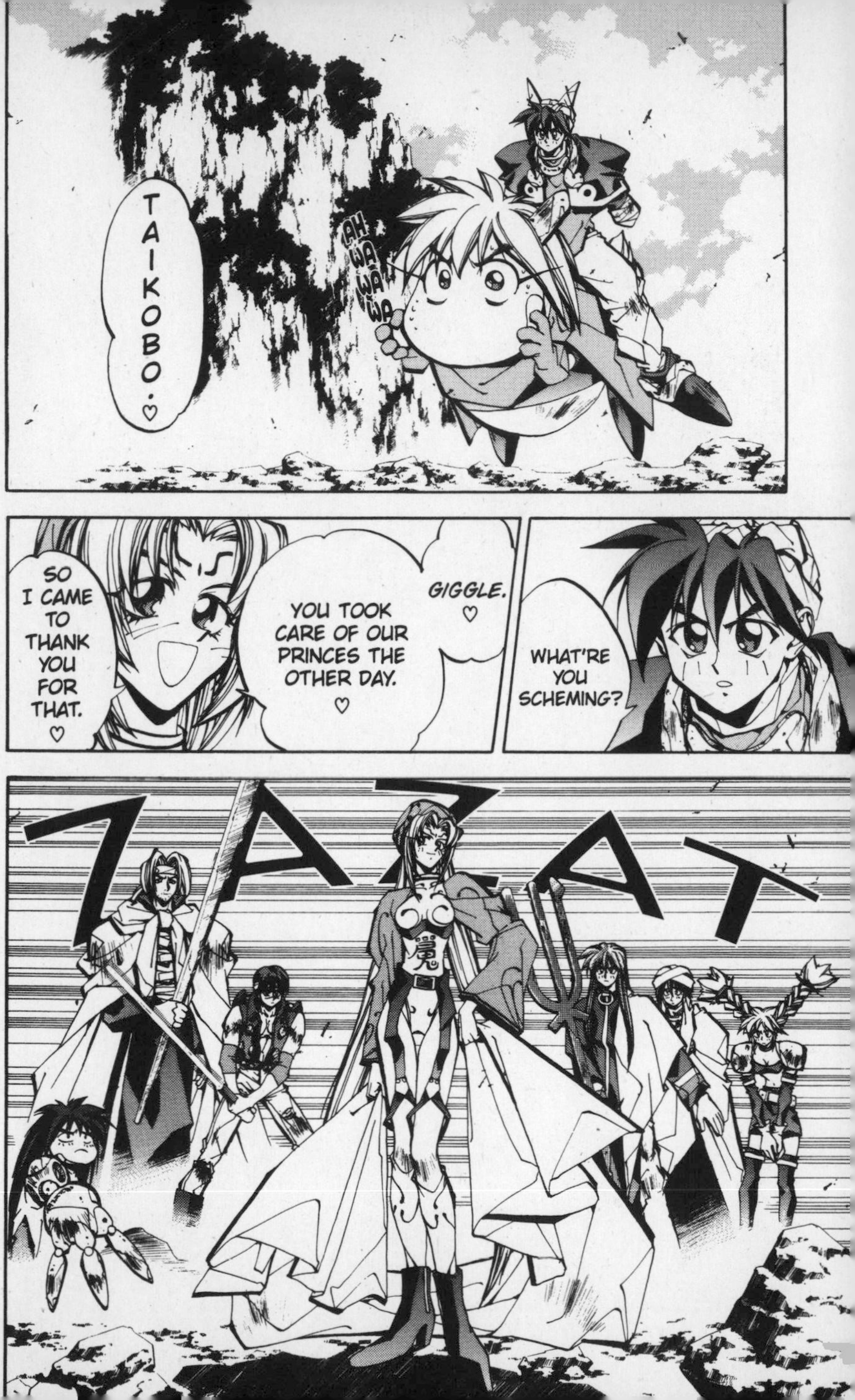
TAIKOBO. ♡
AH WA WA WA WA
WHAT'RE YOU SCHEMING?
GIGGLE. ♡
YOU TOOK CARE OF OUR PRINCES THE OTHER DAY. ♡
SO I CAME TO THANK YOU FOR THAT. ♡
ZAZAT

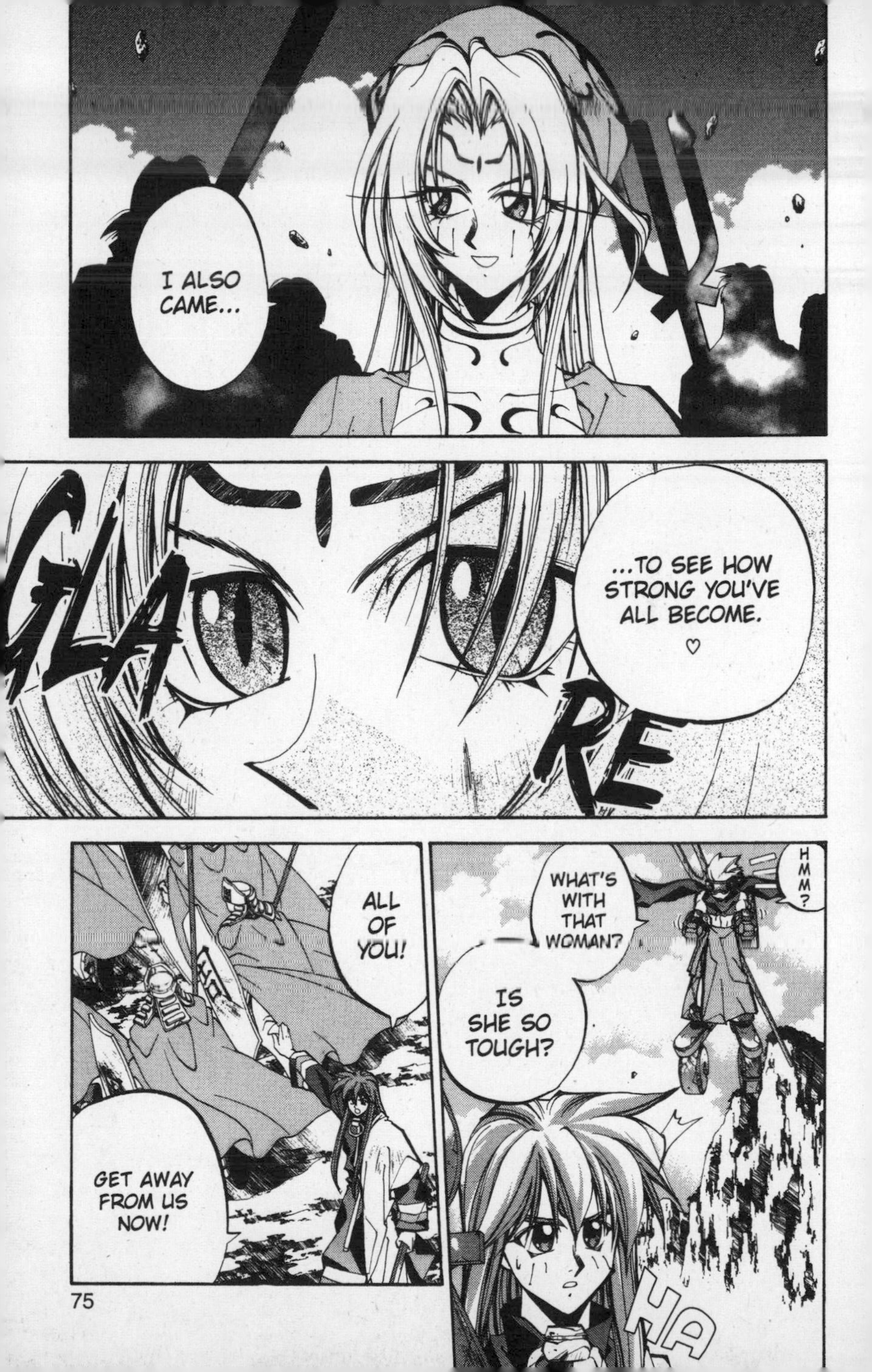
I ALSO CAME...
GLARE
...TO SEE HOW STRONG YOU'VE ALL BECOME. ♡
HMM?
WHAT'S WITH THAT WOMAN?
IS SHE SO TOUGH?
HA
ALL OF YOU!
GET AWAY FROM US NOW!

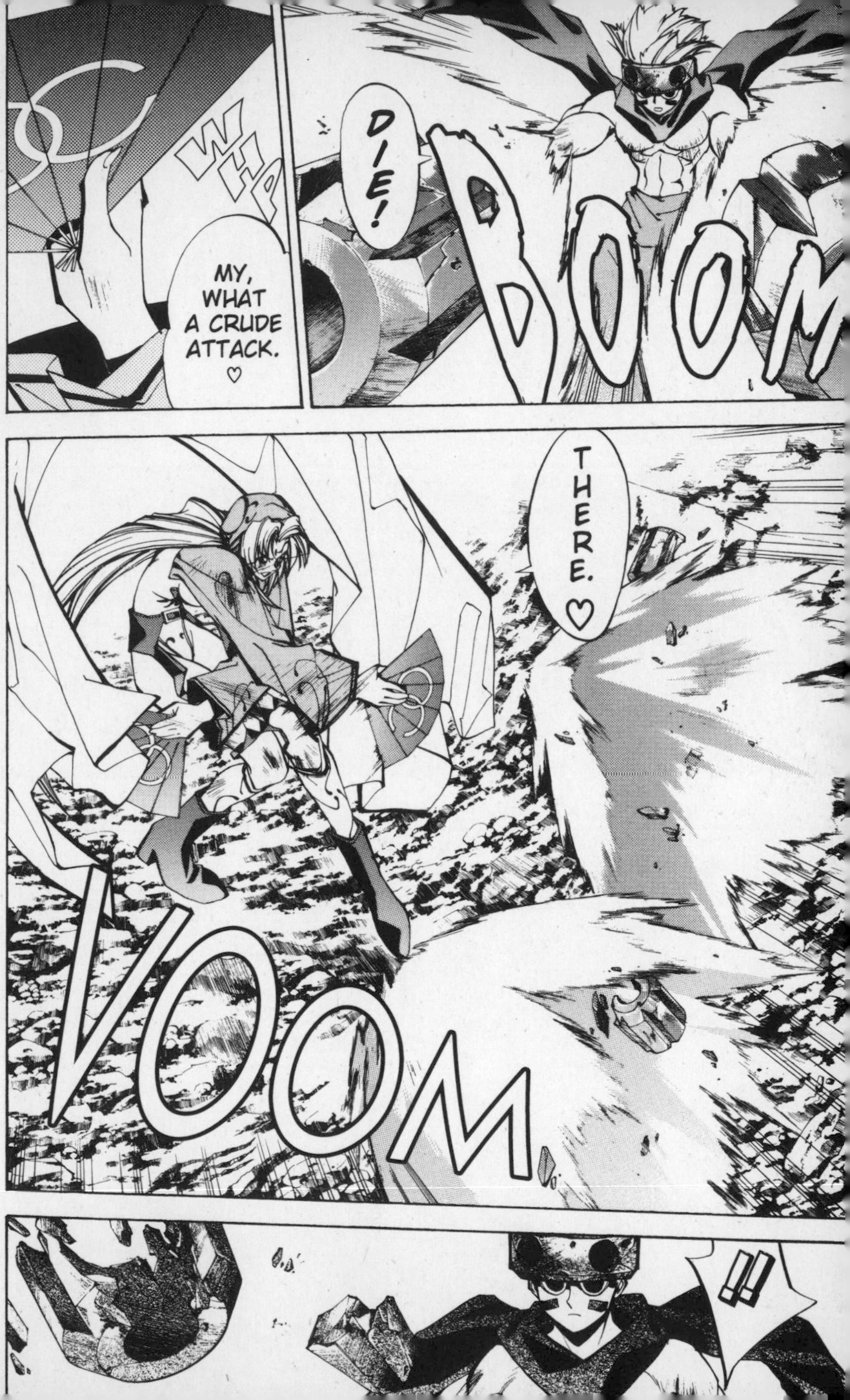
DIE!
BOOM
WHA
MY, WHAT A CRUDE ATTACK. ♡
THERE. ♡
VOOM
!!

READ THIS WAY

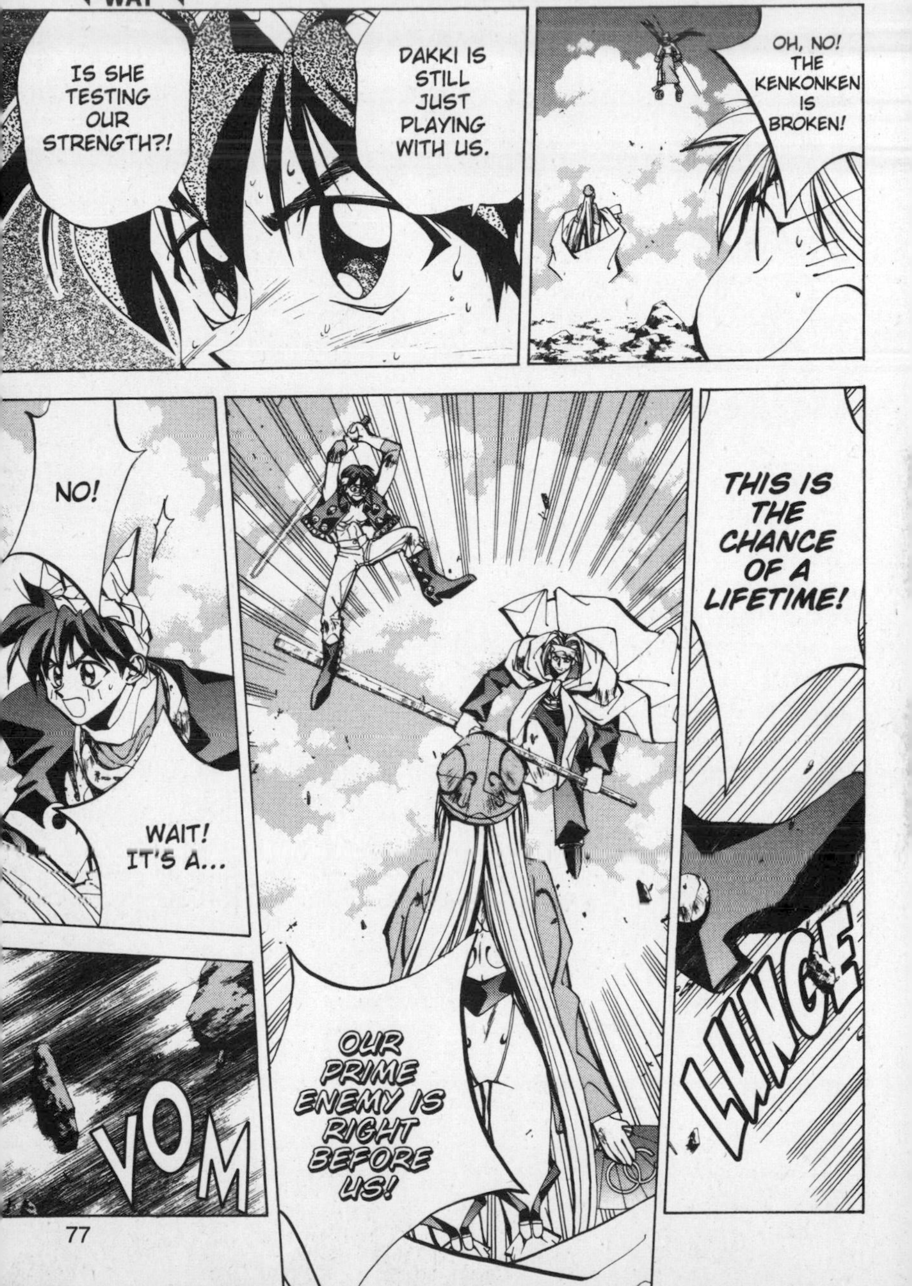

OH, NO! THE KENKONKEN IS BROKEN!
DAKKI IS STILL JUST PLAYING WITH US.
IS SHE TESTING OUR STRENGTH?!
THIS IS THE CHANCE OF A LIFETIME!
LUNGE
OUR PRIME ENEMY IS RIGHT BEFORE US!
NO!
WAIT! IT'S A...
VOM

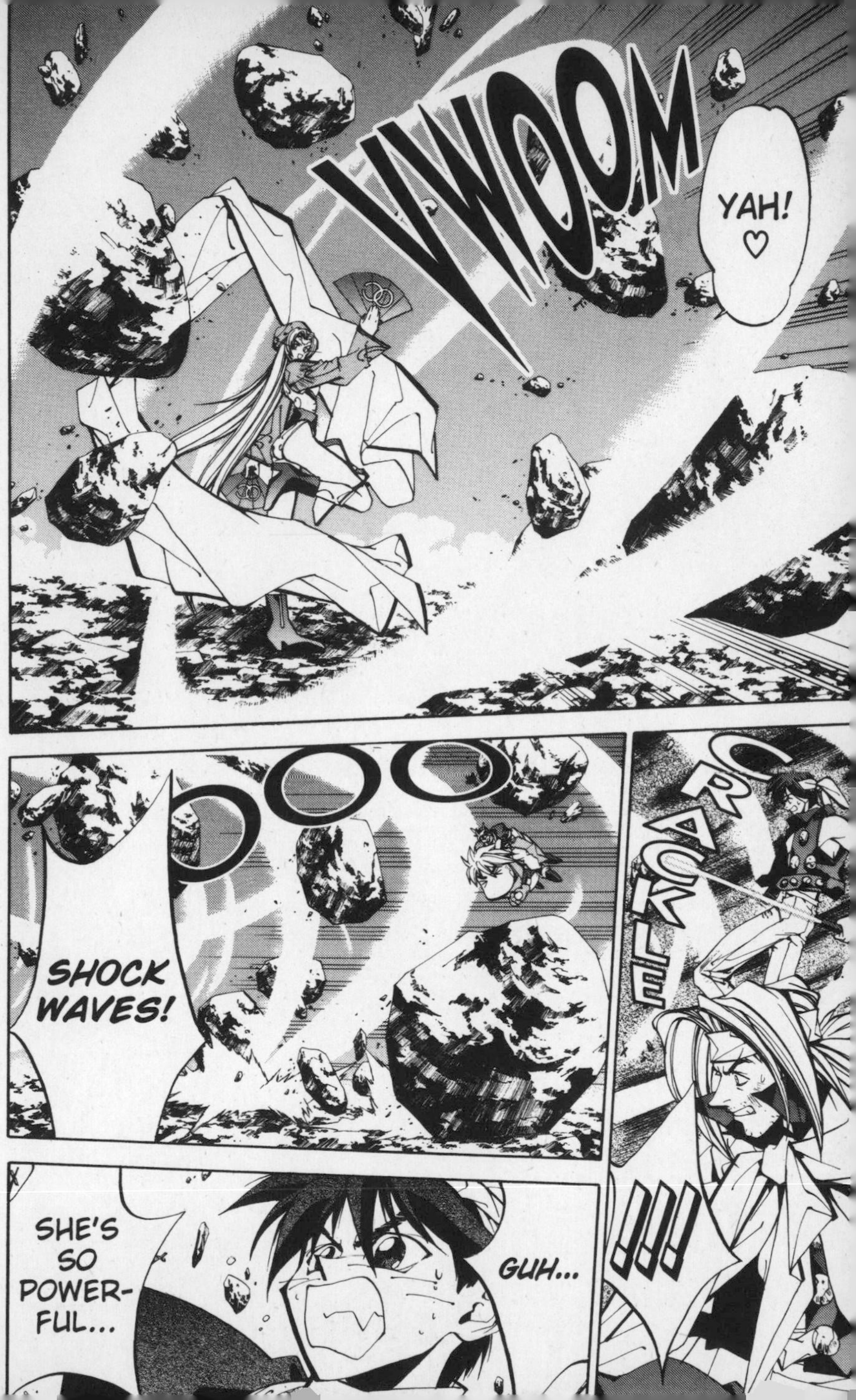
VWOOM
YAH! ♥
CRACKLE
OOO
SHOCK WAVES!
GUH...
SHE'S SO POWER-FUL...

READ THIS WAY

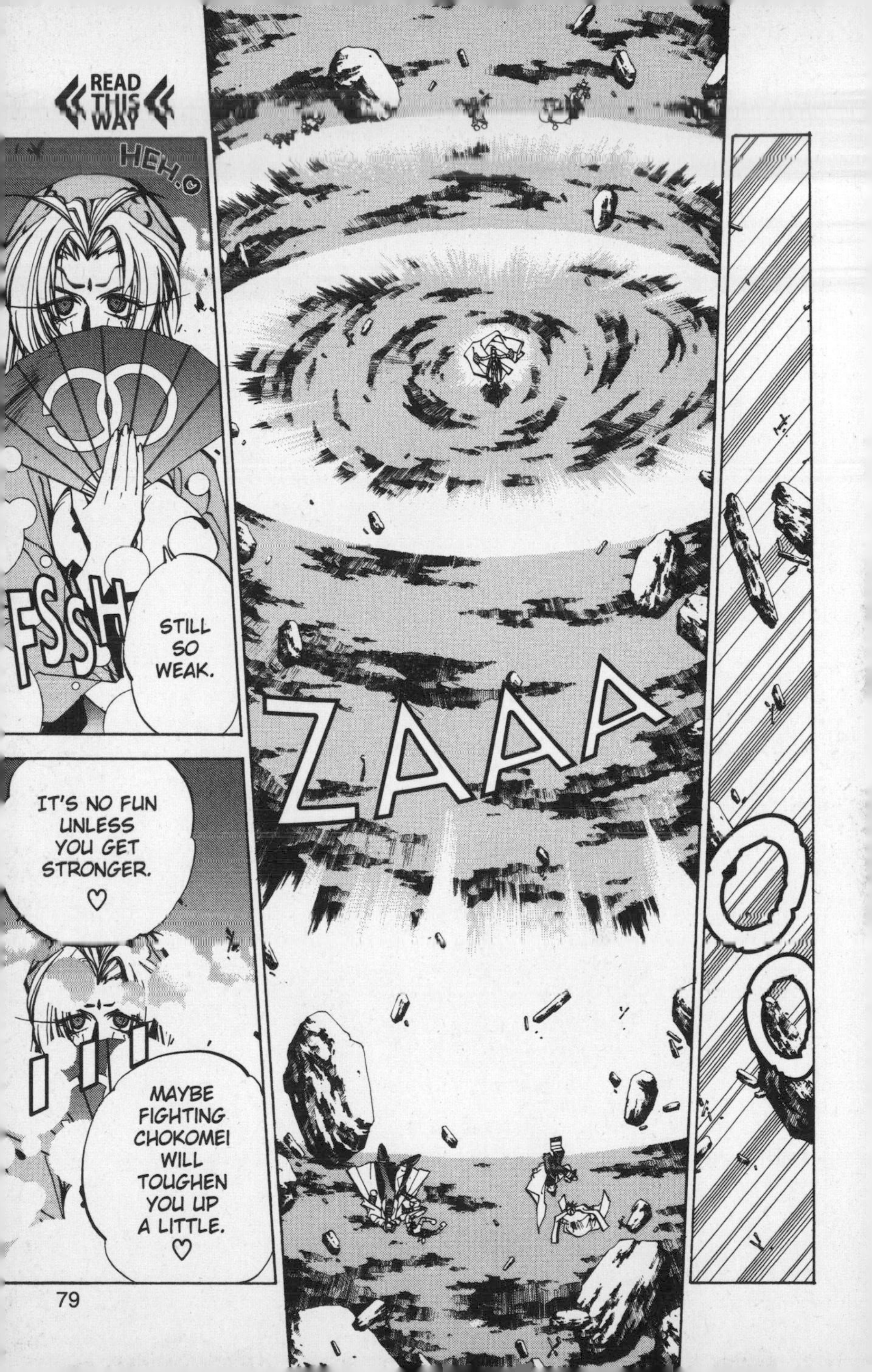
ZAAAOO
HEH.♡
FSSH
STILL SO WEAK.
IT'S NO FUN UNLESS YOU GET STRONGER. ♡
MAYBE FIGHTING CHOKOMEI WILL TOUGHEN YOU UP A LITTLE. ♡

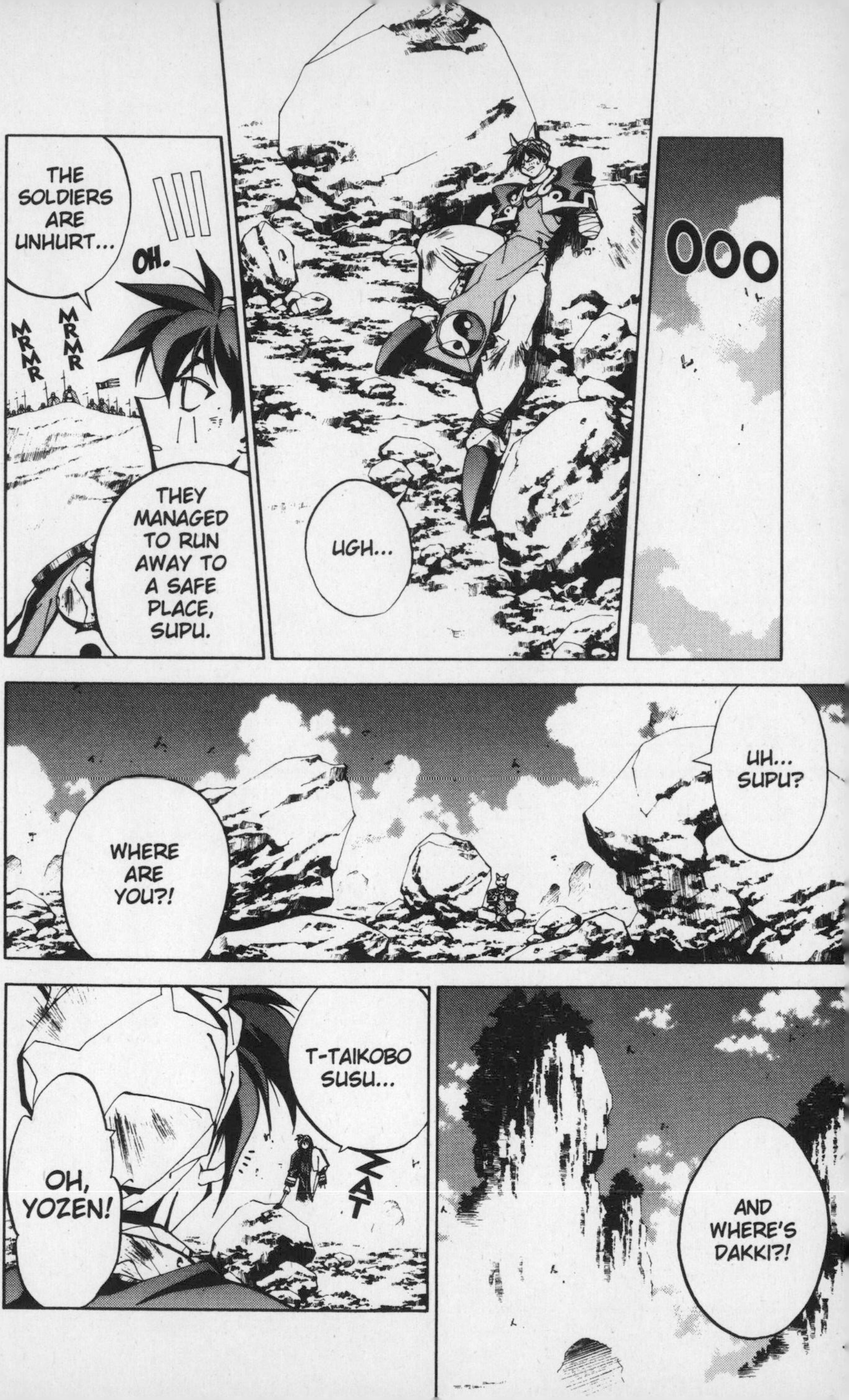
OOO
UGH...
THE SOLDIERS ARE UNHURT...
OH.
MRMR MRMR
THEY MANAGED TO RUN AWAY TO A SAFE PLACE, SUPU.
UH... SUPU?
WHERE ARE YOU?!
AND WHERE'S DAKKI?!
T-TAIKOBO SUSU...
ZAT
OH, YOZEN!

READ THIS WAY

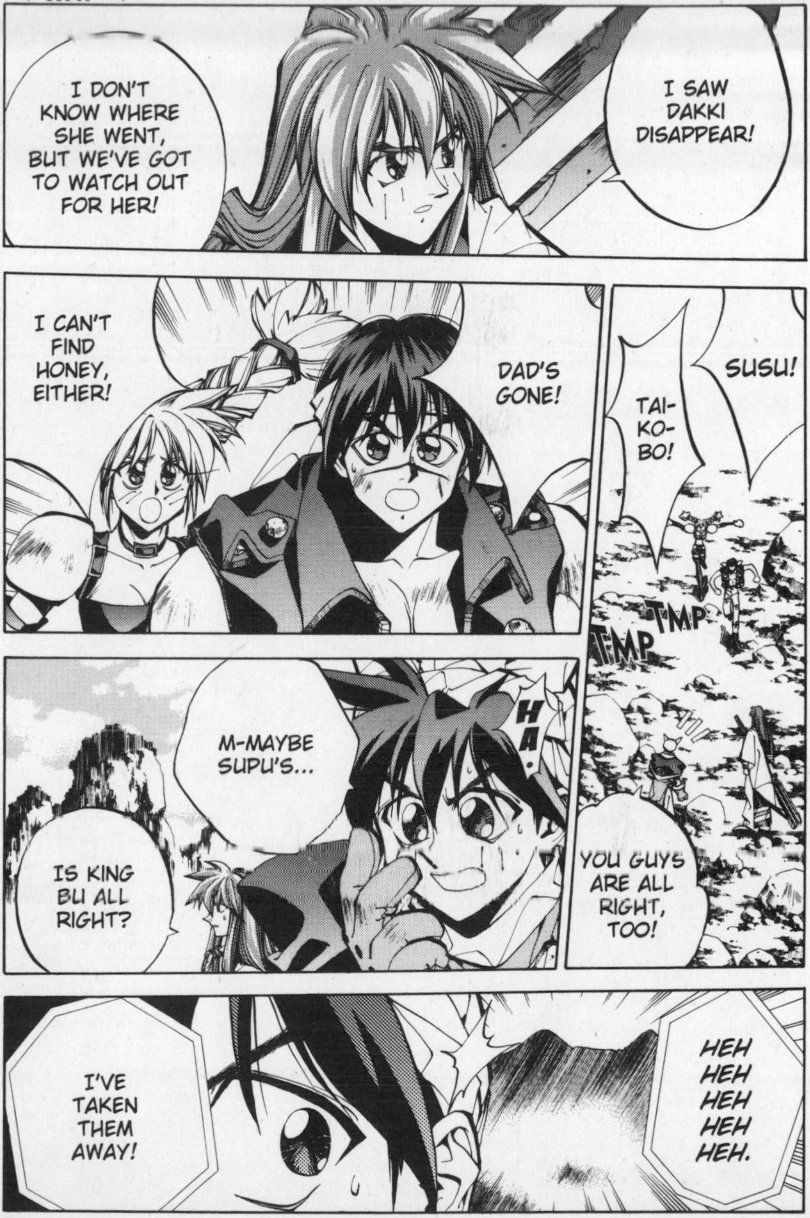
I SAW DAKKI DISAPPEAR!
I DON'T KNOW WHERE SHE WENT, BUT WE'VE GOT TO WATCH OUT FOR HER!
SUSU!
TAIKOBO!
TMP
TMP
YOU GUYS ARE ALL RIGHT, TOO!
DAD'S GONE!
I CAN'T FIND HONEY, EITHER!
HA!
M-MAYBE SUPU'S...
IS KING BU ALL RIGHT?
HEH HEH HEH HEH HEH.
I'VE TAKEN THEM AWAY!

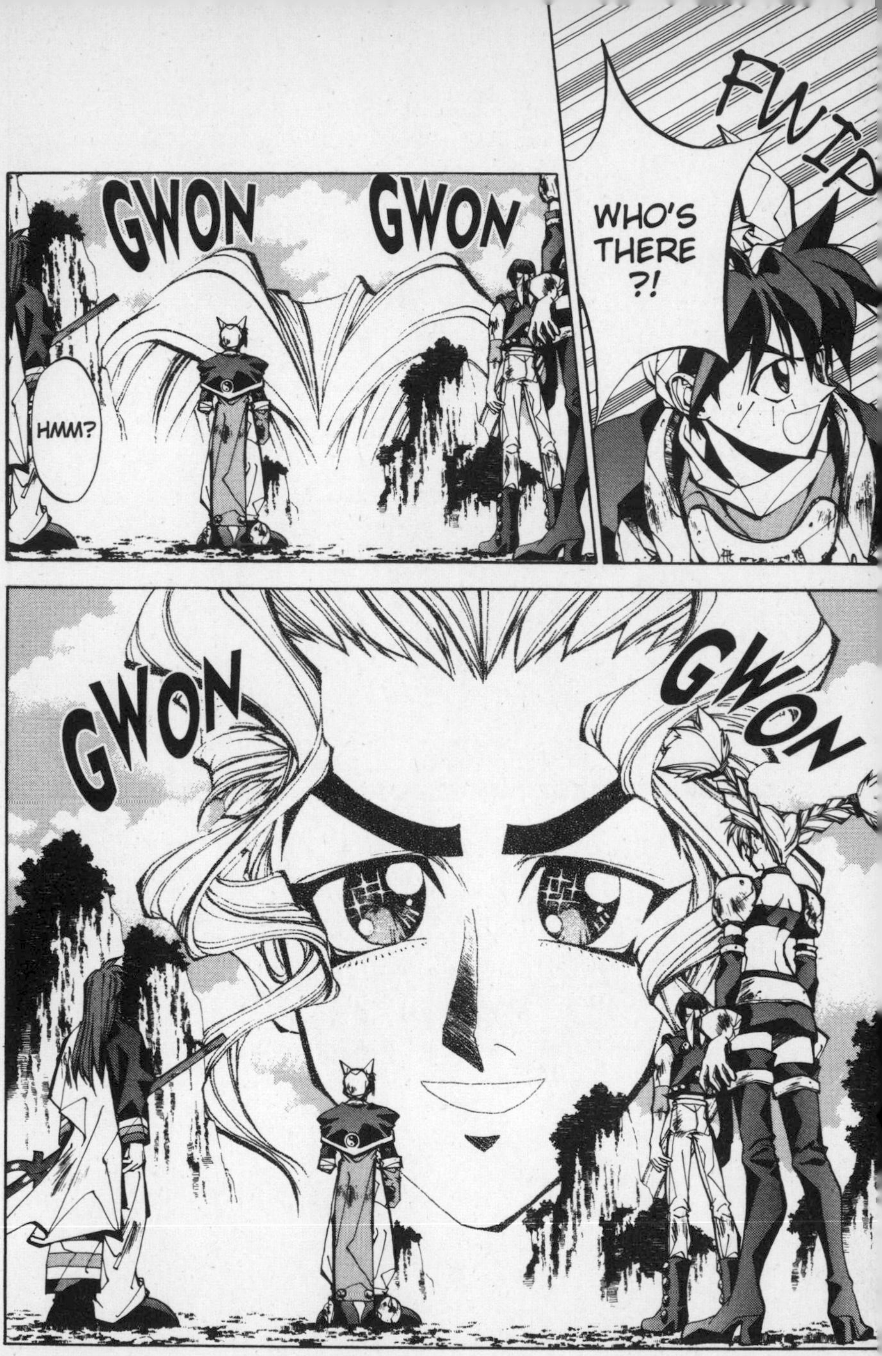
FWIP
WHO'S THERE ?!
GWON
GWON
HMM?
GWON
GWON

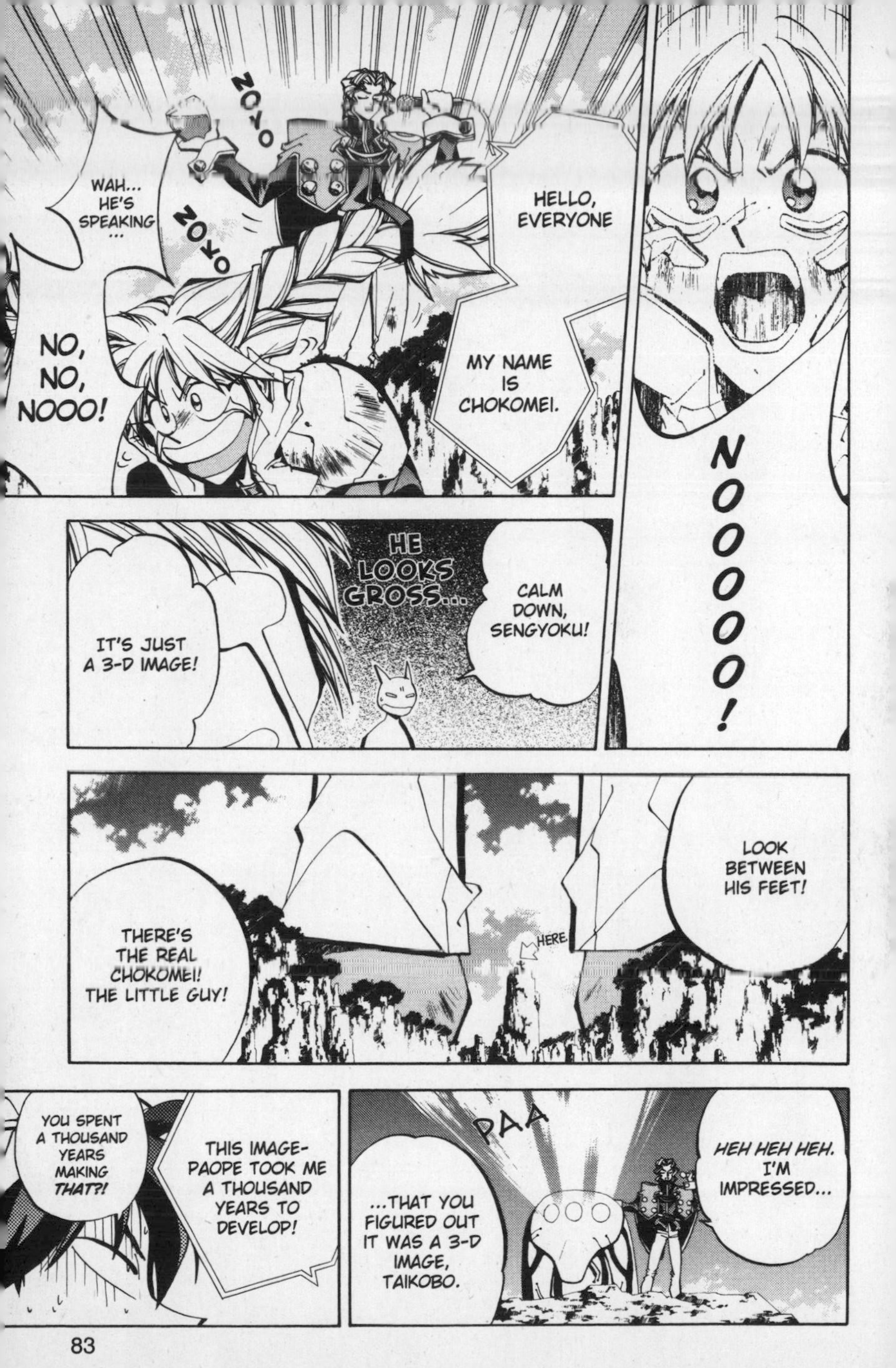
ZOYO
ZOYO
HELLO, EVERYONE
MY NAME IS CHOKOMEI.
WAH... HE'S SPEAKING...
NO, NO, NOOO!
NOOOOOO!
CALM DOWN, SENGYOKU!
HE LOOKS GROSS...
IT'S JUST A 3-D IMAGE!
LOOK BETWEEN HIS FEET!
HERE
THERE'S THE REAL CHOKOMEI! THE LITTLE GUY!
HEH HEH HEH. I'M IMPRESSED...
PAA
...THAT YOU FIGURED OUT IT WAS A 3-D IMAGE, TAIKOBO.
THIS IMAGE-PAOPE TOOK ME A THOUSAND YEARS TO DEVELOP!
YOU SPENT A THOUSAND YEARS MAKING *THAT?!*

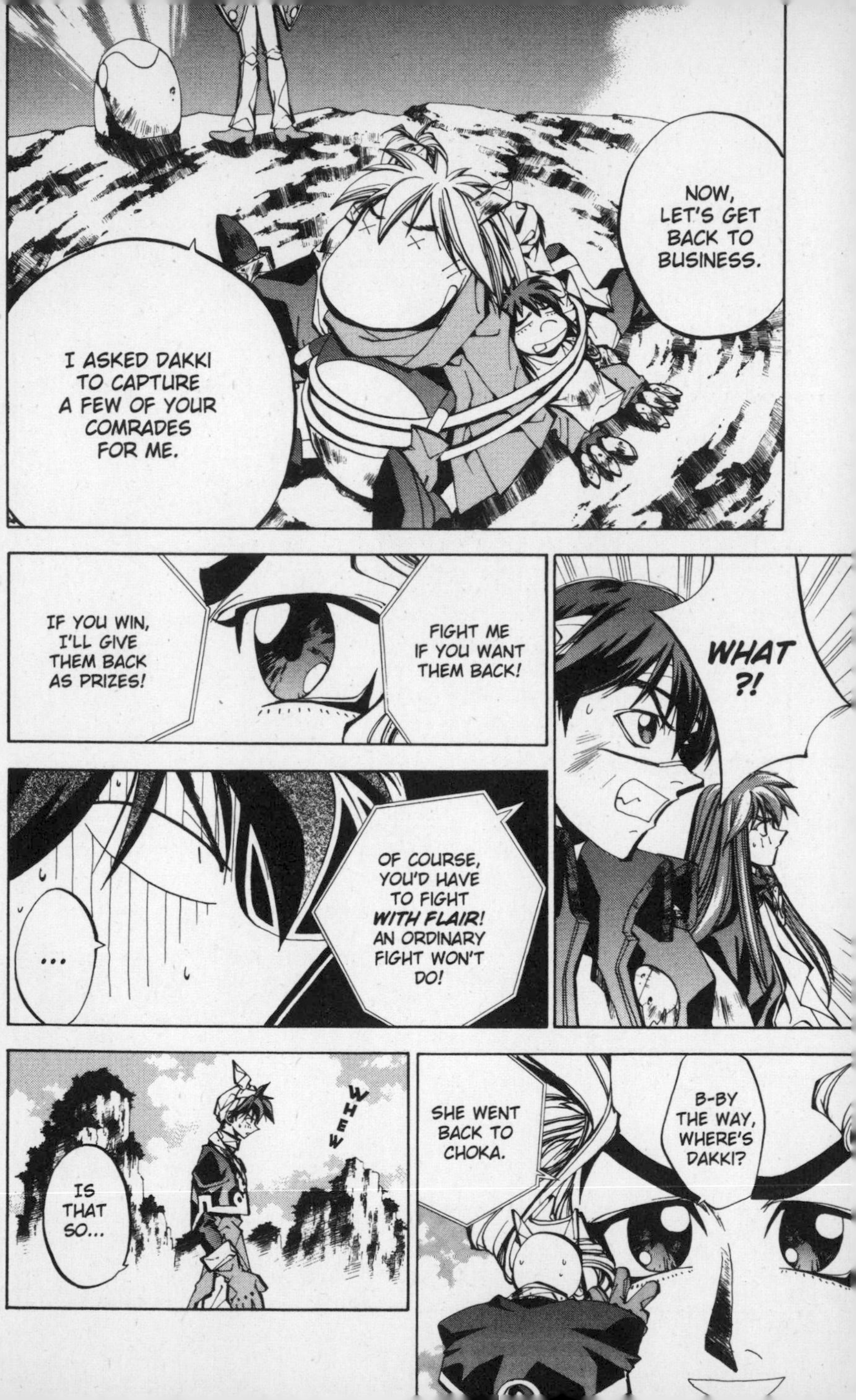
NOW, LET'S GET BACK TO BUSINESS.
I ASKED DAKKI TO CAPTURE A FEW OF YOUR COMRADES FOR ME.
WHAT?!
FIGHT ME IF YOU WANT THEM BACK!
IF YOU WIN, I'LL GIVE THEM BACK AS PRIZES!
OF COURSE, YOU'D HAVE TO FIGHT WITH FLAIR! AN ORDINARY FIGHT WON'T DO!
...
B-BY THE WAY, WHERE'S DAKKI?
SHE WENT BACK TO CHOKA.
WHEW
IS THAT SO...

READ THIS WAY

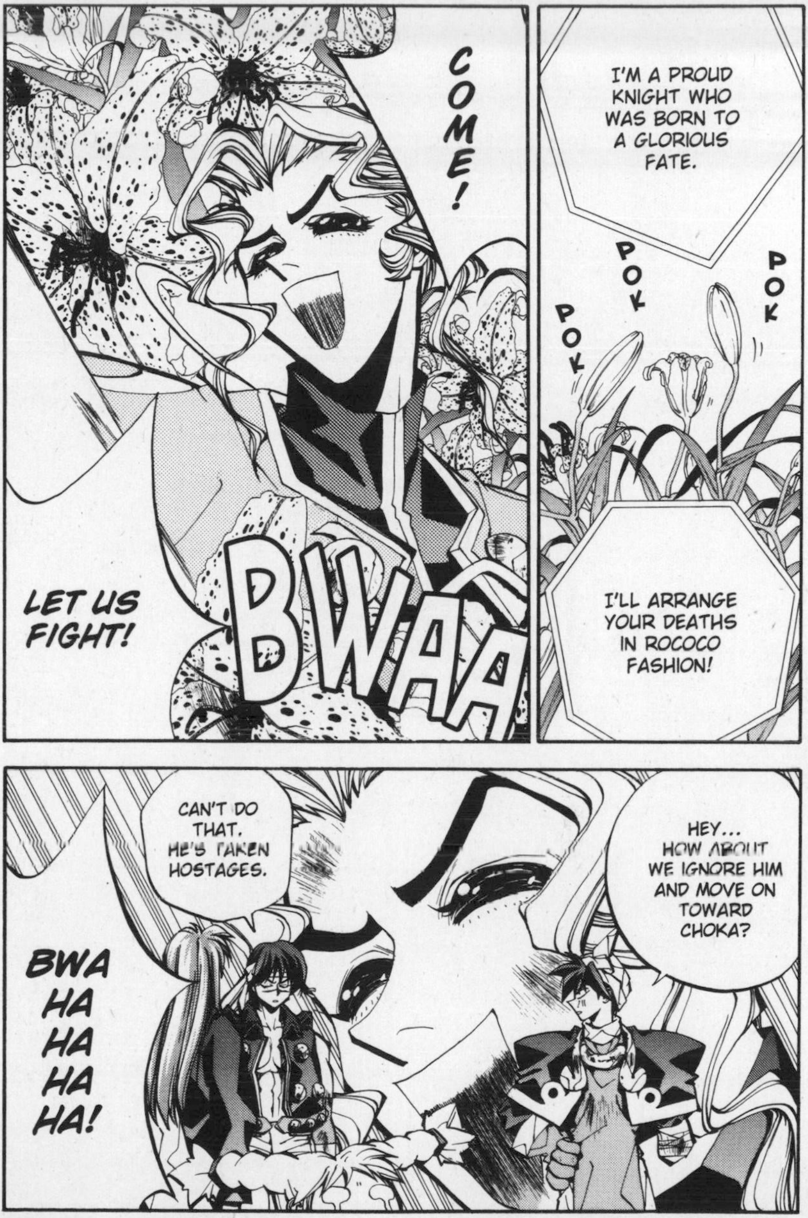

I'M A PROUD KNIGHT WHO WAS BORN TO A GLORIOUS FATE.
POK
POK
POK
I'LL ARRANGE YOUR DEATHS IN ROCOCO FASHION!
COME!
BWAA
LET US FIGHT!
HEY... HOW ABOUT WE IGNORE HIM AND MOVE ON TOWARD CHOKA?
CAN'T DO THAT. HE'S TAKEN HOSTAGES.
BWA HA HA HA HA!

封神演義

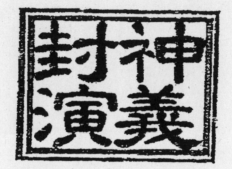

Chapter 84

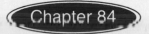

THE LUXURY LINER QUEEN JOKER II

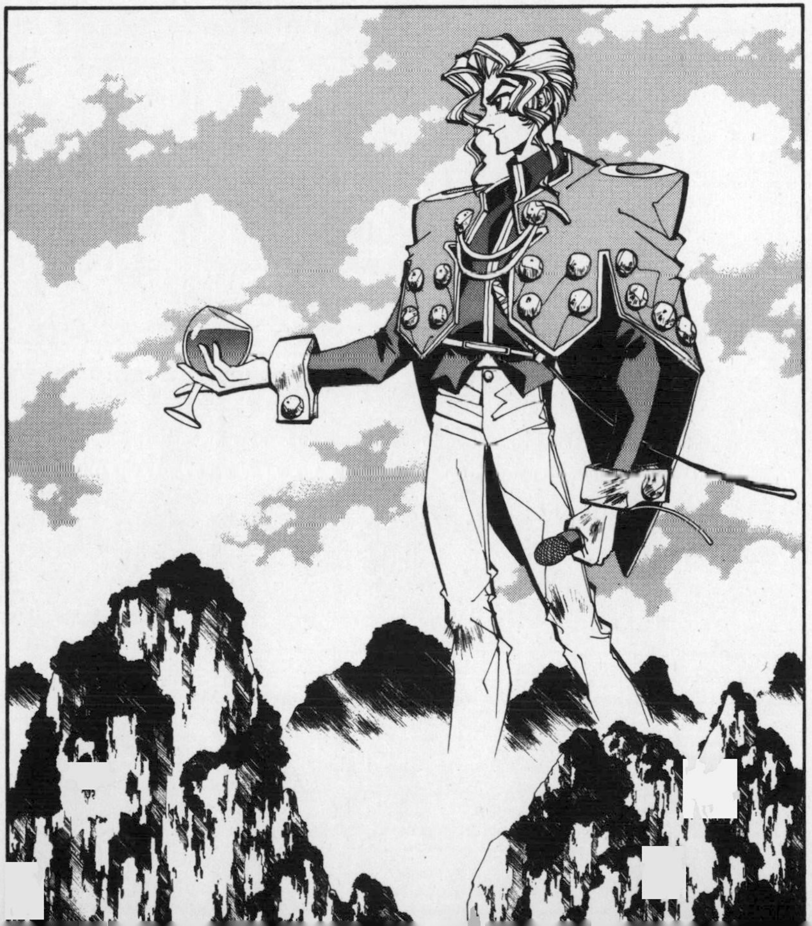

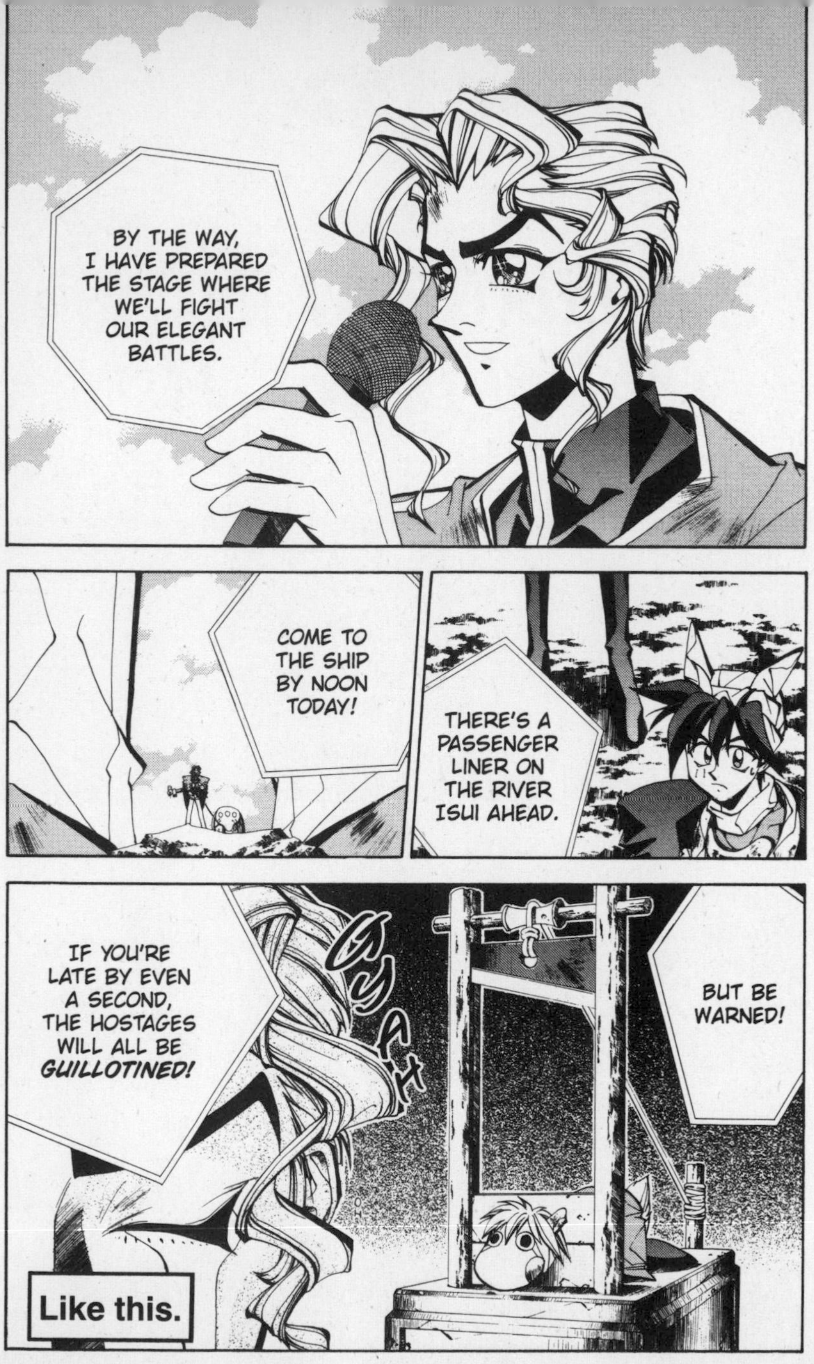
BY THE WAY, I HAVE PREPARED THE STAGE WHERE WE'LL FIGHT OUR ELEGANT BATTLES.
THERE'S A PASSENGER LINER ON THE RIVER ISUI AHEAD.
COME TO THE SHIP BY NOON TODAY!
BUT BE WARNED!
IF YOU'RE LATE BY EVEN A SECOND, THE HOSTAGES WILL ALL BE *GUILLOTINED!*
Like this.

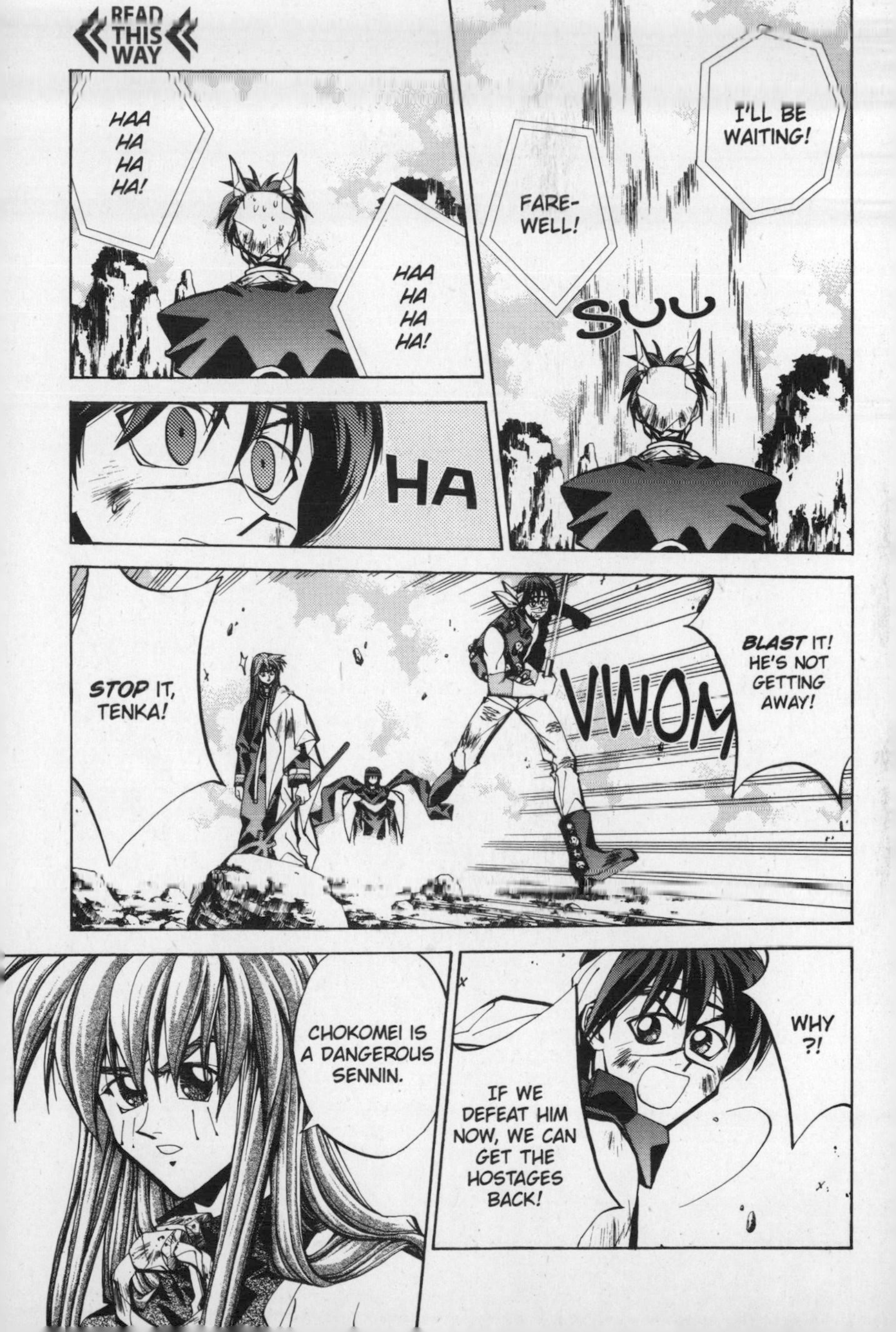
READ THIS WAY
I'LL BE WAITING!
FARE-WELL!
SUU
HAA HA HA HA!
HAA HA HA HA!
HA
BLAST IT! HE'S NOT GETTING AWAY!
VWOM
STOP IT, TENKA!
WHY?!
IF WE DEFEAT HIM NOW, WE CAN GET THE HOSTAGES BACK!
CHOKOMEI IS A DANGEROUS SENNIN.

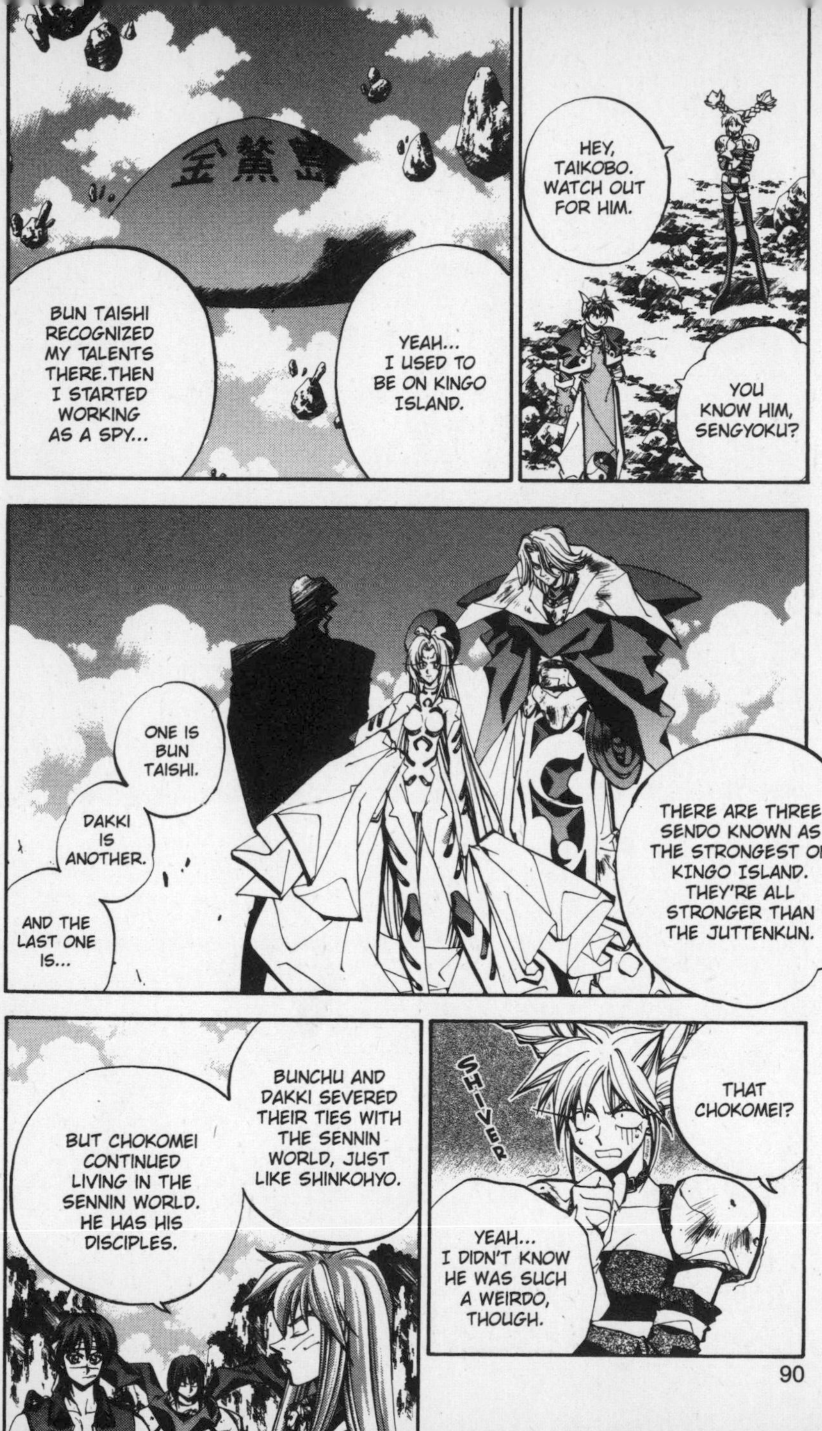
HEY, TAIKOBO. WATCH OUT FOR HIM.
YOU KNOW HIM, SENGYOKU?
金鰲島
YEAH... I USED TO BE ON KINGO ISLAND.
BUN TAISHI RECOGNIZED MY TALENTS THERE.THEN I STARTED WORKING AS A SPY...
THERE ARE THREE SENDO KNOWN AS THE STRONGEST ON KINGO ISLAND. THEY'RE ALL STRONGER THAN THE JUTTENKUN.
ONE IS BUN TAISHI.
DAKKI IS ANOTHER.
AND THE LAST ONE IS...
SHIVER
THAT CHOKOMEI?
YEAH... I DIDN'T KNOW HE WAS SUCH A WEIRDO, THOUGH.
BUNCHU AND DAKKI SEVERED THEIR TIES WITH THE SENNIN WORLD, JUST LIKE SHINKOHYO.
BUT CHOKOMEI CONTINUED LIVING IN THE SENNIN WORLD. HE HAS HIS DISCIPLES.

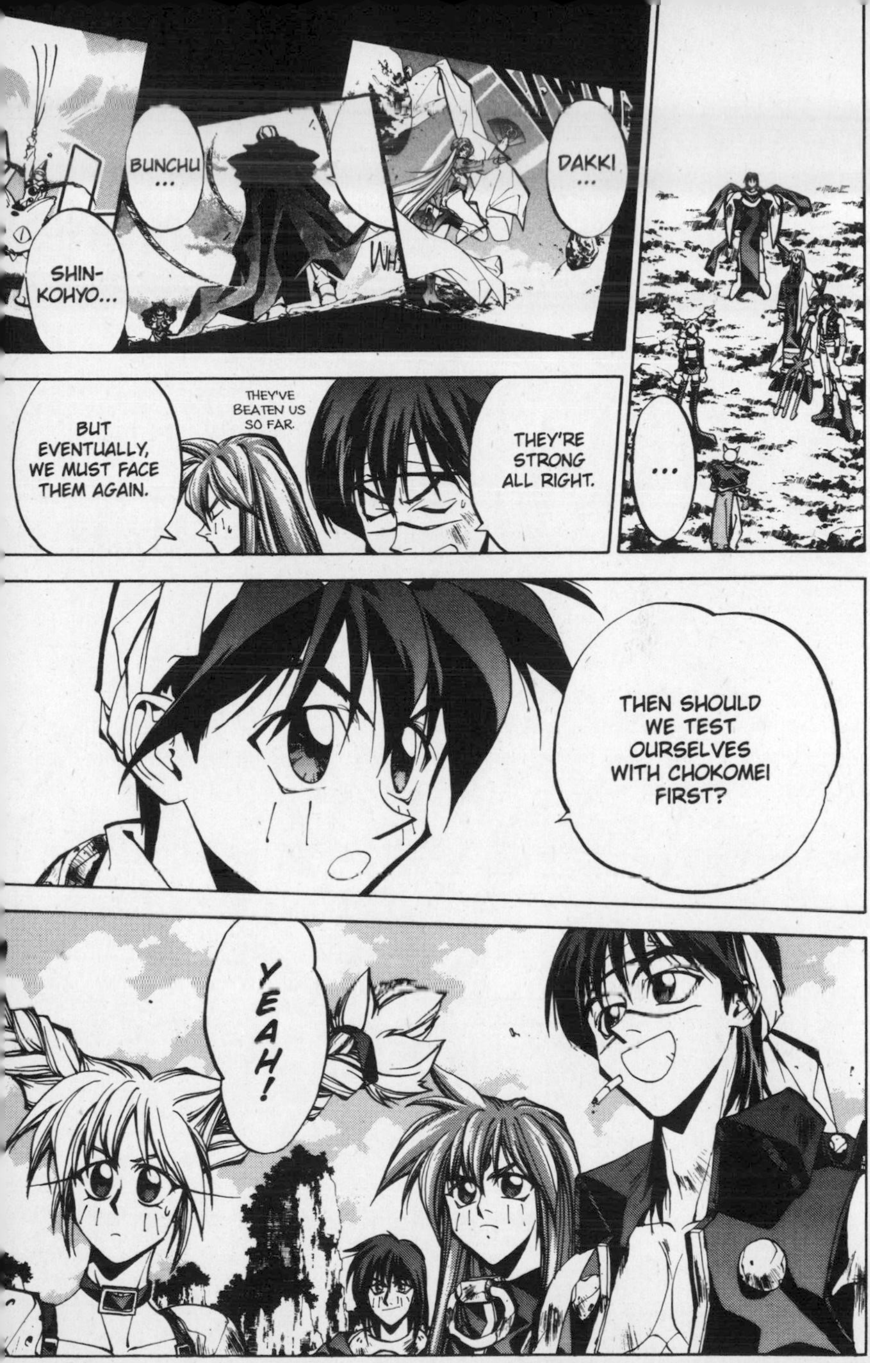
...
DAKKI ...
BUNCHU ...
SHIN-KOHYO...
THEY'RE STRONG ALL RIGHT.
THEY'VE BEATEN US SO FAR.
BUT EVENTUALLY, WE MUST FACE THEM AGAIN.
THEN SHOULD WE TEST OURSELVES WITH CHOKOMEI FIRST?
YEAH!

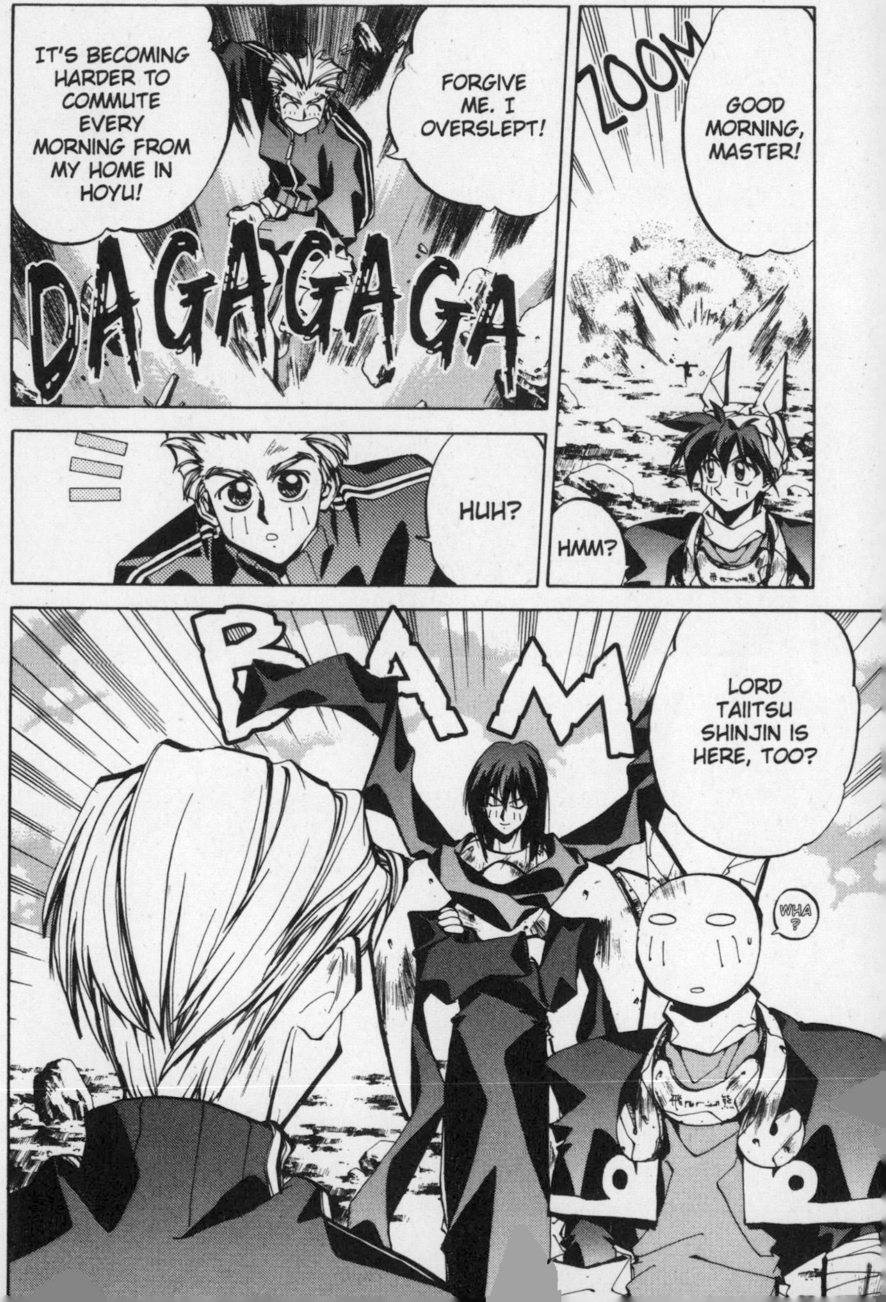
ZOOM
GOOD MORNING, MASTER!
HMM?
FORGIVE ME. I OVERSLEPT!
IT'S BECOMING HARDER TO COMMUTE EVERY MORNING FROM MY HOME IN HOYU!
DAGAGAGA
HUH?
BAM
LORD TAIITSU SHINJIN IS HERE, TOO?
WHA?

READ THIS WAY

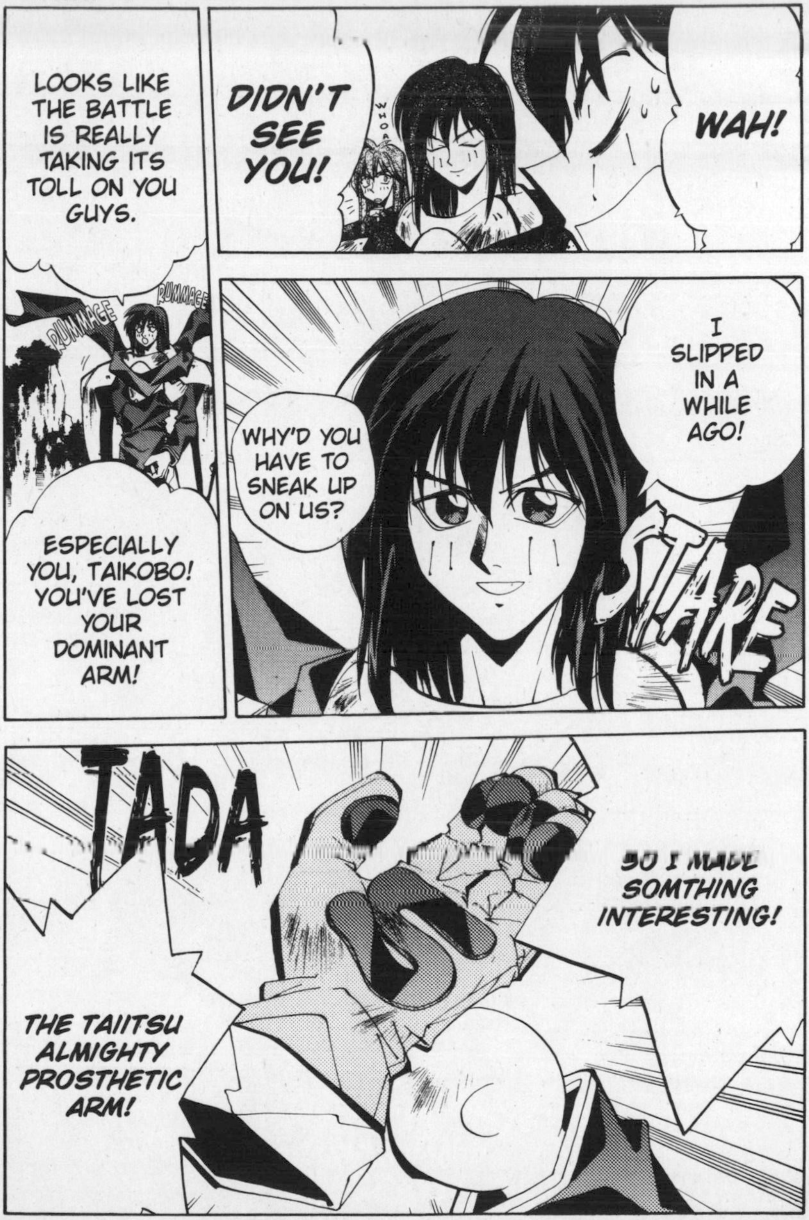
WAH!
DIDN'T SEE YOU!
WHOA
I SLIPPED IN A WHILE AGO!
STARE
WHY'D YOU HAVE TO SNEAK UP ON US?
LOOKS LIKE THE BATTLE IS REALLY TAKING ITS TOLL ON YOU GUYS.
RUMMAGE
RUMMAGE
ESPECIALLY YOU, TAIKOBO! YOU'VE LOST YOUR DOMINANT ARM!
SO I MADE SOMTHING INTERESTING!
TADA
THE TAIITSU ALMIGHTY PROSTHETIC ARM!

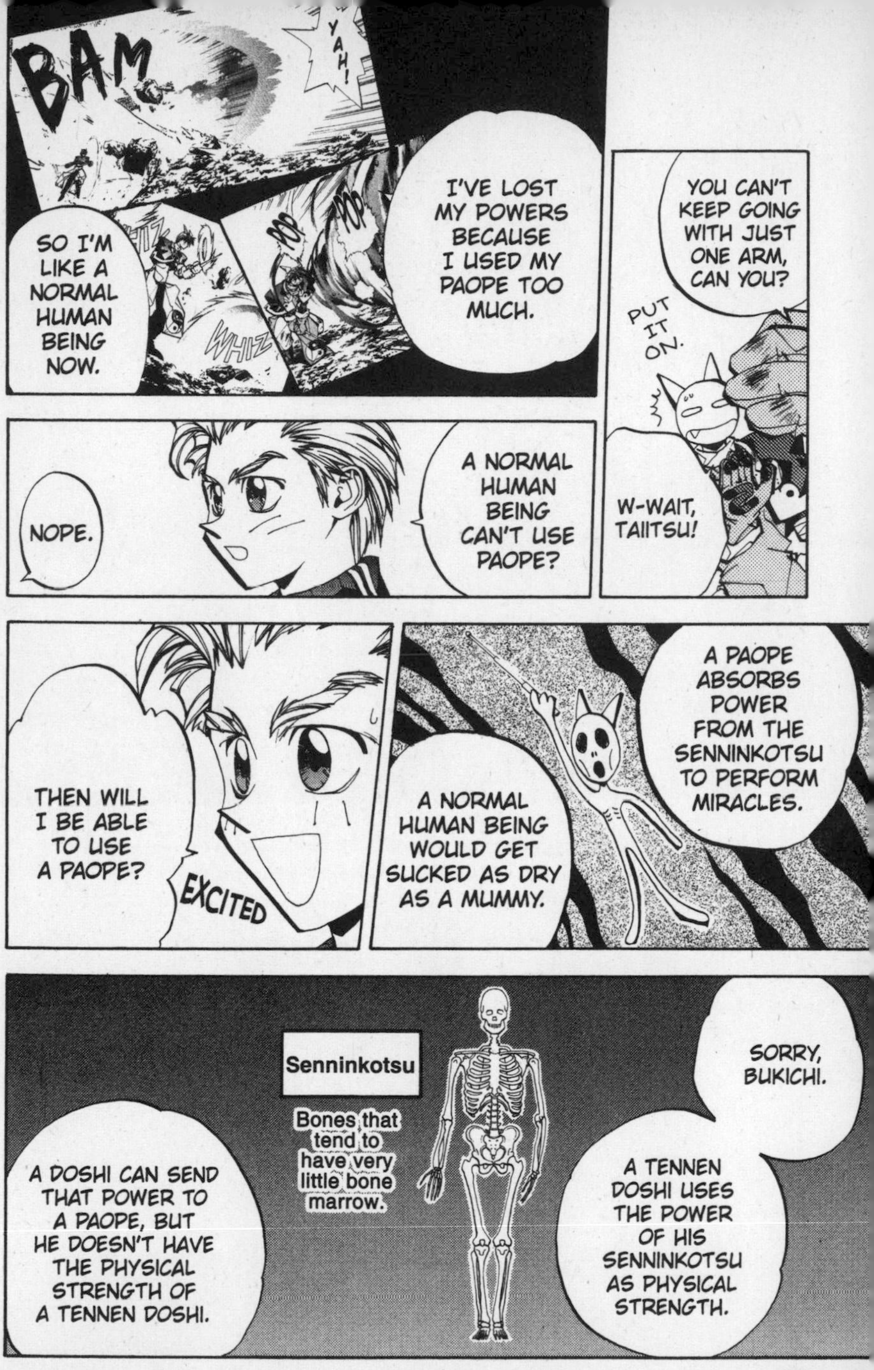
YAH!
BAM
I'VE LOST MY POWERS BECAUSE I USED MY PAOPE TOO MUCH.
POP POP
WHIZ
SO I'M LIKE A NORMAL HUMAN BEING NOW.
YOU CAN'T KEEP GOING WITH JUST ONE ARM, CAN YOU?
PUT IT ON.
W-WAIT, TAIITSU!
A NORMAL HUMAN BEING CAN'T USE PAOPE?
NOPE.
A PAOPE ABSORBS POWER FROM THE SENNINKOTSU TO PERFORM MIRACLES.
A NORMAL HUMAN BEING WOULD GET SUCKED AS DRY AS A MUMMY.
THEN WILL I BE ABLE TO USE A PAOPE?
EXCITED
SORRY, BUKICHI.
A TENNEN DOSHI USES THE POWER OF HIS SENNINKOTSU AS PHYSICAL STRENGTH.
Senninkotsu
Bones that tend to have very little bone marrow.
A DOSHI CAN SEND THAT POWER TO A PAOPE, BUT HE DOESN'T HAVE THE PHYSICAL STRENGTH OF A TENNEN DOSHI.

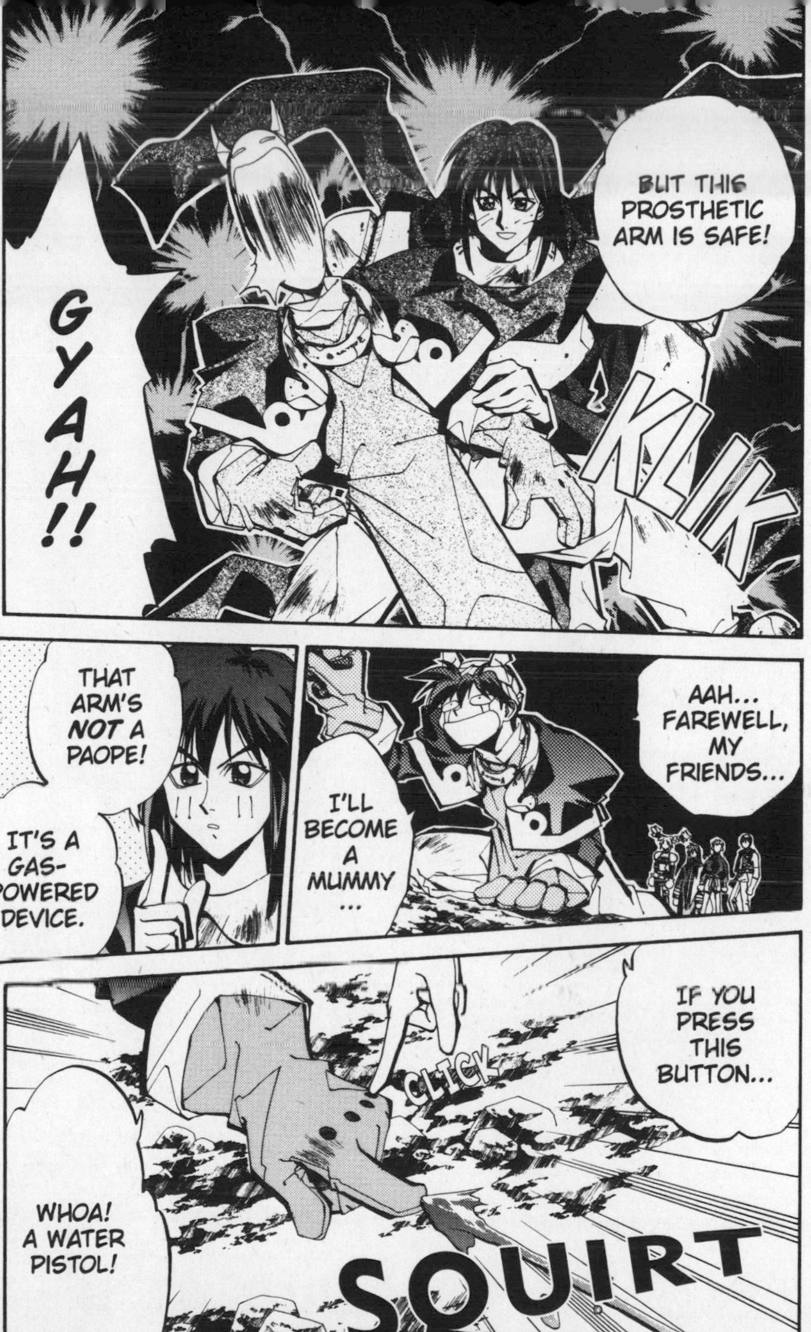
BUT THIS PROSTHETIC ARM IS SAFE!
KLIK
GYAH!!
AAH... FAREWELL, MY FRIENDS...
I'LL BECOME A MUMMY ...
THAT ARM'S *NOT* A PAOPE!
IT'S A GAS-POWERED DEVICE.
IF YOU PRESS THIS BUTTON...
CLICK
WHOA! A WATER PISTOL!
SQUIRT

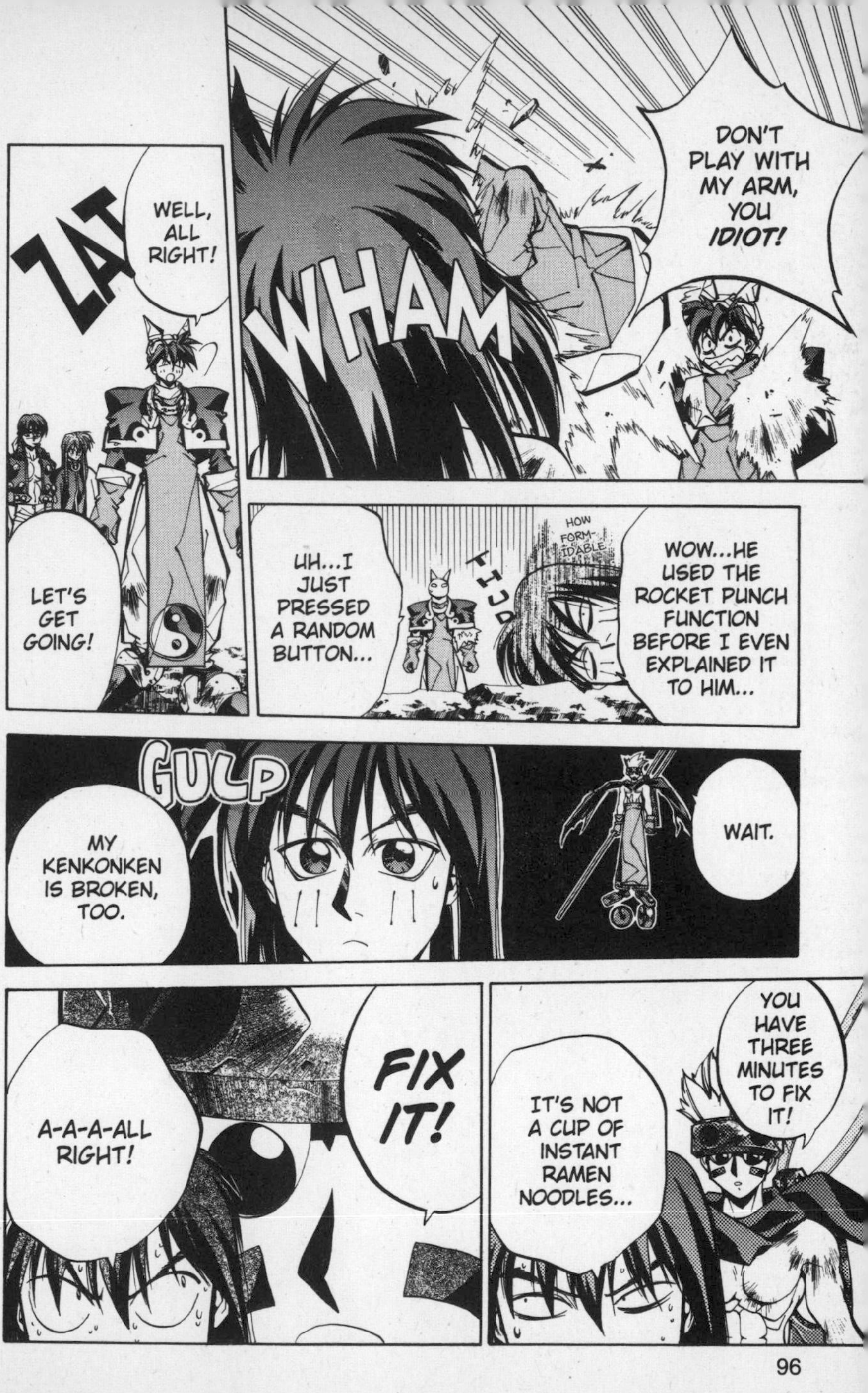
DON'T PLAY WITH MY ARM, YOU *IDIOT!*
WHAM
WOW...HE USED THE ROCKET PUNCH FUNCTION BEFORE I EVEN EXPLAINED IT TO HIM...
HOW FORM-IDABLE
THUD
UH...I JUST PRESSED A RANDOM BUTTON...
ZAT
WELL, ALL RIGHT!
LET'S GET GOING!
WAIT.
GULP
MY KENKONKEN IS BROKEN, TOO.
YOU HAVE THREE MINUTES TO FIX IT!
IT'S NOT A CUP OF INSTANT RAMEN NOODLES...
FIX IT!
A-A-A-ALL RIGHT!

READ THIS WAY

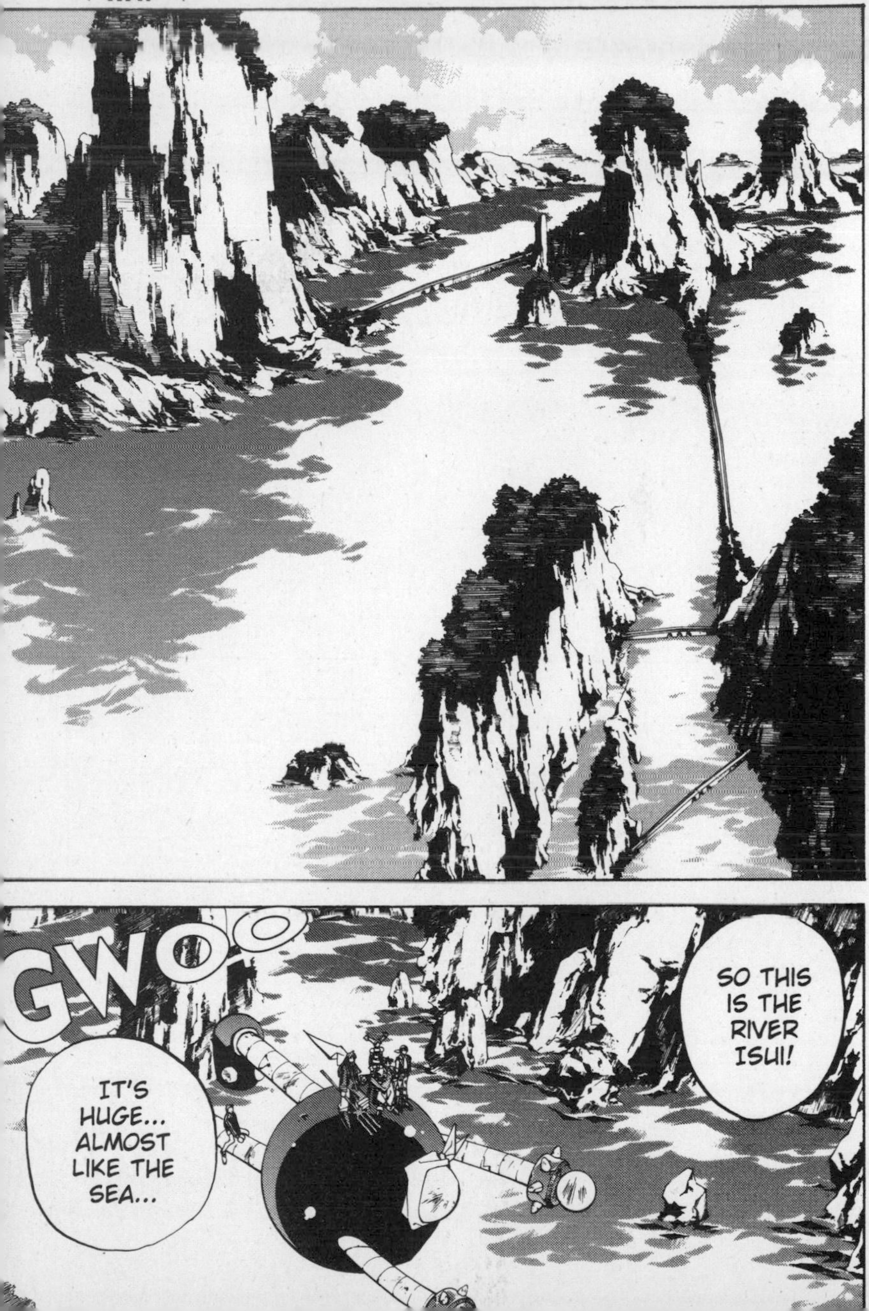
SO THIS IS THE RIVER ISUI!
GWOO
IT'S HUGE... ALMOST LIKE THE SEA...

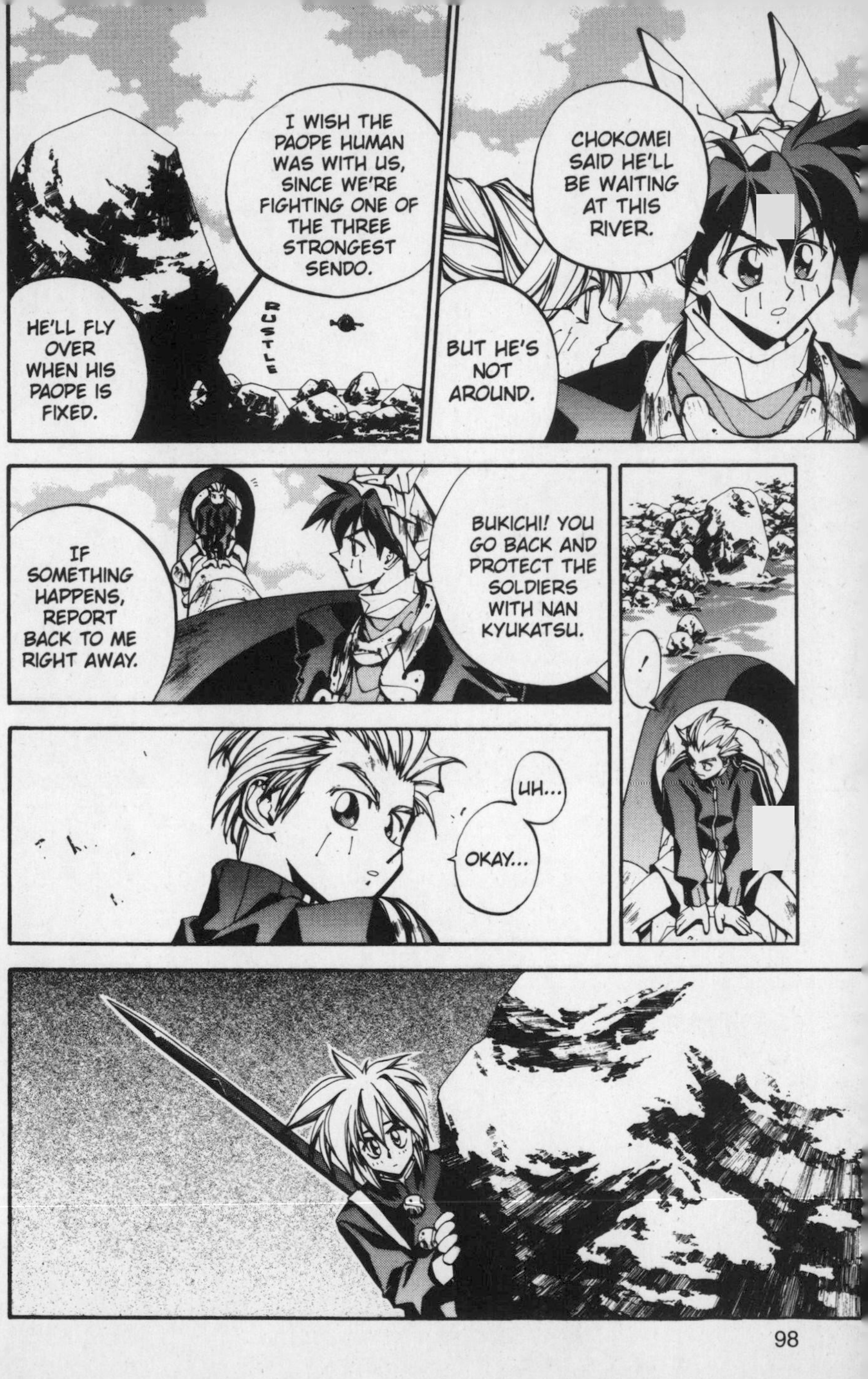
CHOKOMEI SAID HE'LL BE WAITING AT THIS RIVER.
BUT HE'S NOT AROUND.
I WISH THE PAOPE HUMAN WAS WITH US, SINCE WE'RE FIGHTING ONE OF THE THREE STRONGEST SENDO.
RUSTLE
HE'LL FLY OVER WHEN HIS PAOPE IS FIXED.
!
BUKICHI! YOU GO BACK AND PROTECT THE SOLDIERS WITH NAN KYUKATSU.
IF SOMETHING HAPPENS, REPORT BACK TO ME RIGHT AWAY.
UH...
OKAY...

READ THIS WAY

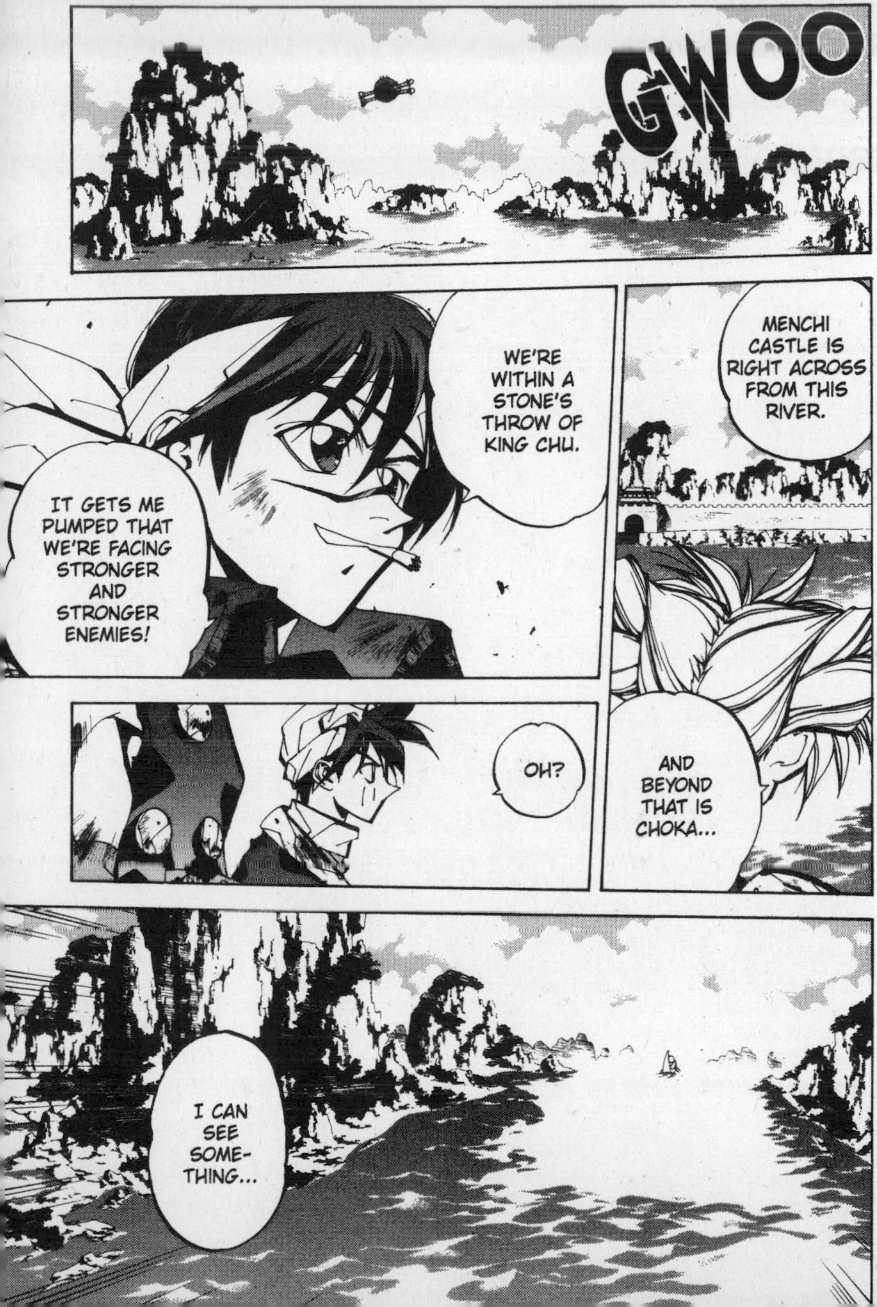
GWOO
MENCHI CASTLE IS RIGHT ACROSS FROM THIS RIVER.
AND BEYOND THAT IS CHOKA...
WE'RE WITHIN A STONE'S THROW OF KING CHU.
IT GETS ME PUMPED THAT WE'RE FACING STRONGER AND STRONGER ENEMIES!
OH?
I CAN SEE SOME-THING...

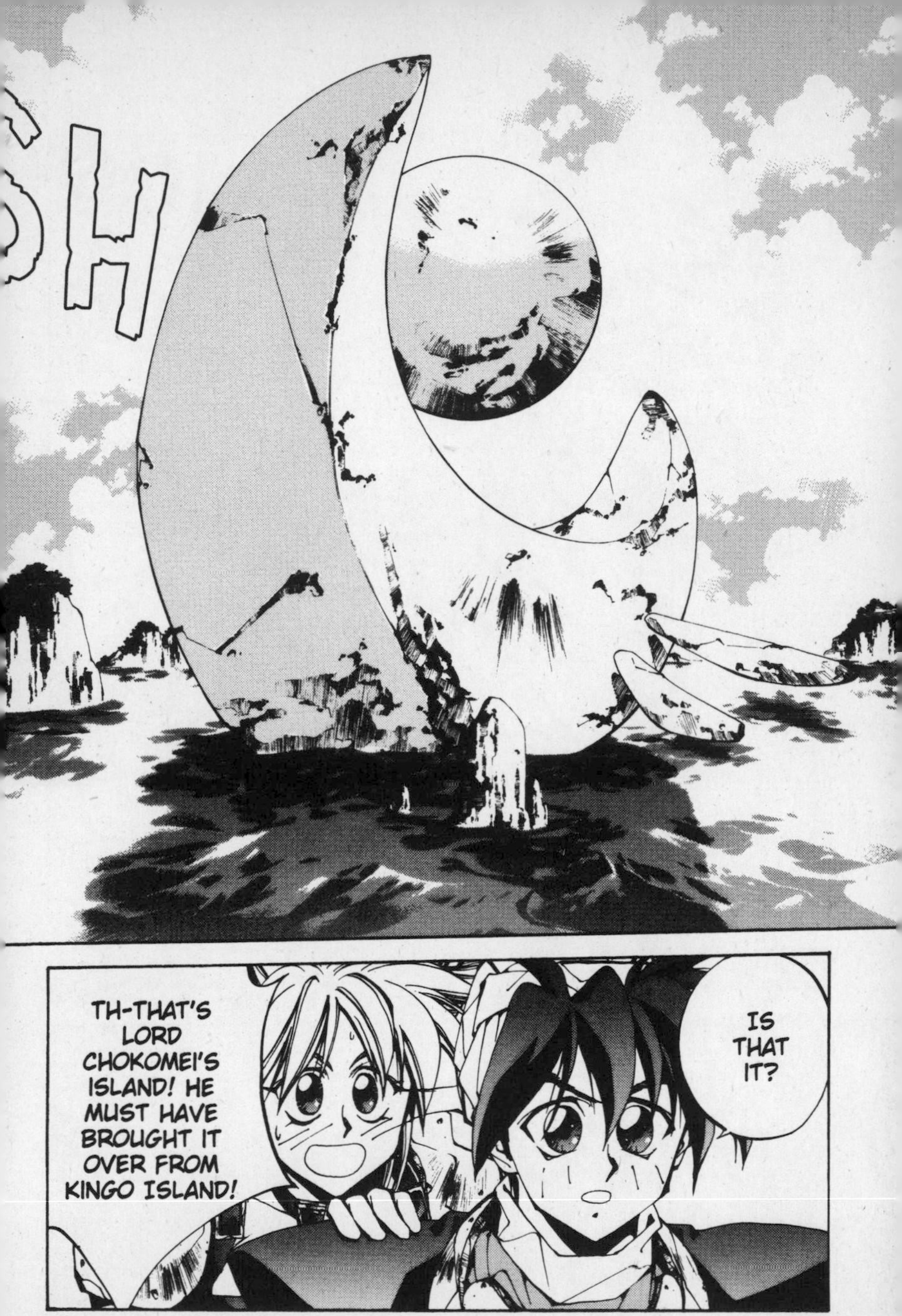
IS THAT IT?
TH-THAT'S LORD CHOKOMEI'S ISLAND! HE MUST HAVE BROUGHT IT OVER FROM KINGO ISLAND!

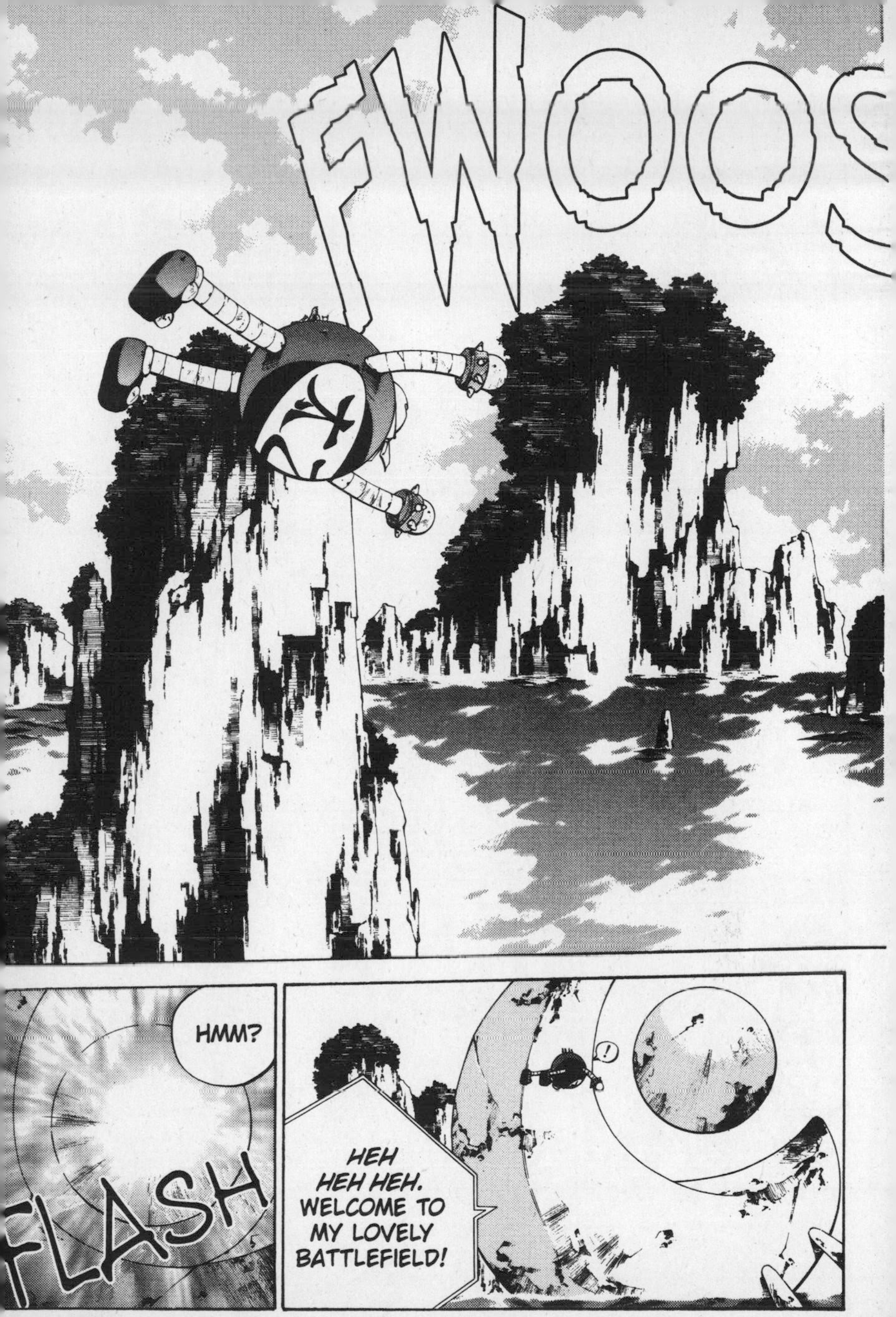
FWOOS
!
HEH HEH HEH. WELCOME TO MY LOVELY BATTLEFIELD!
HMM?
FLASH

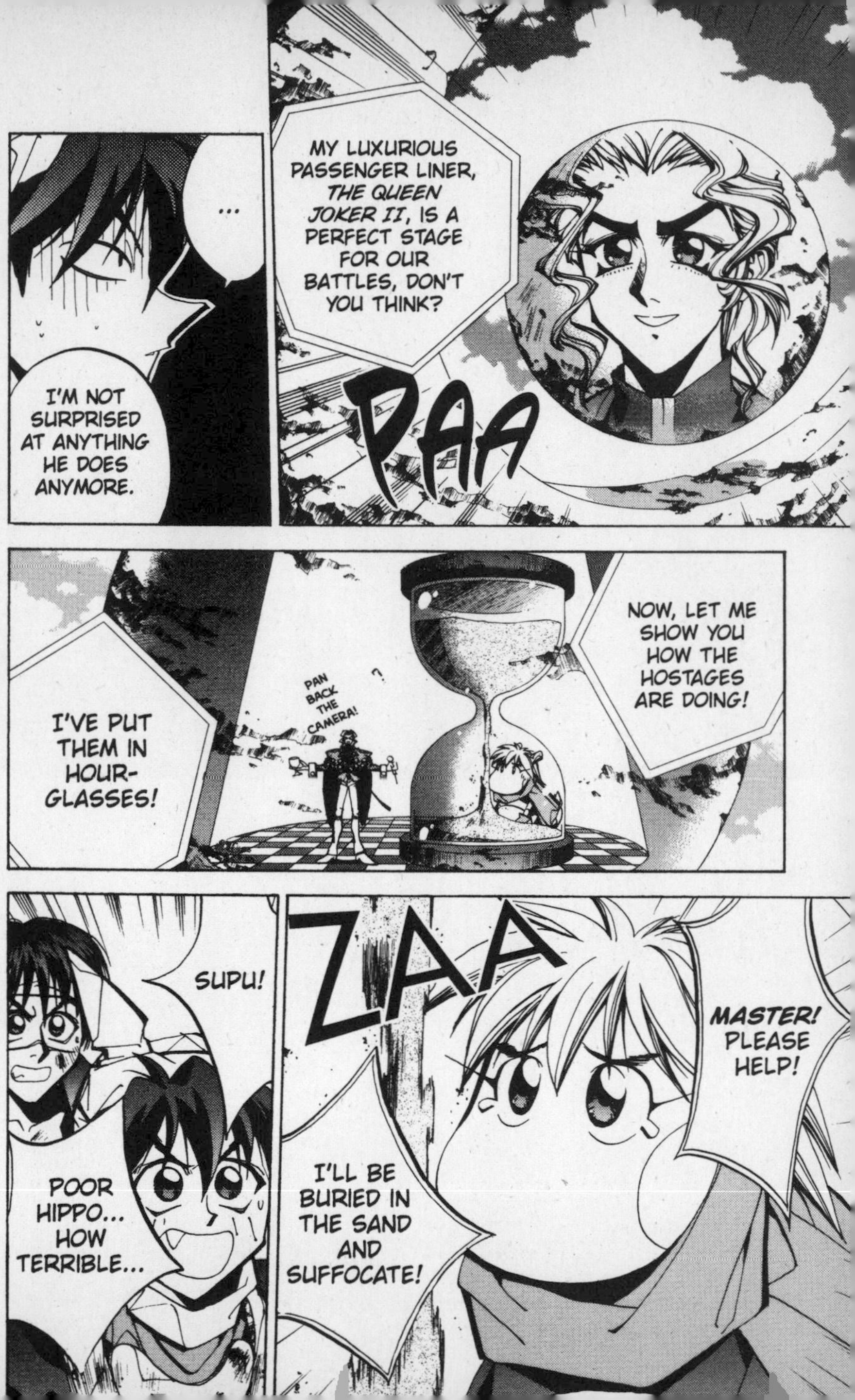
MY LUXURIOUS PASSENGER LINER, *THE QUEEN JOKER II*, IS A PERFECT STAGE FOR OUR BATTLES, DON'T YOU THINK?
PAA
...
I'M NOT SURPRISED AT ANYTHING HE DOES ANYMORE.
NOW, LET ME SHOW YOU HOW THE HOSTAGES ARE DOING!
?
PAN BACK THE CAMERA!
I'VE PUT THEM IN HOUR-GLASSES!
ZAA
MASTER! PLEASE HELP!
I'LL BE BURIED IN THE SAND AND SUFFOCATE!
SUPU!
POOR HIPPO... HOW TERRIBLE...

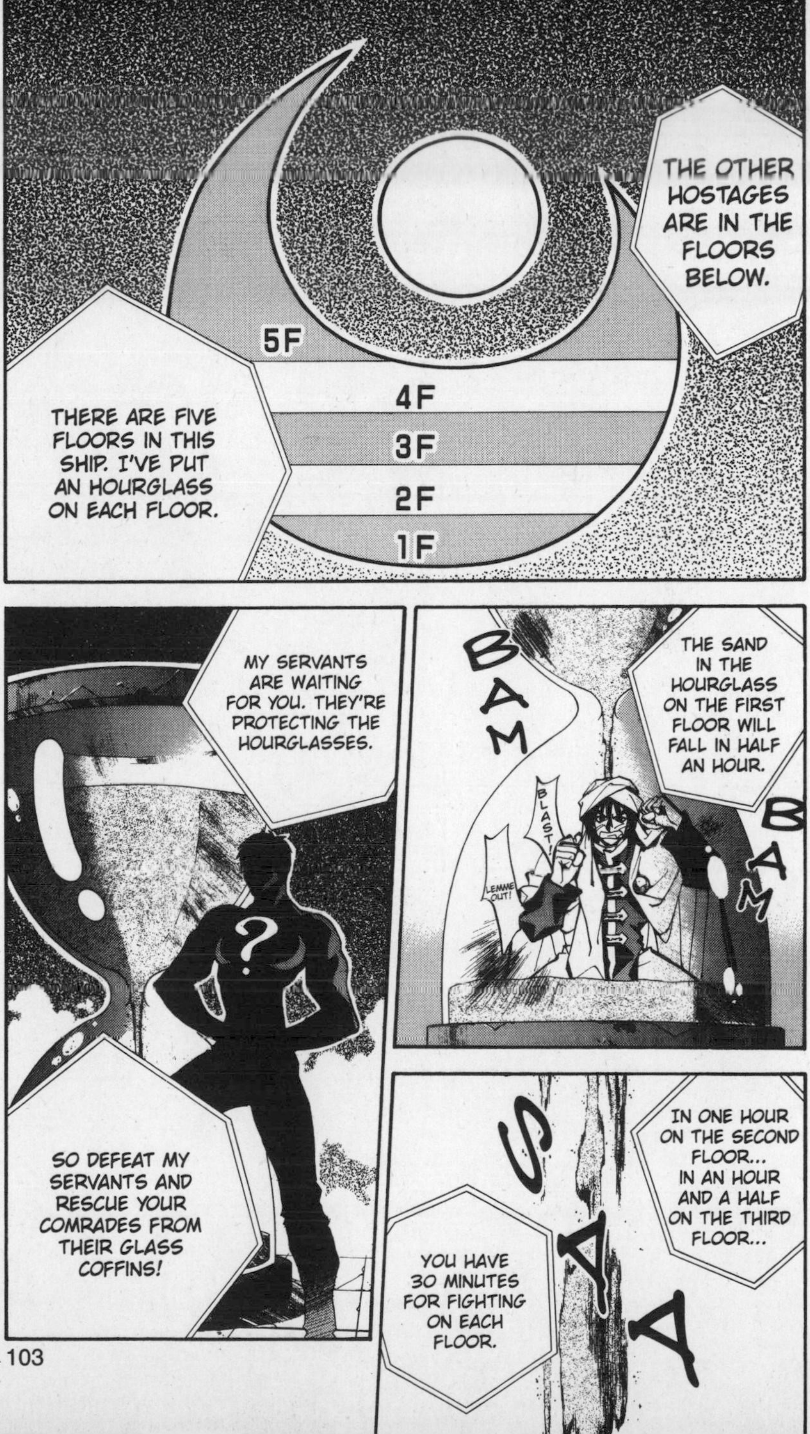
THE OTHER HOSTAGES ARE IN THE FLOORS BELOW.
THERE ARE FIVE FLOORS IN THIS SHIP. I'VE PUT AN HOURGLASS ON EACH FLOOR.
5F
4F
3F
2F
1F
BAM
THE SAND IN THE HOURGLASS ON THE FIRST FLOOR WILL FALL IN HALF AN HOUR.
BLAST!
LEMME OUT!
BAM
IN ONE HOUR ON THE SECOND FLOOR... IN AN HOUR AND A HALF ON THE THIRD FLOOR...
SAA
YOU HAVE 30 MINUTES FOR FIGHTING ON EACH FLOOR.
MY SERVANTS ARE WAITING FOR YOU. THEY'RE PROTECTING THE HOURGLASSES.
SO DEFEAT MY SERVANTS AND RESCUE YOUR COMRADES FROM THEIR GLASS COFFINS!

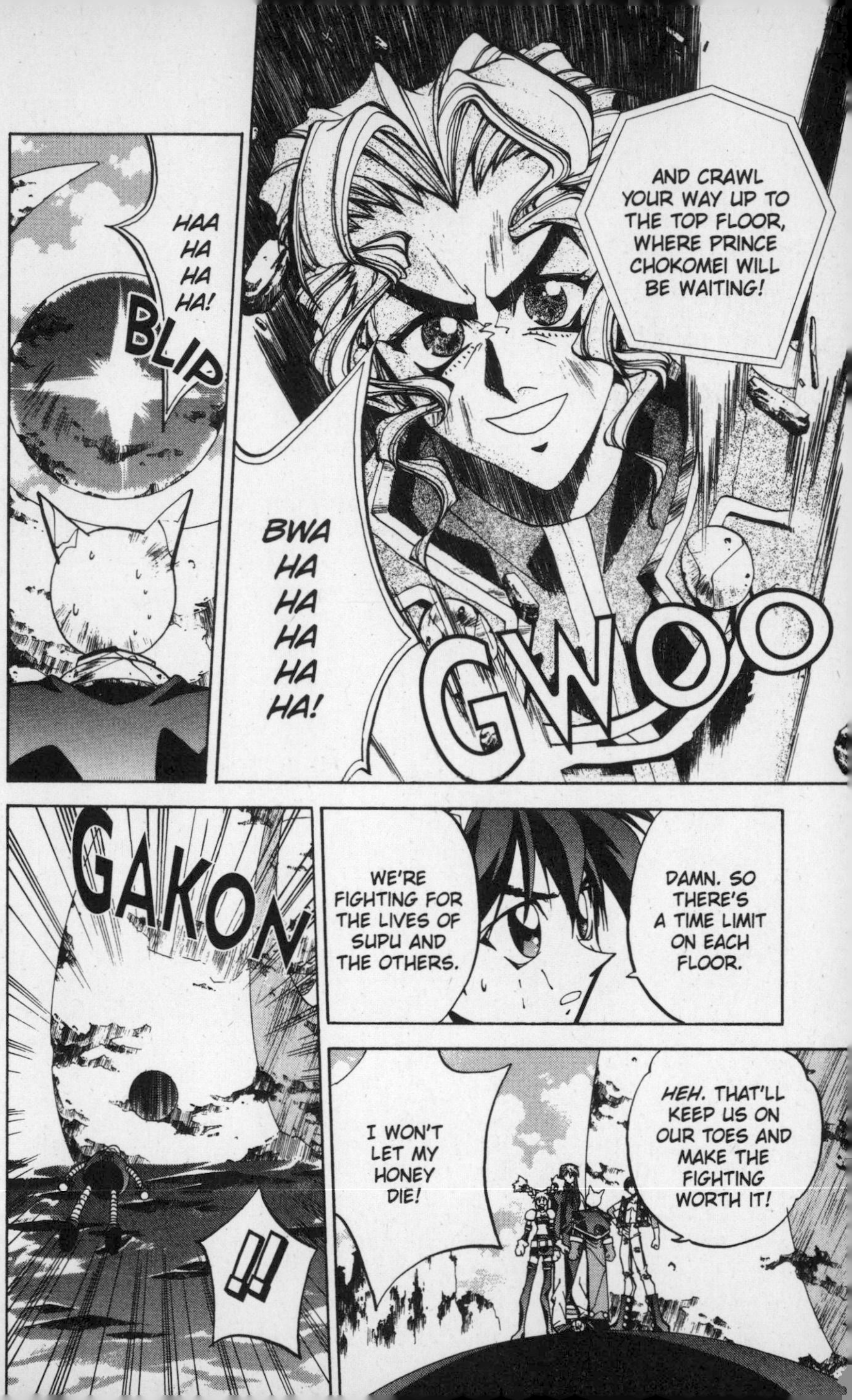
AND CRAWL YOUR WAY UP TO THE TOP FLOOR, WHERE PRINCE CHOKOMEI WILL BE WAITING!
BWA HA HA HA HA HA!
GWOOO
HAA HA HA HA!
BLIP
DAMN. SO THERE'S A TIME LIMIT ON EACH FLOOR.
WE'RE FIGHTING FOR THE LIVES OF SUPU AND THE OTHERS.
HEH. THAT'LL KEEP US ON OUR TOES AND MAKE THE FIGHTING WORTH IT!
I WON'T LET MY HONEY DIE!
GAKON
!!

READ THIS WAY

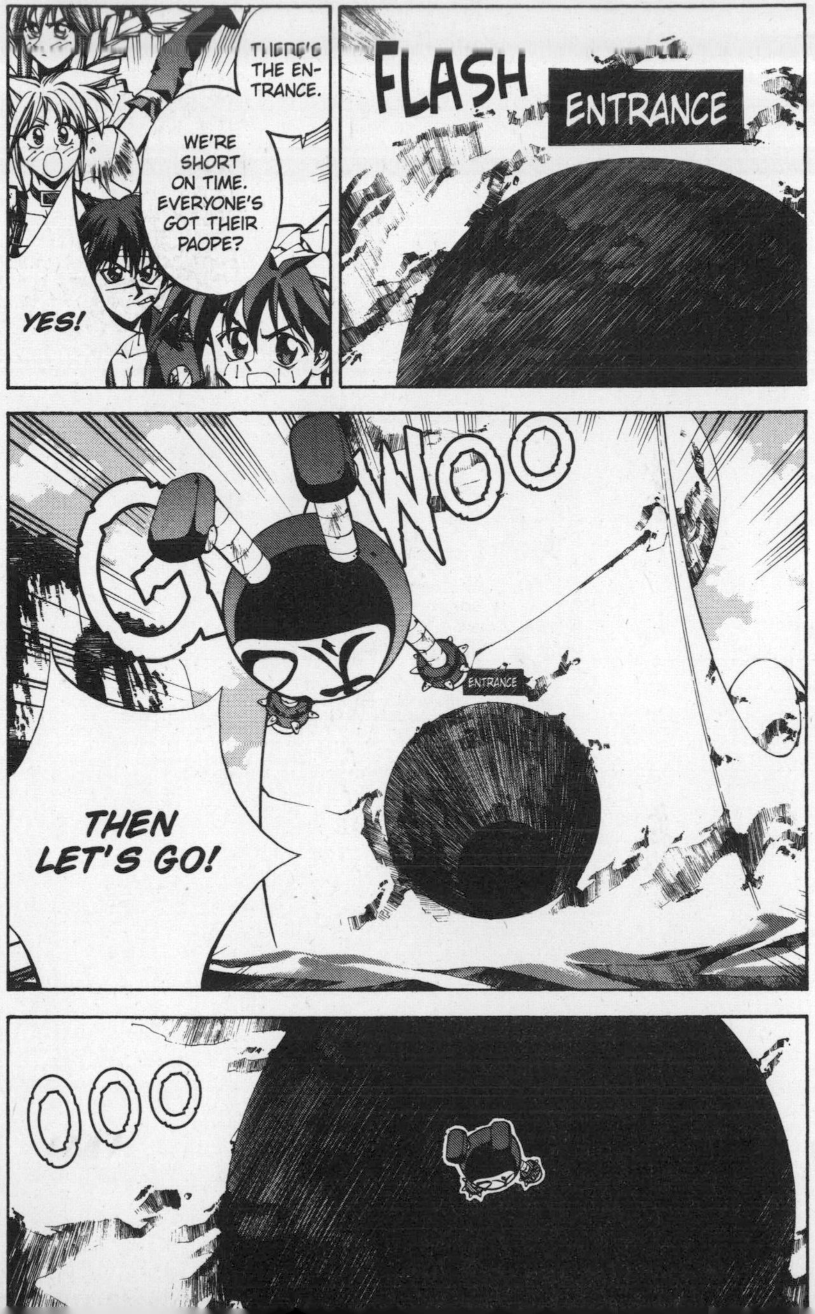
FLASH
ENTRANCE
THERE'S THE EN-TRANCE.
WE'RE SHORT ON TIME. EVERYONE'S GOT THEIR PAOPE?
YES!
GWOO
ENTRANCE
THEN LET'S GO!
OOO

封神演義

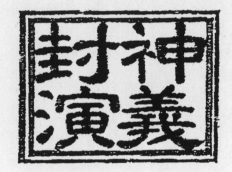

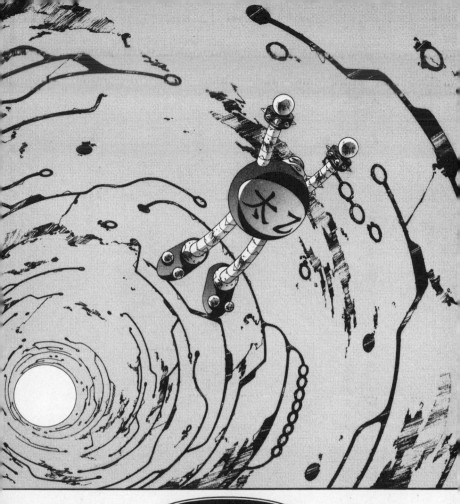

Chapter 85

CONQUERING CHOKOMEI, PART 1
YOZEN IN BIG TROUBLE

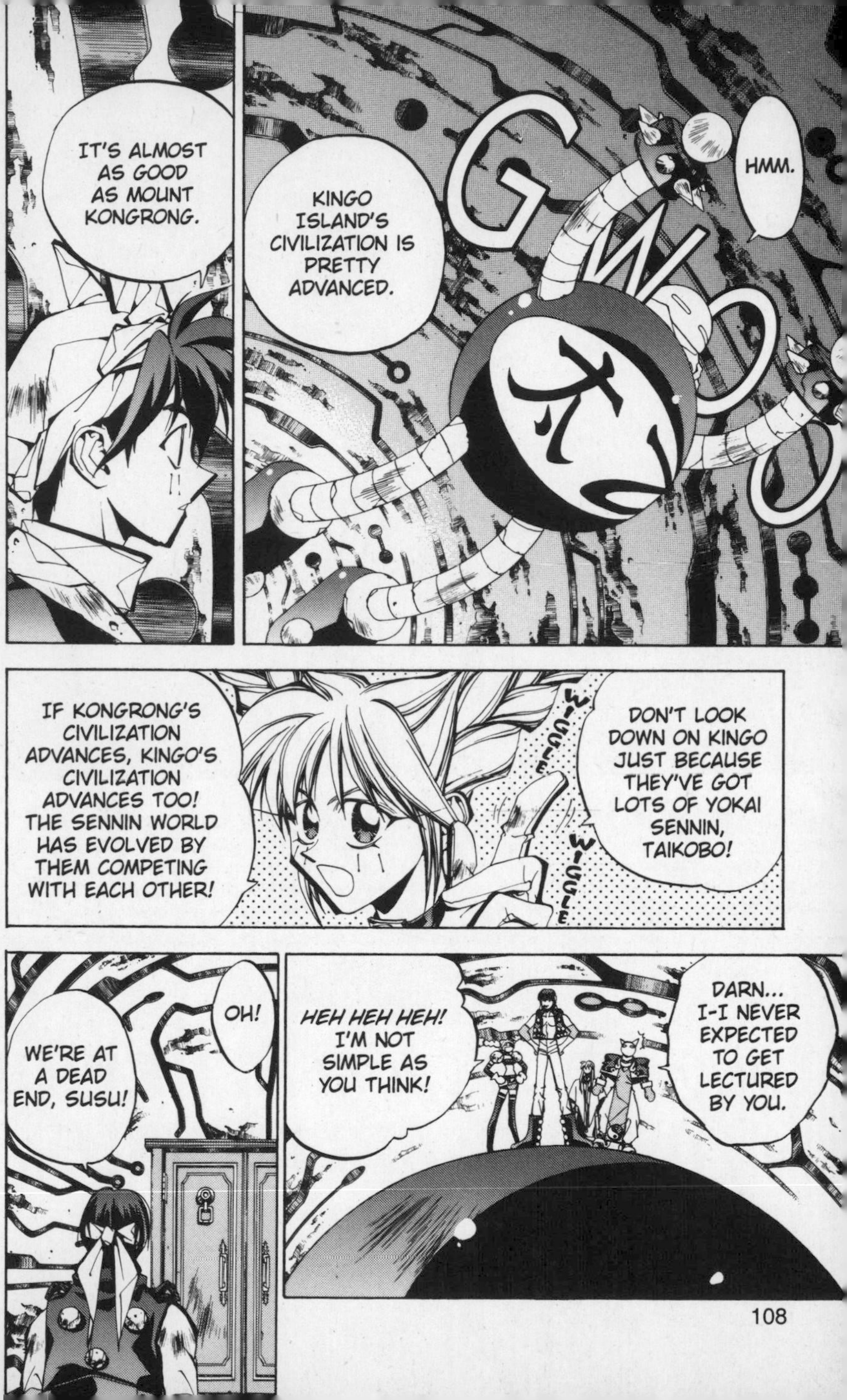
HMM.
KINGO ISLAND'S CIVILIZATION IS PRETTY ADVANCED.
IT'S ALMOST AS GOOD AS MOUNT KONGRONG.
DON'T LOOK DOWN ON KINGO JUST BECAUSE THEY'VE GOT LOTS OF YOKAI SENNIN, TAIKOBO!
WIGGLE
WIGGLE
IF KONGRONG'S CIVILIZATION ADVANCES, KINGO'S CIVILIZATION ADVANCES TOO! THE SENNIN WORLD HAS EVOLVED BY THEM COMPETING WITH EACH OTHER!
DARN... I-I NEVER EXPECTED TO GET LECTURED BY YOU.
HEH HEH HEH! I'M NOT SIMPLE AS YOU THINK!
OH!
WE'RE AT A DEAD END, SUSU!

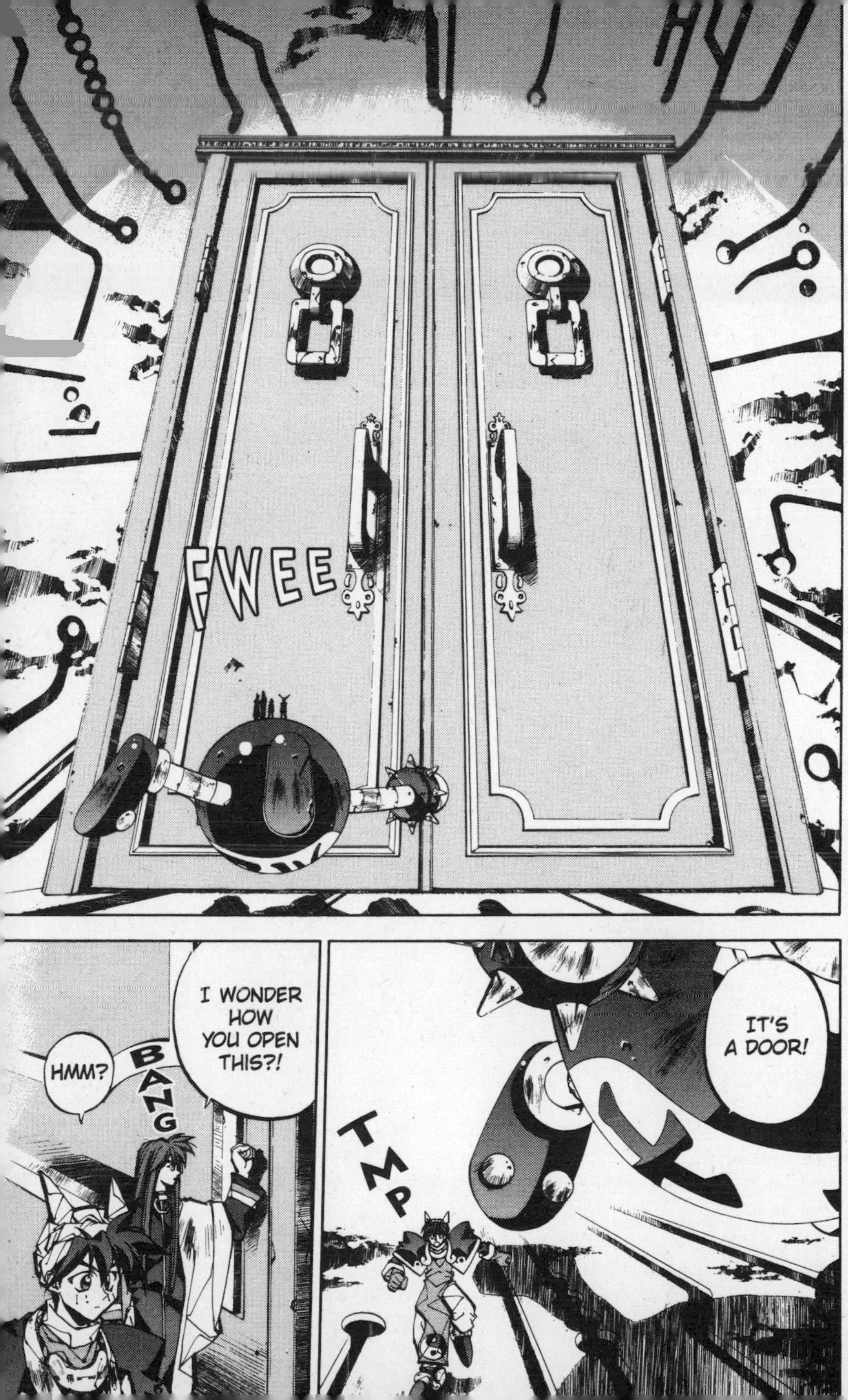
FWEE
IT'S A DOOR!
TMP
I WONDER HOW YOU OPEN THIS?!
BANG
HMM?

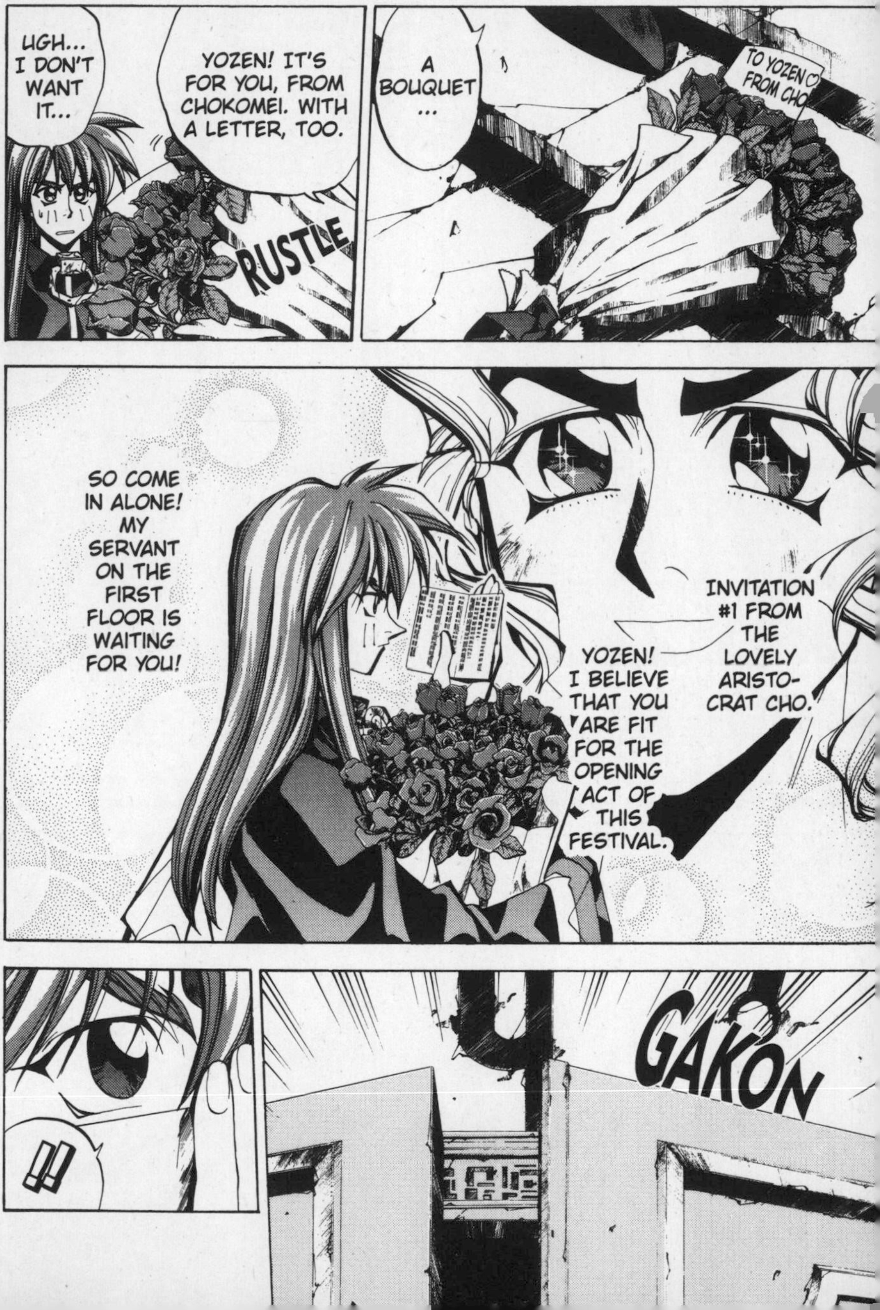
TO YOZEN♡ FROM CHO
A BOUQUET ...
YOZEN! IT'S FOR YOU, FROM CHOKOMEI. WITH A LETTER, TOO.
UGH... I DON'T WANT IT...
RUSTLE
INVITATION #1 FROM THE LOVELY ARISTOCRAT CHO.
YOZEN! I BELIEVE THAT YOU ARE FIT FOR THE OPENING ACT OF THIS FESTIVAL.
SO COME IN ALONE! MY SERVANT ON THE FIRST FLOOR IS WAITING FOR YOU!
GAKON
!!

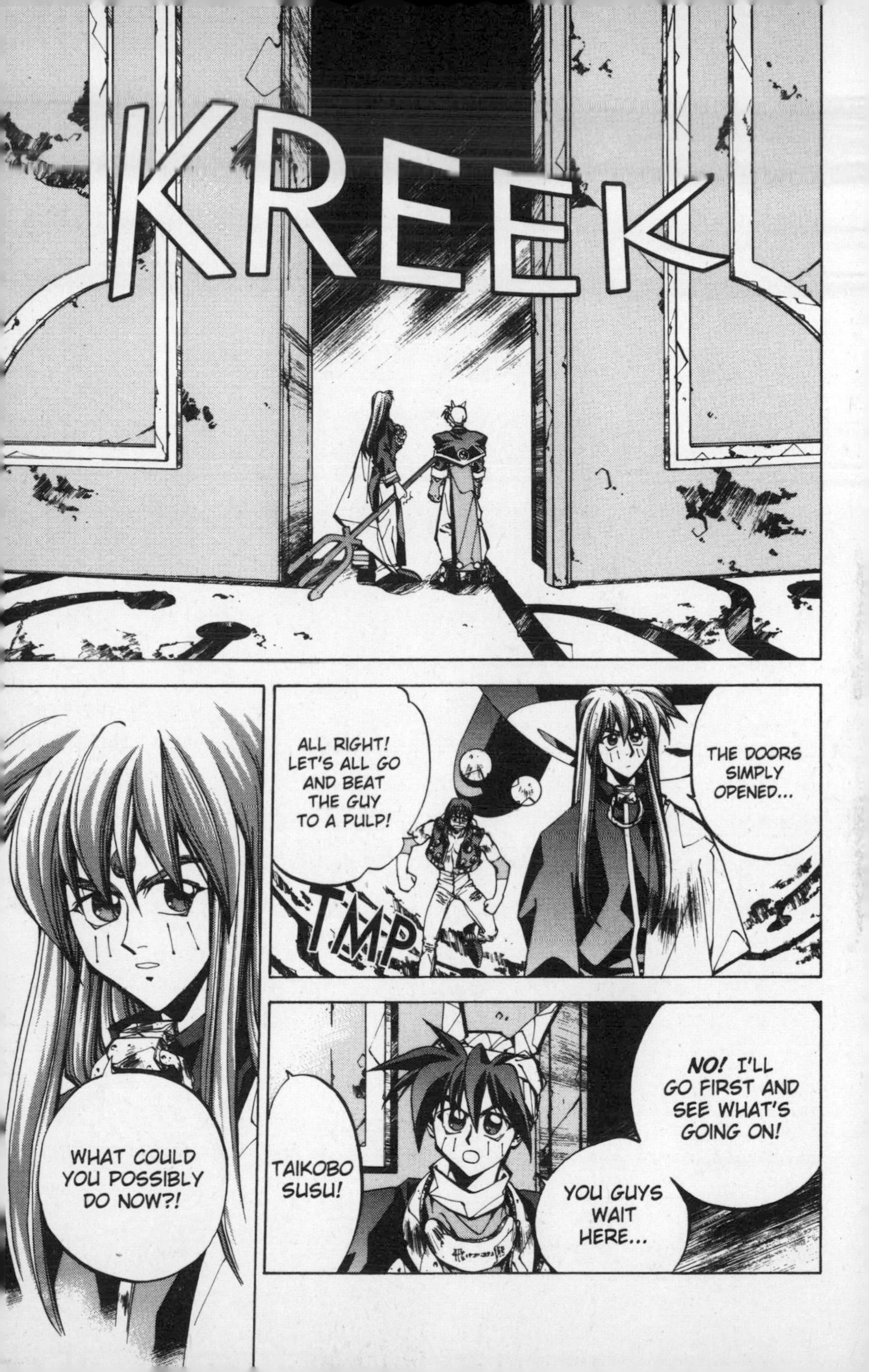
KREEK
THE DOORS SIMPLY OPENED...
ALL RIGHT! LET'S ALL GO AND BEAT THE GUY TO A PULP!
TMP
NO! I'LL GO FIRST AND SEE WHAT'S GOING ON!
YOU GUYS WAIT HERE...
TAIKOBO SUSU!
WHAT COULD YOU POSSIBLY DO NOW?!

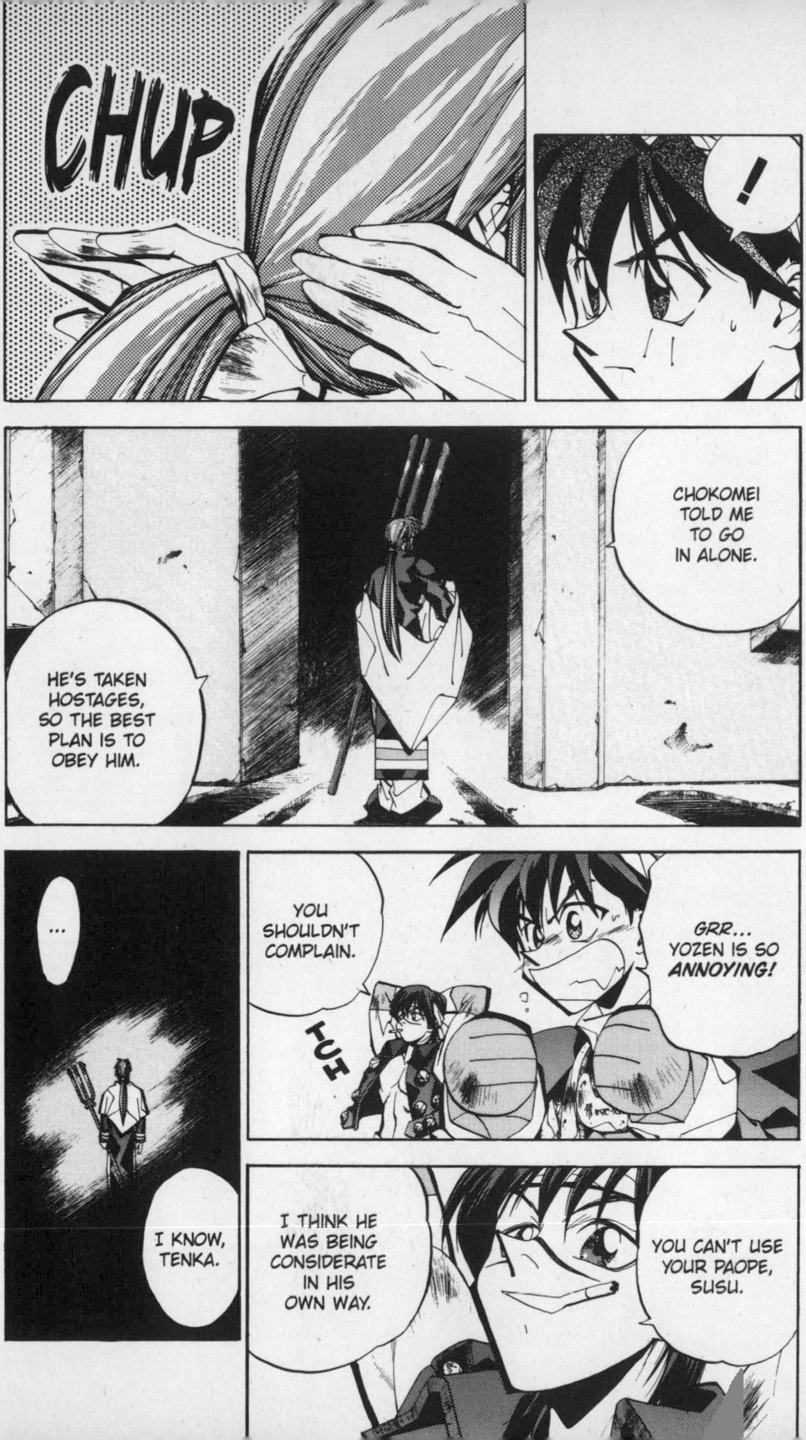
!
CHUP
CHOKOMEI TOLD ME TO GO IN ALONE.
HE'S TAKEN HOSTAGES, SO THE BEST PLAN IS TO OBEY HIM.
GRR... YOZEN IS SO *ANNOYING!*
YOU SHOULDN'T COMPLAIN.
TCH
YOU CAN'T USE YOUR PAOPE, SUSU.
I THINK HE WAS BEING CONSIDERATE IN HIS OWN WAY.
...
I KNOW, TENKA.

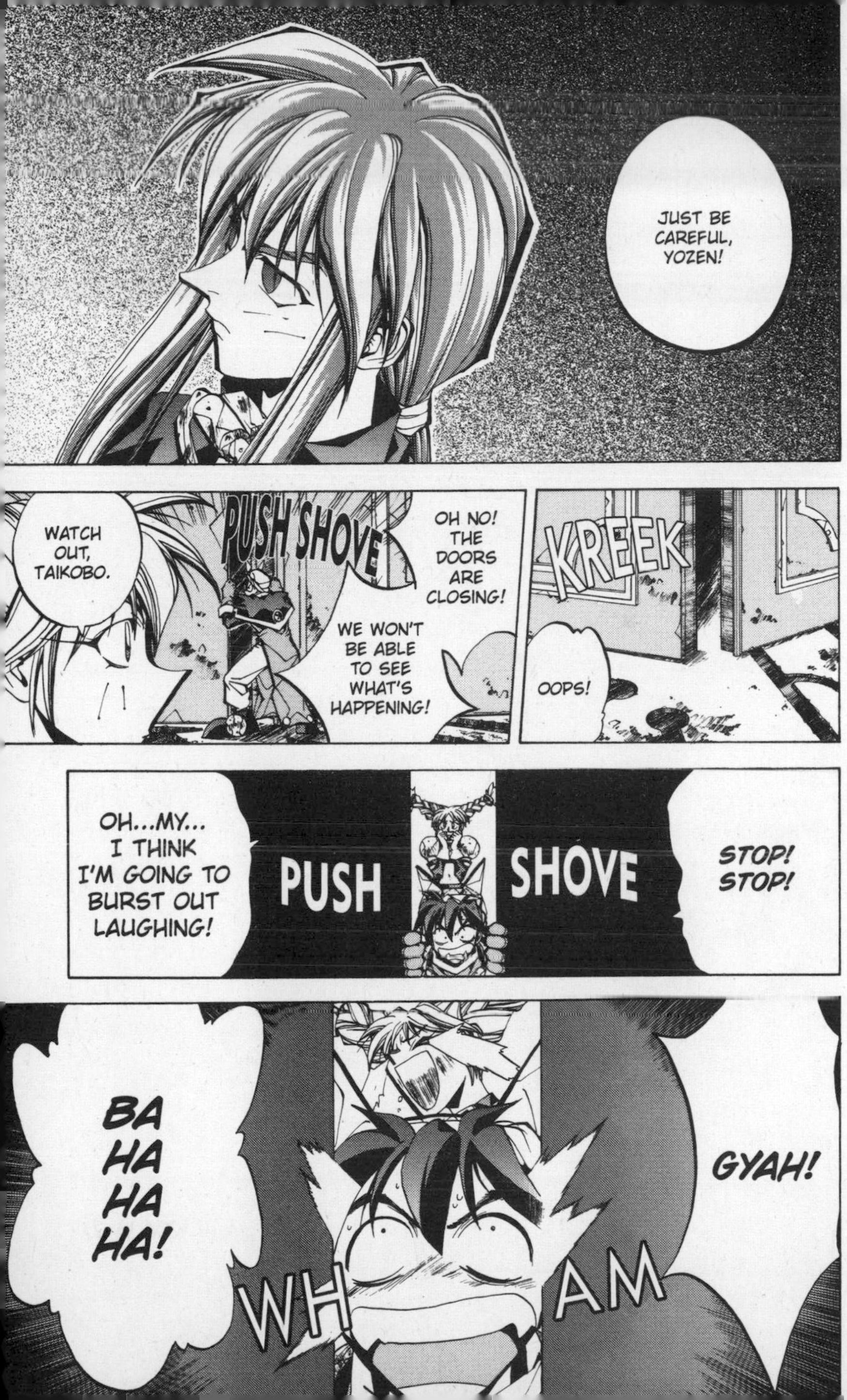
JUST BE CAREFUL, YOZEN!
KREEK
OOPS!
OH NO! THE DOORS ARE CLOSING!
WE WON'T BE ABLE TO SEE WHAT'S HAPPENING!
PUSH SHOVE
WATCH OUT, TAIKOBO.
STOP! STOP!
SHOVE
PUSH
OH...MY... I THINK I'M GOING TO BURST OUT LAUGHING!
GYAH!
WH AM
BA HA HA HA!

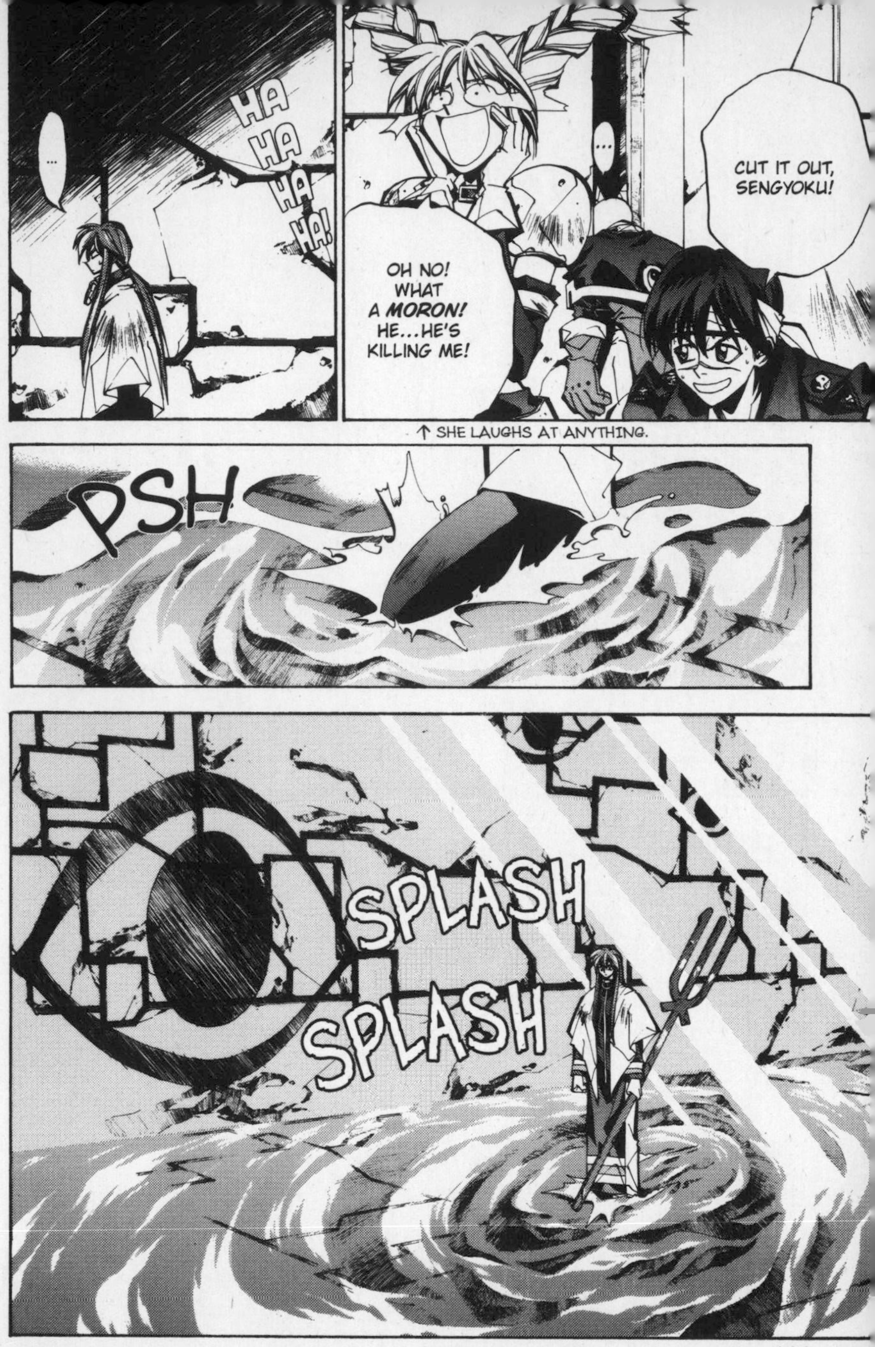
CUT IT OUT, SENGYOKU!
...
OH NO! WHAT A MORON! HE...HE'S KILLING ME!
HA HA HA HA!
...
↑ SHE LAUGHS AT ANYTHING.
PSH
SPLASH
SPLASH

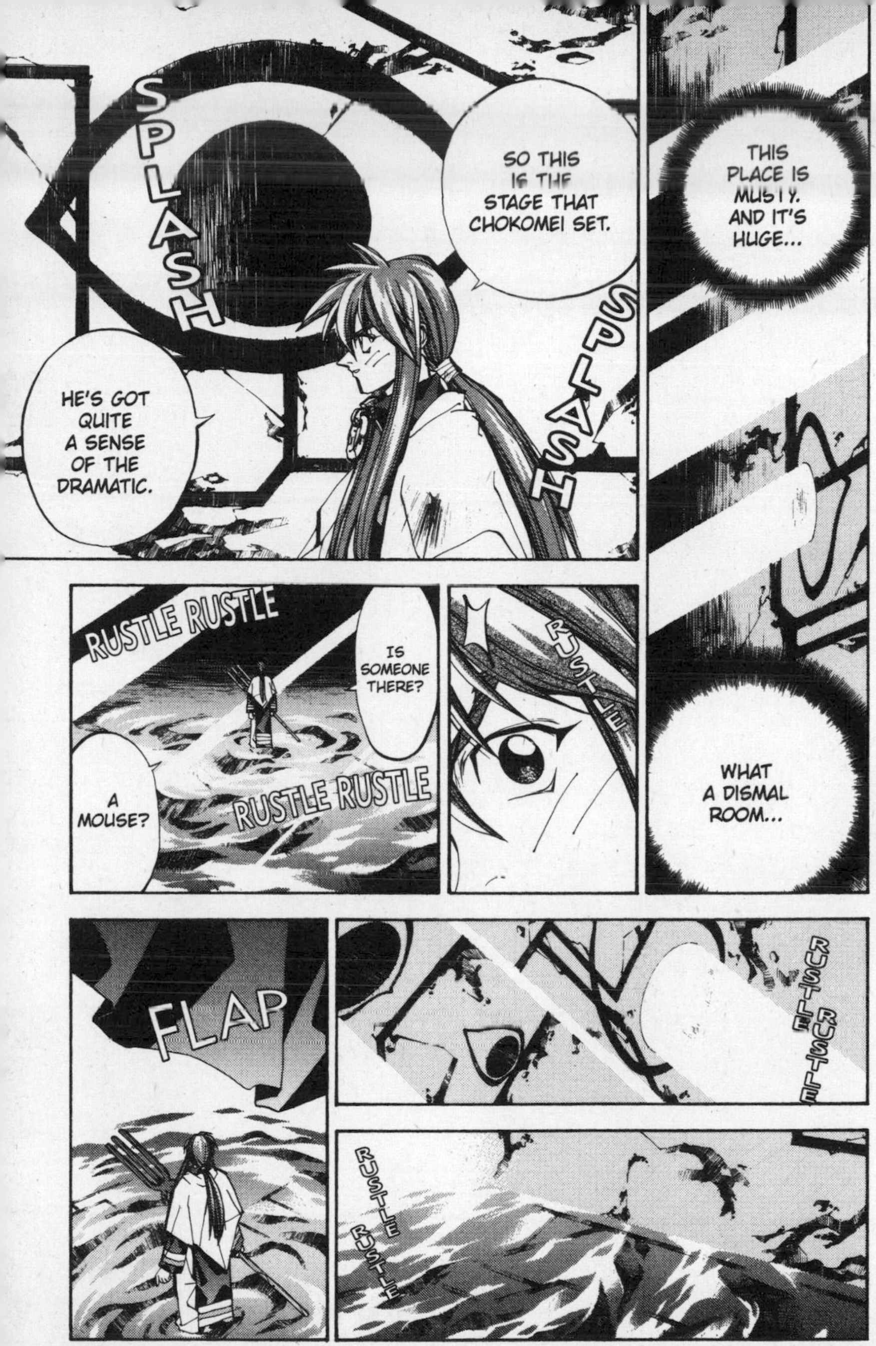
THIS PLACE IS MUSTY. AND IT'S HUGE...
WHAT A DISMAL ROOM...
SPLASH
SO THIS IS THE STAGE THAT CHOKOMEI SET.
SPLASH
HE'S GOT QUITE A SENSE OF THE DRAMATIC.
RUSTLE
IS SOMEONE THERE?
RUSTLE RUSTLE
A MOUSE?
RUSTLE RUSTLE
RUSTLE RUSTLE
RUSTLE RUSTLE
FLAP

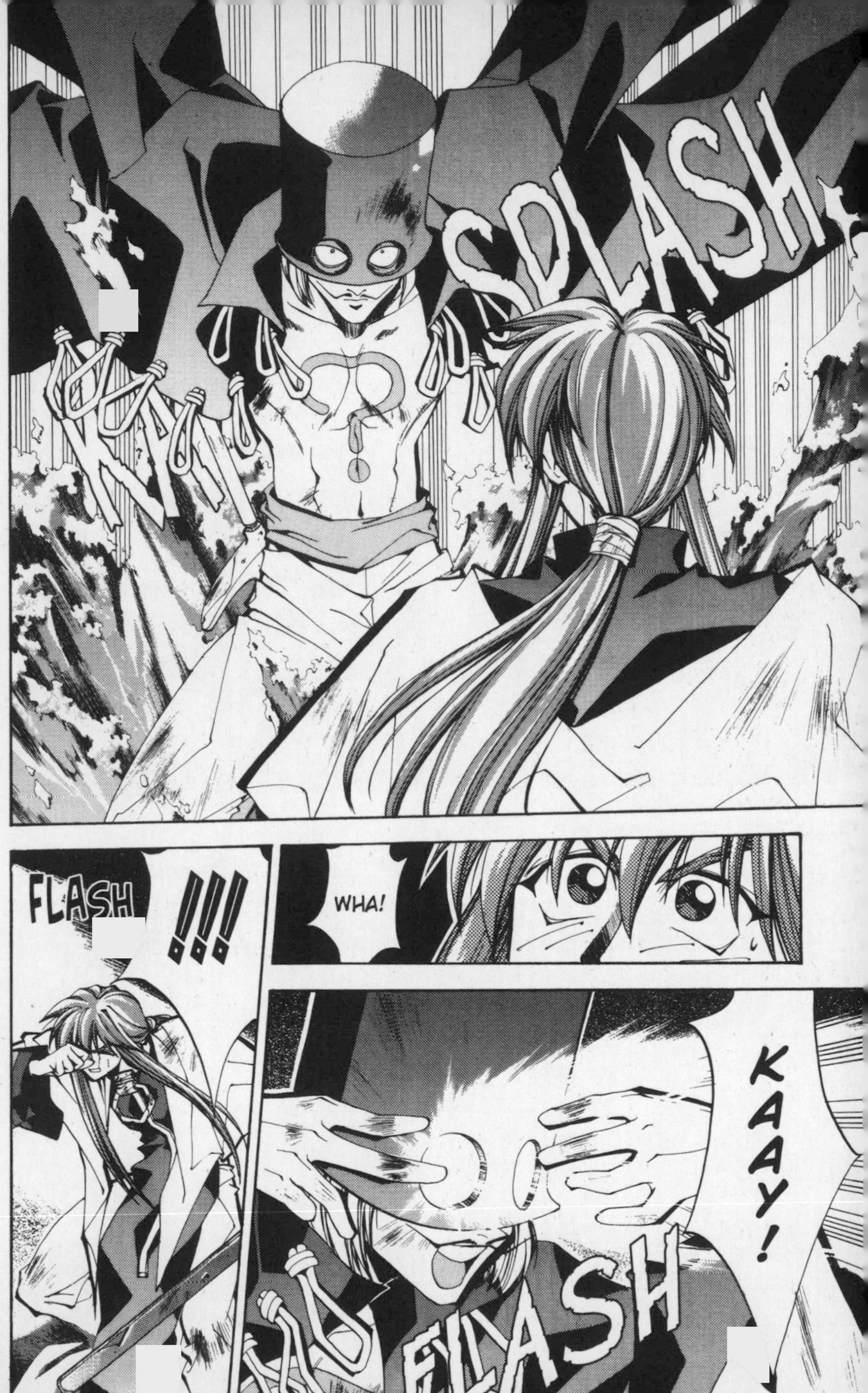
SPLASH
WHA!
FLASH
!!!
KAAY!
FLASH

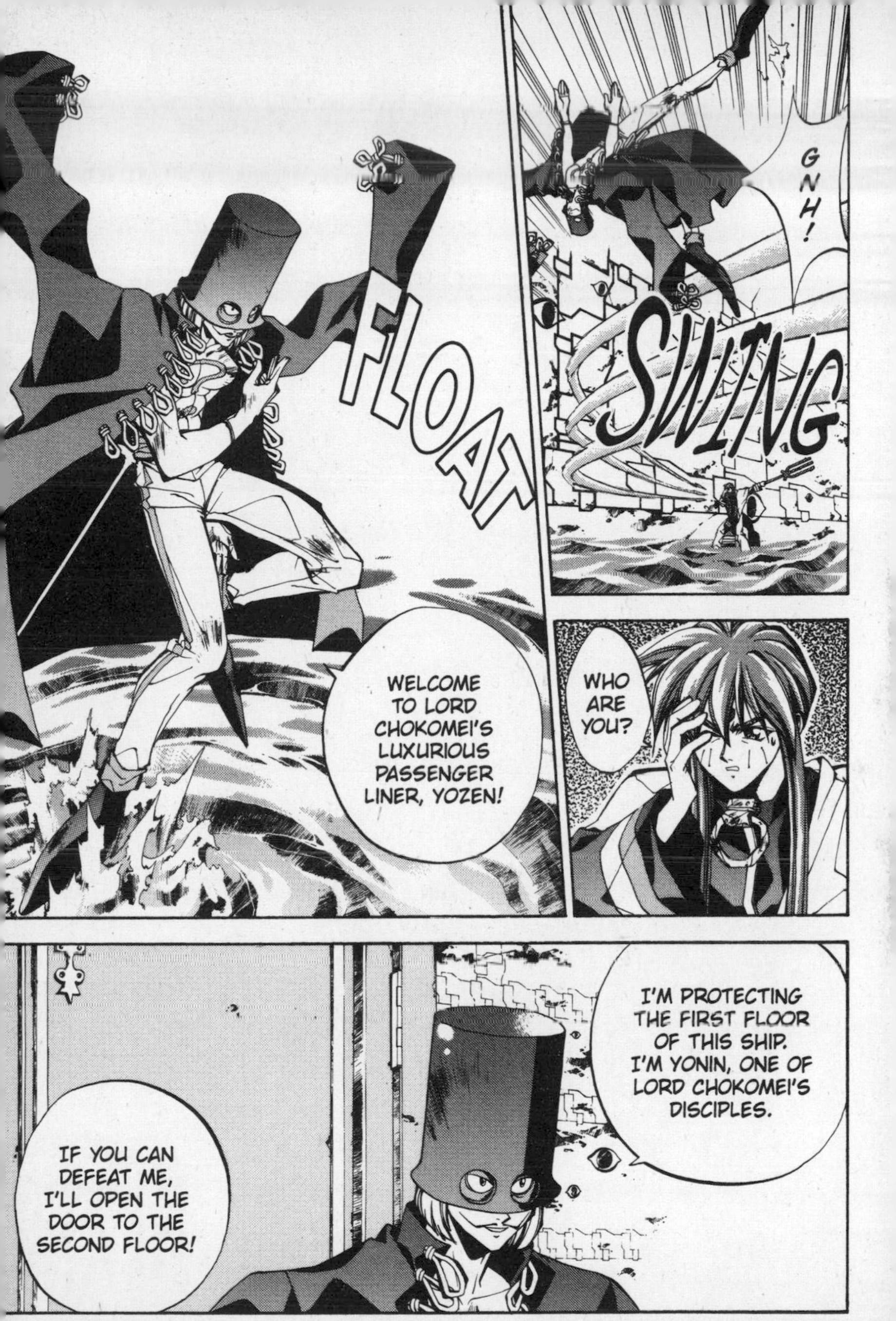
GNH!
SWING
WHO ARE YOU?
FLOAT
WELCOME TO LORD CHOKOMEI'S LUXURIOUS PASSENGER LINER, YOZEN!
I'M PROTECTING THE FIRST FLOOR OF THIS SHIP. I'M YONIN, ONE OF LORD CHOKOMEI'S DISCIPLES.
IF YOU CAN DEFEAT ME, I'LL OPEN THE DOOR TO THE SECOND FLOOR!

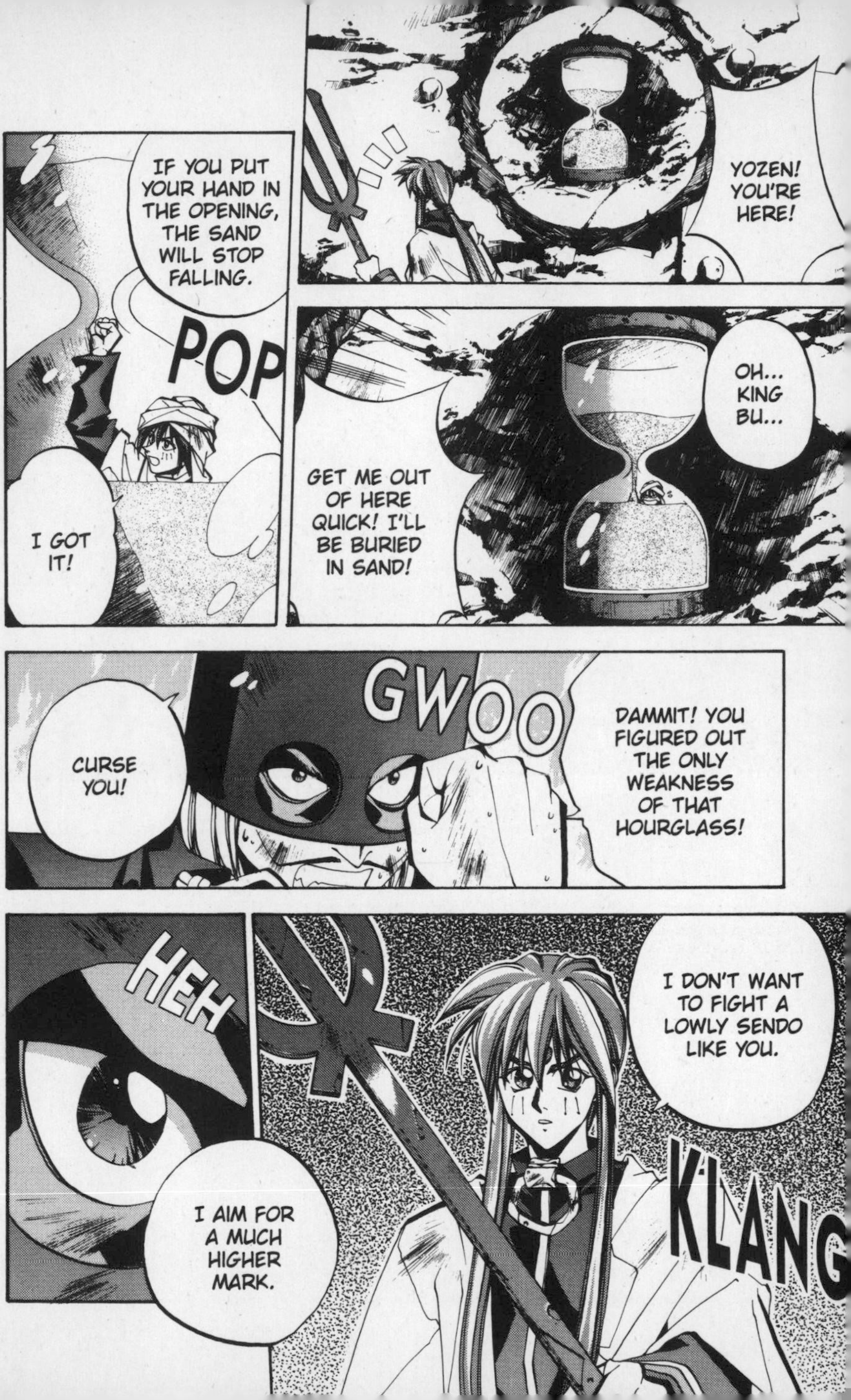
YOZEN! YOU'RE HERE!
OH... KING BU...
GET ME OUT OF HERE QUICK! I'LL BE BURIED IN SAND!
IF YOU PUT YOUR HAND IN THE OPENING, THE SAND WILL STOP FALLING.
POP
I GOT IT!
DAMMIT! YOU FIGURED OUT THE ONLY WEAKNESS OF THAT HOURGLASS!
GWOO
CURSE YOU!
I DON'T WANT TO FIGHT A LOWLY SENDO LIKE YOU.
KLANG
HEH
I AIM FOR A MUCH HIGHER MARK.

READ THIS WAY

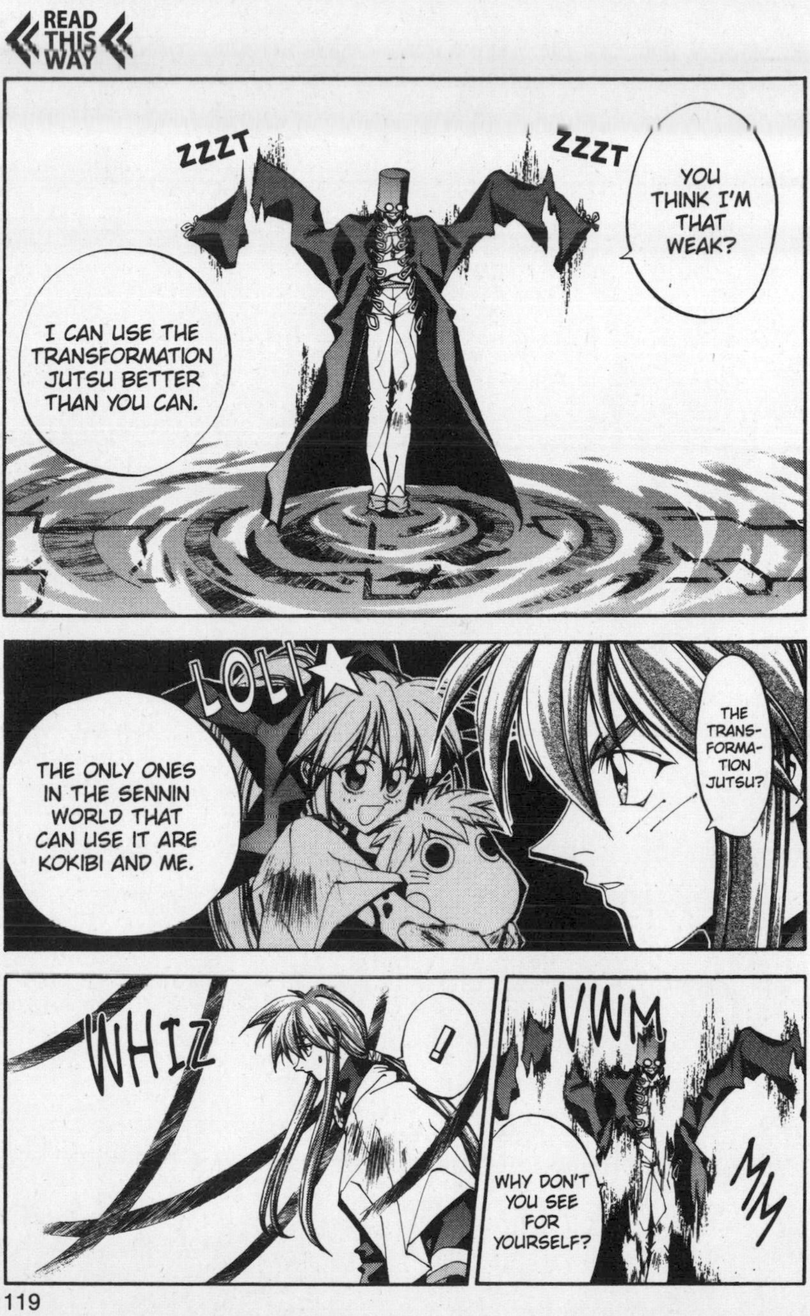
ZZZT
ZZZT
YOU THINK I'M THAT WEAK?
I CAN USE THE TRANSFORMATION JUTSU BETTER THAN YOU CAN.
THE TRANSFORMATION JUTSU?
LOL!
THE ONLY ONES IN THE SENNIN WORLD THAT CAN USE IT ARE KOKIBI AND ME.
VWM
MM
WHY DON'T YOU SEE FOR YOURSELF?
WHIZ
!

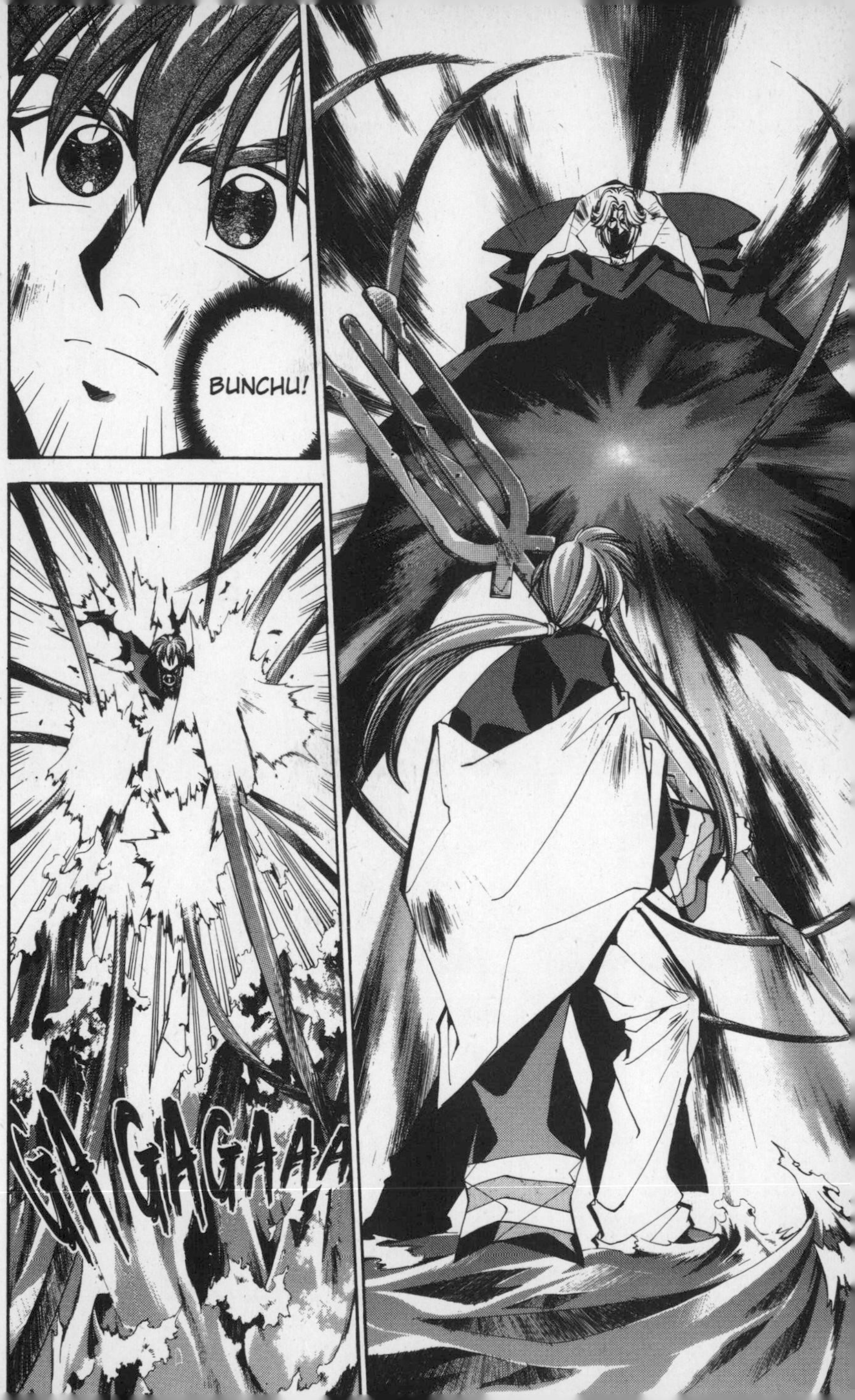
BUNCHU!
GAGAGAA

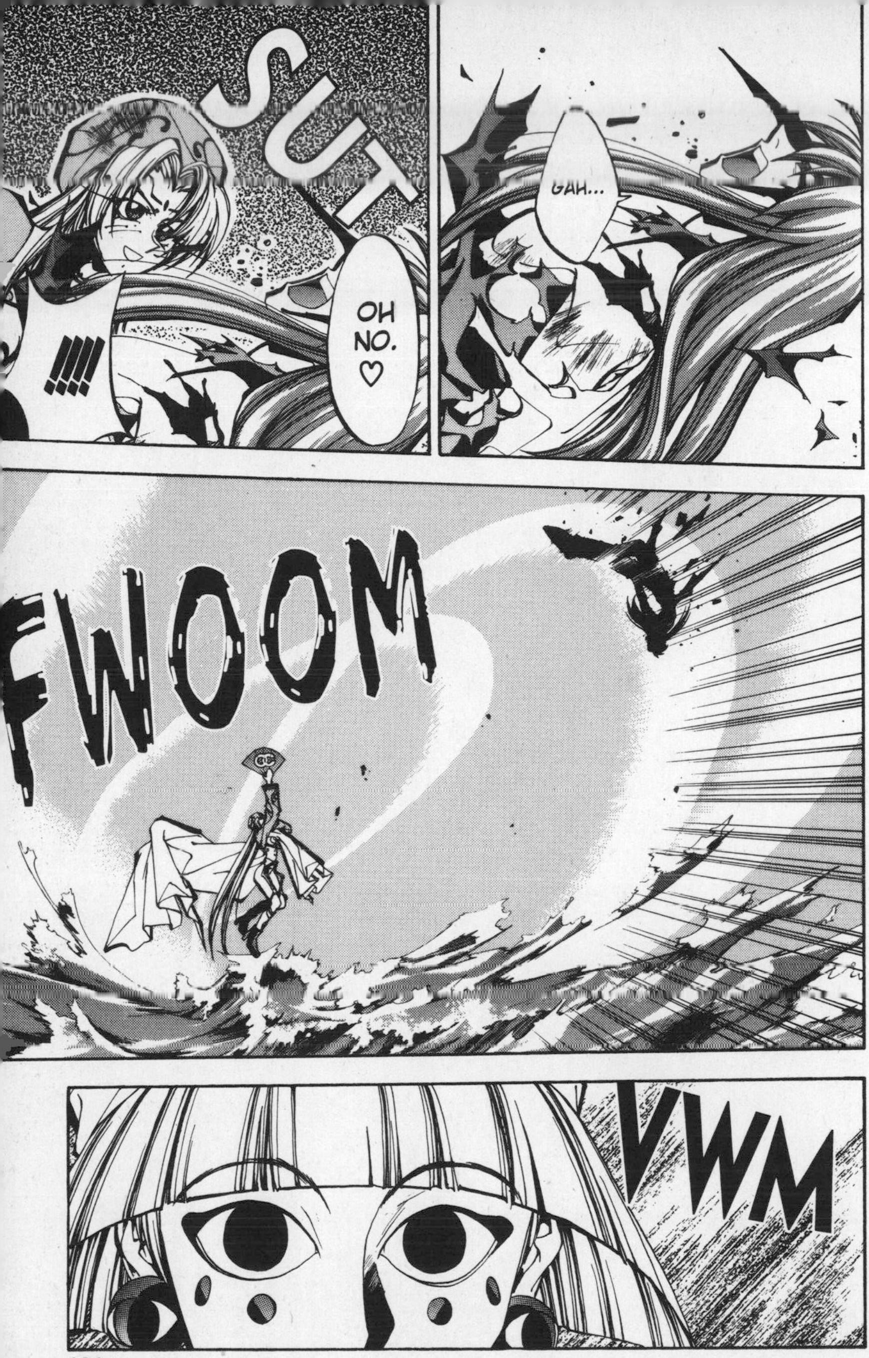
GAH...
SUT
OH NO. ♡
!!!!!
FWOOM
VWM

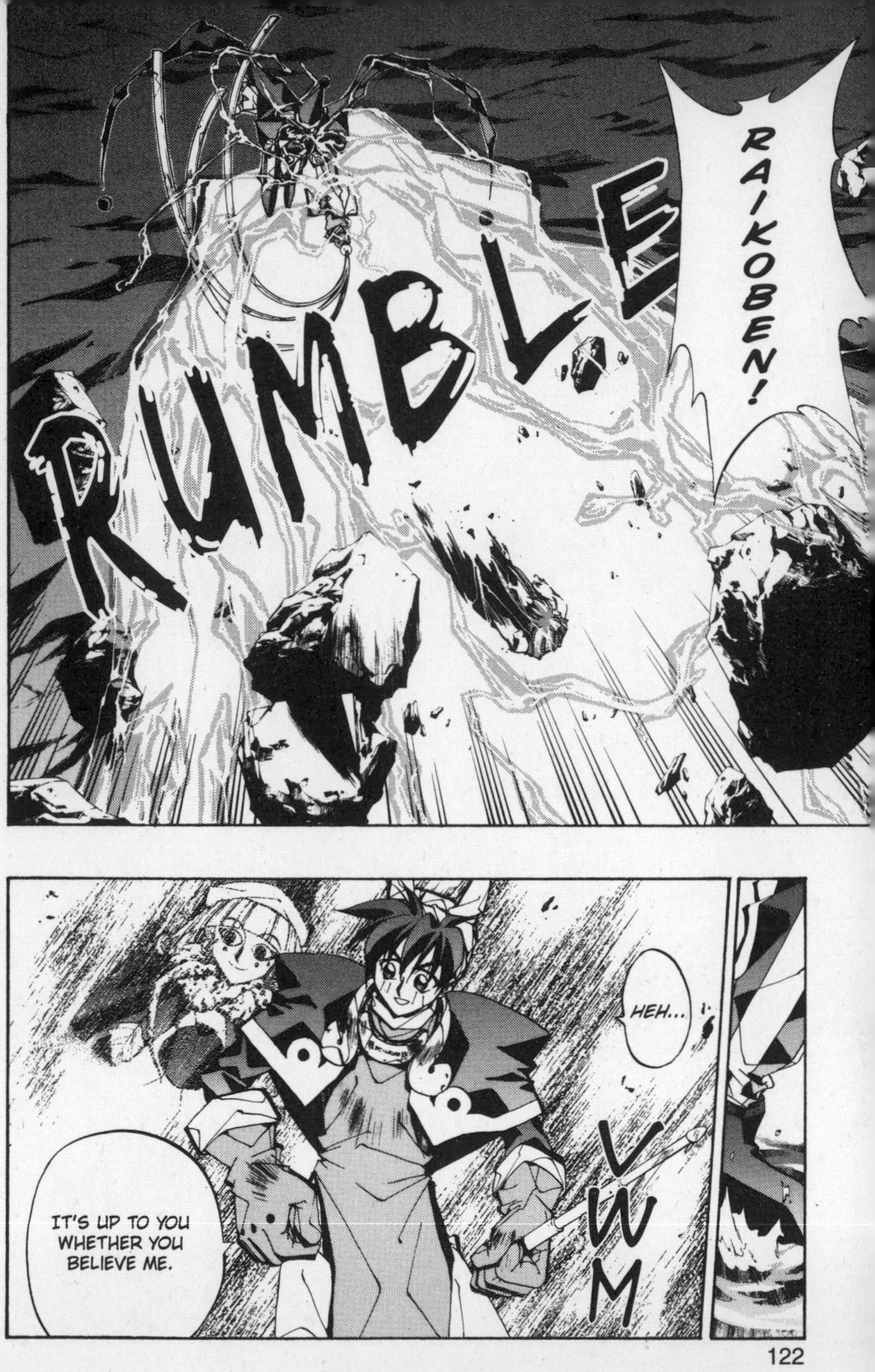
RAIKOBEN!
RUMBLE
HEH...
VWM
IT'S UP TO YOU WHETHER YOU BELIEVE ME.

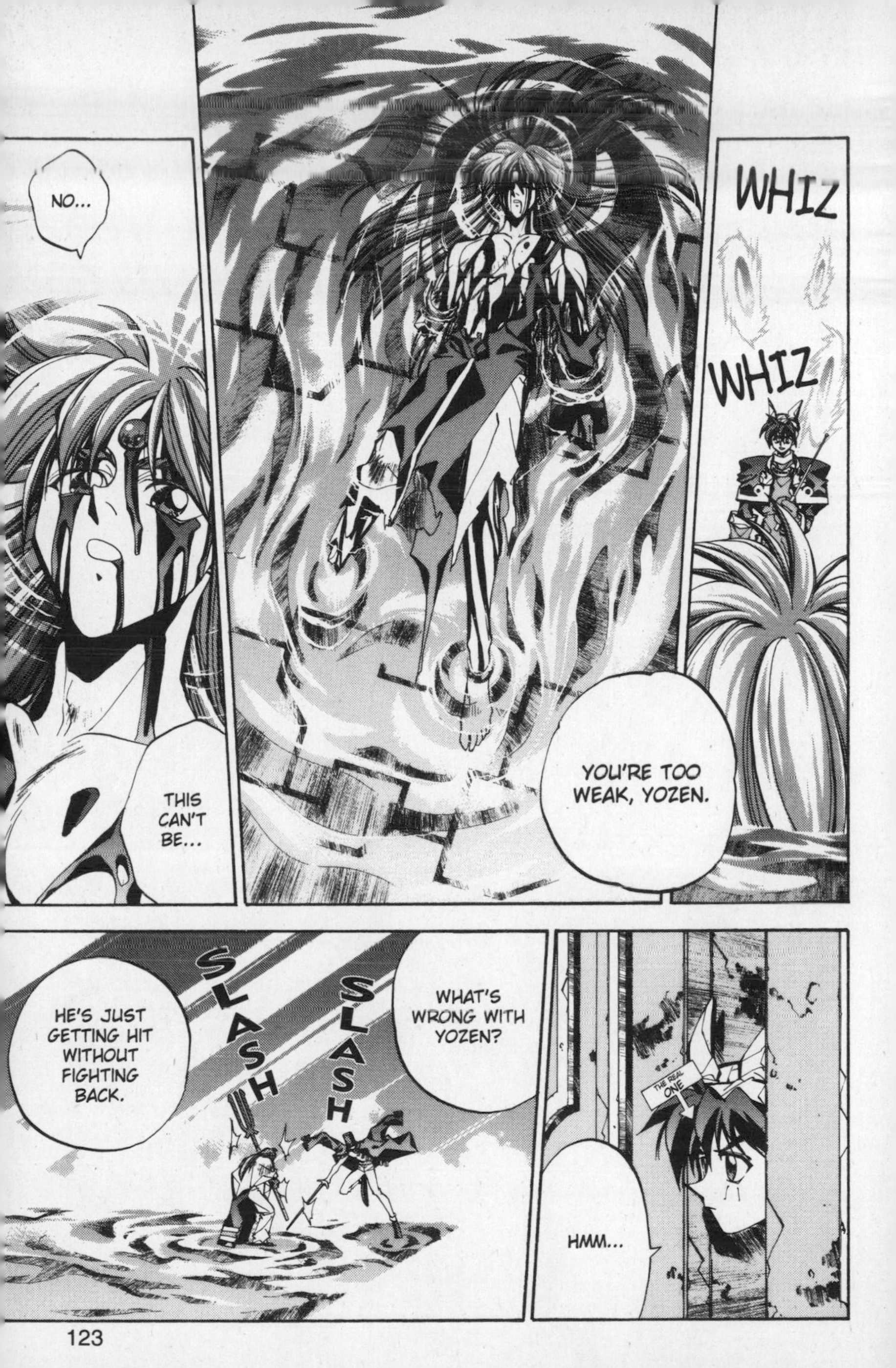
WHIZ
WHIZ
YOU'RE TOO WEAK, YOZEN.
NO...
THIS CAN'T BE...
THE REAL ONE
HMM...
WHAT'S WRONG WITH YOZEN?
SLASH
SLASH
HE'S JUST GETTING HIT WITHOUT FIGHTING BACK.

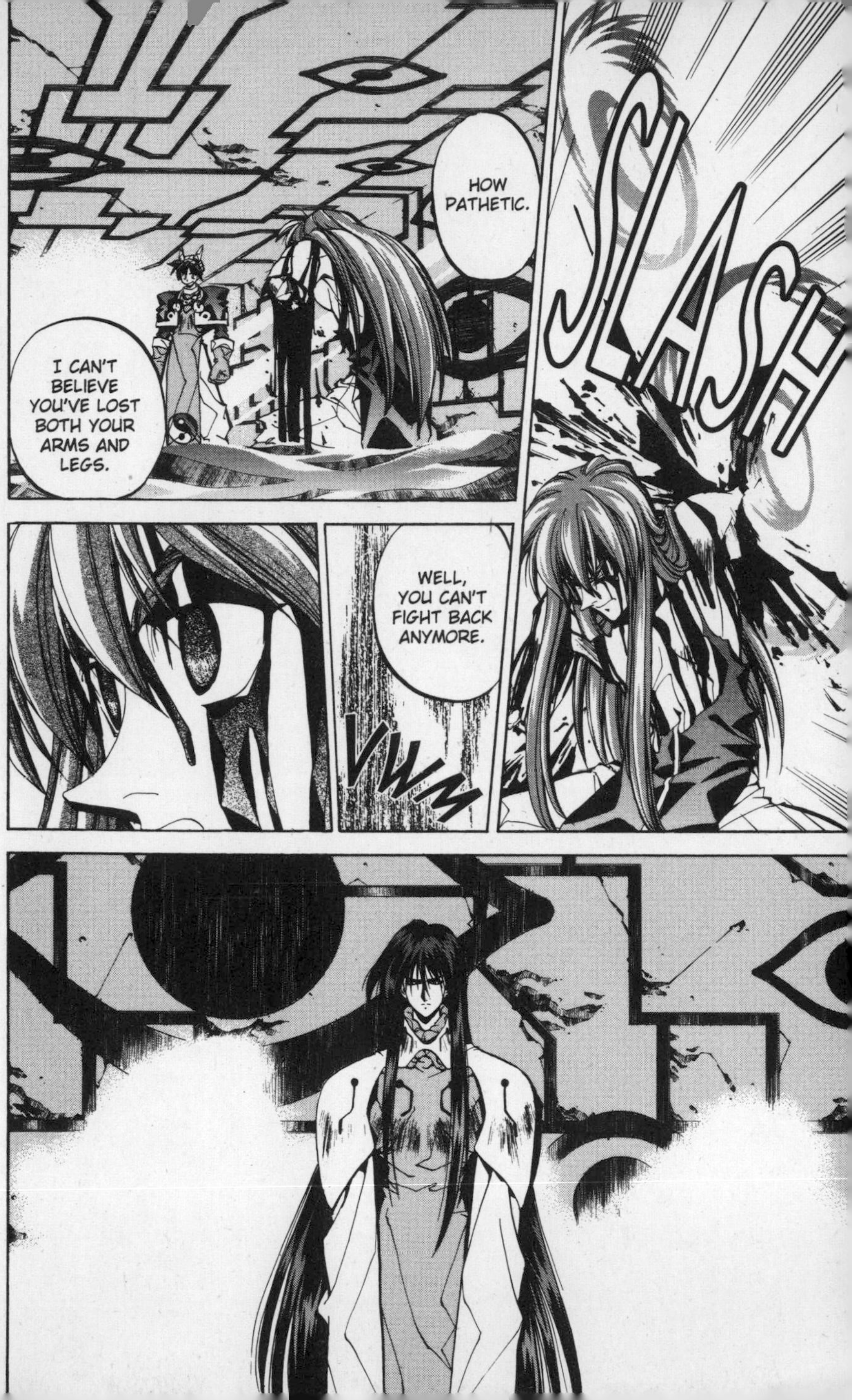
SLASH
HOW PATHETIC.
I CAN'T BELIEVE YOU'VE LOST BOTH YOUR ARMS AND LEGS.
WELL, YOU CAN'T FIGHT BACK ANYMORE.
VWM

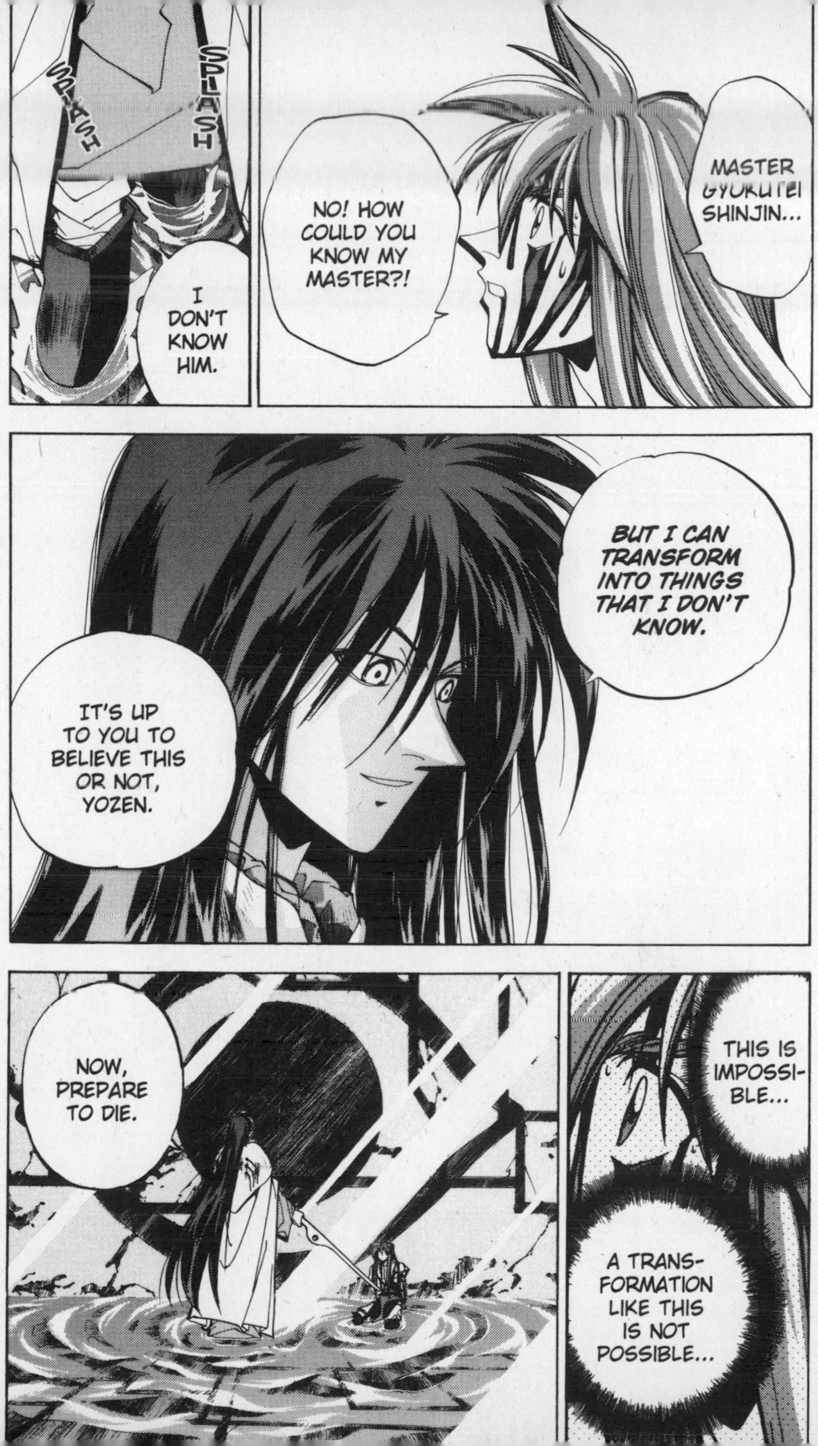
MASTER GYOKUTEI SHINJIN...
NO! HOW COULD YOU KNOW MY MASTER?!
SPLASH
SPLASH
I DON'T KNOW HIM.
BUT I CAN TRANSFORM INTO THINGS THAT I DON'T KNOW.
IT'S UP TO YOU TO BELIEVE THIS OR NOT, YOZEN.
THIS IS IMPOSSI-BLE...
A TRANS-FORMATION LIKE THIS IS NOT POSSIBLE...
NOW, PREPARE TO DIE.

封神演義

Chapter 86

CONQUERING CHOKOMEI, PART 2
MIND CONTROL

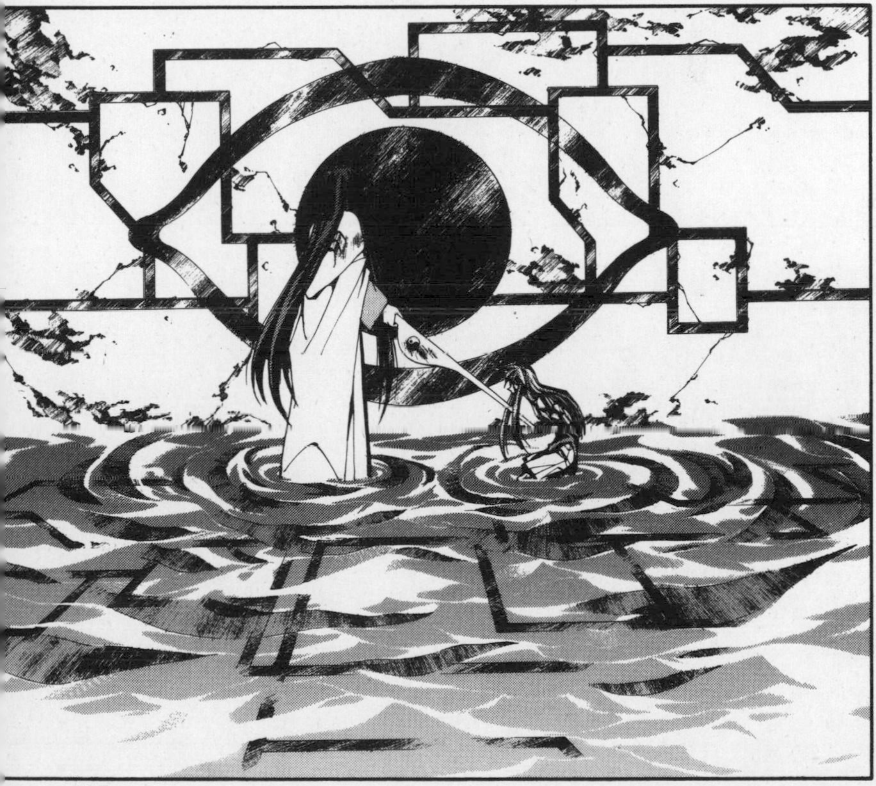

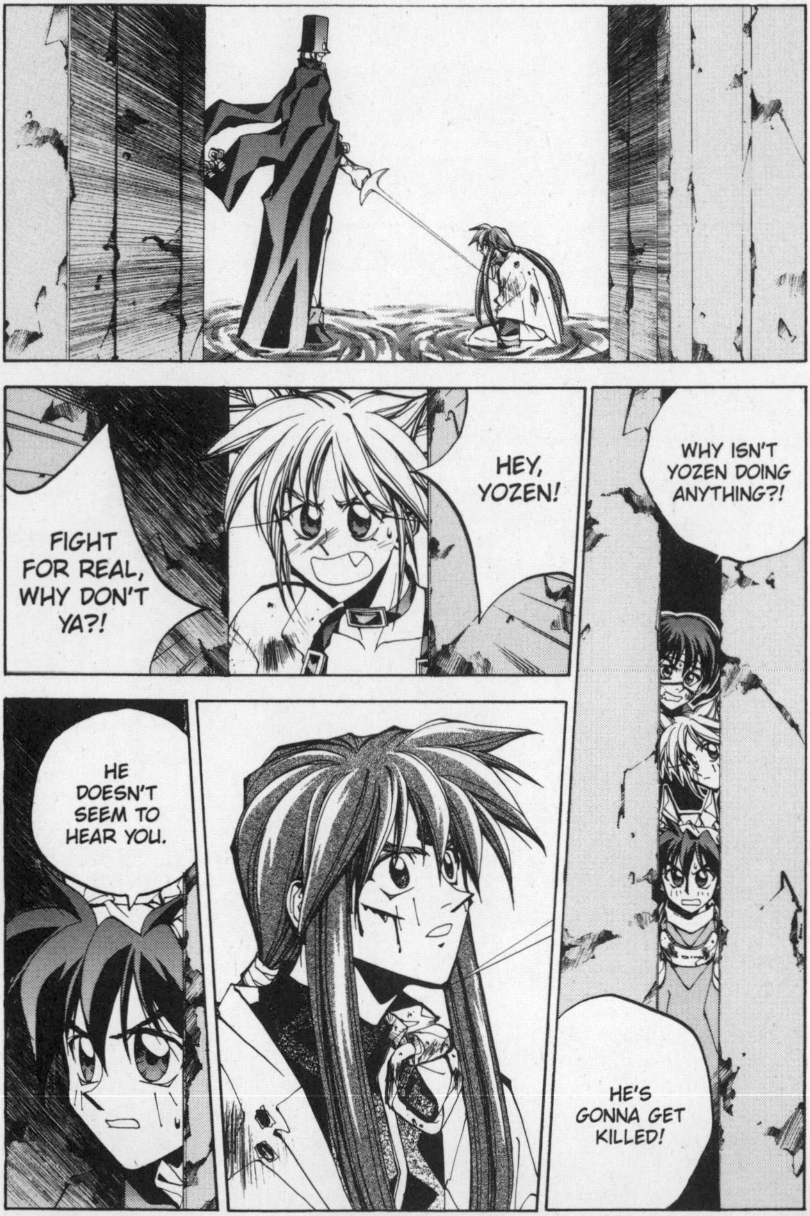
WHY ISN'T YOZEN DOING ANYTHING?!
HE'S GONNA GET KILLED!
HEY, YOZEN!
FIGHT FOR REAL, WHY DON'T YA?!
HE DOESN'T SEEM TO HEAR YOU.

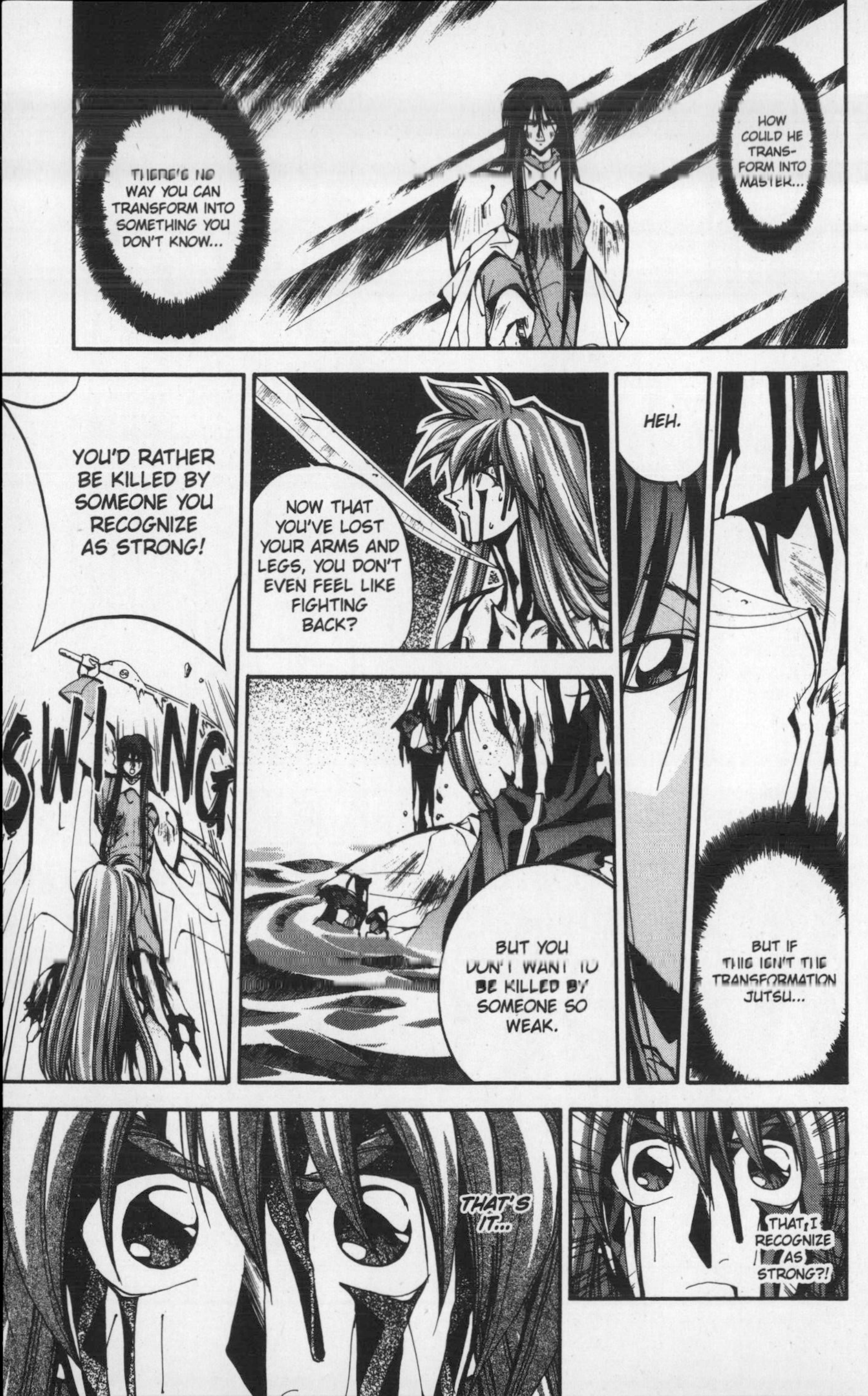
HOW COULD HE TRANS-FORM INTO MASTER...
THERE'S NO WAY YOU CAN TRANSFORM INTO SOMETHING YOU DON'T KNOW...
BUT IF THIS ISN'T THE TRANSFORMATION JUTSU...
HEH.
NOW THAT YOU'VE LOST YOUR ARMS AND LEGS, YOU DON'T EVEN FEEL LIKE FIGHTING BACK?
BUT YOU DON'T WANT TO BE KILLED BY SOMEONE SO WEAK.
YOU'D RATHER BE KILLED BY SOMEONE YOU RECOGNIZE AS STRONG!
SWING
THAT I RECOGNIZE AS STRONG?!
THAT'S IT...

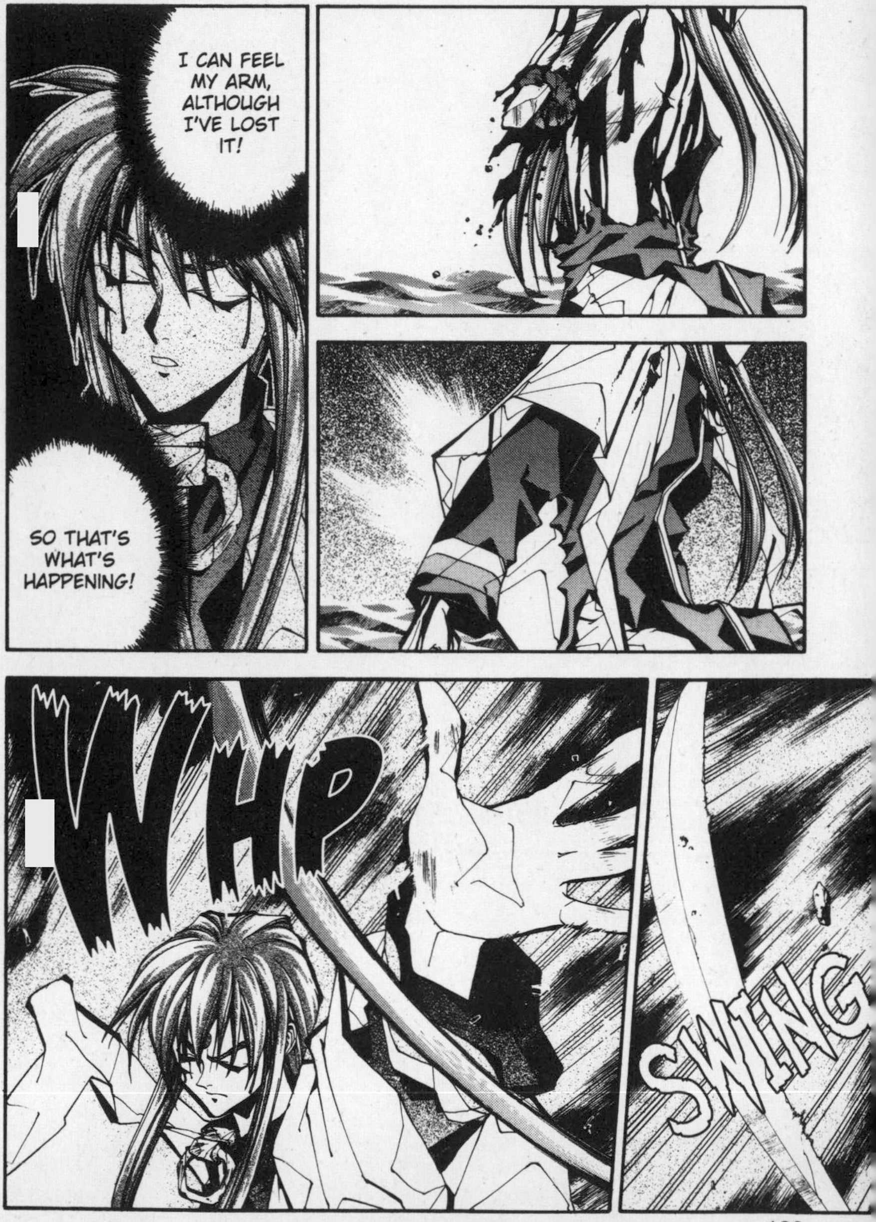
I CAN FEEL MY ARM, ALTHOUGH I'VE LOST IT!
SO THAT'S WHAT'S HAPPENING!
SWING
WHP

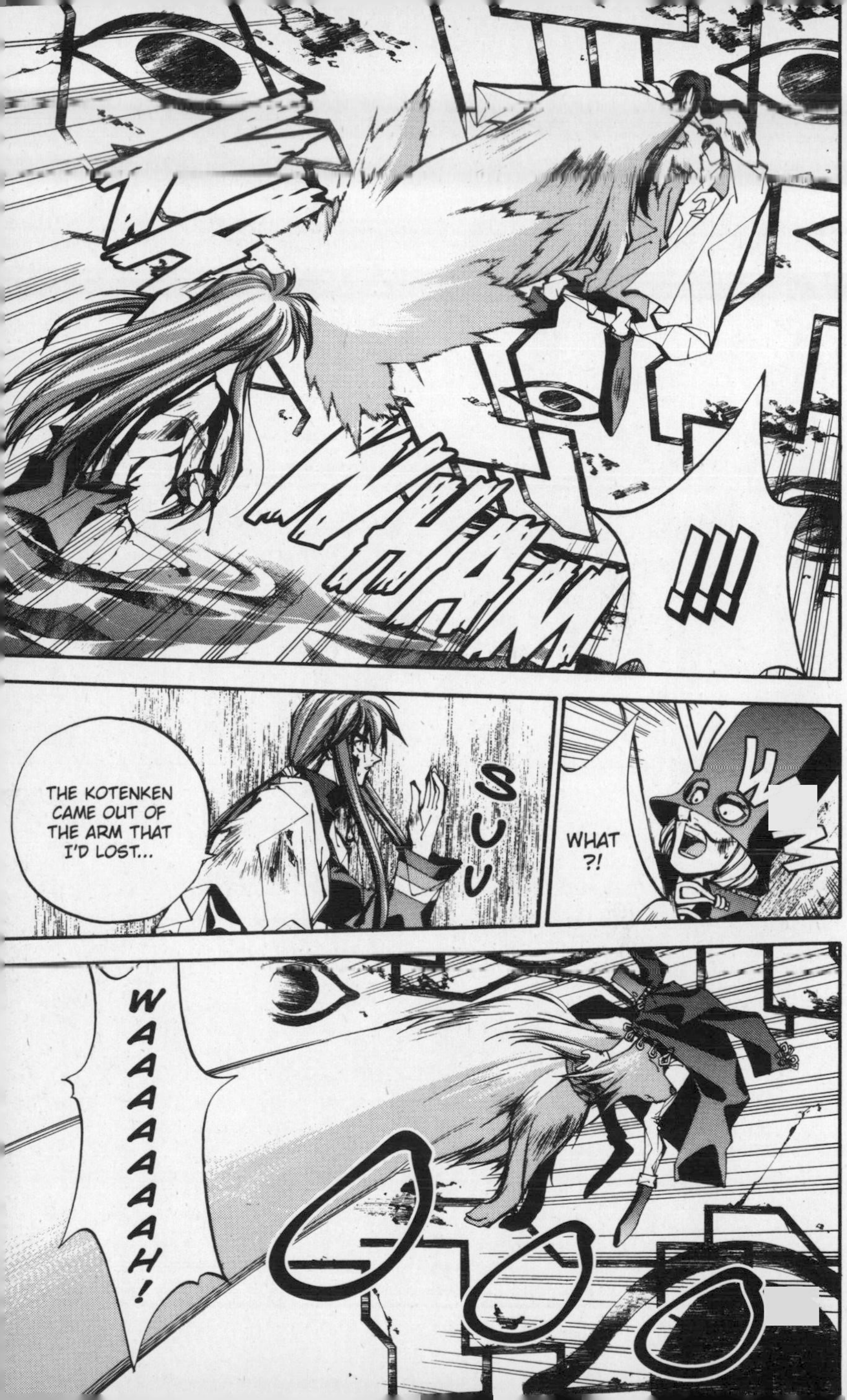
WHAM!!!
VWM
WHAT ?!
SUU
THE KOTENKEN CAME OUT OF THE ARM THAT I'D LOST...
WAAAAAAAAAH!

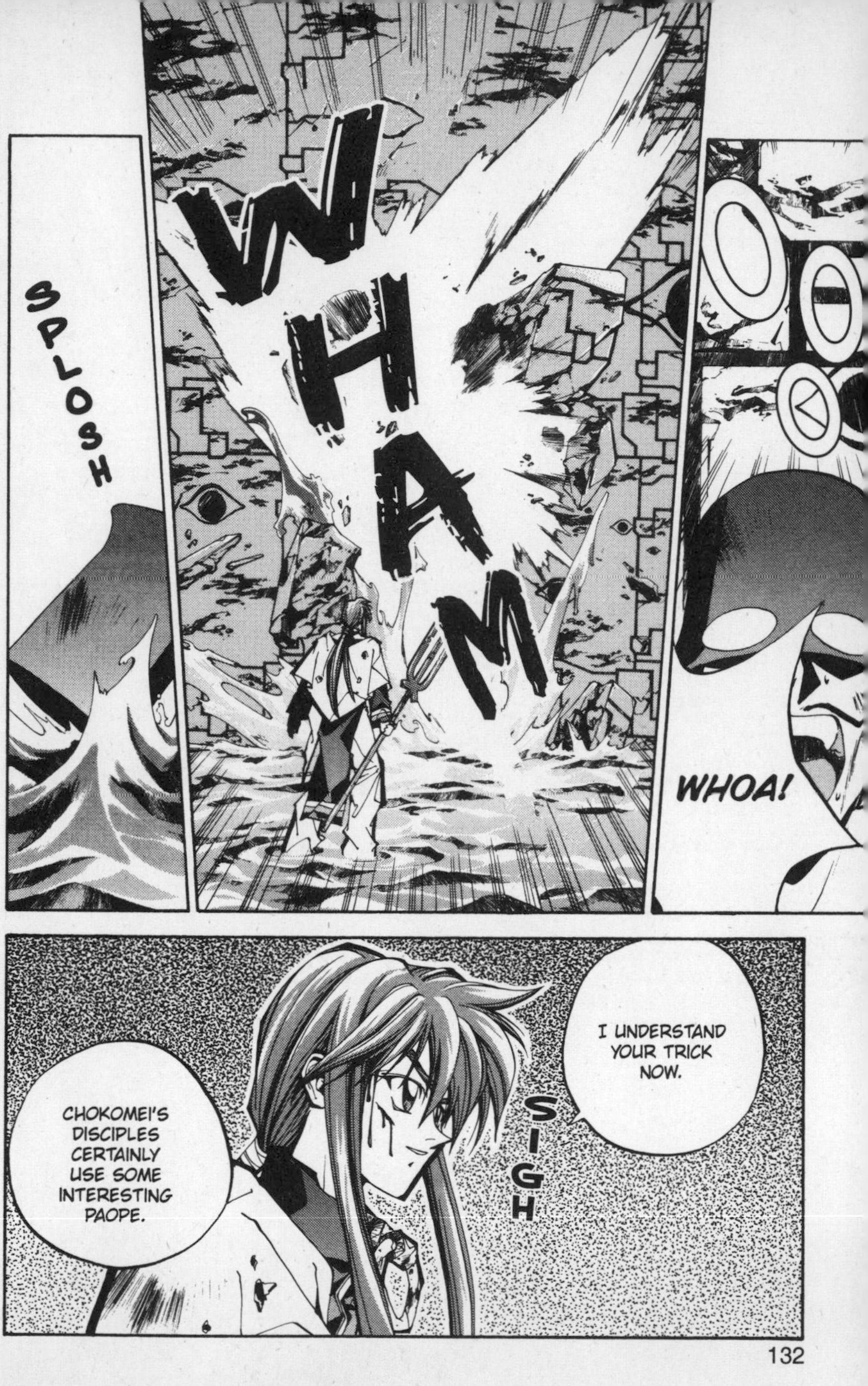
WHOA!
WHAM
SPLOSH
I UNDERSTAND YOUR TRICK NOW.
SIGH
CHOKOMEI'S DISCIPLES CERTAINLY USE SOME INTERESTING PAOPE.

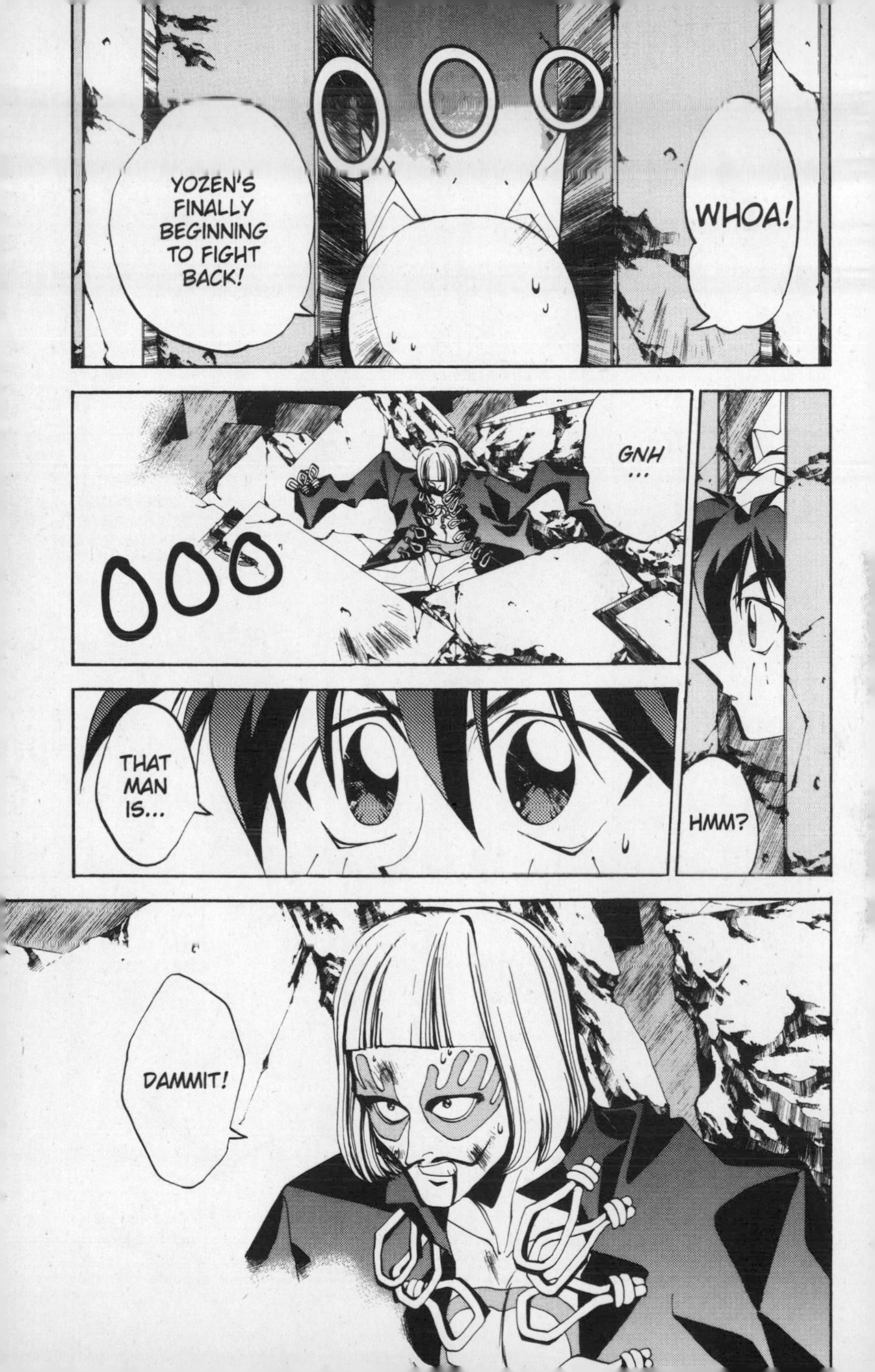
WHOA!
YOZEN'S FINALLY BEGINNING TO FIGHT BACK!
HMM?
GNH ...
OOO
THAT MAN IS...
DAMMIT!

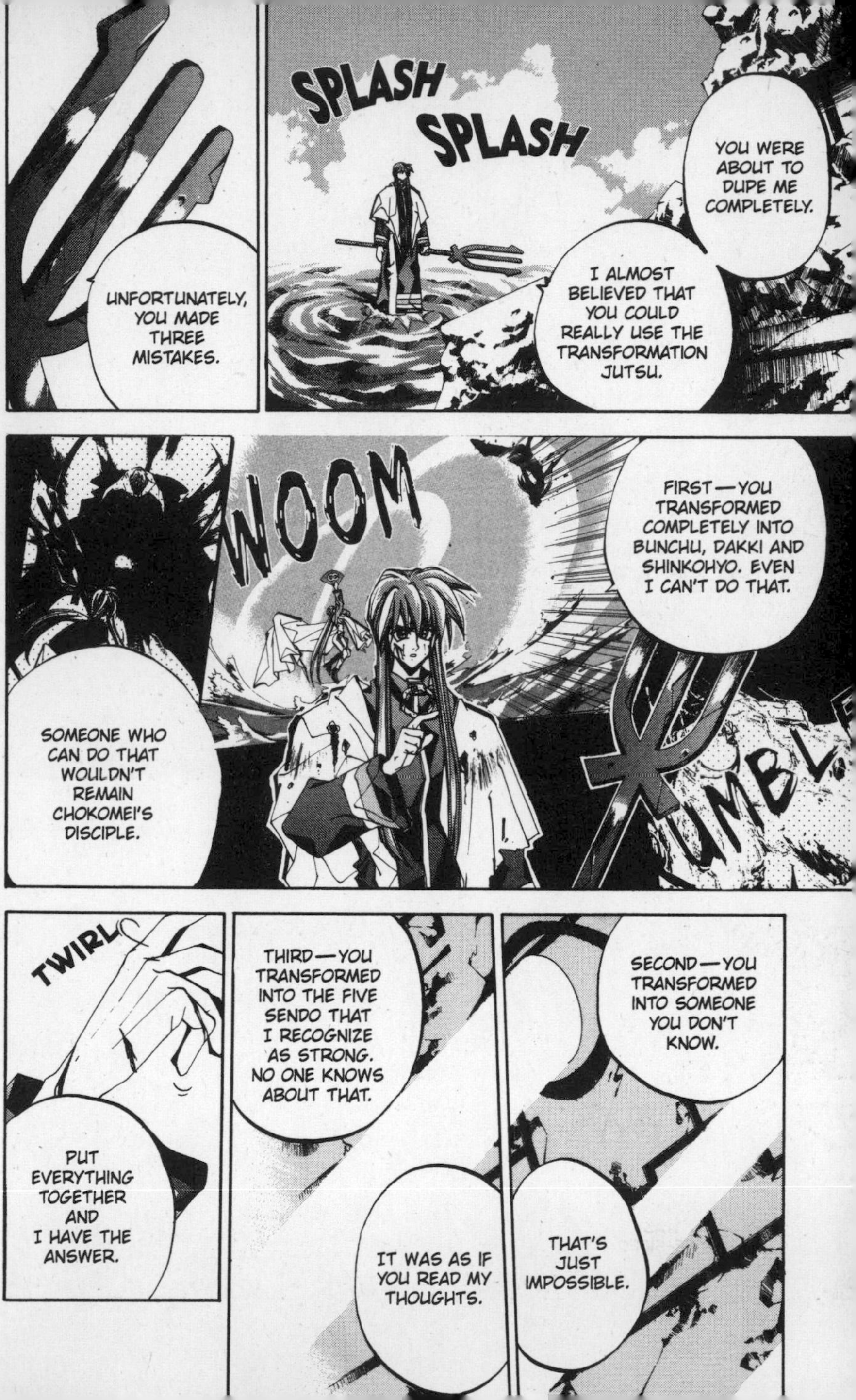
SPLASH
SPLASH
YOU WERE ABOUT TO DUPE ME COMPLETELY.
I ALMOST BELIEVED THAT YOU COULD REALLY USE THE TRANSFORMATION JUTSU.
UNFORTUNATELY, YOU MADE THREE MISTAKES.
WOOM
FIRST—YOU TRANSFORMED COMPLETELY INTO BUNCHU, DAKKI AND SHINKOHYO. EVEN I CAN'T DO THAT.
UMBLE
SOMEONE WHO CAN DO THAT WOULDN'T REMAIN CHOKOMEI'S DISCIPLE.
SECOND—YOU TRANSFORMED INTO SOMEONE YOU DON'T KNOW.
THAT'S JUST IMPOSSIBLE.
THIRD—YOU TRANSFORMED INTO THE FIVE SENDO THAT I RECOGNIZE AS STRONG. NO ONE KNOWS ABOUT THAT.
IT WAS AS IF YOU READ MY THOUGHTS.
TWIRL
PUT EVERYTHING TOGETHER AND I HAVE THE ANSWER.

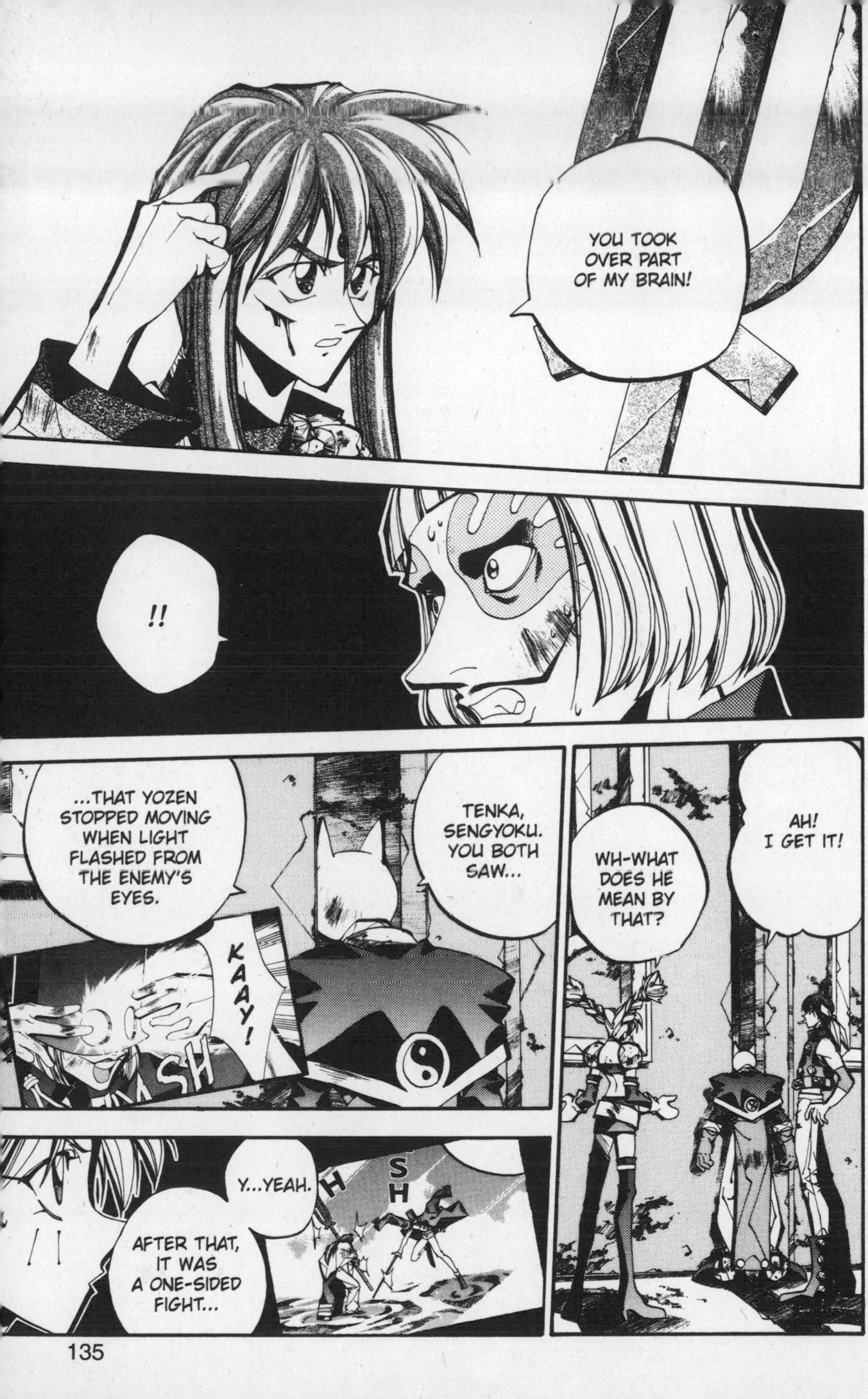
YOU TOOK OVER PART OF MY BRAIN!
!!
AH! I GET IT!
WH-WHAT DOES HE MEAN BY THAT?
TENKA, SENGYOKU. YOU BOTH SAW...
...THAT YOZEN STOPPED MOVING WHEN LIGHT FLASHED FROM THE ENEMY'S EYES.
KAAY!
Y...YEAH.
AFTER THAT, IT WAS A ONE-SIDED FIGHT...

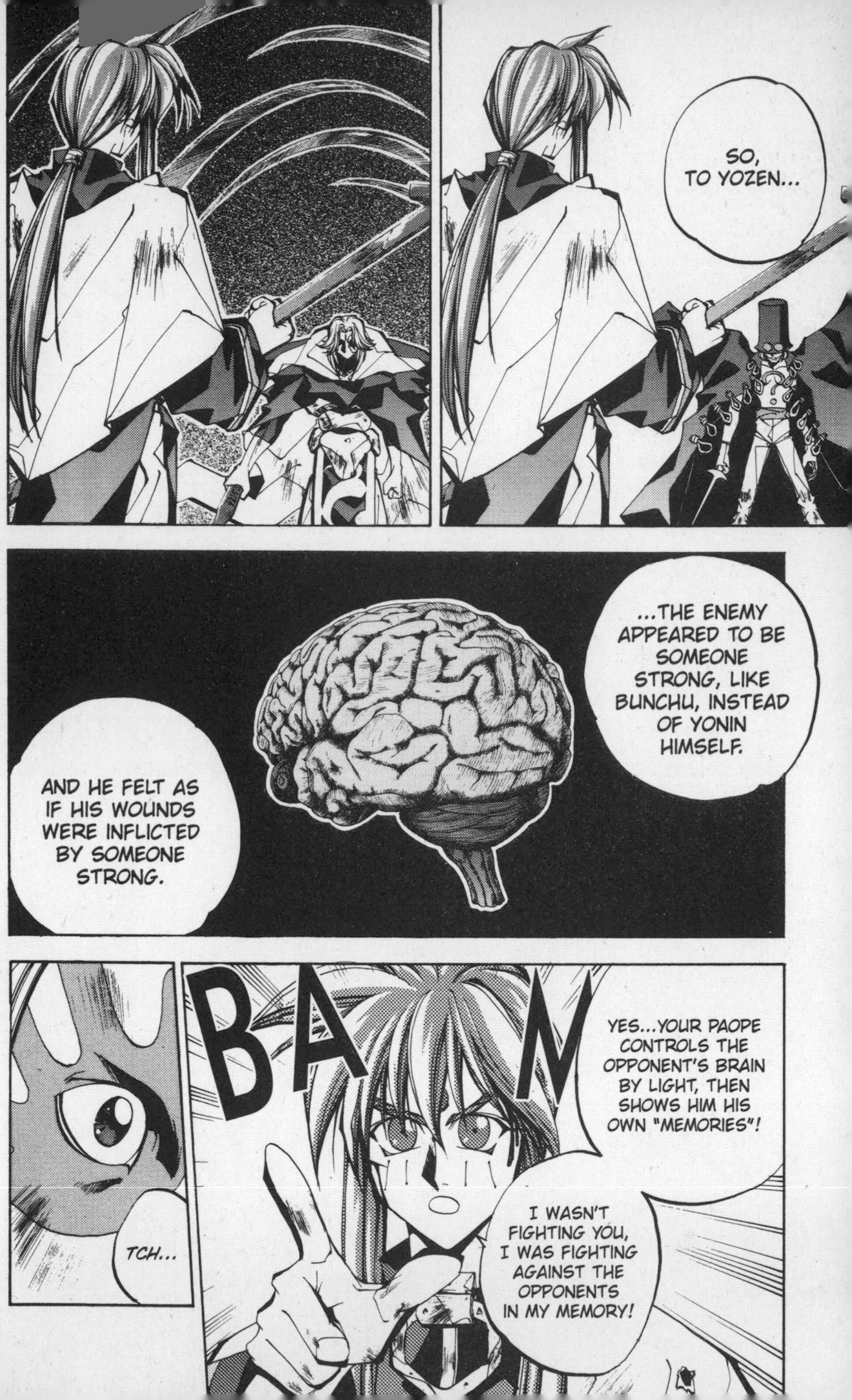
SO, TO YOZEN...
...THE ENEMY APPEARED TO BE SOMEONE STRONG, LIKE BUNCHU, INSTEAD OF YONIN HIMSELF.
AND HE FELT AS IF HIS WOUNDS WERE INFLICTED BY SOMEONE STRONG.
BAM
YES...YOUR PAOPE CONTROLS THE OPPONENT'S BRAIN BY LIGHT, THEN SHOWS HIM HIS OWN "MEMORIES"!
I WASN'T FIGHTING YOU, I WAS FIGHTING AGAINST THE OPPONENTS IN MY MEMORY!
TCH...

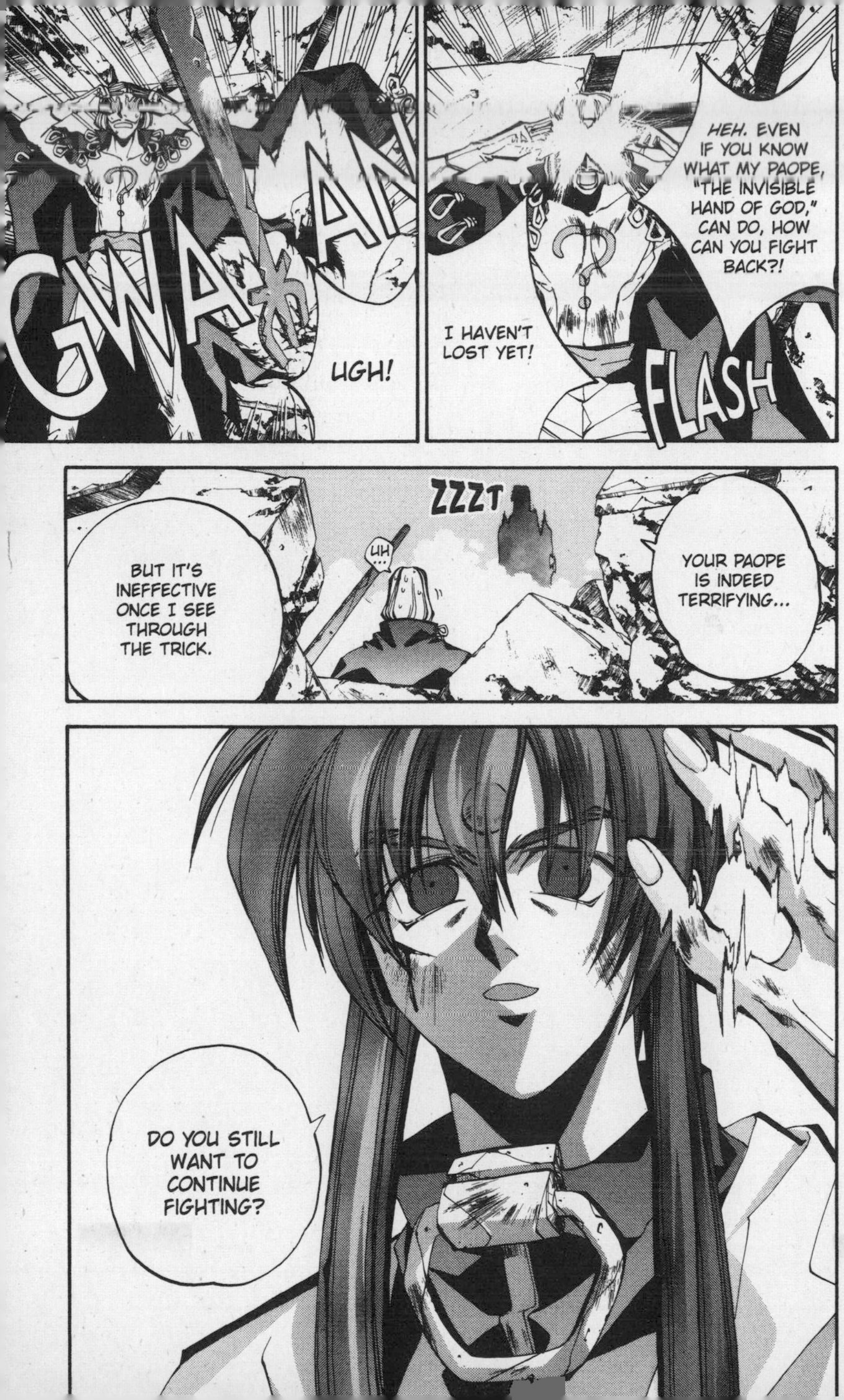
HEH. EVEN IF YOU KNOW WHAT MY PAOPE, "THE INVISIBLE HAND OF GOD," CAN DO, HOW CAN YOU FIGHT BACK?!
I HAVEN'T LOST YET!
FLASH
GWAAN
UGH!
YOUR PAOPE IS INDEED TERRIFYING...
ZZZT
UH...
BUT IT'S INEFFECTIVE ONCE I SEE THROUGH THE TRICK.
DO YOU STILL WANT TO CONTINUE FIGHTING?

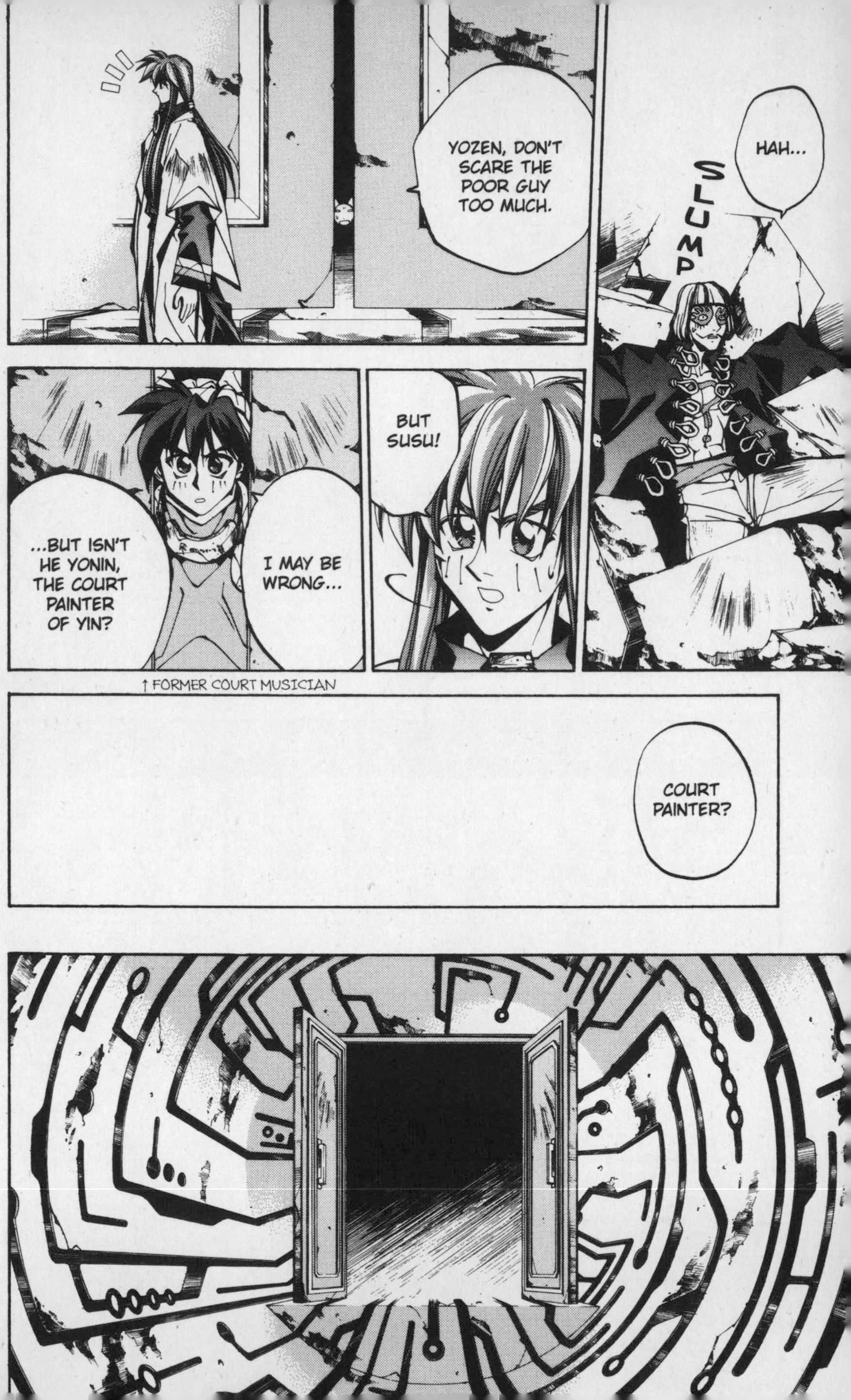
HAH...
SLUMP
YOZEN, DON'T SCARE THE POOR GUY TOO MUCH.
BUT SUSU!
I MAY BE WRONG...
...BUT ISN'T HE YONIN, THE COURT PAINTER OF YIN?
↑FORMER COURT MUSICIAN
COURT PAINTER?

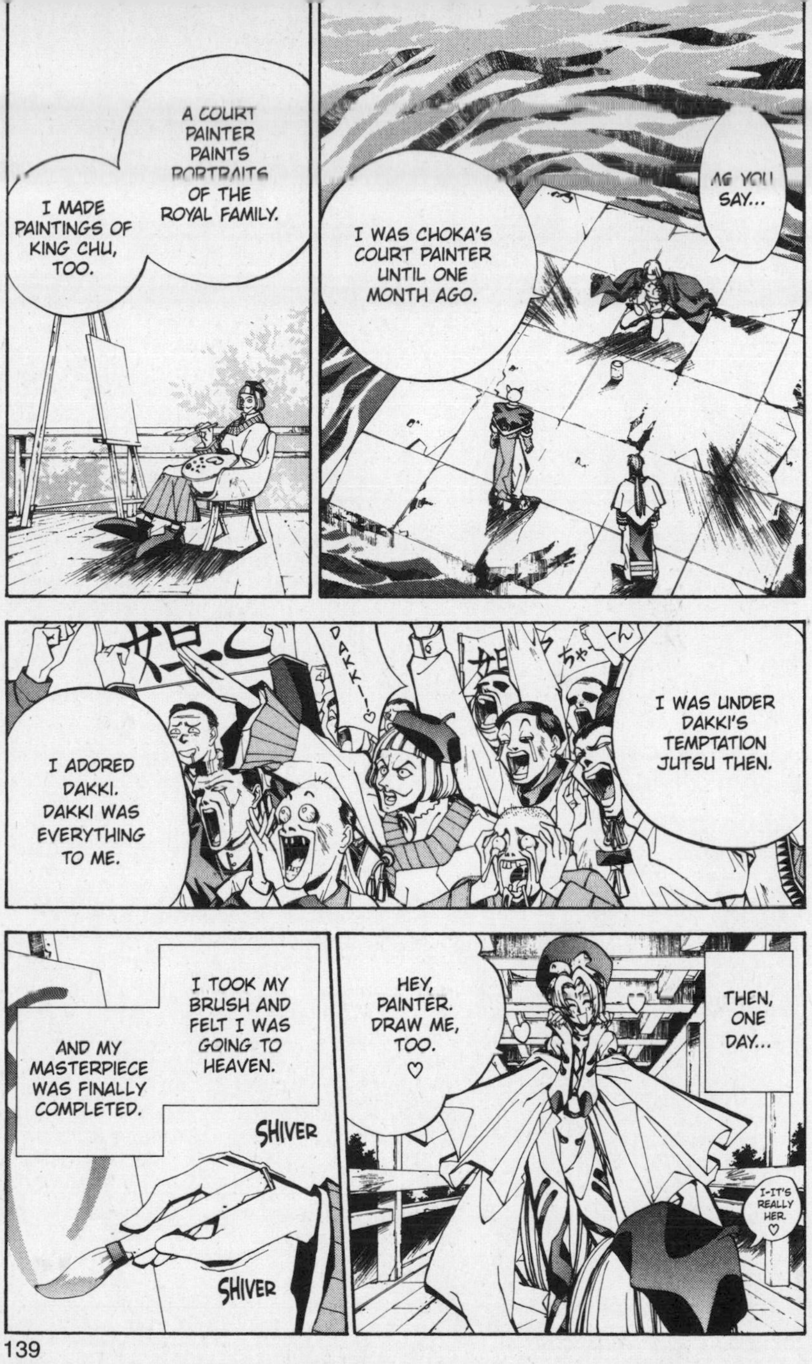
AS YOU SAY...
I WAS CHOKA'S COURT PAINTER UNTIL ONE MONTH AGO.
A COURT PAINTER PAINTS PORTRAITS OF THE ROYAL FAMILY.
I MADE PAINTINGS OF KING CHU, TOO.
I WAS UNDER DAKKI'S TEMPTATION JUTSU THEN.
DAKKI-! ♡
I ADORED DAKKI. DAKKI WAS EVERYTHING TO ME.
THEN, ONE DAY...
HEY, PAINTER. DRAW ME, TOO. ♡
I-IT'S REALLY HER. ♡
I TOOK MY BRUSH AND FELT I WAS GOING TO HEAVEN.
AND MY MASTERPIECE WAS FINALLY COMPLETED.
SHIVER
SHIVER

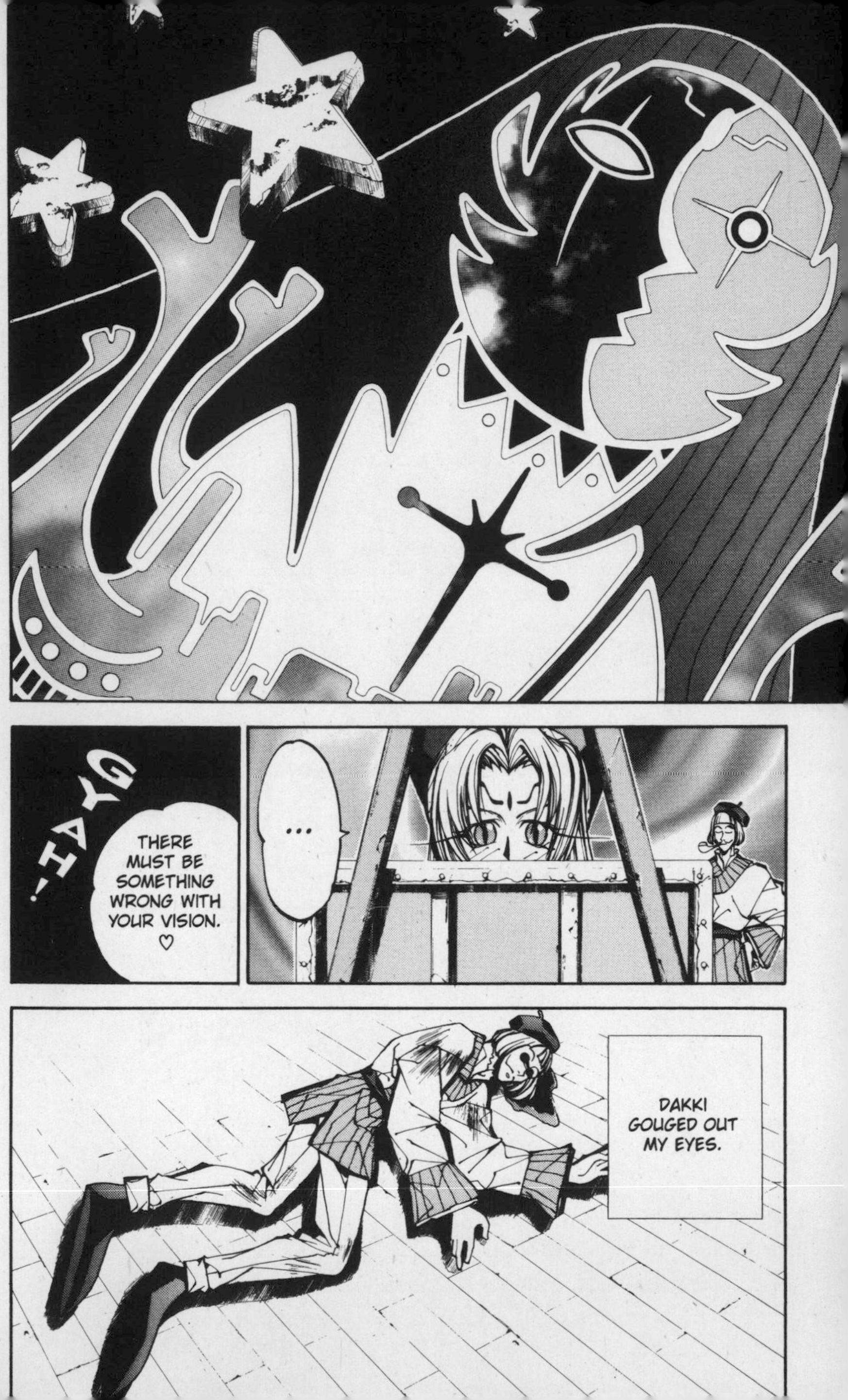
...
GYAH!
THERE MUST BE SOMETHING WRONG WITH YOUR VISION. ♡
DAKKI GOUGED OUT MY EYES.

READ THIS WAY

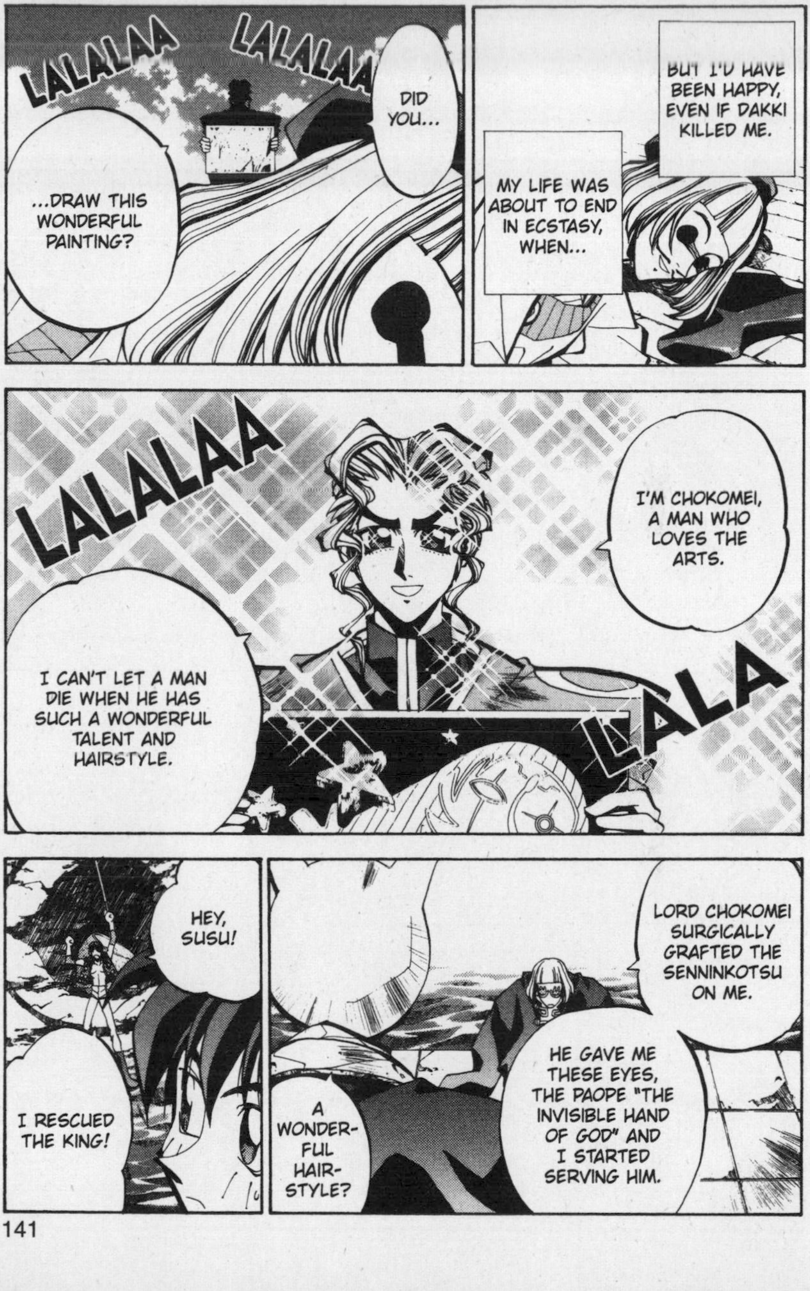

BUT I'D HAVE BEEN HAPPY, EVEN IF DAKKI KILLED ME.
MY LIFE WAS ABOUT TO END IN ECSTASY, WHEN...
LALALAA
LALALAA
DID YOU...
...DRAW THIS WONDERFUL PAINTING?
I'M CHOKOMEI, A MAN WHO LOVES THE ARTS.
LALALAA
LALA
I CAN'T LET A MAN DIE WHEN HE HAS SUCH A WONDERFUL TALENT AND HAIRSTYLE.
LORD CHOKOMEI SURGICALLY GRAFTED THE SENNINKOTSU ON ME.
HE GAVE ME THESE EYES, THE PAOPE "THE INVISIBLE HAND OF GOD" AND I STARTED SERVING HIM.
A WONDERFUL HAIRSTYLE?
HEY, SUSU!
I RESCUED THE KING!

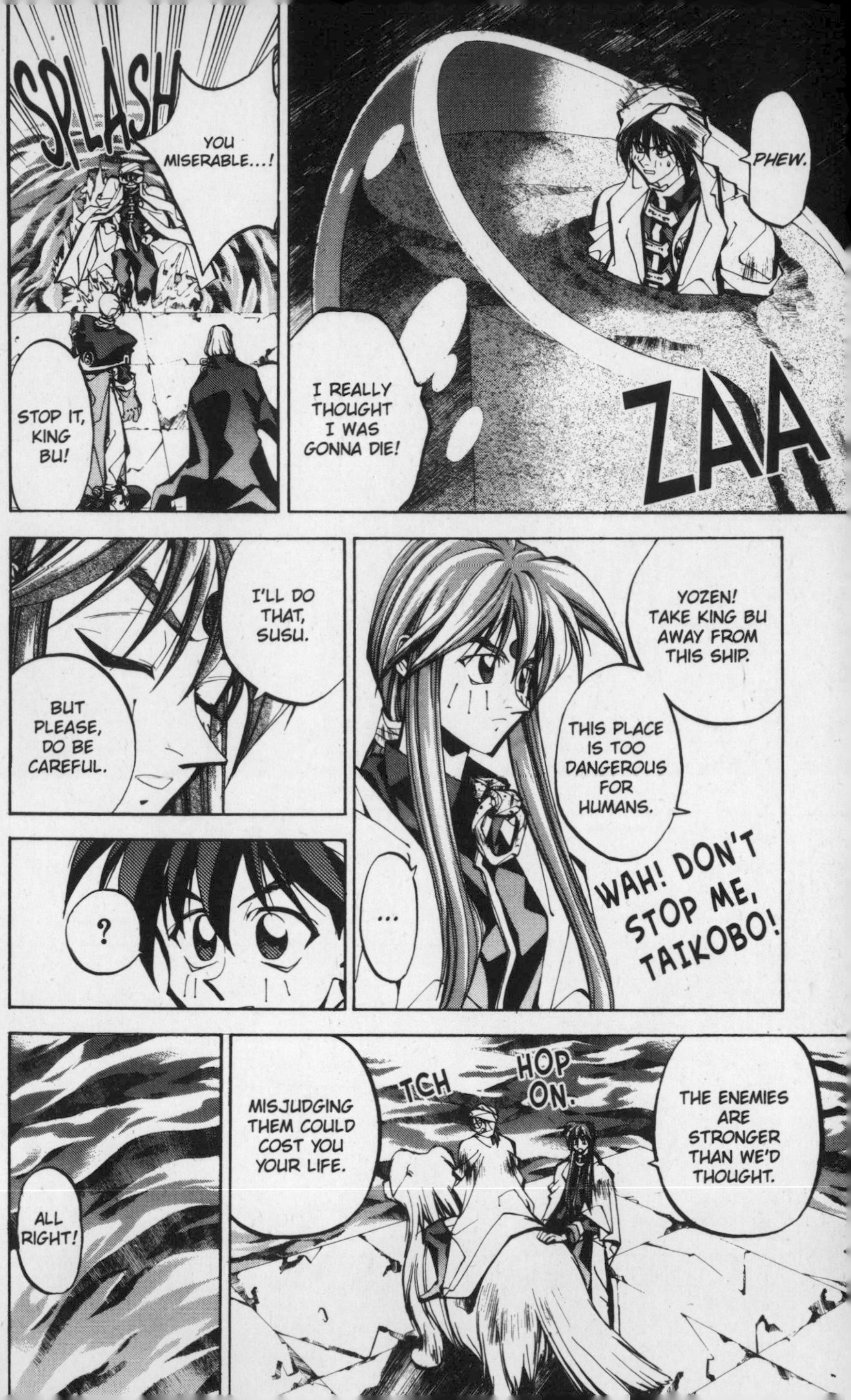
PHEW.
ZAA
I REALLY THOUGHT I WAS GONNA DIE!
SPLASH
YOU MISERABLE...!
STOP IT, KING BU!
YOZEN! TAKE KING BU AWAY FROM THIS SHIP.
THIS PLACE IS TOO DANGEROUS FOR HUMANS.
WAH! DON'T STOP ME, TAIKOBO!
...
I'LL DO THAT, SUSU.
BUT PLEASE, DO BE CAREFUL.
?
THE ENEMIES ARE STRONGER THAN WE'D THOUGHT.
HOP ON.
TCH
MISJUDGING THEM COULD COST YOU YOUR LIFE.
ALL RIGHT!

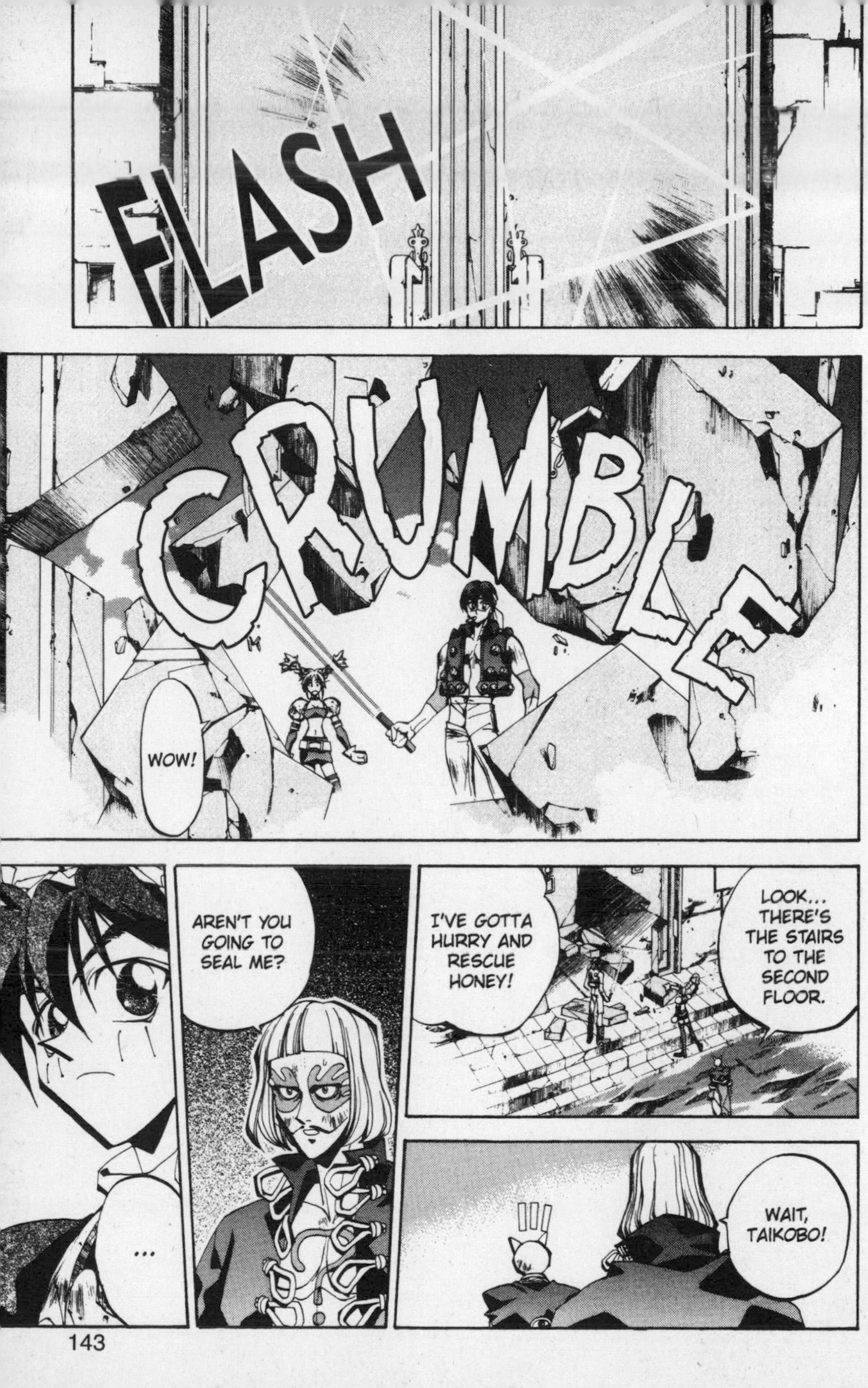
FLASH
CRUMBLE
WOW!
LOOK... THERE'S THE STAIRS TO THE SECOND FLOOR.
I'VE GOTTA HURRY AND RESCUE HONEY!
WAIT, TAIKOBO!
AREN'T YOU GOING TO SEAL ME?
...

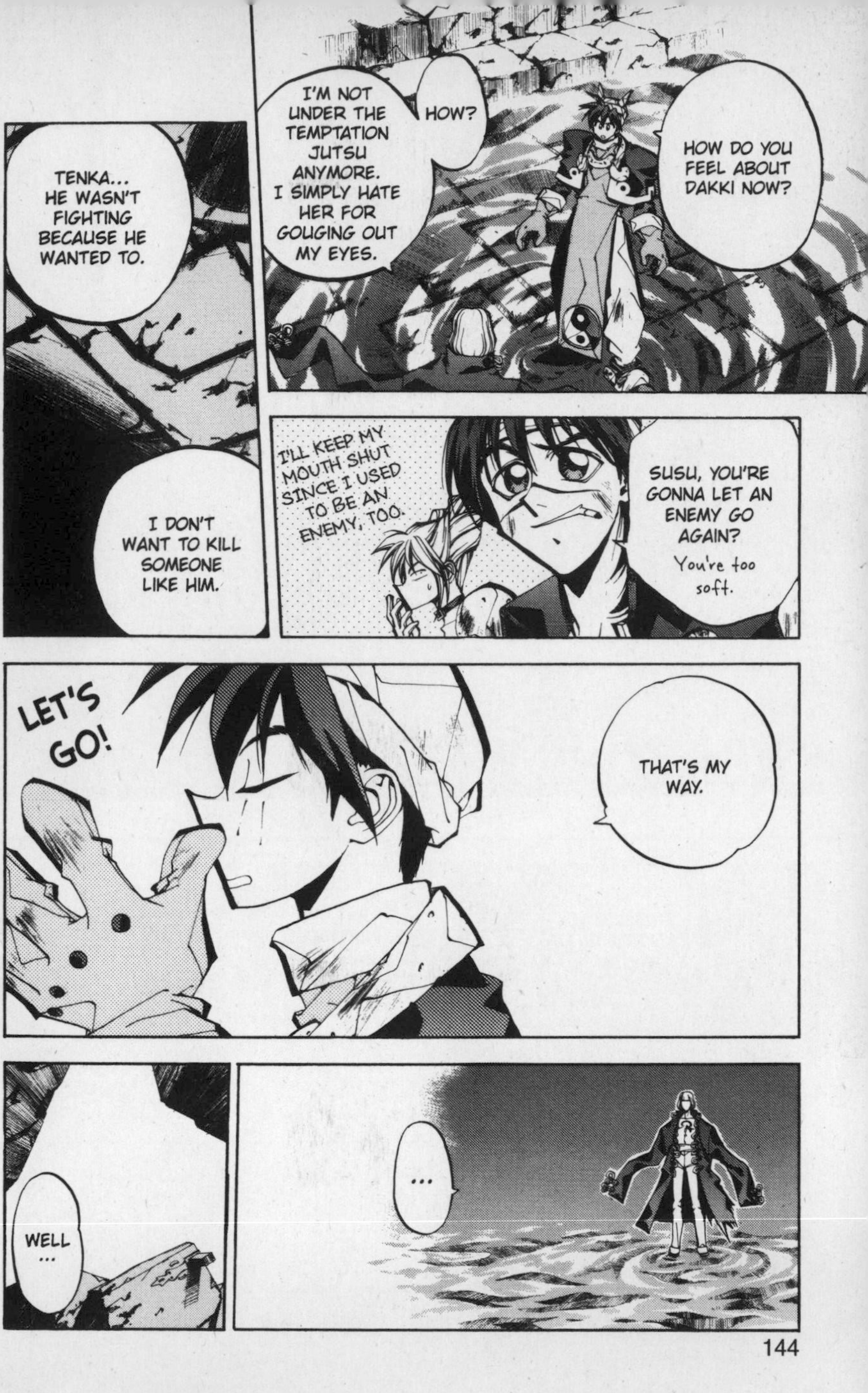
HOW DO YOU FEEL ABOUT DAKKI NOW?
HOW?
I'M NOT UNDER THE TEMPTATION JUTSU ANYMORE. I SIMPLY HATE HER FOR GOUGING OUT MY EYES.
SUSU, YOU'RE GONNA LET AN ENEMY GO AGAIN?
You're too soft.
I'LL KEEP MY MOUTH SHUT SINCE I USED TO BE AN ENEMY, TOO.
TENKA... HE WASN'T FIGHTING BECAUSE HE WANTED TO.
I DON'T WANT TO KILL SOMEONE LIKE HIM.
THAT'S MY WAY.
LET'S GO!
...
WELL ...

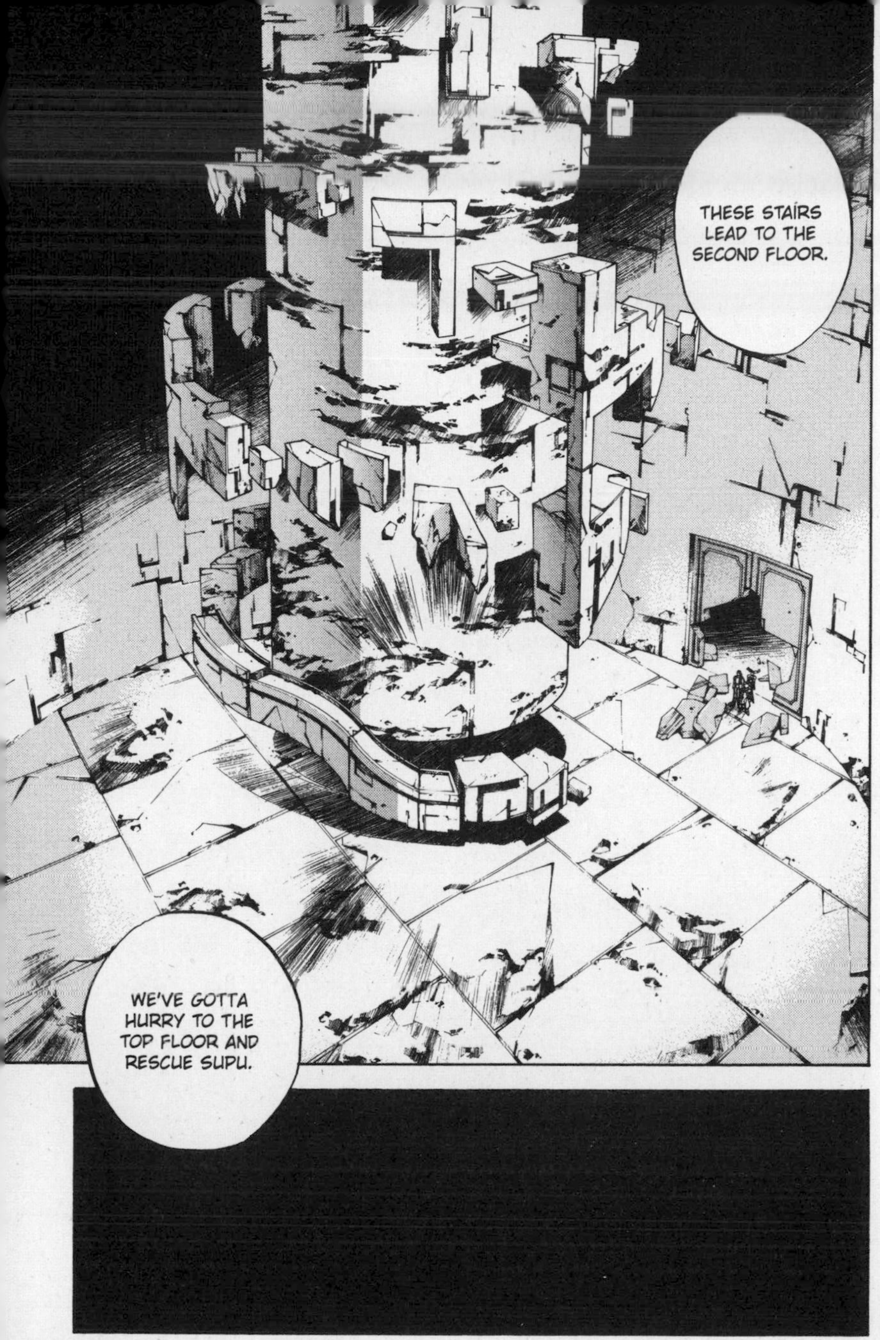
THESE STAIRS LEAD TO THE SECOND FLOOR.
WE'VE GOTTA HURRY TO THE TOP FLOOR AND RESCUE SUPU.

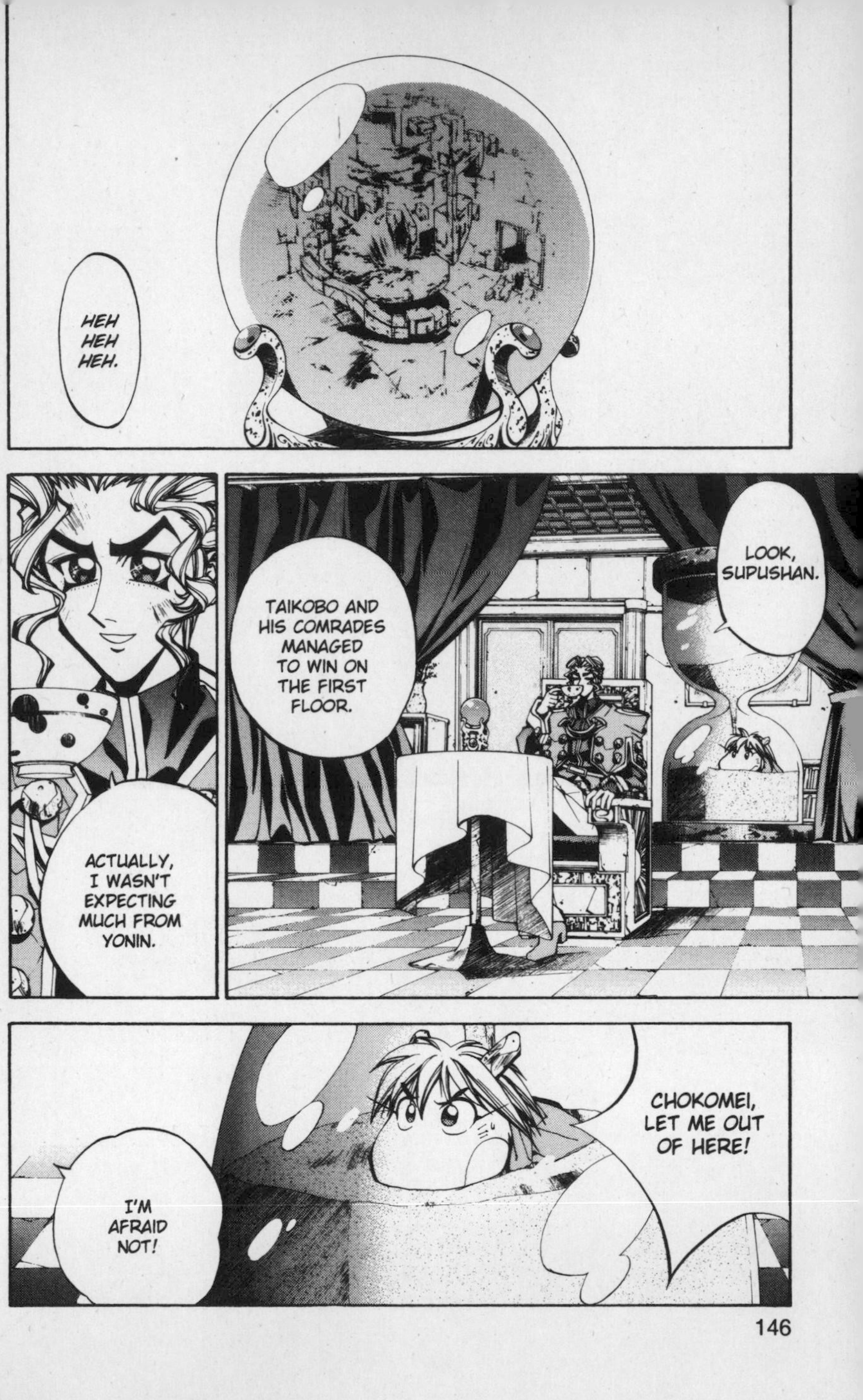
HEH HEH HEH.
LOOK, SUPUSHAN.
TAIKOBO AND HIS COMRADES MANAGED TO WIN ON THE FIRST FLOOR.
ACTUALLY, I WASN'T EXPECTING MUCH FROM YONIN.
CHOKOMEI, LET ME OUT OF HERE!
I'M AFRAID NOT!

READ THIS WAY

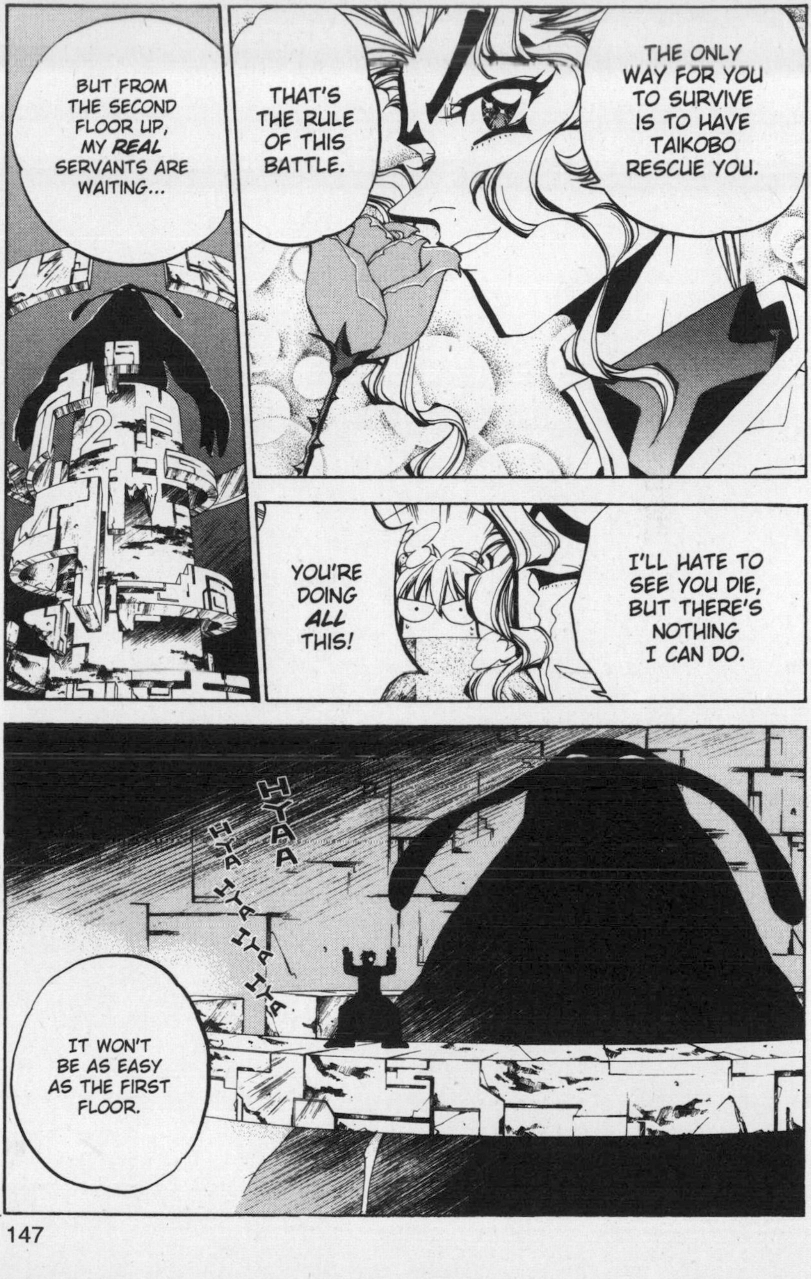

THE ONLY WAY FOR YOU TO SURVIVE IS TO HAVE TAIKOBO RESCUE YOU.
THAT'S THE RULE OF THIS BATTLE.
I'LL HATE TO SEE YOU DIE, BUT THERE'S NOTHING I CAN DO.
YOU'RE DOING *ALL* THIS!
BUT FROM THE SECOND FLOOR UP, MY *REAL* SERVANTS ARE WAITING...
2F
HYAA
HYA HYA HYA HYA
IT WON'T BE AS EASY AS THE FIRST FLOOR.

封神演義

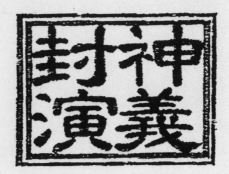

Chapter 87

CONQUERING CHOKOMEI, PART 3
KINGO'S PAOPE HUMAN

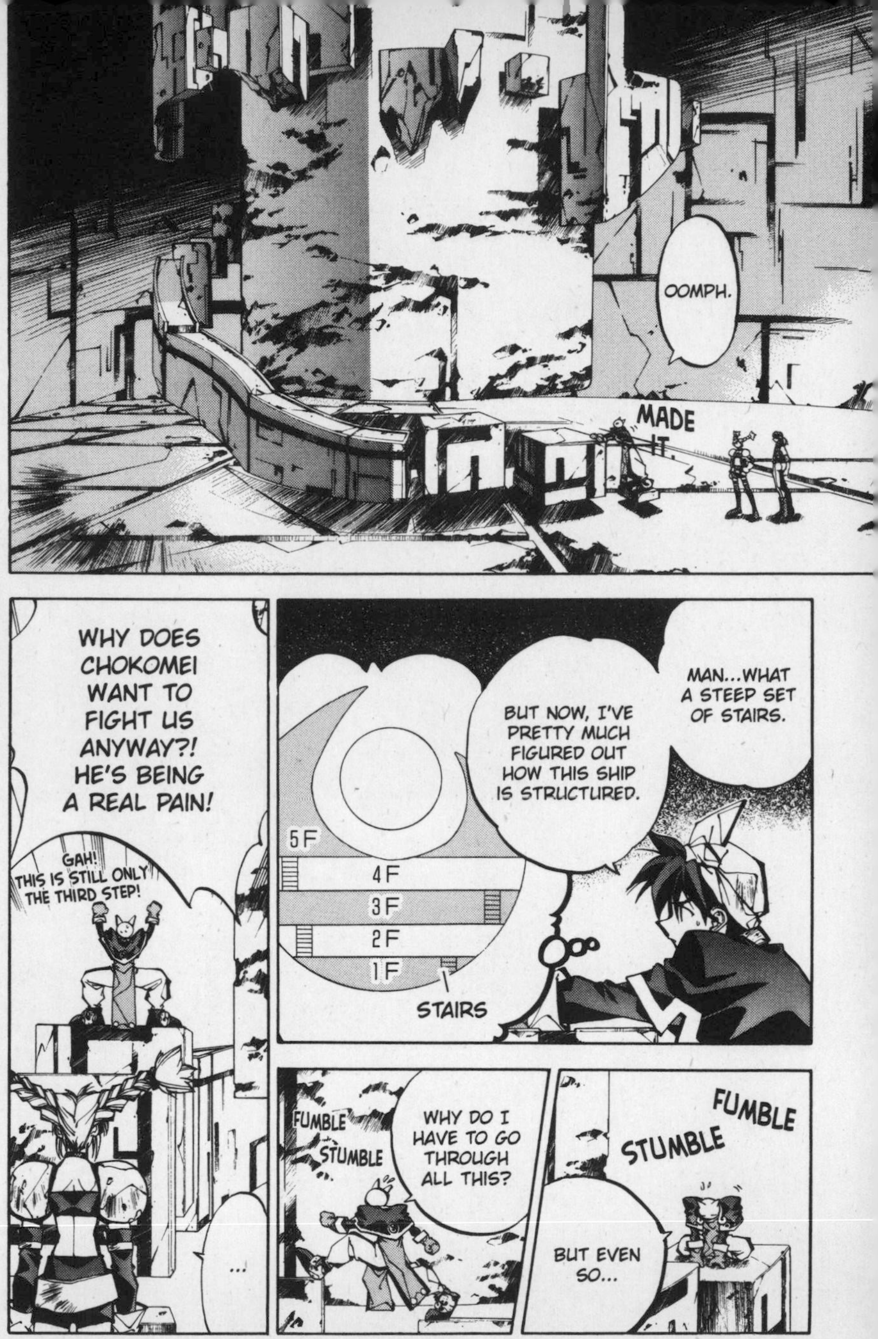
OOMPH.
MADE IT.
MAN...WHAT A STEEP SET OF STAIRS.
BUT NOW, I'VE PRETTY MUCH FIGURED OUT HOW THIS SHIP IS STRUCTURED.
5F
4F
3F
2F
1F
STAIRS
FUMBLE
STUMBLE
BUT EVEN SO...
FUMBLE
STUMBLE
WHY DO I HAVE TO GO THROUGH ALL THIS?
WHY DOES CHOKOMEI WANT TO FIGHT US ANYWAY?! HE'S BEING A REAL PAIN!
GAH! THIS IS STILL ONLY THE THIRD STEP!
...

READ THIS WAY

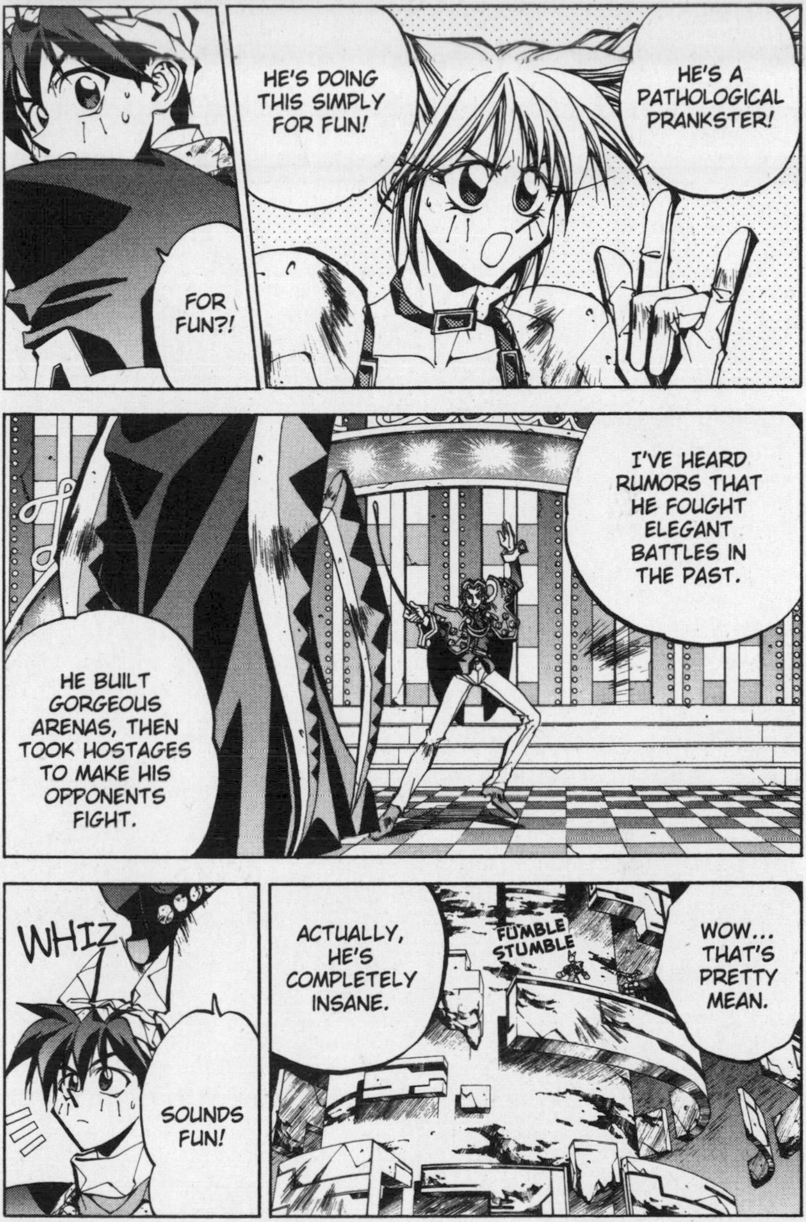

HE'S A PATHOLOGICAL PRANKSTER!
HE'S DOING THIS SIMPLY FOR FUN!
FOR FUN?!
I'VE HEARD RUMORS THAT HE FOUGHT ELEGANT BATTLES IN THE PAST.
HE BUILT GORGEOUS ARENAS, THEN TOOK HOSTAGES TO MAKE HIS OPPONENTS FIGHT.
WOW... THAT'S PRETTY MEAN.
FUMBLE STUMBLE
ACTUALLY, HE'S COMPLETELY INSANE.
WHIZ
SOUNDS FUN!

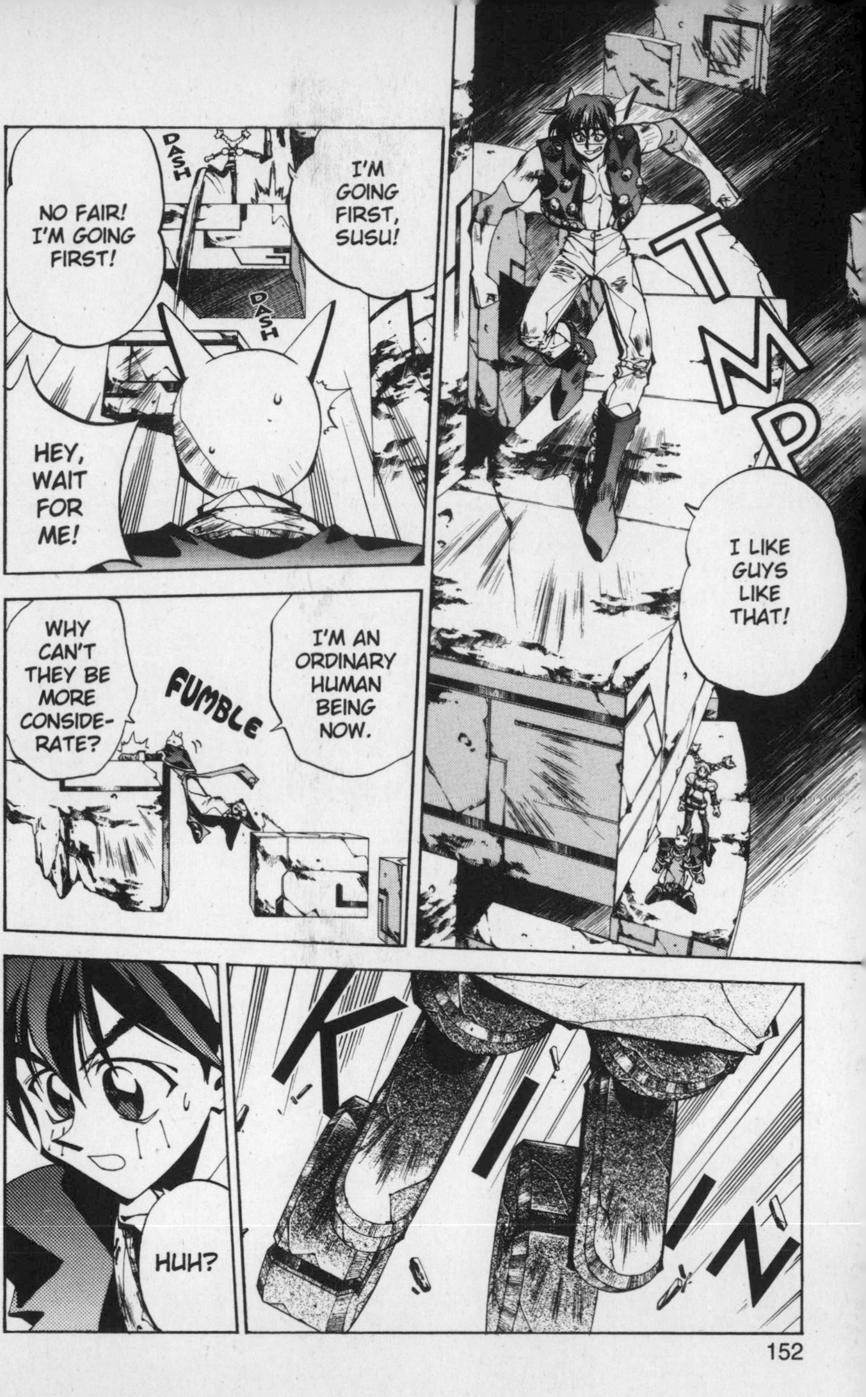
TMP
I LIKE GUYS LIKE THAT!
I'M GOING FIRST, SUSU!
DASH
NO FAIR! I'M GOING FIRST!
DASH
HEY, WAIT FOR ME!
I'M AN ORDINARY HUMAN BEING NOW.
FUMBLE
WHY CAN'T THEY BE MORE CONSIDE-RATE?
KIIIN
HUH?

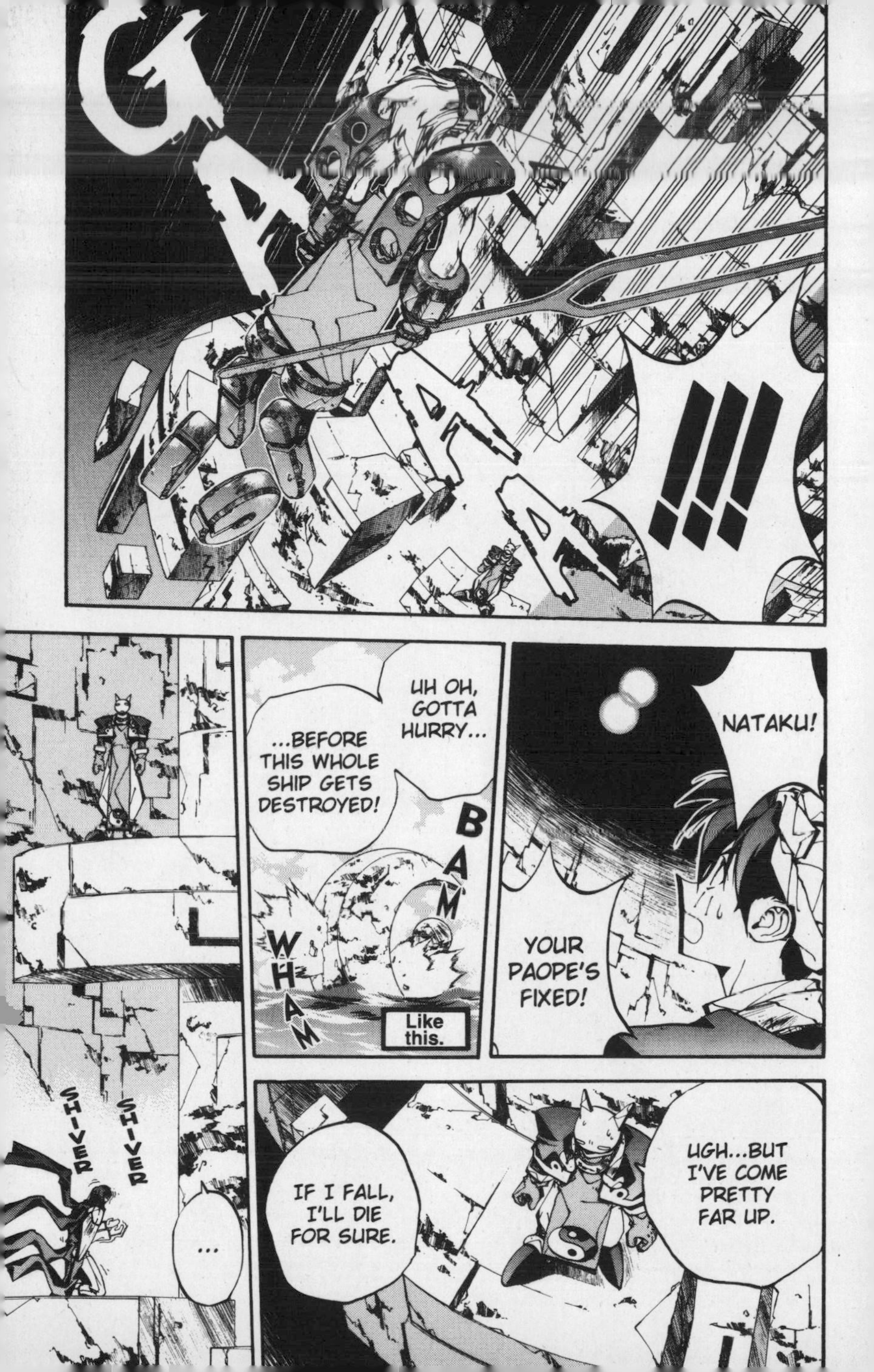
GAAA!!!!
NATAKU!
YOUR PAOPE'S FIXED!
UH OH, GOTTA HURRY...
...BEFORE THIS WHOLE SHIP GETS DESTROYED!
BAM
WHAM
Like this.
UGH...BUT I'VE COME PRETTY FAR UP.
IF I FALL, I'LL DIE FOR SURE.
SHIVER
SHIVER
...

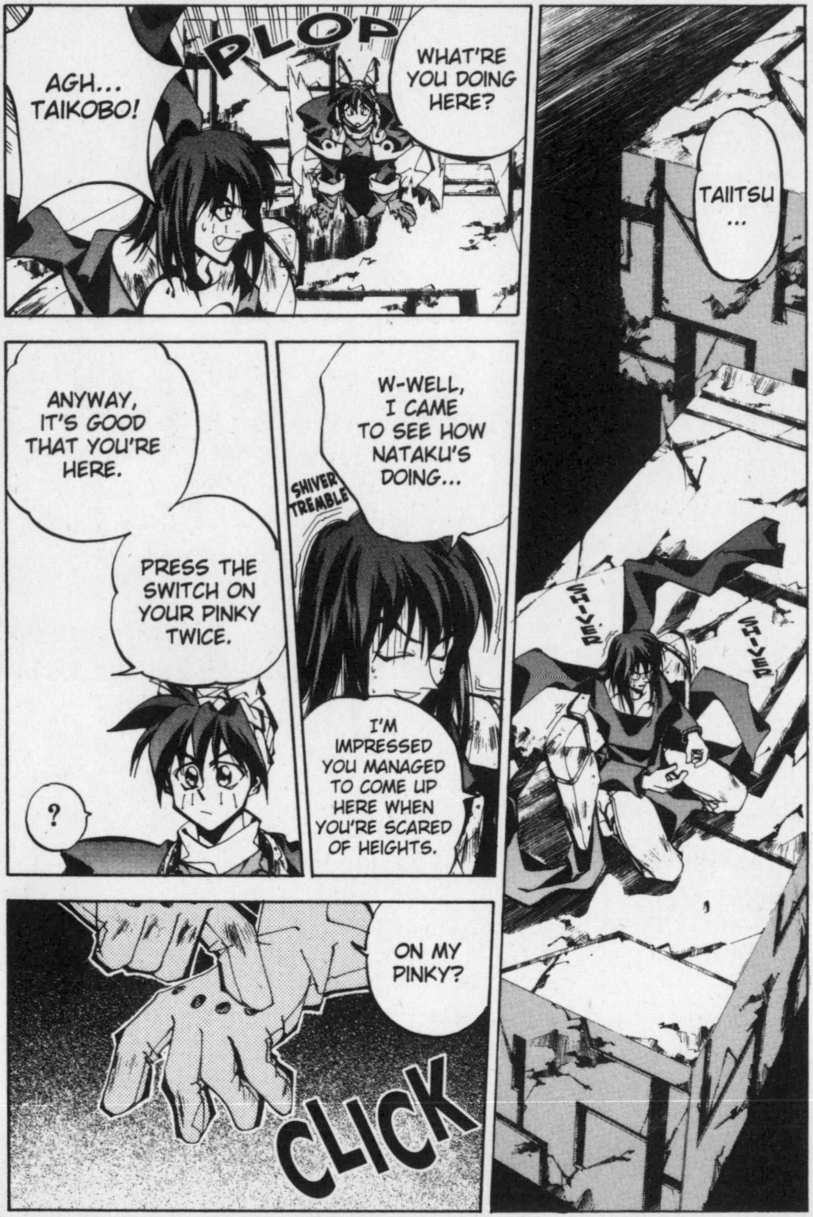
TAIITSU ...
SHIVER
SHIVER
WHAT'RE YOU DOING HERE?
PLOP
AGH... TAIKOBO!
W-WELL, I CAME TO SEE HOW NATAKU'S DOING...
SHIVER TREMBLE
I'M IMPRESSED YOU MANAGED TO COME UP HERE WHEN YOU'RE SCARED OF HEIGHTS.
ANYWAY, IT'S GOOD THAT YOU'RE HERE.
PRESS THE SWITCH ON YOUR PINKY TWICE.
?
ON MY PINKY?
CLICK

READ THIS WAY

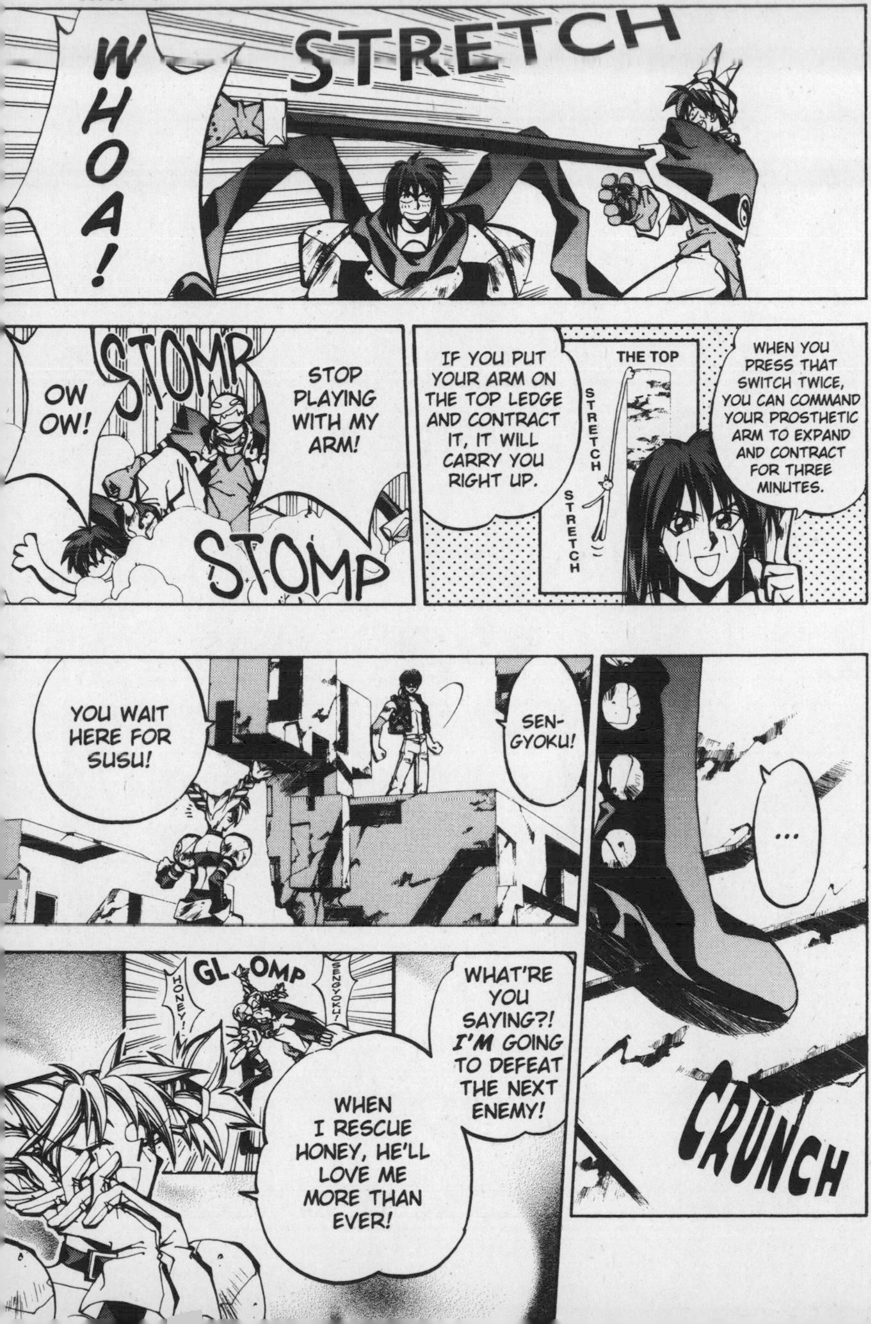

STRETCH
WHOA!
WHEN YOU PRESS THAT SWITCH TWICE, YOU CAN COMMAND YOUR PROSTHETIC ARM TO EXPAND AND CONTRACT FOR THREE MINUTES.
THE TOP
STRETCH
STRETCH
IF YOU PUT YOUR ARM ON THE TOP LEDGE AND CONTRACT IT, IT WILL CARRY YOU RIGHT UP.
STOP PLAYING WITH MY ARM!
STOMP
OW OW!
STOMP
...
CRUNCH
SEN-GYOKU!
YOU WAIT HERE FOR SUSU!
WHAT'RE YOU SAYING?! *I'M* GOING TO DEFEAT THE NEXT ENEMY!
SENGYOKU!
GLOMP
HONEY!
WHEN I RESCUE HONEY, HE'LL LOVE ME MORE THAN EVER!

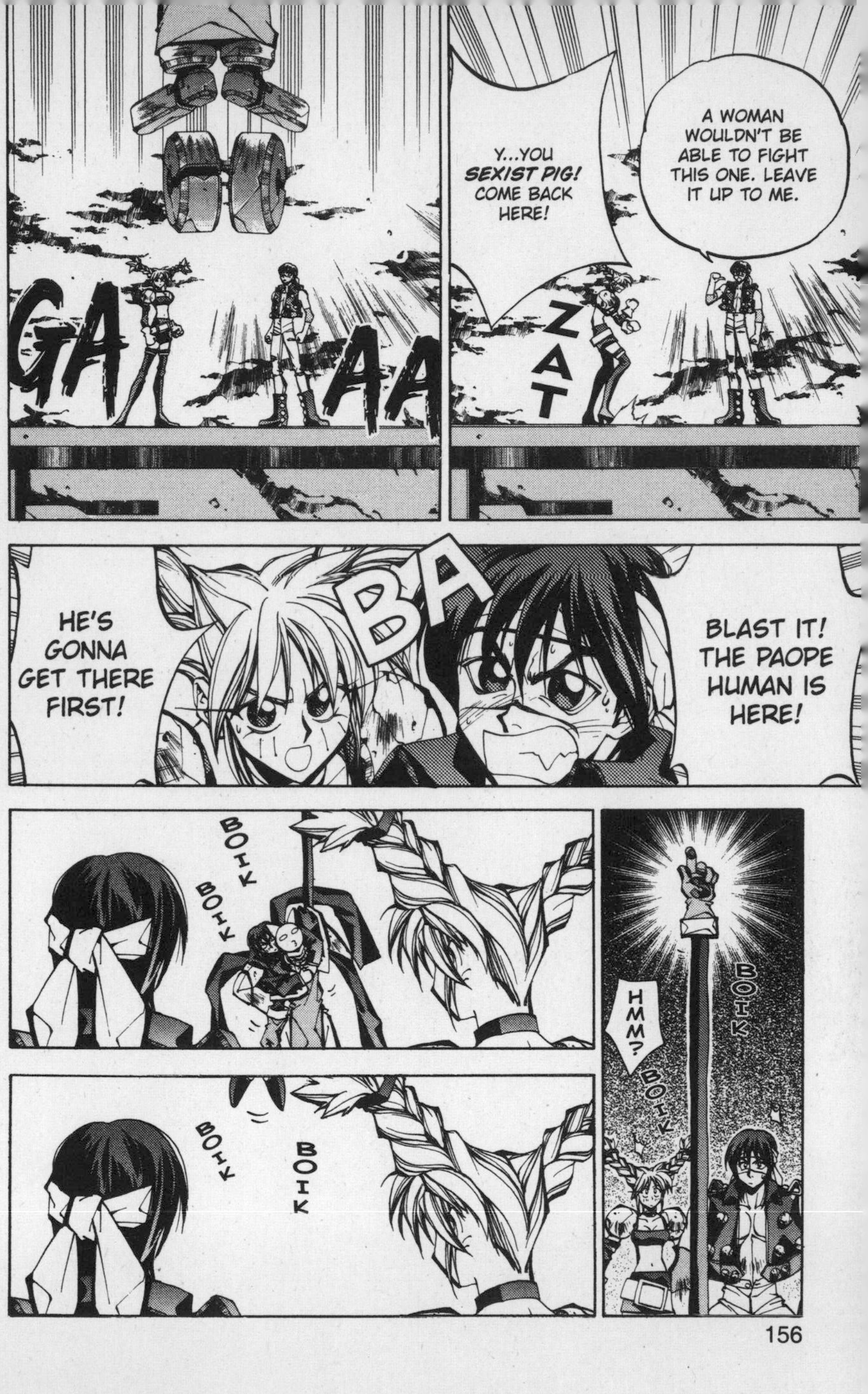
A WOMAN WOULDN'T BE ABLE TO FIGHT THIS ONE. LEAVE IT UP TO ME.
Y...YOU *SEXIST PIG!* COME BACK HERE!
ZAT
GA
AA
BLAST IT! THE PAOPE HUMAN IS HERE!
BA
HE'S GONNA GET THERE FIRST!
BOIK
HMM?
BOIK
BOIK
BOIK
BOIK
BOIK

READ THIS WAY

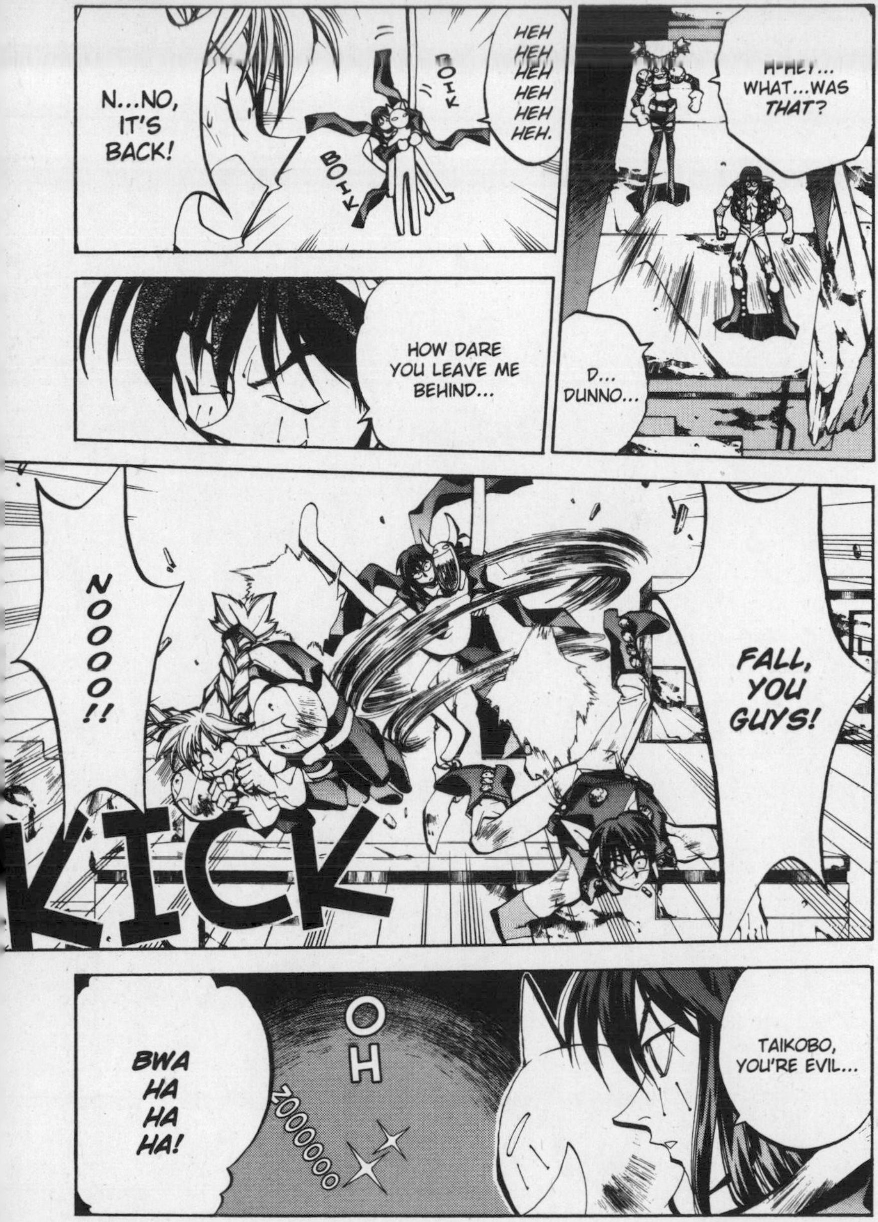
H-HEY... WHAT...WAS THAT?
D... DUNNO...
HEH HEH HEH HEH HEH HEH.
BOIK
BOIK
N...NO, IT'S BACK!
HOW DARE YOU LEAVE ME BEHIND...
FALL, YOU GUYS!
KICK
NOOOOO!!
TAIKOBO, YOU'RE EVIL...
OH
ZOOOOOO
BWA HA HA HA!

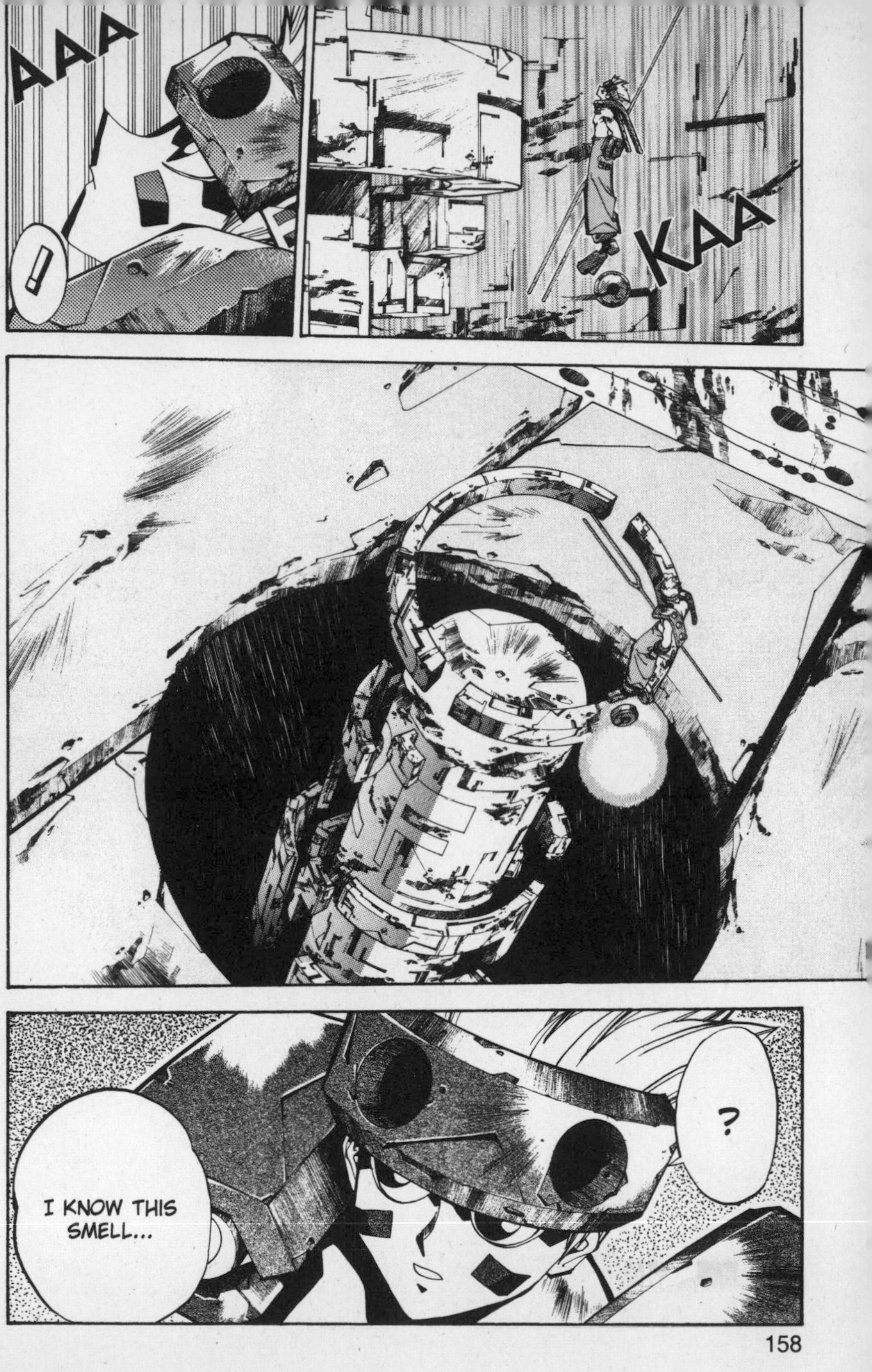
KAA
AAA
!
?
I KNOW THIS SMELL...

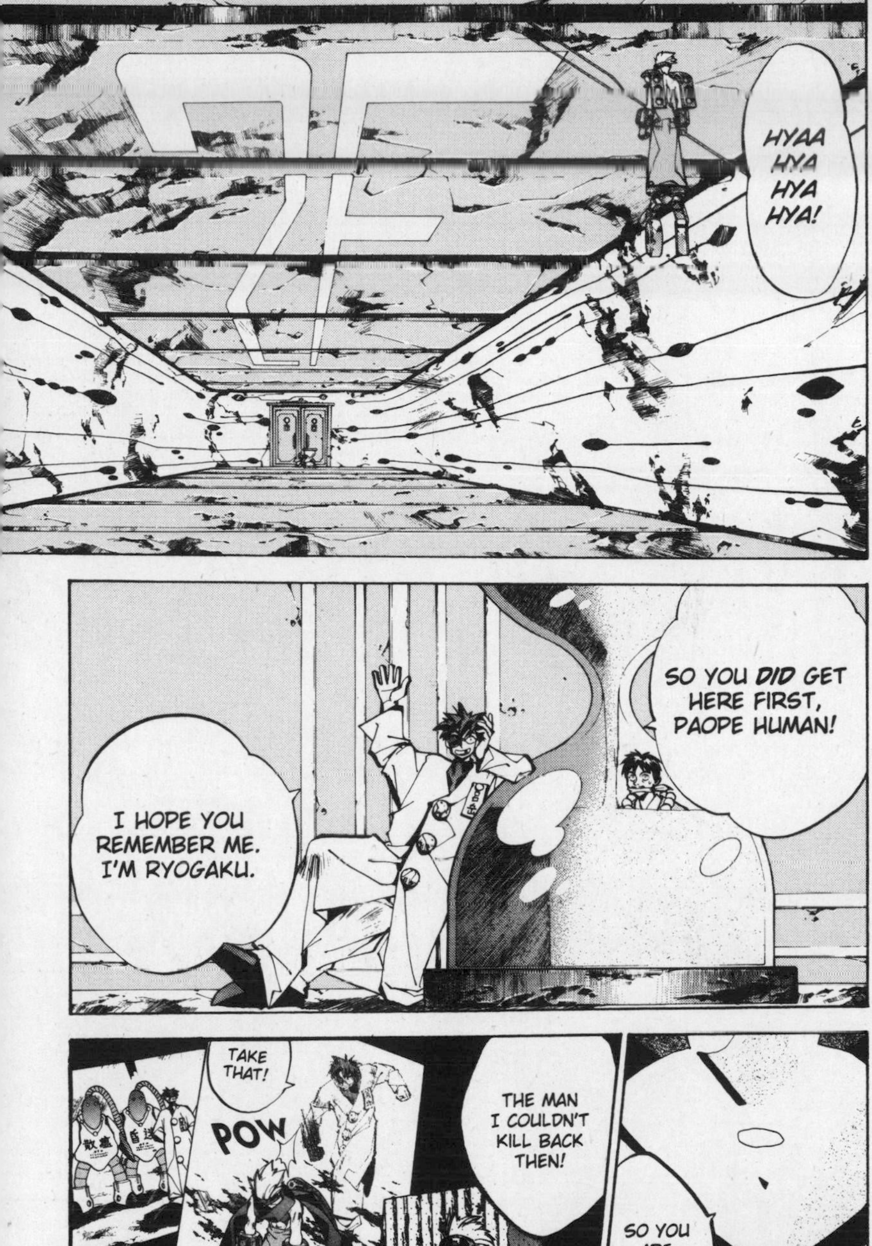
HYAA HYA HYA HYA!
SO YOU *DID* GET HERE FIRST, PAOPE HUMAN!
I HOPE YOU REMEMBER ME. I'M RYOGAKU.
SO YOU ARE ALIVE...
THE MAN I COULDN'T KILL BACK THEN!
TAKE THAT!
POW

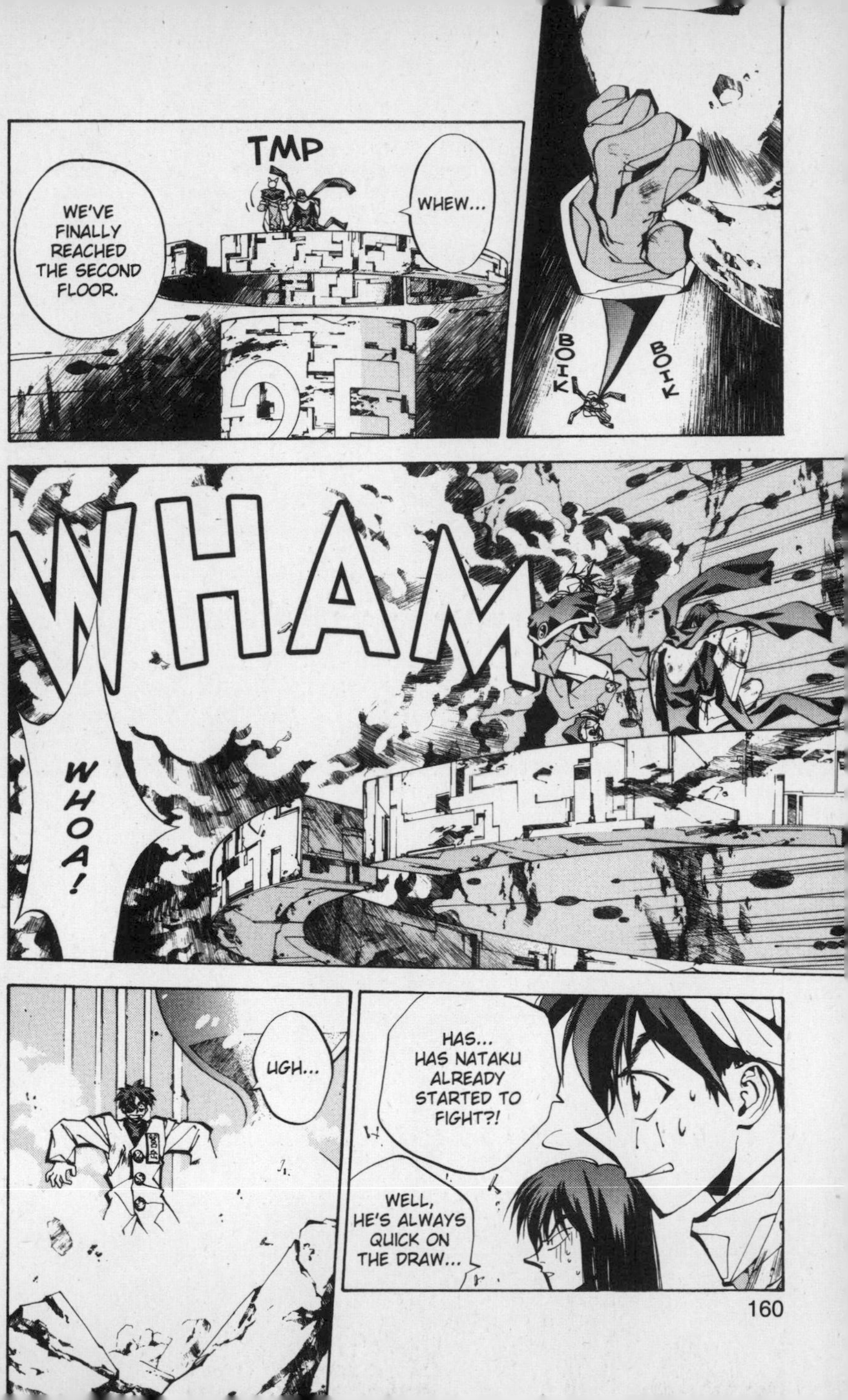
BOIK
BOIK
WHEW...
TMP
WE'VE FINALLY REACHED THE SECOND FLOOR.
WHAM
WHOA!
HAS... HAS NATAKU ALREADY STARTED TO FIGHT?!
WELL, HE'S ALWAYS QUICK ON THE DRAW...
UGH...

READ THIS WAY

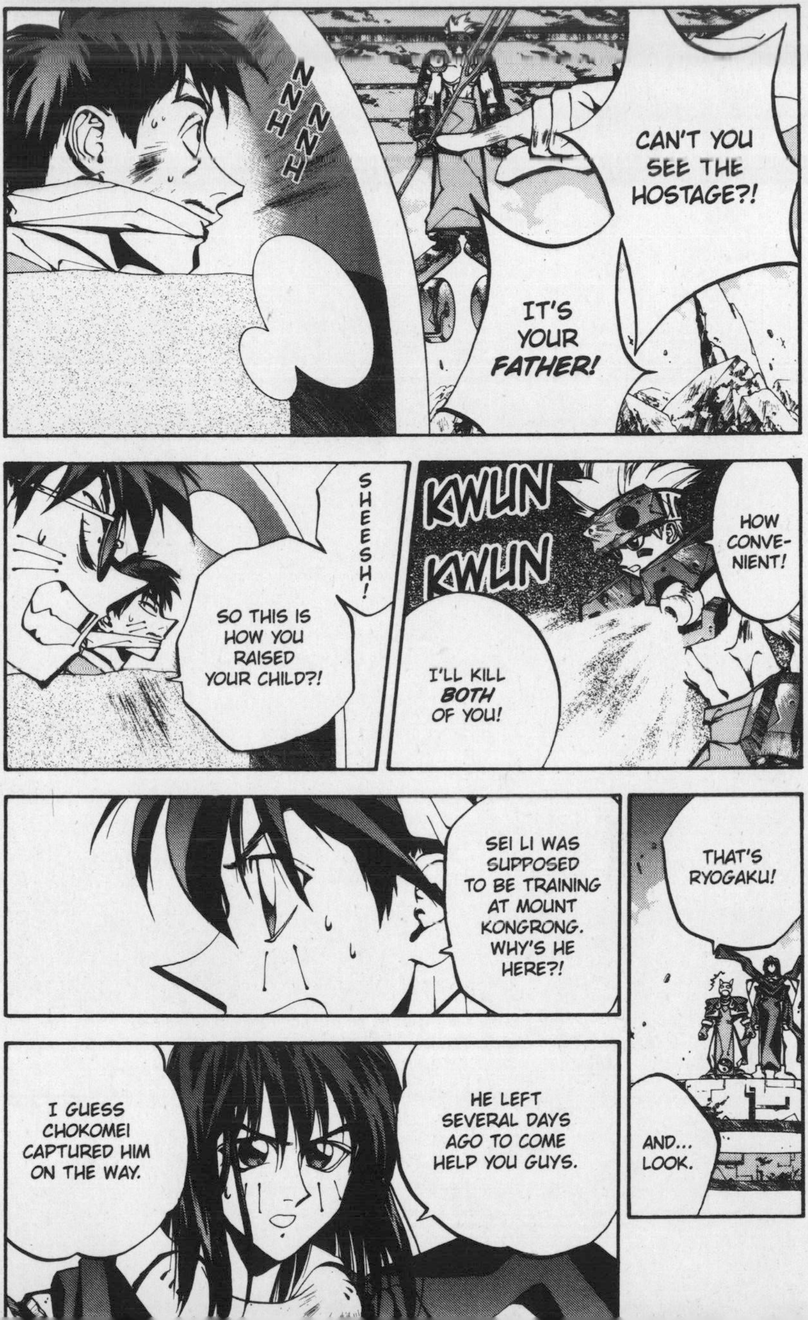

CAN'T YOU SEE THE HOSTAGE?!
IT'S YOUR *FATHER!*
NNNH NNNH
HOW CONVE-NIENT!
KWUN KWUN
I'LL KILL *BOTH* OF YOU!
SHEESH!
SO THIS IS HOW YOU RAISED YOUR CHILD?!
THAT'S RYOGAKU!
AND... LOOK.
SEI LI WAS SUPPOSED TO BE TRAINING AT MOUNT KONGRONG. WHY'S HE HERE?!
HE LEFT SEVERAL DAYS AGO TO COME HELP YOU GUYS.
I GUESS CHOKOMEI CAPTURED HIM ON THE WAY.

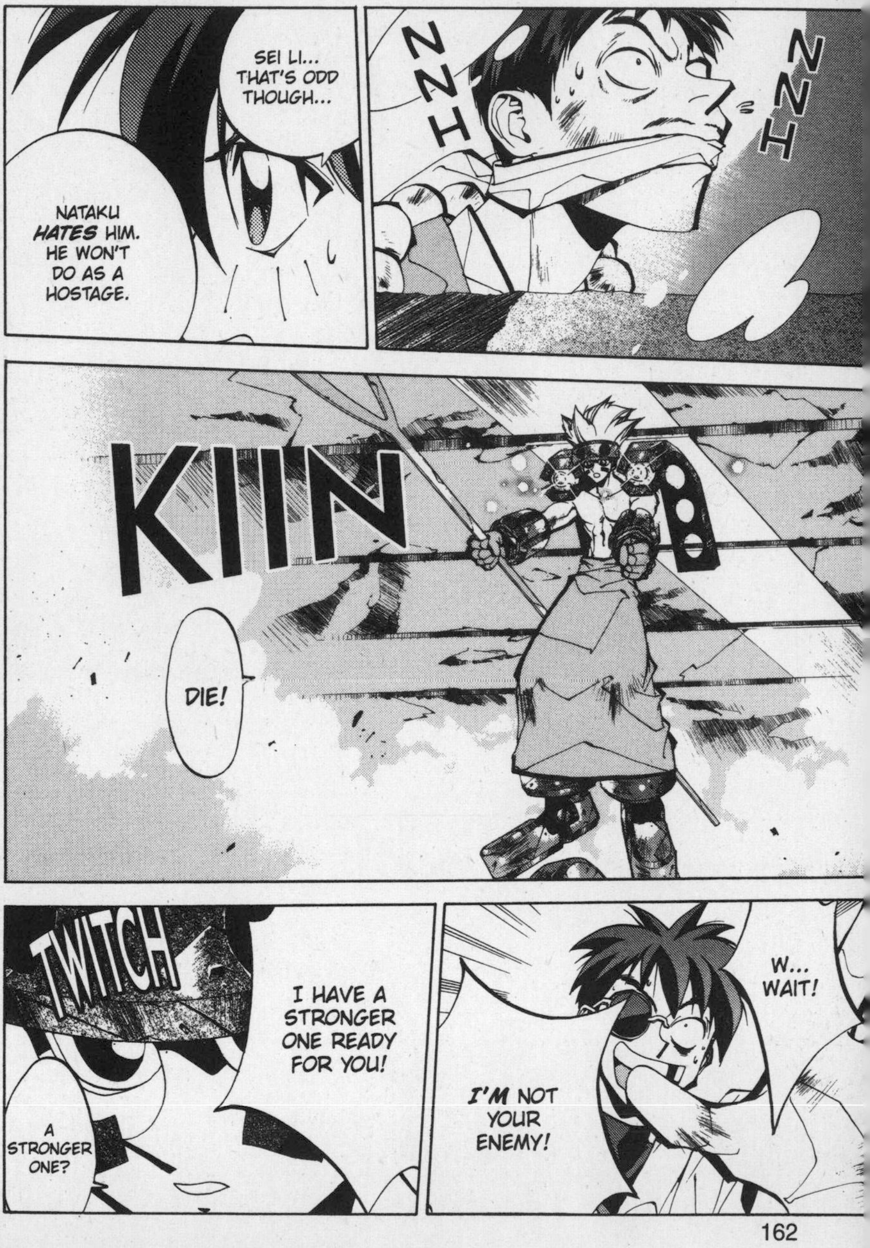
SEI LI... THAT'S ODD THOUGH...
NATAKU HATES HIM. HE WON'T DO AS A HOSTAGE.
KIIN
DIE!
W... WAIT!
I'M NOT YOUR ENEMY!
TWITCH
I HAVE A STRONGER ONE READY FOR YOU!
A STRONGER ONE?

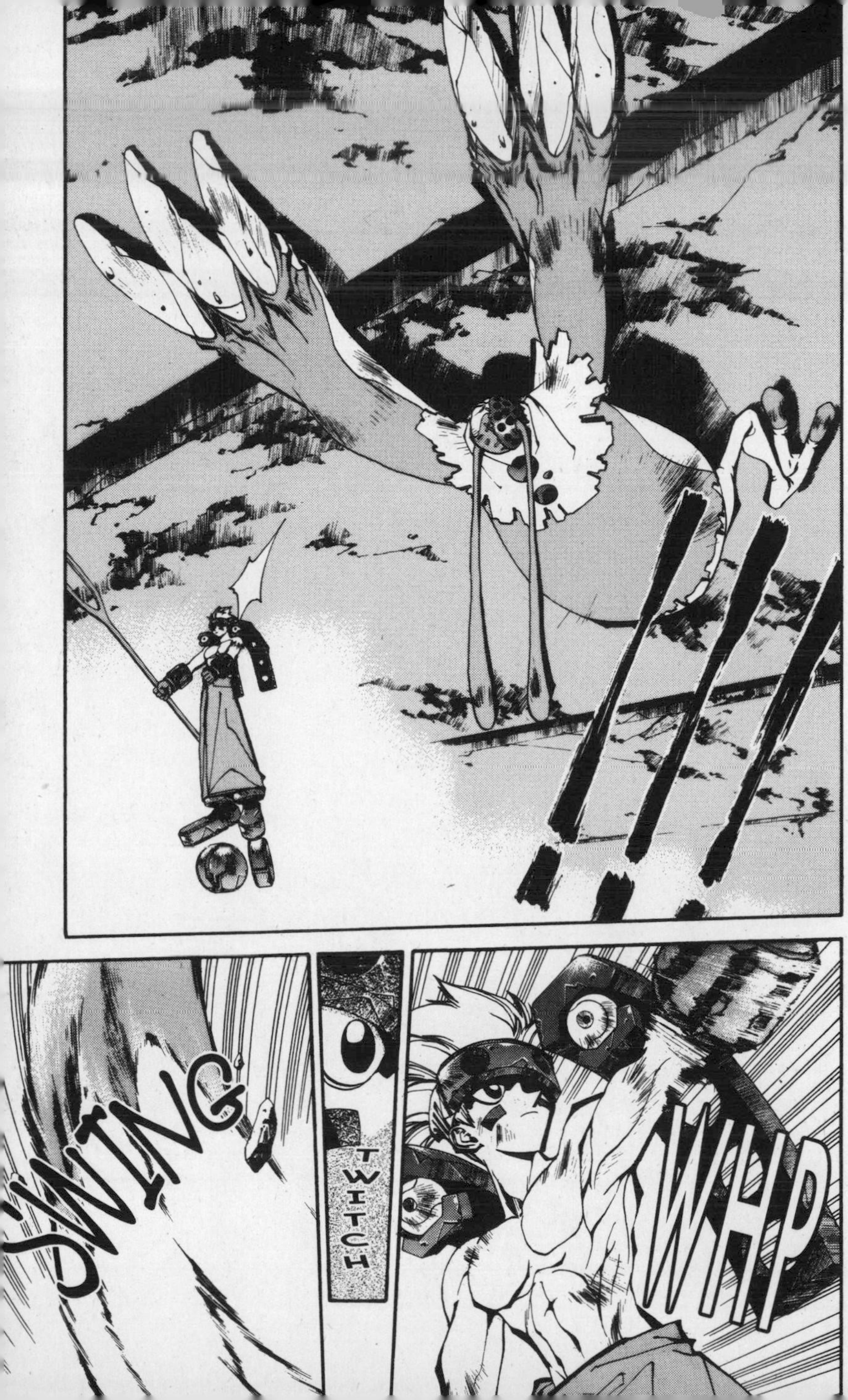
WHP
TWITCH
SWING

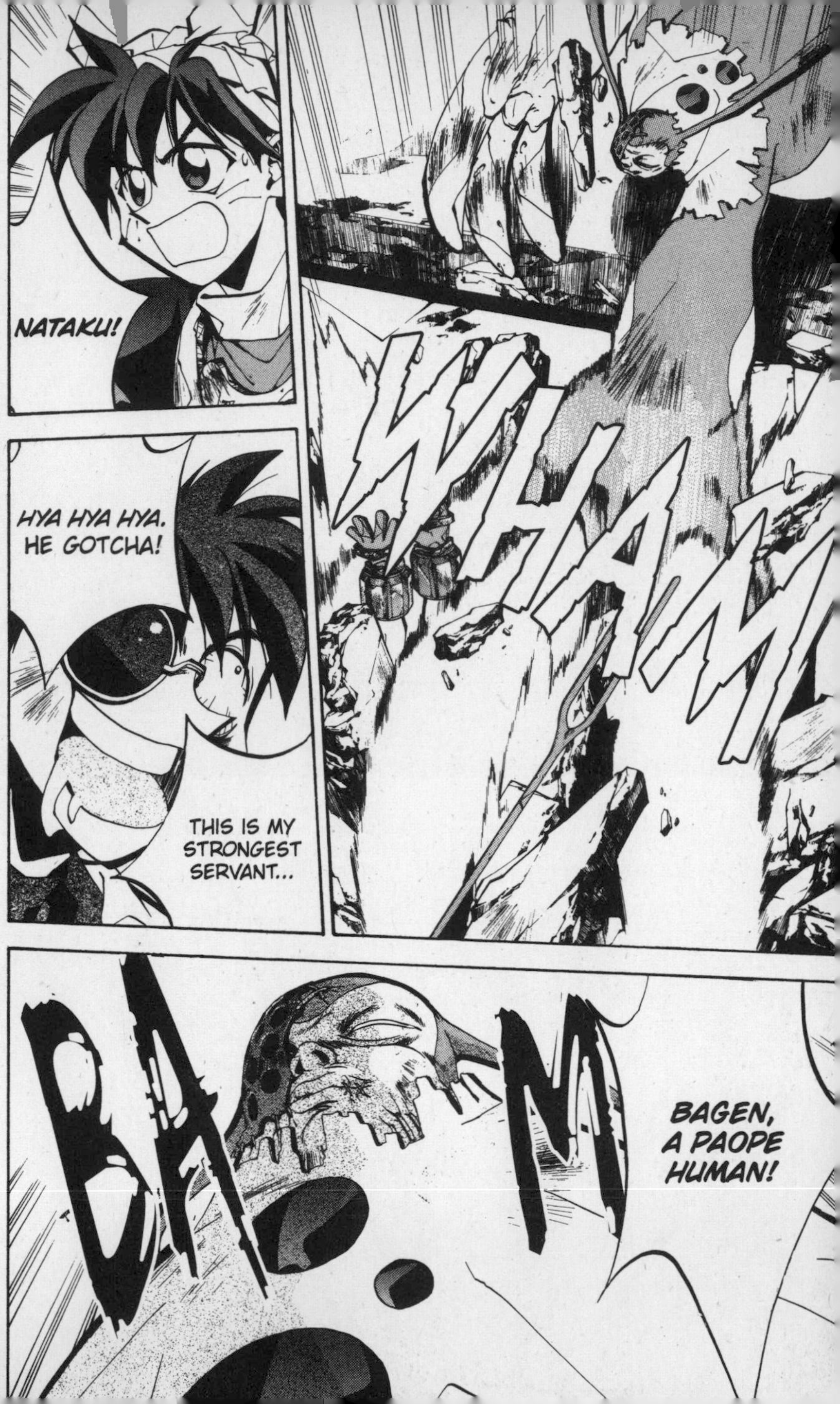
WHAM
NATAKU!
HYA HYA HYA.
HE GOTCHA!
THIS IS MY
STRONGEST
SERVANT...
BAM
BAGEN,
A PAOPE
HUMAN!

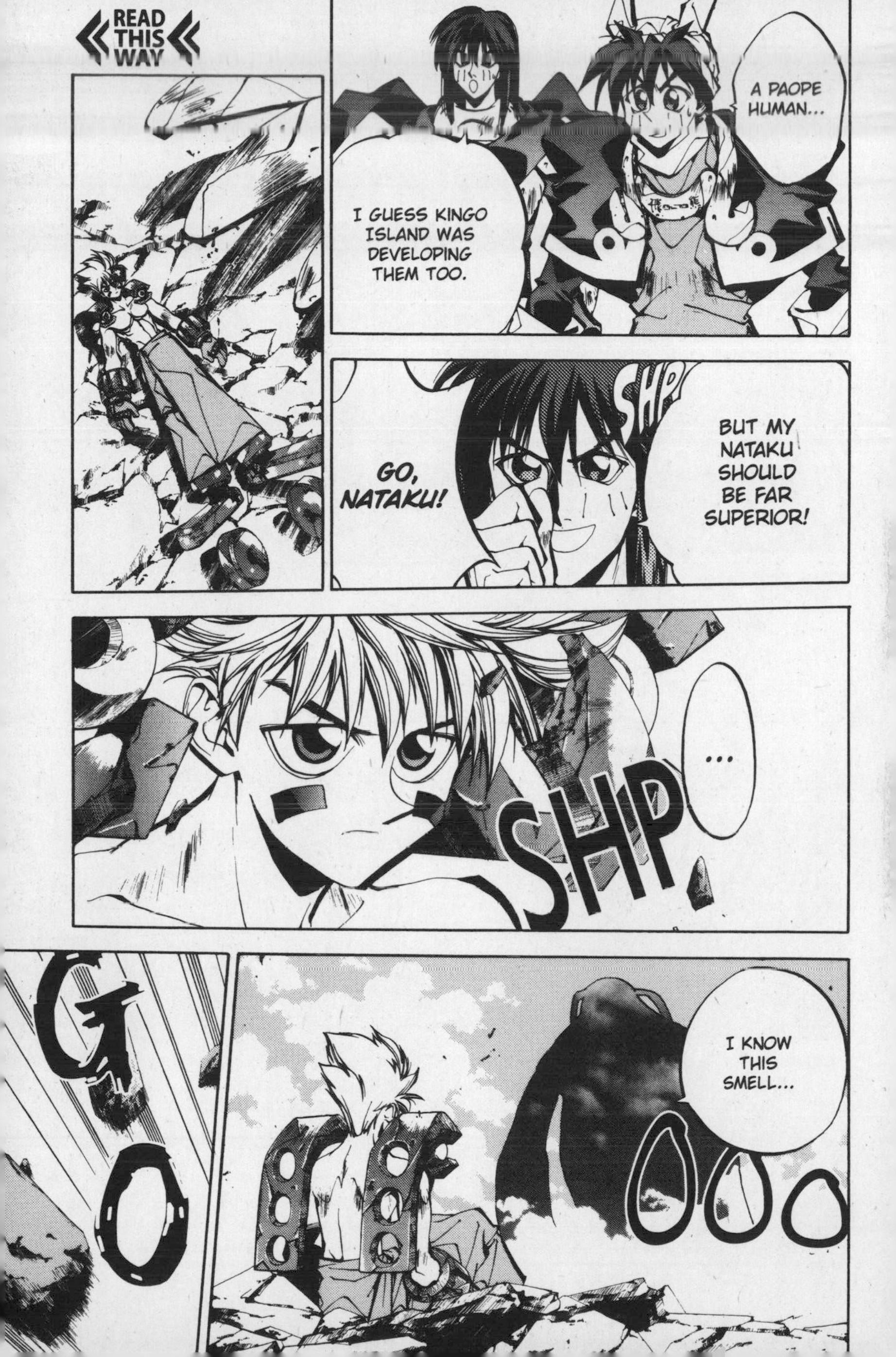
READ THIS WAY
A PAOPE HUMAN...
I GUESS KINGO ISLAND WAS DEVELOPING THEM TOO.
BUT MY NATAKU SHOULD BE FAR SUPERIOR!
SHP
GO, NATAKU!
...
SHP
I KNOW THIS SMELL...
OOOO
GO

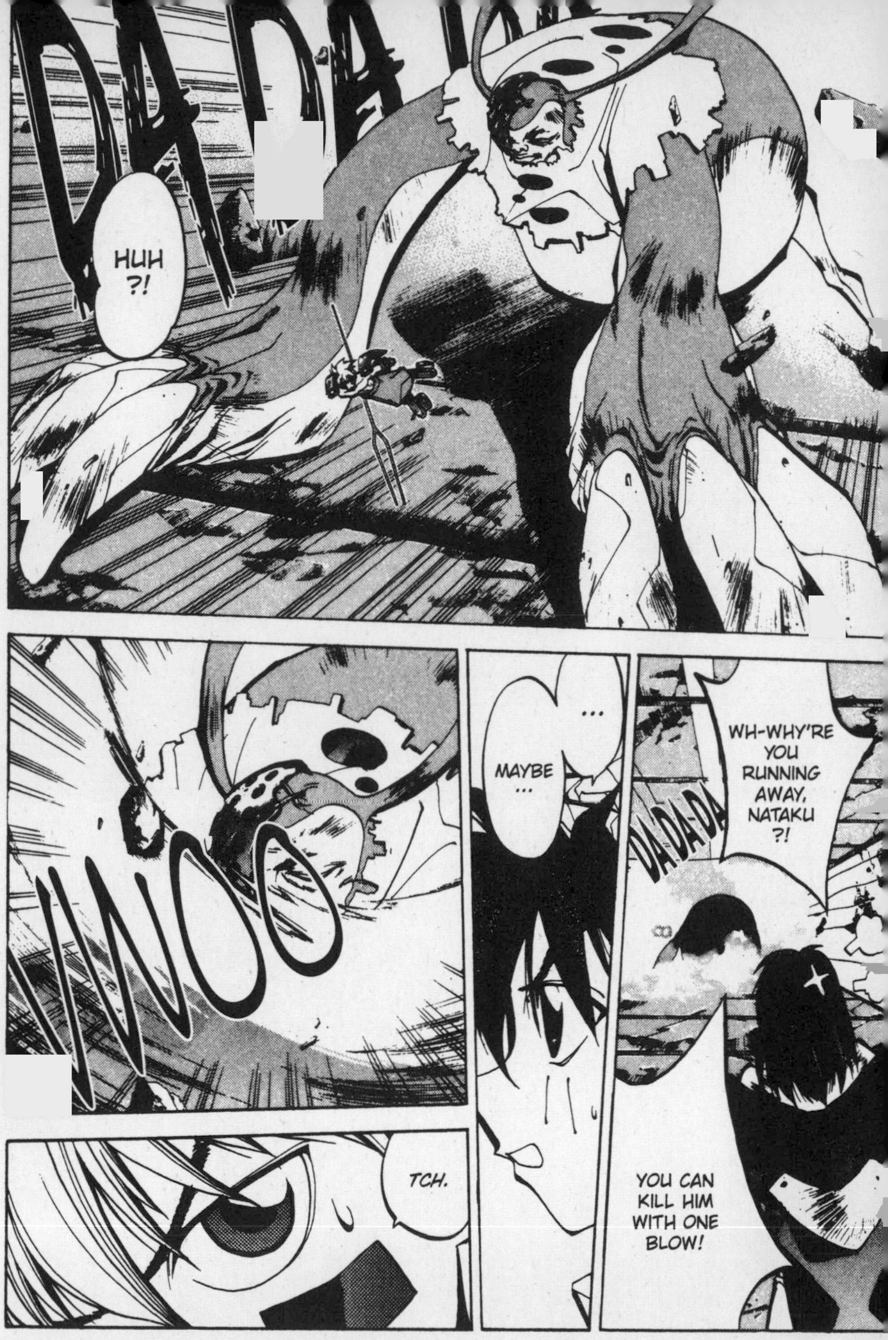
DA DA
HUH ?!
WH-WHY'RE YOU RUNNING AWAY, NATAKU ?!
DA DA DA
YOU CAN KILL HIM WITH ONE BLOW!
...
MAYBE ...
WOO
TCH.

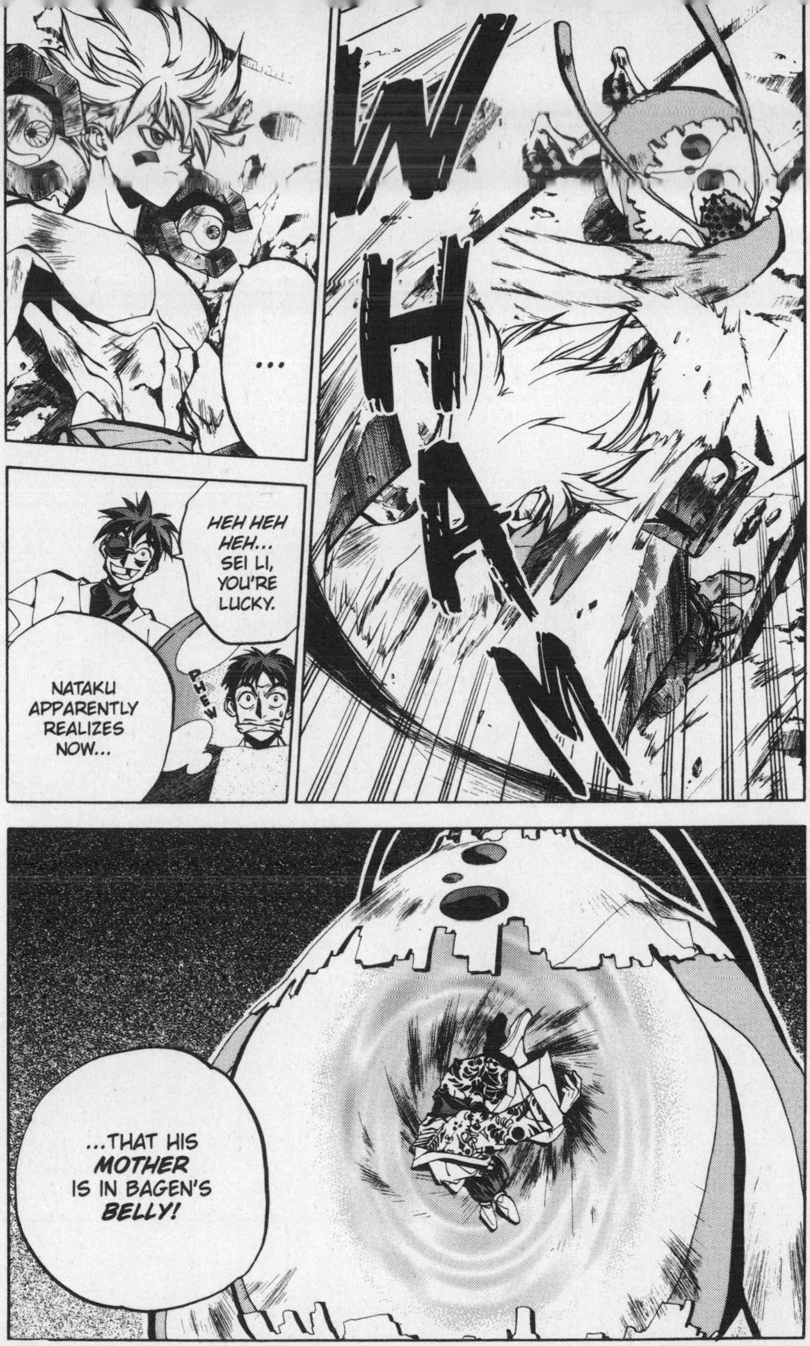
WHAM
...
HEH HEH HEH... SEI LI, YOU'RE LUCKY.
PHEW
NATAKU APPARENTLY REALIZES NOW...
...THAT HIS *MOTHER* IS IN BAGEN'S *BELLY!*

封神演義

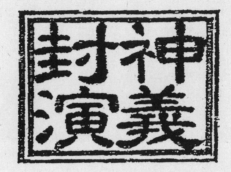

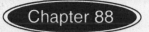

Chapter 88

CONQUERING CHOKOMEI, PART 4
PROOF OF HUMANITY, PART 1

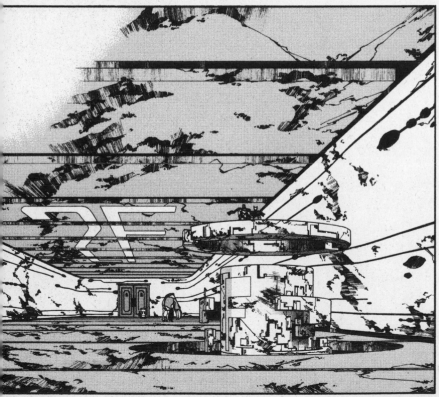

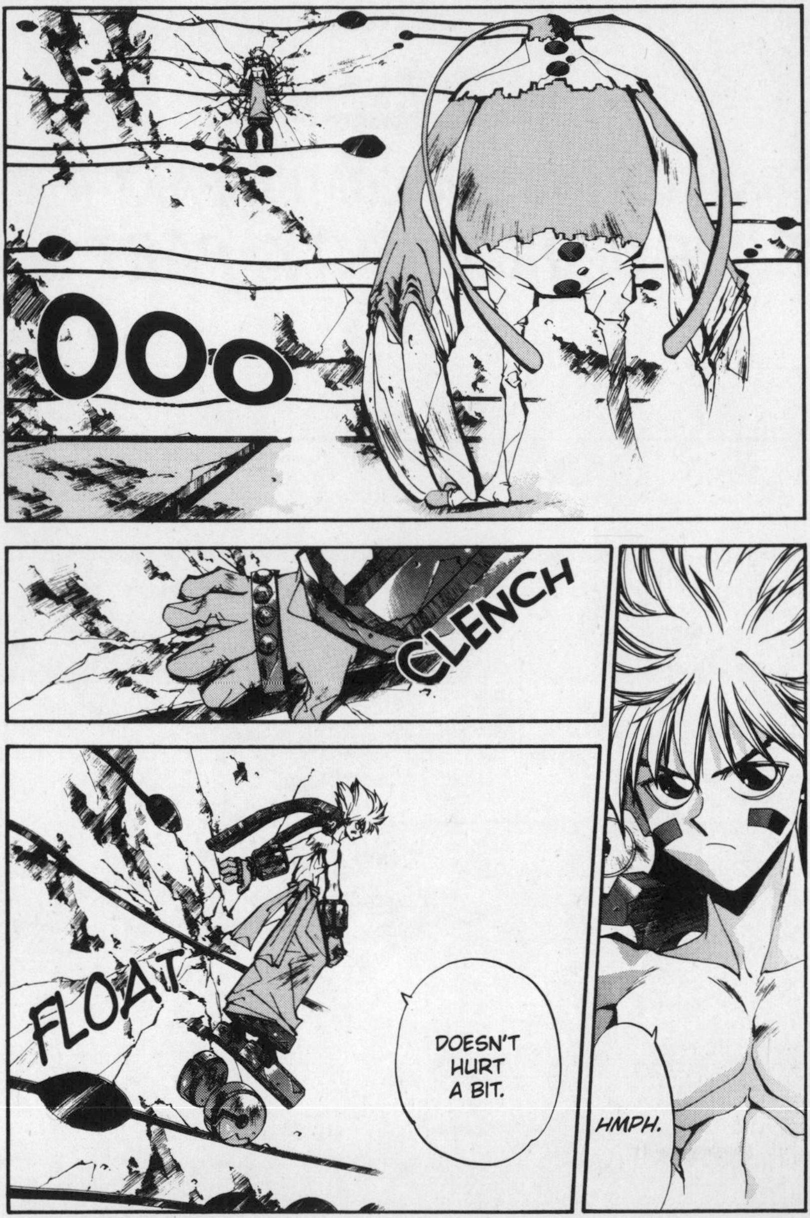
OOO
HMPH.
CLENCH
DOESN'T HURT A BIT.
FLOAT

READ THIS WAY

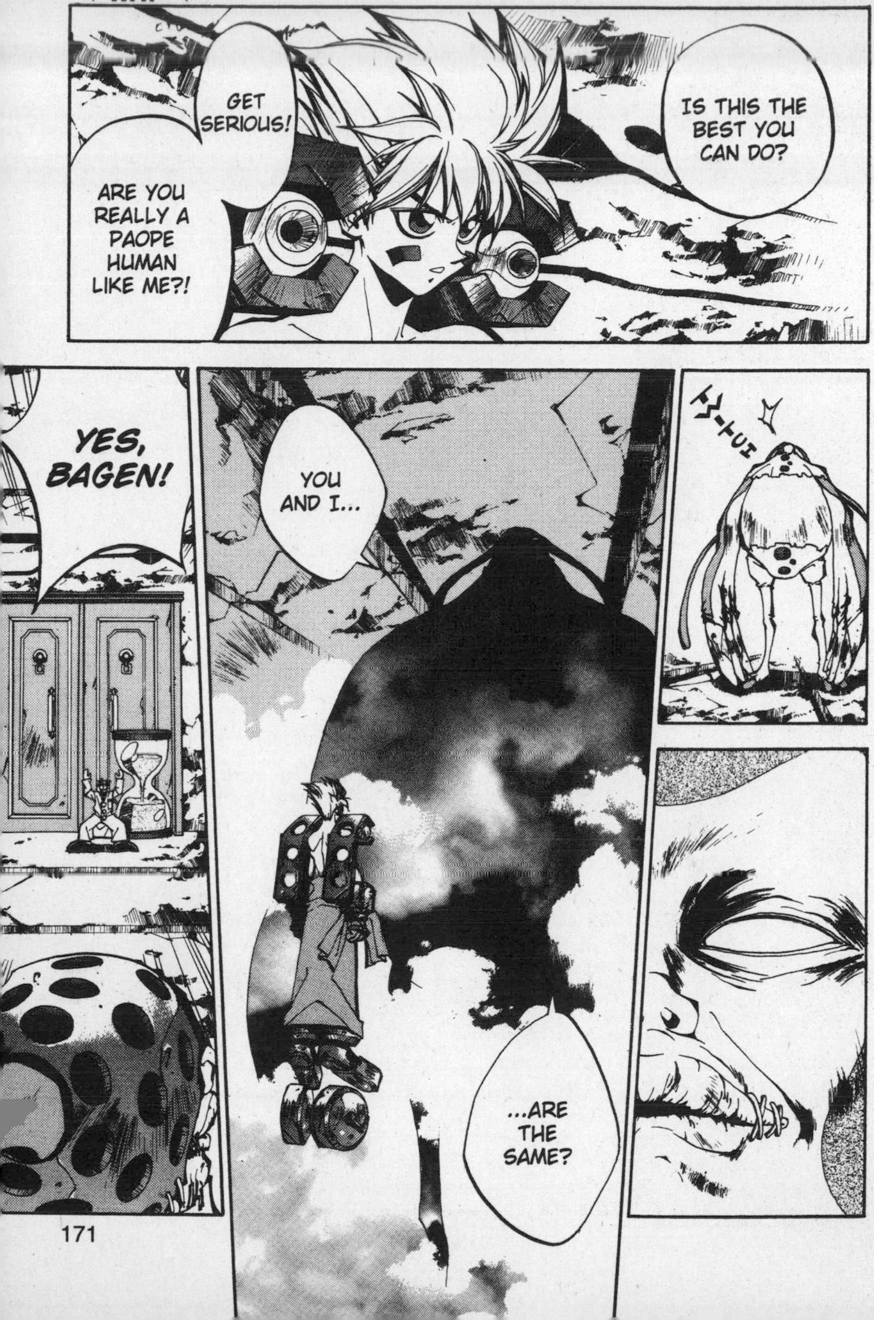

IS THIS THE BEST YOU CAN DO?
GET SERIOUS!
ARE YOU REALLY A PAOPE HUMAN LIKE ME?!
YOU AND I...
...ARE THE SAME?
YES, BAGEN!

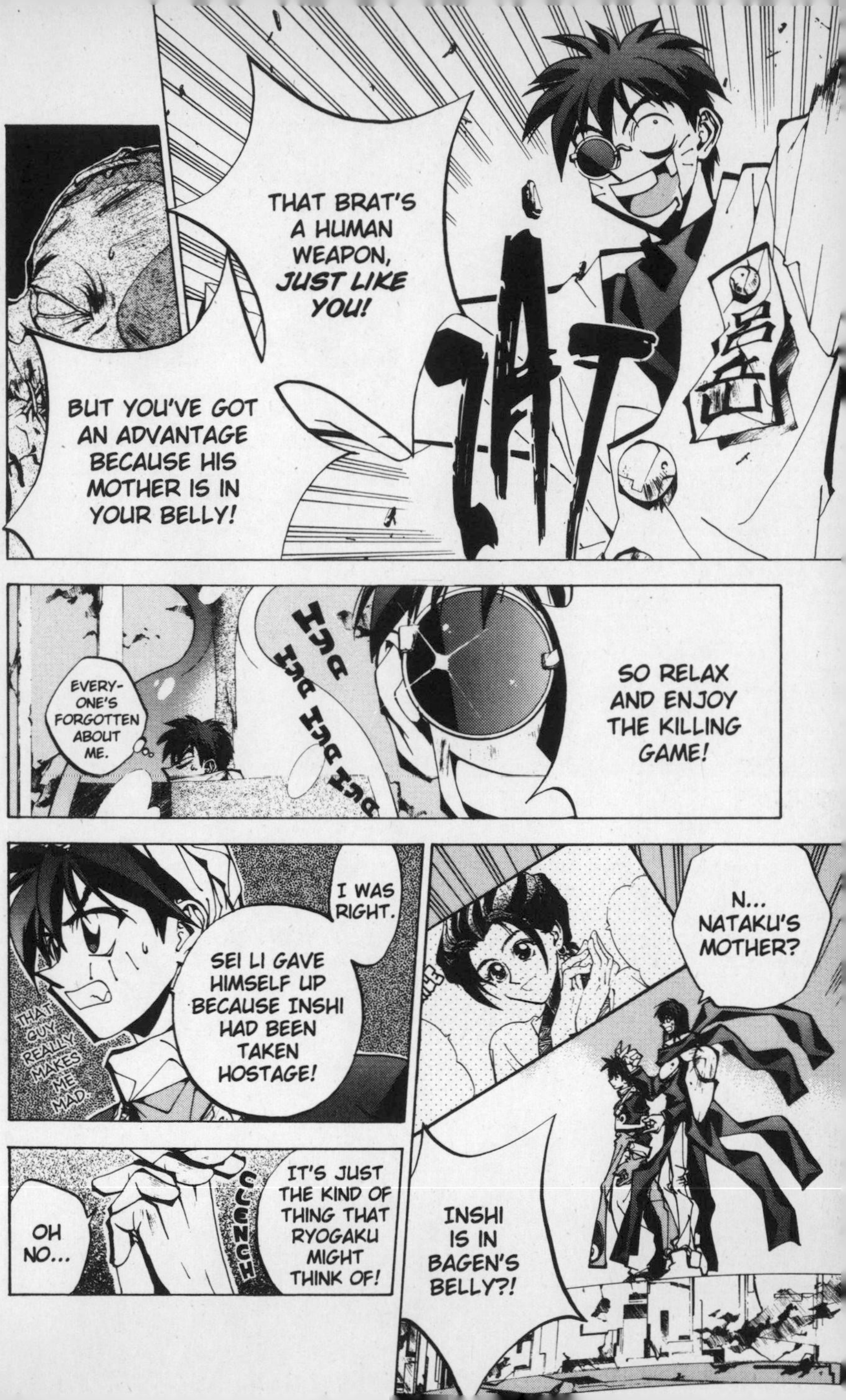
THAT BRAT'S A HUMAN WEAPON, JUST LIKE YOU!
BUT YOU'VE GOT AN ADVANTAGE BECAUSE HIS MOTHER IS IN YOUR BELLY!
SO RELAX AND ENJOY THE KILLING GAME!
HYA HYA HYA HYA
EVERY-ONE'S FORGOTTEN ABOUT ME.
N... NATAKU'S MOTHER?
INSHI IS IN BAGEN'S BELLY?!
I WAS RIGHT.
SEI LI GAVE HIMSELF UP BECAUSE INSHI HAD BEEN TAKEN HOSTAGE!
THAT GUY REALLY MAKES ME MAD.
IT'S JUST THE KIND OF THING THAT RYOGAKU MIGHT THINK OF!
CLENCH
OH NO...

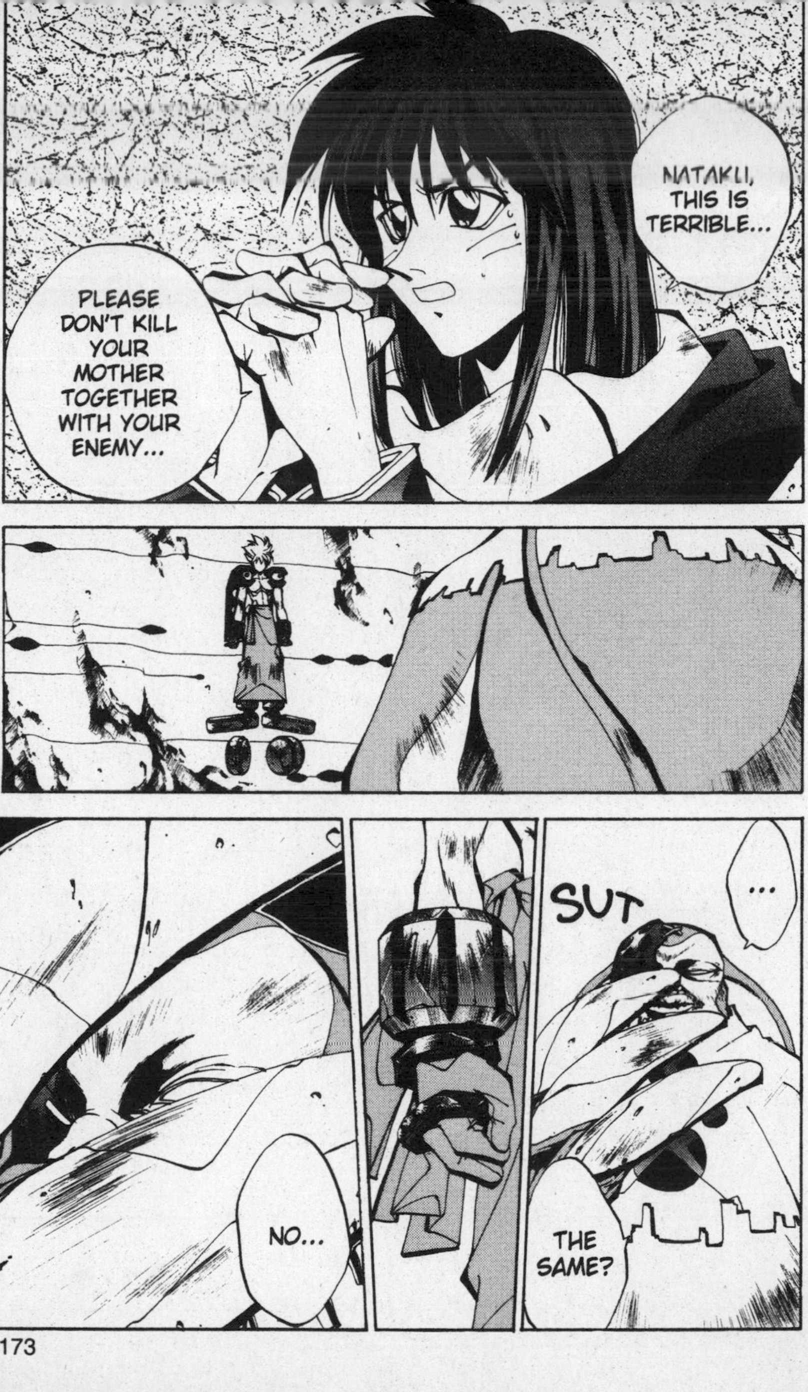
NATAKU, THIS IS TERRIBLE...
PLEASE DON'T KILL YOUR MOTHER TOGETHER WITH YOUR ENEMY...
...
SUT
THE SAME?
NO...

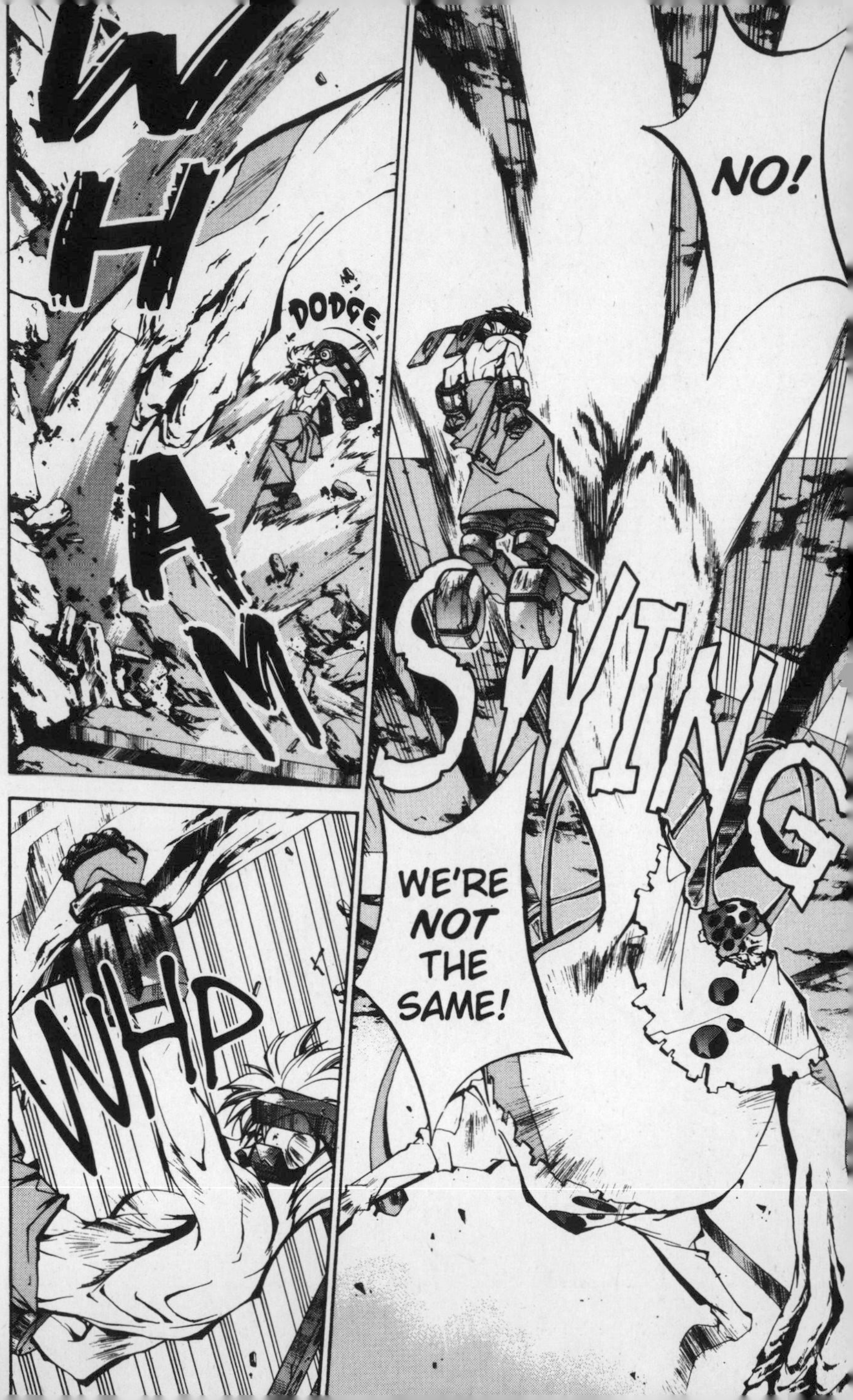
NO!
SWING
WE'RE *NOT* THE SAME!
WHAM
DODGE
WHP

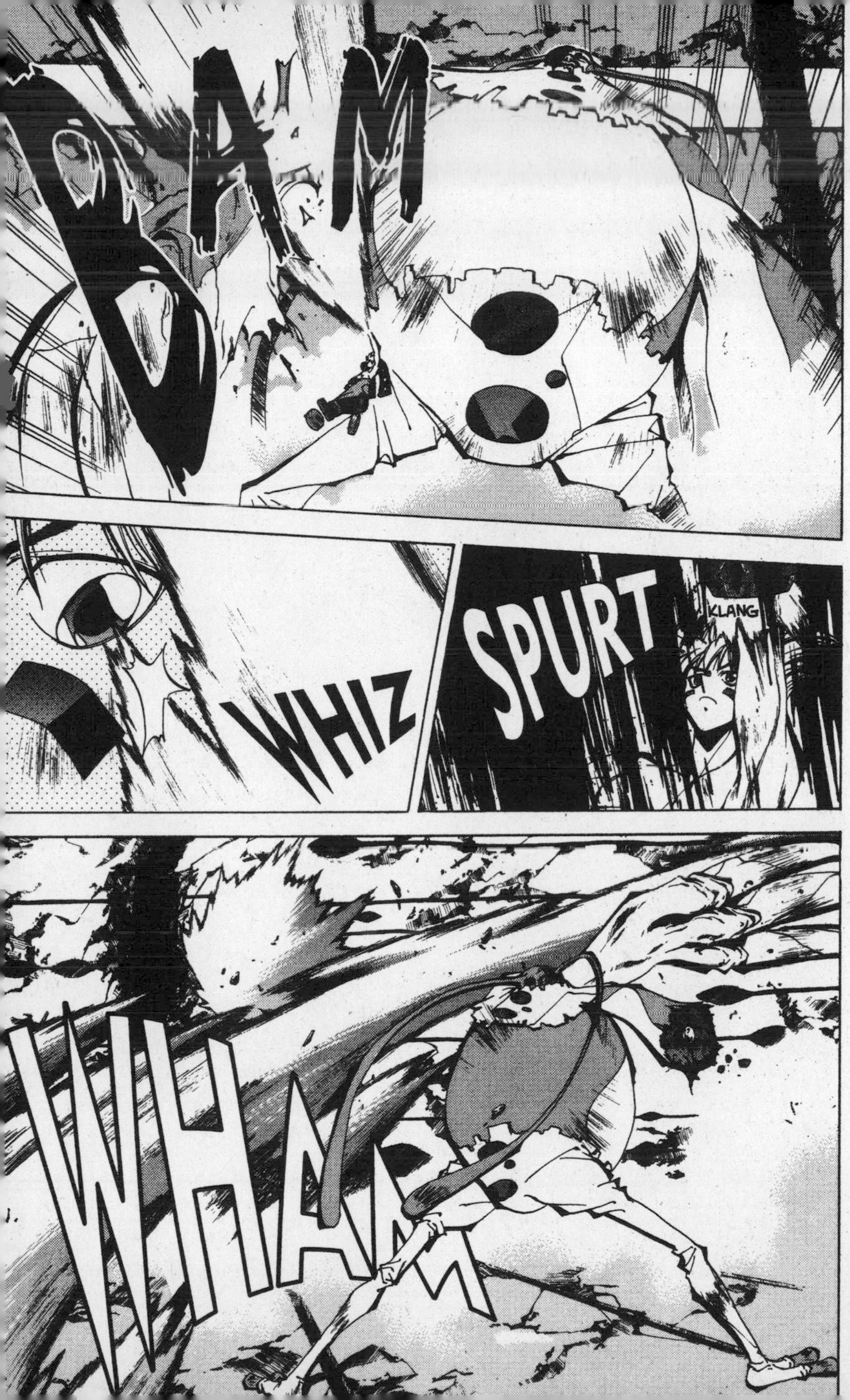
BAM
KLANG
SPURT
WHIZ
WHAM

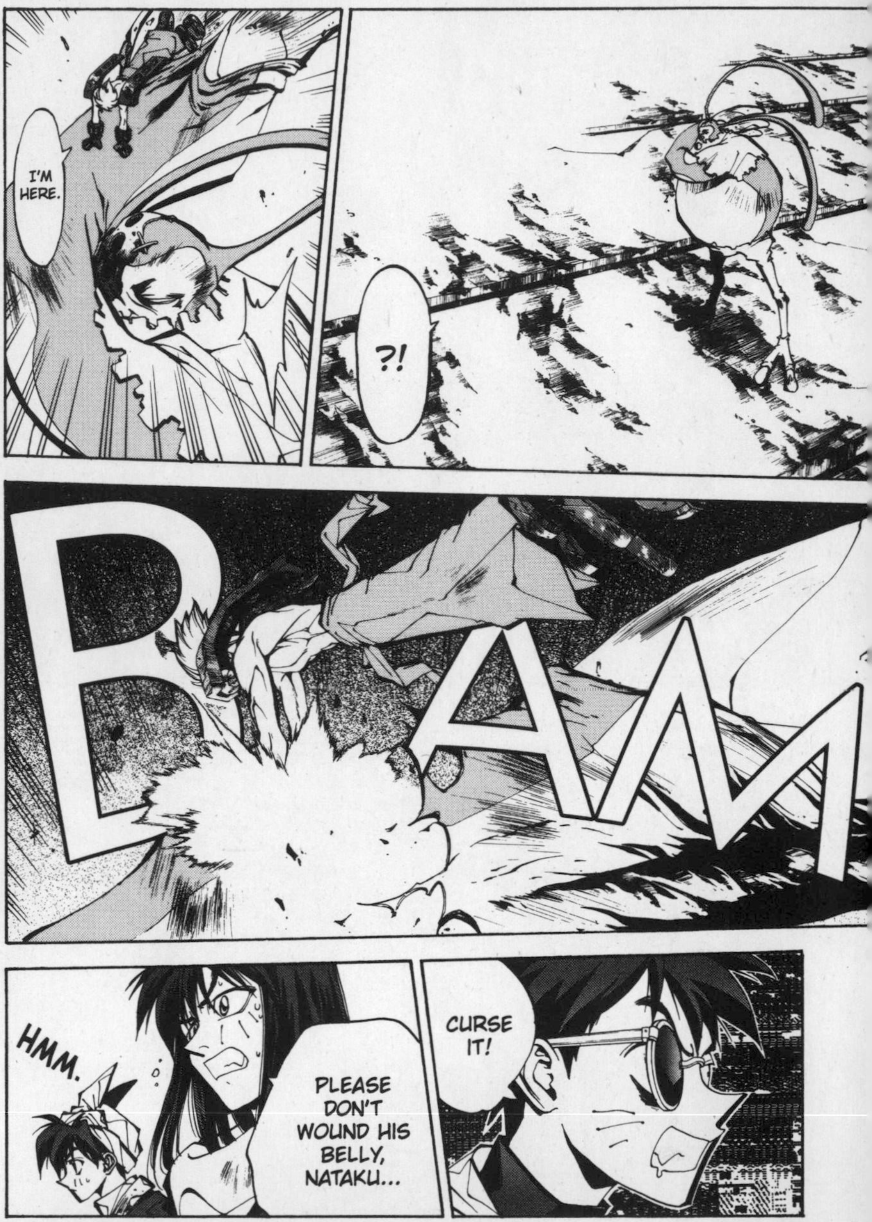
?!
I'M HERE.
BAM
CURSE IT!
PLEASE DON'T WOUND HIS BELLY, NATAKU...
HMM.

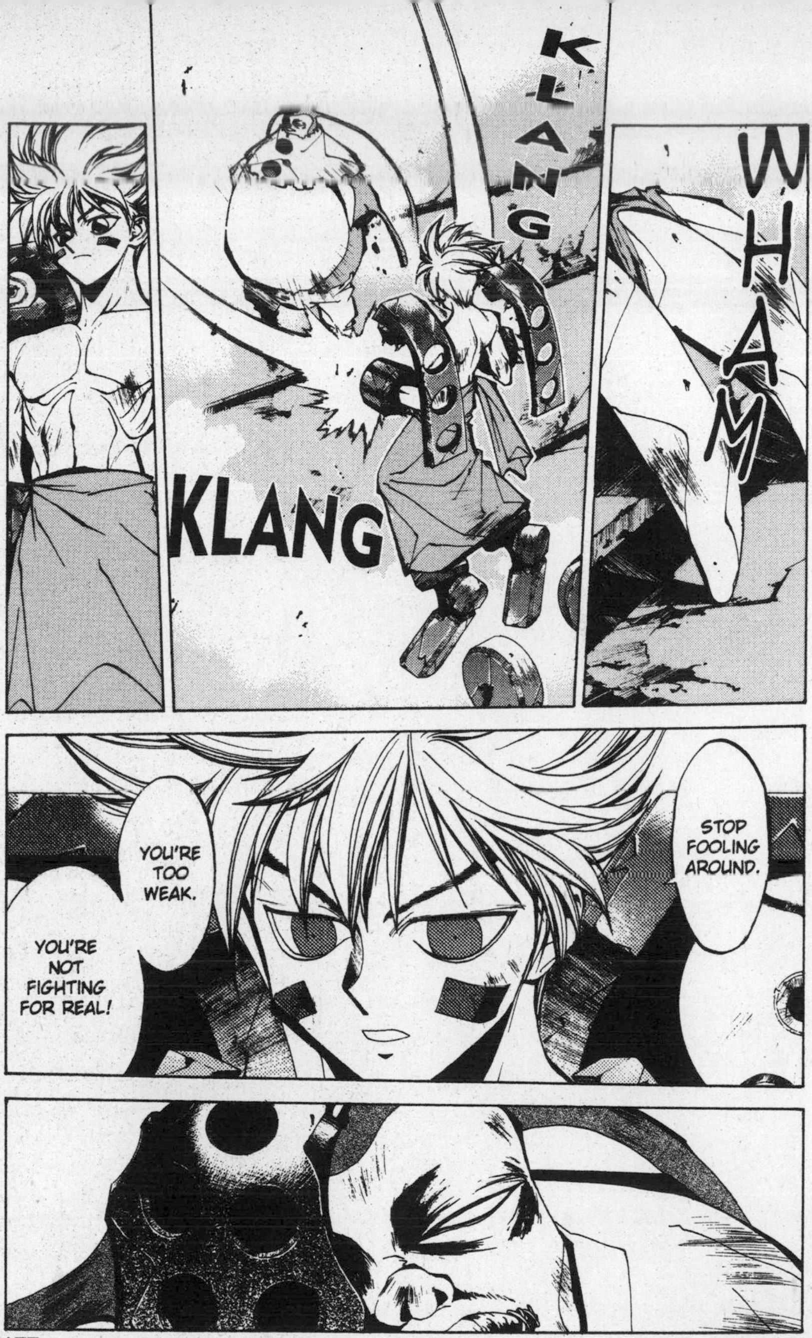
WHAM
KLANG
KLANG
STOP FOOLING AROUND.
YOU'RE TOO WEAK.
YOU'RE NOT FIGHTING FOR REAL!

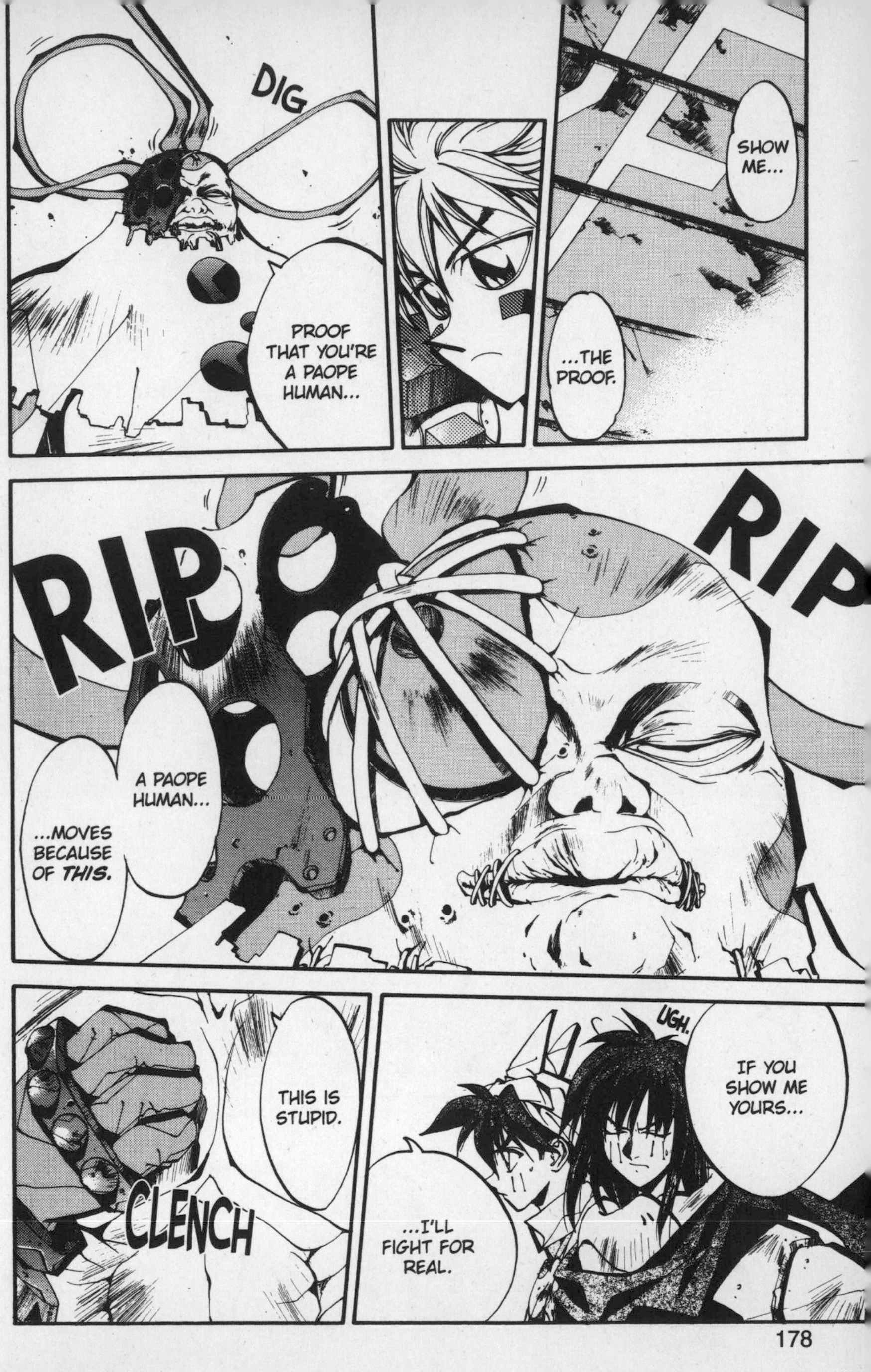
SHOW ME...
...THE PROOF.
DIG
PROOF THAT YOU'RE A PAOPE HUMAN...
RIP
RIP
A PAOPE HUMAN...
...MOVES BECAUSE OF *THIS.*
UGH.
IF YOU SHOW ME YOURS...
...I'LL FIGHT FOR REAL.
THIS IS STUPID.
CLENCH

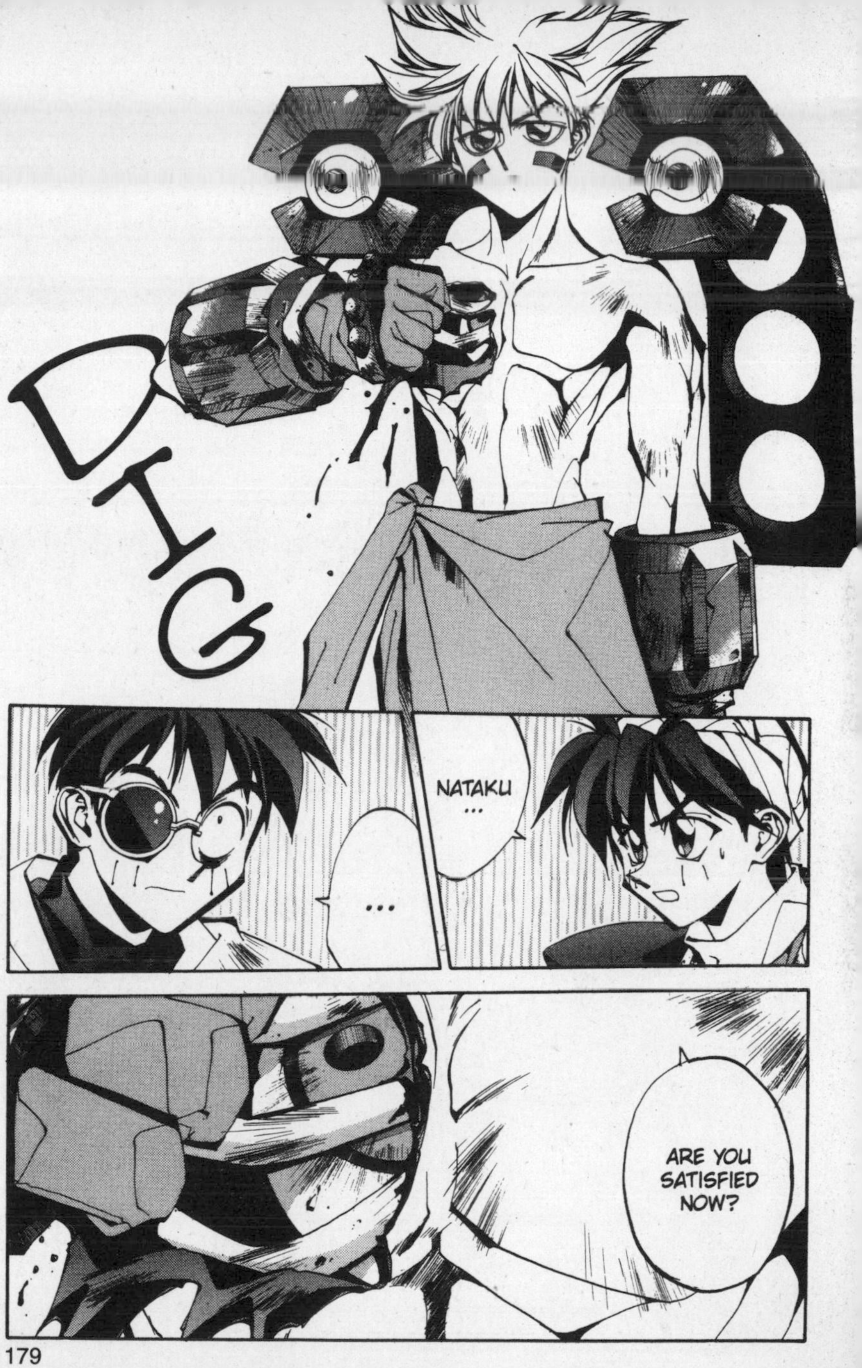
DIG
NATAKU ...
...
ARE YOU SATISFIED NOW?

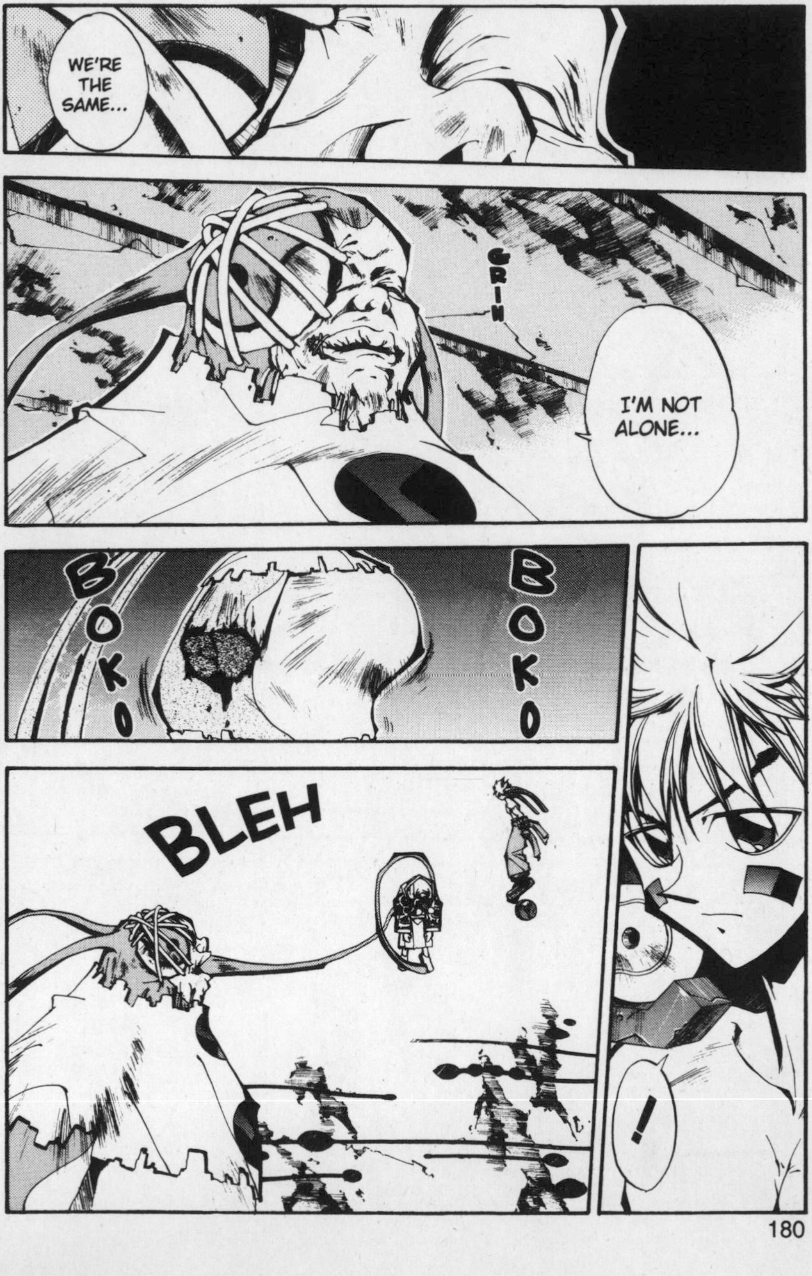
WE'RE THE SAME...
GRIN
I'M NOT ALONE...
!
BOKO
BOKO
BLEH

READ THIS WAY

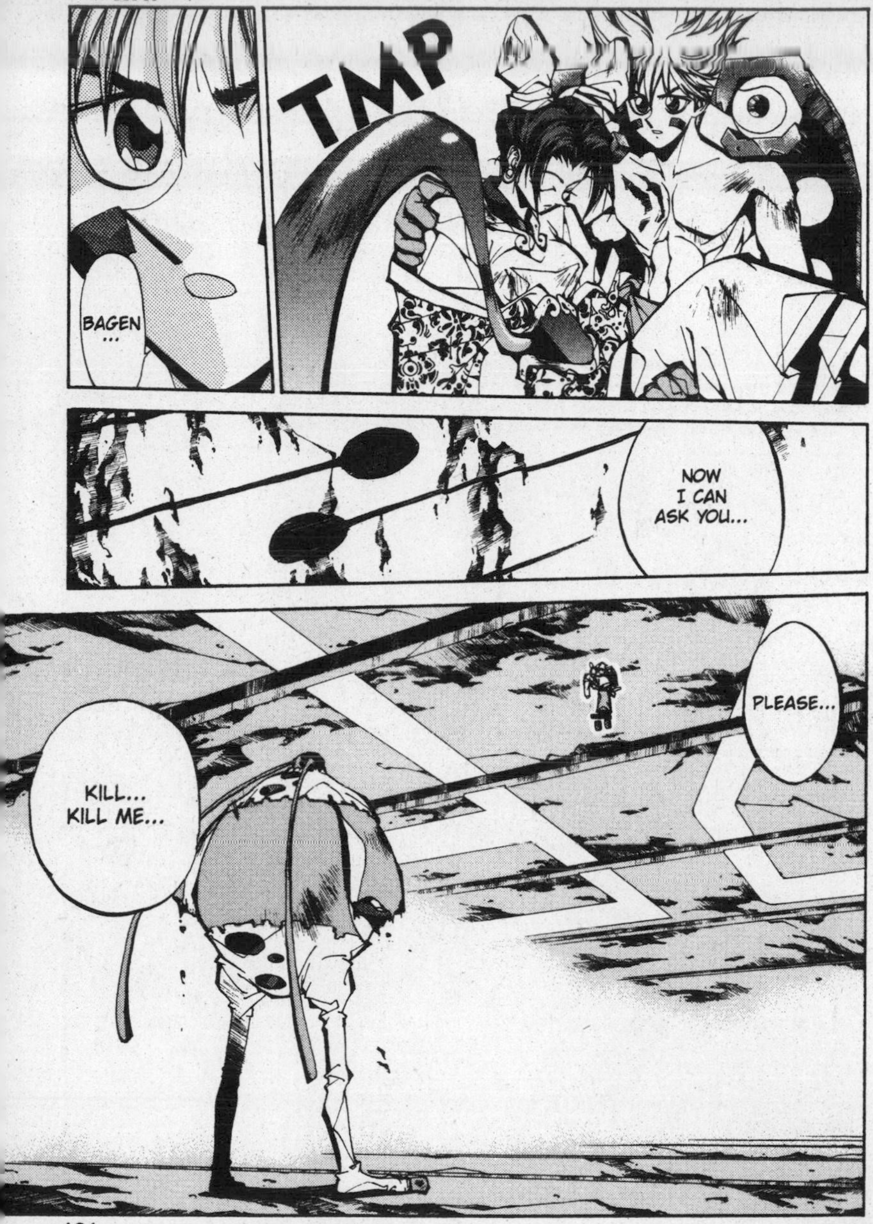
TMP
BAGEN...
NOW I CAN ASK YOU...
PLEASE...
KILL... KILL ME...

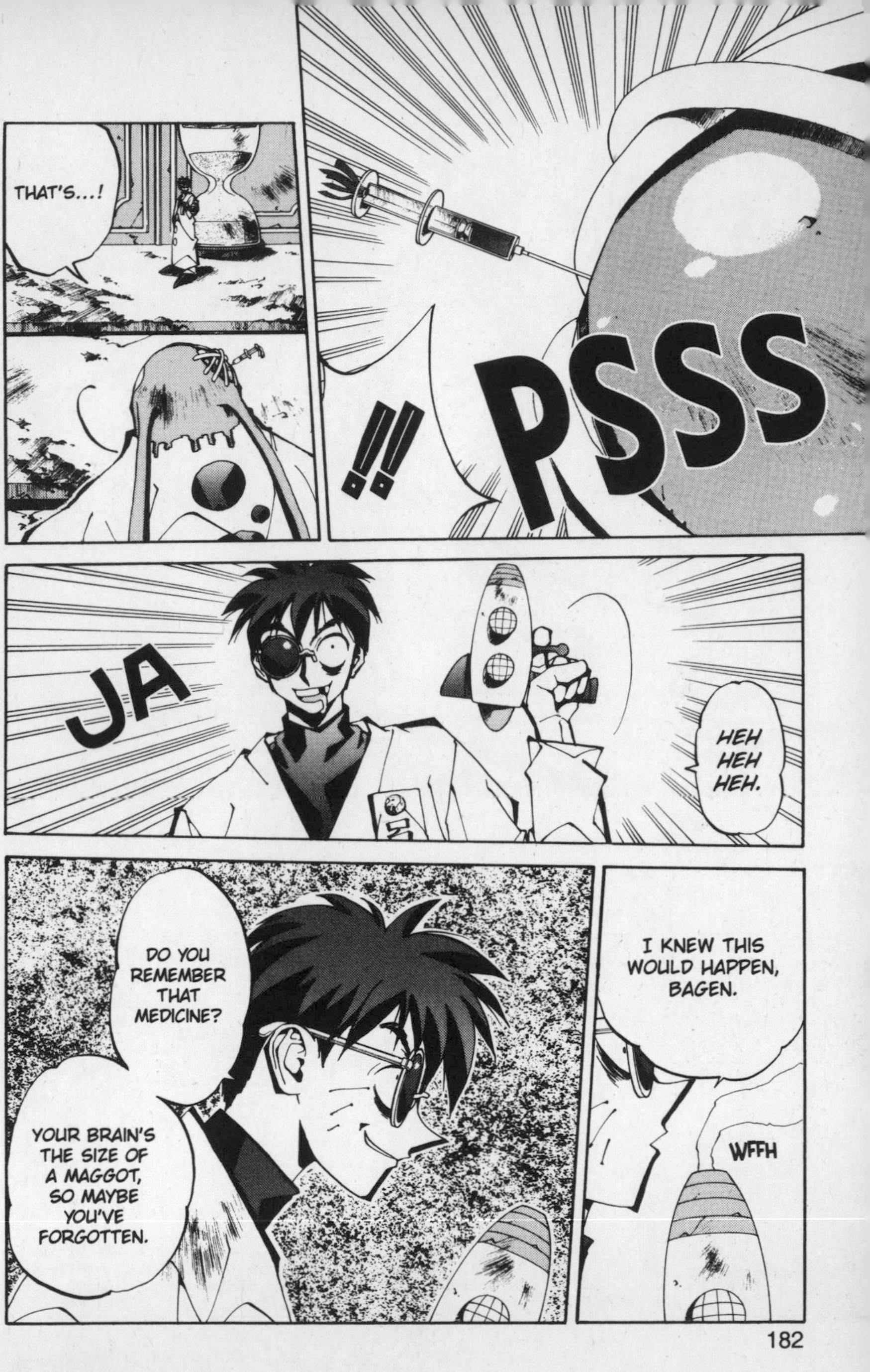
PSSS
!!
THAT'S...!
HEH HEH HEH.
JA
I KNEW THIS WOULD HAPPEN, BAGEN.
WFFH
DO YOU REMEMBER THAT MEDICINE?
YOUR BRAIN'S THE SIZE OF A MAGGOT, SO MAYBE YOU'VE FORGOTTEN.

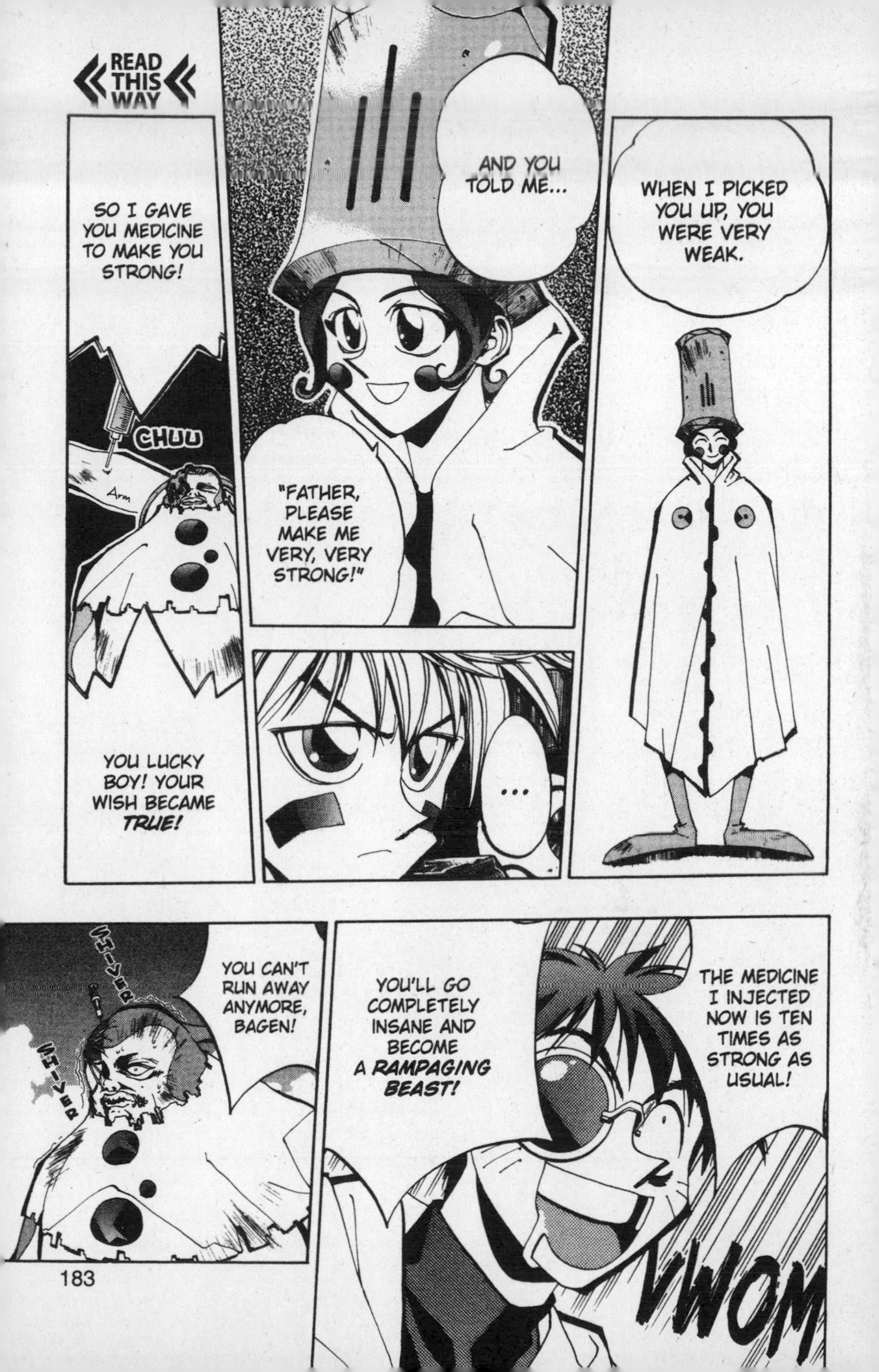
READ THIS WAY
WHEN I PICKED YOU UP, YOU WERE VERY WEAK.
AND YOU TOLD ME...
"FATHER, PLEASE MAKE ME VERY, VERY STRONG!"
...
SO I GAVE YOU MEDICINE TO MAKE YOU STRONG!
CHUU
Arm
YOU LUCKY BOY! YOUR WISH BECAME *TRUE!*
THE MEDICINE I INJECTED NOW IS TEN TIMES AS STRONG AS USUAL!
YOU'LL GO COMPLETELY INSANE AND BECOME A *RAMPAGING BEAST!*
VWOM
SHIVER
SHIVER
YOU CAN'T RUN AWAY ANYMORE, BAGEN!

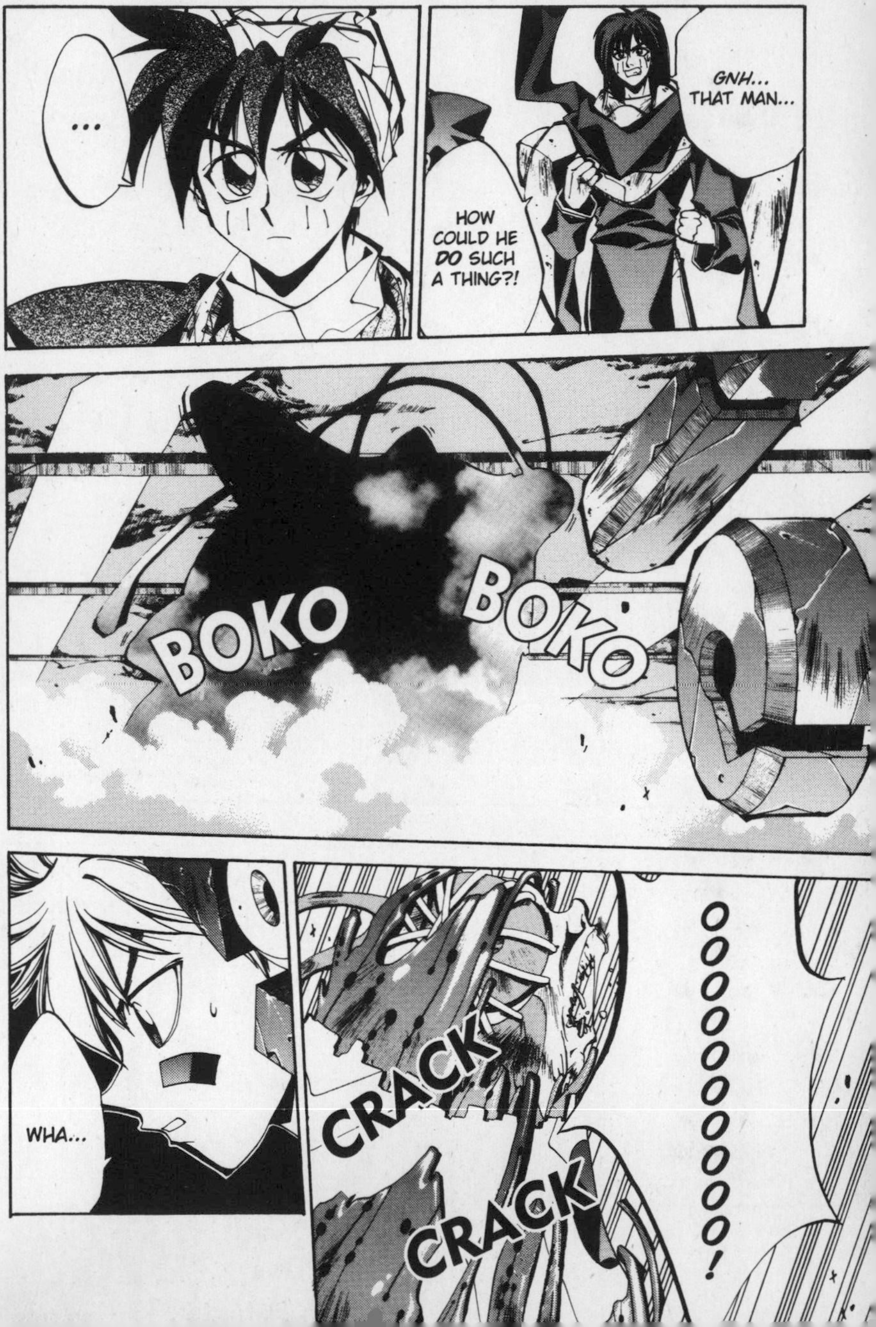
GNH... THAT MAN...
HOW COULD HE DO SUCH A THING?!
...
BOKO
BOKO
OOOOOOOOOOOO!
CRACK
CRACK
WHA...

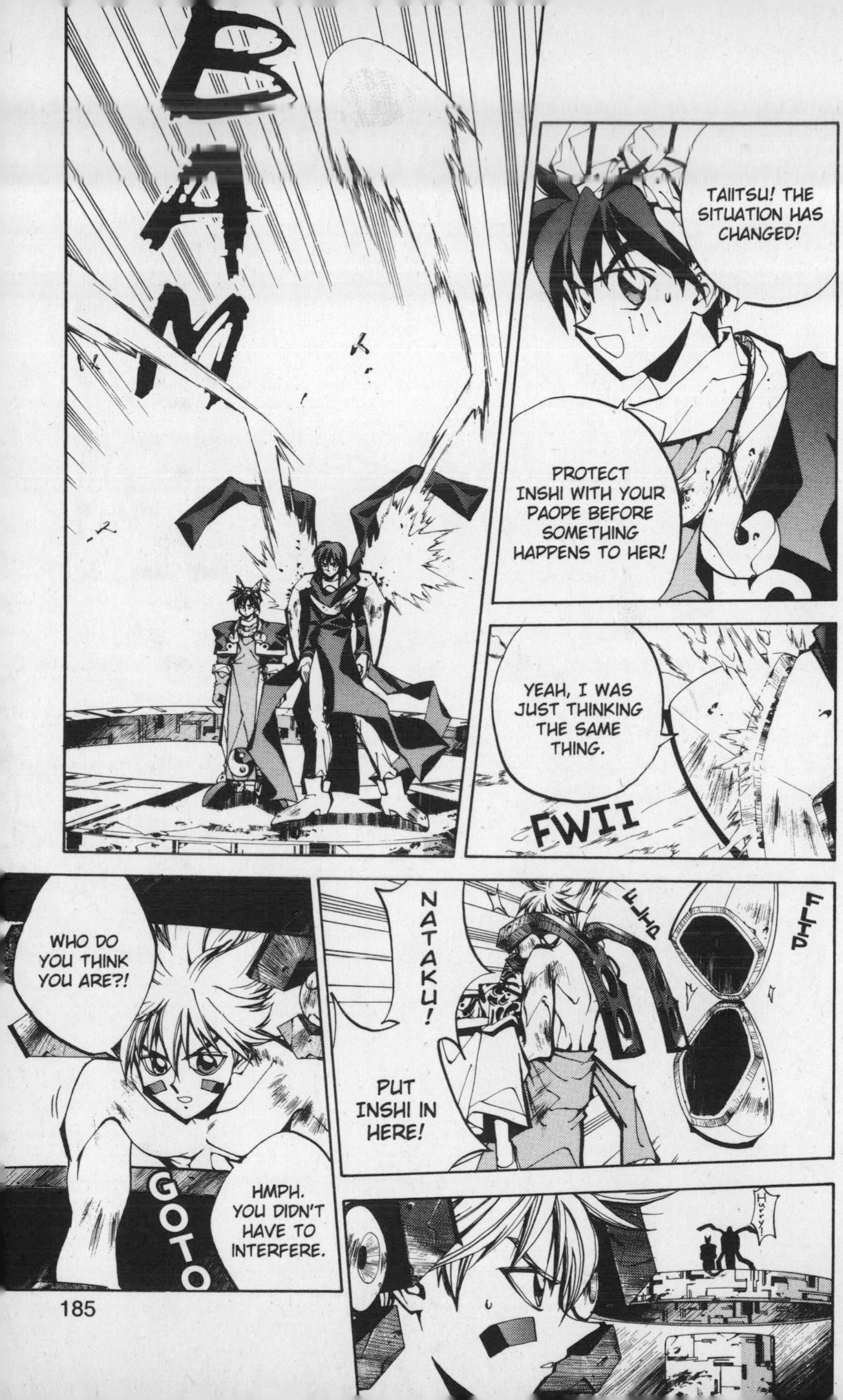
TAIITSU! THE SITUATION HAS CHANGED!
PROTECT INSHI WITH YOUR PAOPE BEFORE SOMETHING HAPPENS TO HER!
YEAH, I WAS JUST THINKING THE SAME THING.
FWII
BAM
NATAKU!
FLIP
FLIP
PUT INSHI IN HERE!
HURRY!
WHO DO YOU THINK YOU ARE?!
HMPH. YOU DIDN'T HAVE TO INTERFERE.
GOTO

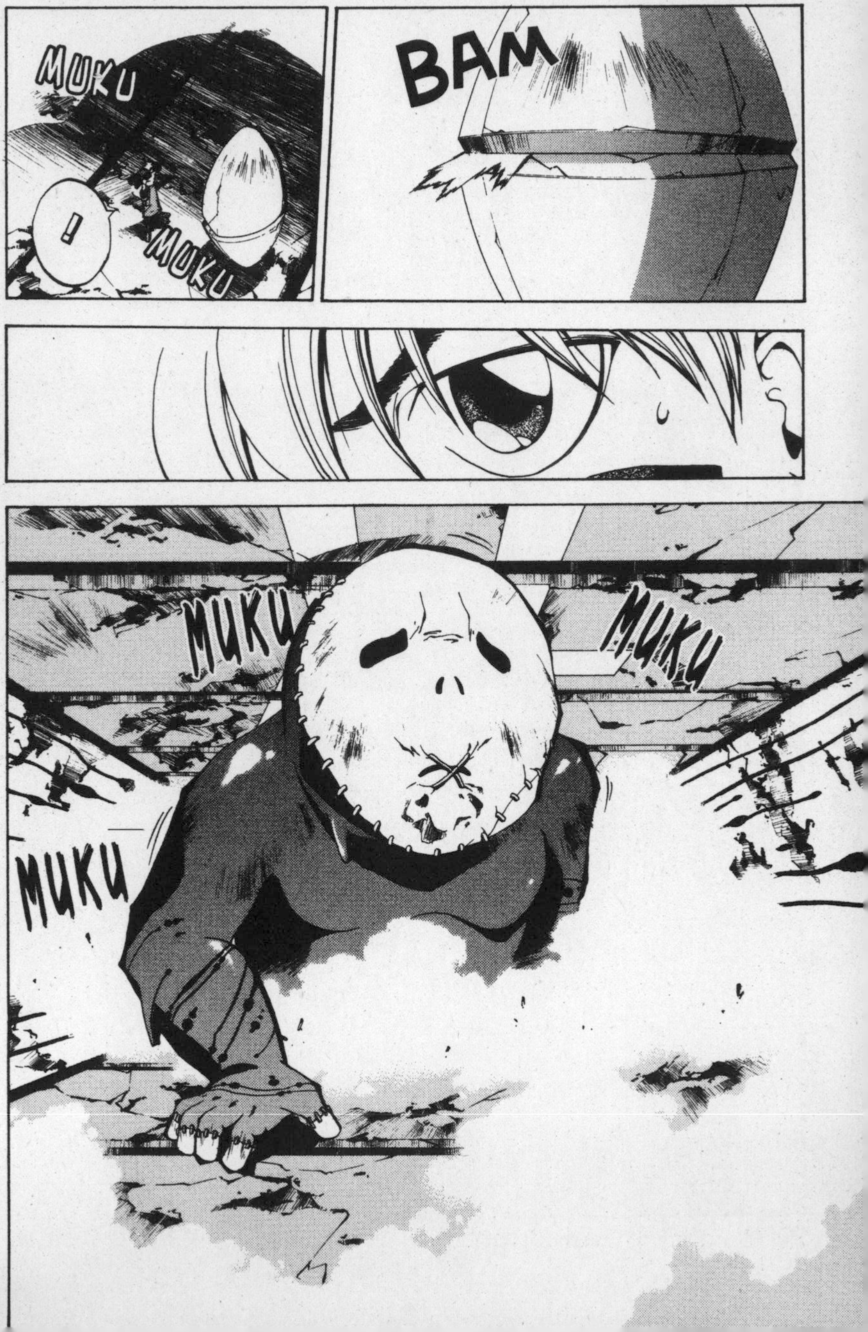
BAM
MUKU
!
MUKU
MUKU MUKU
MUKU
MUKU

READ THIS WAY

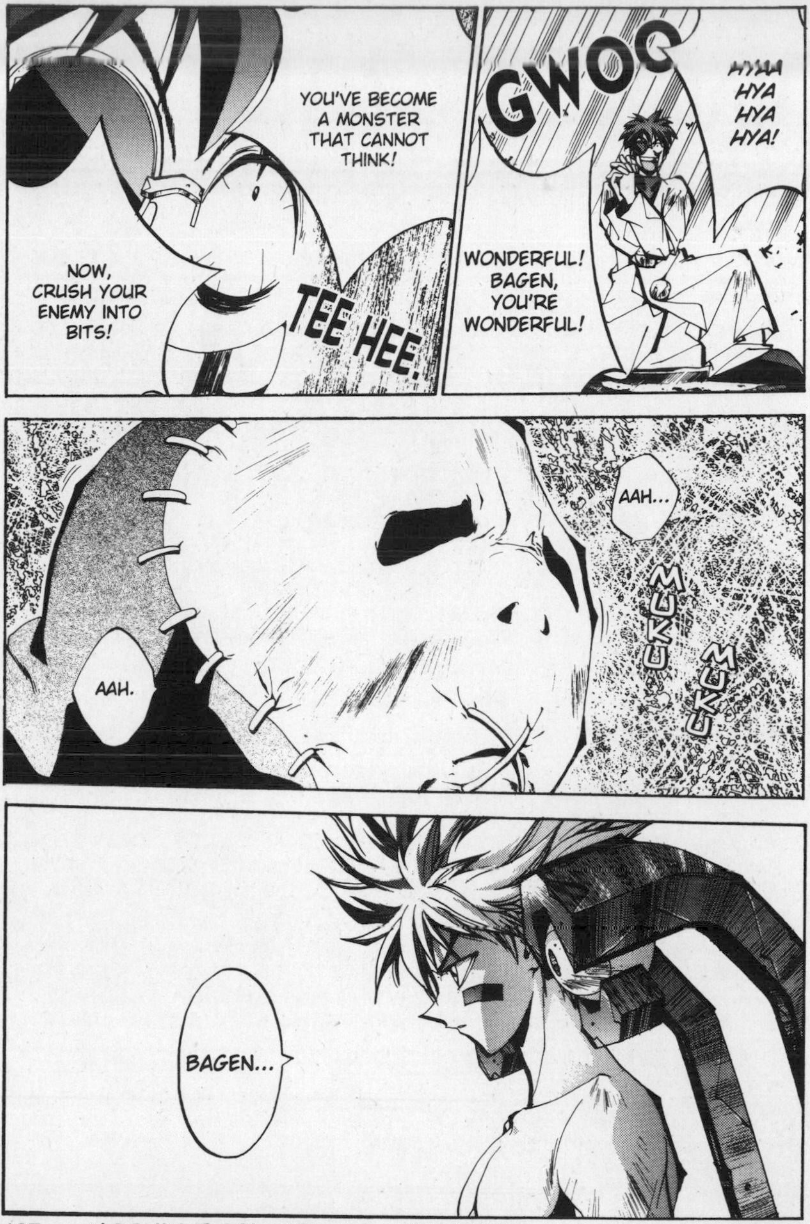
GWOC
HYA HYA HYA HYA!
WONDERFUL! BAGEN, YOU'RE WONDERFUL!
YOU'VE BECOME A MONSTER THAT CANNOT THINK!
TEE HEE.
NOW, CRUSH YOUR ENEMY INTO BITS!
AAH...
MUKU MUKU
AAH.
BAGEN...

YOU DON'T HAVE TO READ IT, BUT SINCE THERE'S AN EXTRA PAGE:

HACK WRITING VIII

△ THERE ARE MANY *MANGAKA* LIVING IN NERIMA-KU, TOKYO. FUJISAKI LIVES THERE, TOO.

△ WHY DID I CHOOSE THAT PLACE IN NERIMA-KU? IT'S SIMPLE. ONE REASON IS THAT THERE'S AN ART SUPPLY SHOP IN THE NEIGHBORHOOD THAT'S OPEN UNTIL 2AM. THE SECOND REASON IS THAT, BECAUSE THE POPULATION DENSITY OF *MANGAKA* IS HIGH, REAL ESTATE AGENTS AREN'T SURPRISED AT MY OCCUPATION. (IN TOWNS THAT DON'T HAVE MANY *MANGAKA*, AGENTS MAY REFUSE TO RENT A ROOM TO ONE.) THAT WAS ALL I HAD IN MIND WHEN I MADE MY DECISION. I DIDN'T HAVE MUCH OF A CHOICE.

△ THERE ARE OTHER PLACES WHERE I'D LIKE TO LIVE.

△ FOR EXAMPLE, A WHITE WESTERN-STYLE MANSION ON A HILL WITH A LAWN, WHERE I COULD SEE THE SEA AND THE CLIMATE IS MILD. I'D DO MY WORK ON A BIG WOODEN DESK BY THE WINDOW, WHERE I COULD LOOK OUT INTO THE SEA. MY PET DOG SHIGERU OYAMA (LABRADOR RETRIEVER, MALE, FOUR YEARS OLD) WOULD SOMETIMES RUB AGAINST MY LEGS WHEN HE'S HUNGRY. WHEN I'M TIRED, A MAID WOULD BRING ME HOT ORANGE PEKOE AND CREPES. AND WHEN THE SUN SETS, I'D LISTEN TO THE SOUND OF THE WAVES AND FALL ASLEEP WITH THE MOONLIGHT AS THE LIGHT THAT STAYS ON ALL NIGHT...

△ I'LL NEVER HAVE SUCH A LIFE, THOUGH.

△ SO WHAT'S REALITY LIKE?

△ THE PLACE WHERE I LIVE IS VERY DIFFERENT FROM THE PLACE I DESCRIBED ABOVE. I LIVE IN A SHOPPING ARCADE THAT'S LIKE A MAZE. SOMETIMES I CAN SMELL CRAB OMELETS FROM THE WINDOW. THERE'S A *MANGAKA* FOR ANOTHER MAGAZINE LIVING ON THE FIRST FLOOR. THERE'S A FRUIT STORE THAT'S FULL OF WHAT LOOKS LIKE OVERSIZE TRASH. (IT SEEMS TO HAVE GONE OUT OF BUSINESS NOW.) THERE ARE NO PARKS. THERE'S A FUNERAL HALL NEARBY, AND MANY FISH SHOPS.

△ BUT MAYBE THIS IS THE WAY THINGS ARE. YOU CAN ALWAYS WANT SOMETHING BETTER. AND THERE ARE BETTER PLACES (LIKE PLACES WITH BETTER TRANSPORTATION ACCESS). NOWADAYS, I THINK THAT THIS IS THE BEST CHOICE AMONG THE FEW ALTERNATIVES I HAVE. AND I CAN RELAX HERE.

△ THE EXPRESSION "THERE IS NO PLACE LIKE HOME" SUDDENLY POPPED IN MY MIND.

△ MAYBE THAT'S THE WAY IT IS.

△ PROBABLY.

END OF HACK WRITING

YOU DON'T HAVE TO READ IT, BUT SINCE THERE'S AN EXTRA PAGE:

HACK WRITING IX

△ I'VE WRITTEN TWO COLUMNS THIS TIME.

△ DO YOU KNOW ABOUT THE "PERIOD WHEN YOU DON'T WANT MEAT"?

△ IF THERE WERE TEN MILLION PEOPLE, 9,999,999 OF THEM WOULDN'T KNOW ABOUT IT. THAT'S BECAUSE FUJISAKI MADE THIS PHRASE UP.

△ I WROTE THAT I'M A PICKY EATER. SOMETIMES I EVEN STOP EATING MEAT. THIS IS THE "PERIOD WHEN I DON'T WANT MEAT." I HATE FISH, SO WHEN THIS PERIOD COMES, I CAN ONLY TAKE ANIMAL PROTEIN FROM EGGS. BUT WHEN THINGS ARE REALLY BAD, I DON'T EVEN WANT TO EAT EGGS. IT MAY NOT BE AN ILLNESS, BUT STILL...

△ WHY DOES THIS HAPPEN?

△ I KNOW THE REASON WHY. I FIND IT SOMEWHAT GROSS. I FIND ANIMAL FLESH VERY GROSS, AND I JUST CANNOT, *CANNOT* EAT IT! THOSE VEINS! THOSE FATS! MEAT DISGUSTS ME, AS IF THE MONK-LIKE PART OF MY HEART SUDDENLY RAISED ITS HEAD. I LIKE VEGETABLES AND FRUIT, SO I SIMPLY EAT THOSE FOODS FOR THREE OR FOUR DAYS. I THINK THAT I'LL NEVER EAT MEAT AGAIN, EVER.

△ BUT FUJISAKI ISN'T A SAINT. AT THE END OF THAT PERIOD, I WANT TO EAT HAMBURGERS. I ESPECIALLY LIKE HAMBURGERS WITH GRATED *DAIKON*. THEN THE FUJISAKI THAT CAN EAT MEAT COMES BACK. BUT I DON'T LIKE STEAK OR GRILLED MEAT TOO MUCH, SO I CHOOSE MEAT DISHES OTHER THAN THOSE. I LOVE BACON AND SAUSAGES.

△ BY THE WAY, I HATE MUSHROOMS, BUT I RECENTLY FOUND A TRICK TO EAT THEM. I SAY TO MYSELF, "THESE AREN'T MUSHROOMS, THEY'RE 'KINOKO NO YAMA!'" [NOTE: KINOKO NO YAMA IS NAME OF A MUSHROOM-SHAPED CHOCOLATE SNACK.] THEN YOU CAN EAT THEM. IF YOU DON'T LIKE MUSHROOMS, TRY IT OUT.

END OF HACK WRITING

THE SHEER PRECIPICE, WHERE IS IT NOW? 13

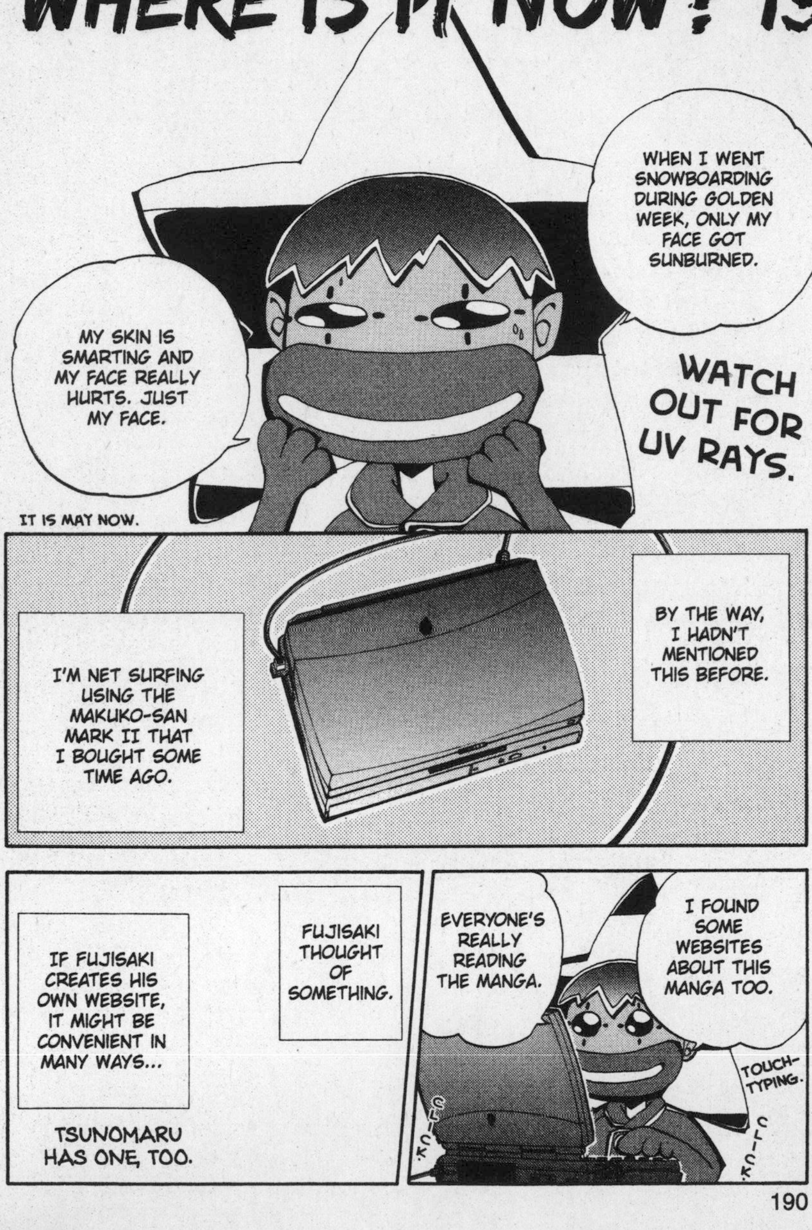
WHEN I WENT SNOWBOARDING DURING GOLDEN WEEK, ONLY MY FACE GOT SUNBURNED.
MY SKIN IS SMARTING AND MY FACE REALLY HURTS. JUST MY FACE.
WATCH OUT FOR UV RAYS.
IT IS MAY NOW.
BY THE WAY, I HADN'T MENTIONED THIS BEFORE.
I'M NET SURFING USING THE MAKUKO-SAN MARK II THAT I BOUGHT SOME TIME AGO.
I FOUND SOME WEBSITES ABOUT THIS MANGA TOO.
EVERYONE'S REALLY READING THE MANGA.
TOUCH-TYPING.
CLICK
CLICK
FUJISAKI THOUGHT OF SOMETHING.
IF FUJISAKI CREATES HIS OWN WEBSITE, IT MIGHT BE CONVENIENT IN MANY WAYS...
TSUNOMARU HAS ONE, TOO.

READ THIS WAY

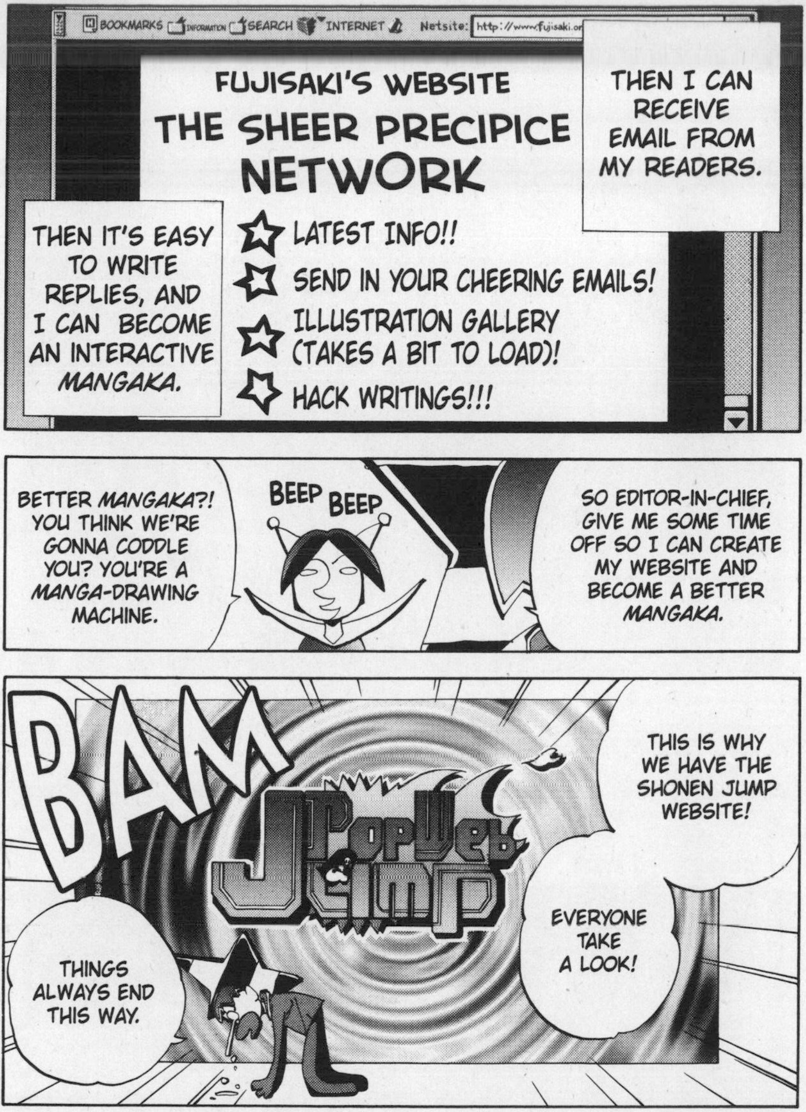
BOOKMARKS INFORMATION SEARCH INTERNET Netsite: http://www.fujisaki.or
THEN I CAN RECEIVE EMAIL FROM MY READERS.
FUJISAKI'S WEBSITE
THE SHEER PRECIPICE NETWORK
LATEST INFO!!
SEND IN YOUR CHEERING EMAILS!
ILLUSTRATION GALLERY (TAKES A BIT TO LOAD)!
HACK WRITINGS!!!
THEN IT'S EASY TO WRITE REPLIES, AND I CAN BECOME AN INTERACTIVE *MANGAKA*.
SO EDITOR-IN-CHIEF, GIVE ME SOME TIME OFF SO I CAN CREATE MY WEBSITE AND BECOME A BETTER *MANGAKA*.
BEEP BEEP
BETTER *MANGAKA*?! YOU THINK WE'RE GONNA CODDLE YOU? YOU'RE A *MANGA*-DRAWING MACHINE.
THIS IS WHY WE HAVE THE SHONEN JUMP WEBSITE!
BAM
EVERYONE TAKE A LOOK!
THINGS ALWAYS END THIS WAY.

[NOTE: THIS IS THE CURRENT URL FOR THE SJ WEBSITE]

http://jump.shueisha.co.jp/

Hoshin Engi: The Rank File!

You'll find as you read *Hoshin Engi* that there are titles and ranks that you are probably unfamiliar with. While it may seem confusing, there is an order to the madness that is pulled from ancient Chinese mythology, Japanese culture, other manga, and, of course, the incredible mind of *Hoshin Engi* creator Ryu Fujisaki.

Where we think it will help, we give you a hint in the margin on the page the name appears. But in addition, here's a quick primer on the titles you'll find in *Hoshin Engi* and what they mean:

Japanese	Title	Job Description
武成王	Buseio	Chief commanding officer
宰相	Saisho	Premier
大師	Taishi	The king's advisor/tutor
大金剛	Dai Kongo	Great Vassals
軍師	Gunshi	Military tactician
大諸侯	Daishoko	Great feudal lord
東伯侯	Tohakuko	Lord of the east region
西伯侯	Seihakuko	Lord of the west region
北伯侯	Hokuhakuko	Lord of the north region
南伯侯	Nanhakuko	Lord of the south region

Hoshin Engi: The Immortal File

Also, you'll probably find the hierarchy of the Sennin, Sendo and Doshi somewhat complicated. Here, we spell it out the easiest way possible!

Japanese	Title	Description
道士	Doshi	Someone training to become Sennin
仙道	Sendo	Used to describe both Sennin and Doshi
仙人	Sennin	Those who have mastered the way. Once you "go Sennin" you are forever changed.
妖孽	Yogetsu	A Yosei who can transform into a human
妖怪仙人	Yokai Sennin	A Sennin whose original form is not human
妖精	Yosei	An animal or object exposed to moonlight and sunlight for more than 1,000 years

Hoshin Engi: The Magical File

Paope (宝貝) are powerful magical items used by Sennin and Doshi. Sometimes they look like regular objects, like a veil or hat. These are just a few of the magical items, both paope and otherwise, that you'll encounter in *Hoshin Engi!*

Japanese	Magic	Description
打神鞭	Dashinben	Known as the God-Striking Whip, Taikobo's paope manipulates the air and wind.
霊獣	Reiju	A magical flying beast that Sennin and Doshi use for transportation and support. Taikobo's reiju is his pal Supu.
雷公鞭	Raikoben	Reduces an opponent to ashes with a huge cla[p] thunder.
哮天犬	Kotenken	The Howling Dog can fly and be used as an attack paope.
莫邪の宝剣	Bakuya no Hoken	Tenka's weapon, a light saber.
禁鞭	Kinben	A powerful whip that can attack anything in a diameter of several kilometers.
花狐貂	Kakoten	An object that consumes people and cities for its energy source.
青雲剣	Seiunken	A sword with a blade that splits into many b[lad]es when swung.
五光石	Gokoseki	A rock that changes the face of whomever it strikes into a "weirdly erotic-looking" face.
鑽心釘	Sanshintei	Dagger-like version of Bakuya no Hoken.
火鴉壺	Kako	Lava that becomes a flaming bird and attacks t[he] enemy.
十絶陣	Juzetsujin	Alternate dimension created by the Juttenkun. Each of the Juttenkun can create a different "jin" (dimension field). "Juzetsujin" is a term that refers to all those "jin" the Juttenkun can create.
落魂陣	Rakkonjin	An alternate dimension with huge talismans in it. Anyone hit with the light of the "talisman of Rakkon" loses their soul.
番天印	Bantenin	Kills all enemies that the paope stamps.
陰陽鏡	Onmyokyo	A weapon that attacks the enemy by light rays emitted from multiple mirrors.
杏黄旗	Kyokoki	A flag that receives power from the Kongron Mountains to make Taikobo stronger.
映像宝貝	Image paope	Chokomei's illusion projector.

Coming Next Volume:
Conquering Chokomei, Part 2

The battle in Chokomei's tower of death continue as Taikobo and his allies continue to fight their way to the upper levels. But each new floor brings greater and greater dangers! Will they make it to the top?!

AVAILABLE FEBRUARY 2009!

Read Any Good Books Lately?

Hoshin Engi is based on *Fengshen Yanji* (*The Creation of the Gods*, written in the 1500s by Xu Zhonglin) one of China's four classic fantastical novels of adventure, magic and mystery. The other three are *Saiyuki* (*Journey to the West* by Cheng'en Wu, late 1500s), *Sangokushi Engi* (*Romance of the Three Kingdoms* by Guanzhong Luo), and *Shui Hu Zhuan* (*Outlaws of the Marsh*, by Shi Nai'an, mid-1500s).

Want to read these books? You can! They're all still in print, more than 500 years later!

These books are North American in-print editions only.

Tell us what you think about SHONEN JUMP manga!

Our survey is now available online.
Go to: www.*SHONENJUMP*.com/mangasurvey

Help us make our product offering better!

Save 50% OFF the cover price!

SHONEN JUMP™

THE WORLD'S MOST POPULAR MANGA

Over **300 pages** per issue!

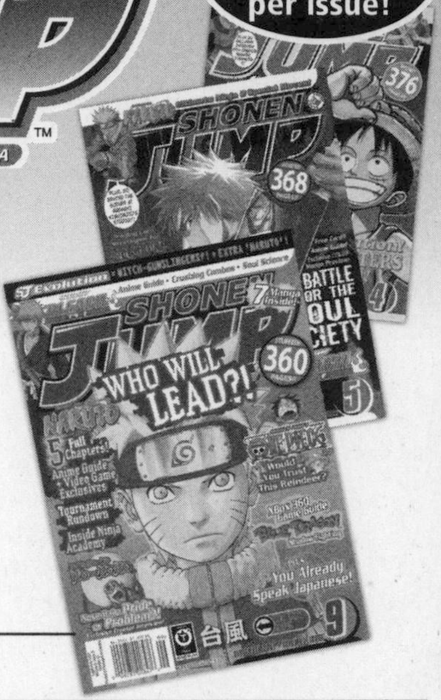
SHONEN JUMP
376
368
360
WHO WILL LEAD?!

Each issue of SHONEN JUMP contains the coolest manga available in the U.S., anime news, and info on video & card games, toys AND more!

☑ **YES!** Please enter my one-year subscription (12 HUGE issues) to **SHONEN JUMP** at the LOW SUBSCRIPTION RATE of **$29.95!**

NAME

ADDRESS

CITY **STATE** **ZIP**

E-MAIL ADDRESS P7GNC1

☐ **MY CHECK IS ENCLOSED (PAYABLE TO SHONEN JUMP)** ☐ **BILL ME LATER**

CREDIT CARD: ☐ **VISA** ☐ **MASTERCARD**

ACCOUNT # **EXP. DATE**

SIGNATURE

CLIP AND MAIL TO

SHONEN JUMP
Subscriptions Service Dept.
P.O. Box 515
Mount Morris, IL 61054-0515

Make checks payable to: **SHONEN JUMP**. Canada price for 12 issues: $41.95 USD, including GST, HST and QST. US/CAN orders only. Allow 6-8 weeks for delivery.

RATED T FOR TEEN ratings.viz.com